GENERAL LEE'S IMMORTALS

The Battles and Campaigns of the
Branch-Lane Brigade in the Army of Northern Virginia,
1861–1865

Michael C. Hardy

SB
Savas Beatie
California

Library of Congress Cataloging-in-Publication Data

Names: Hardy, Michael C., author.
Title: General Lee's Immortals: The Battles and Campaigns of the Branch-Lane Brigade in the Army of Northern Virginia, 1861-1865 / by Michael C. Hardy.
Description: First edition. | El Dorado Hills, California : Savas Beatie LLC, 2017. | Includes bibliographical references and index.
Identifiers: LCCN 2017033751| ISBN 9781611213621 (alk. paper) | ISBN 9781611213638 (ebk.)
Subjects: LCSH: Confederate States of America. Army. Branch-Lane Brigade. | North Carolina—History—Civil War, 1861-1865—Regimental histories. | United States—History—Civil War, 1861-1865—Regimental histories. | United States—History—Civil War, 1861-1865—Campaigns. | Branch, Lawrence O'B. (Lawrence O'Bryan), 1820-1862. | Lane, James Henry, 1833-1907.
Classification: LCC E573.4.B73 H37 2017 | DDC 973.7/13—dc23
LC record available at https://lccn.loc.gov/2017033751

ISBN-13: 978-1-61121-448-2
First paperback edition, first printing

SB

Savas Beatie LLC
989 Governor Drive, Suite 102
El Dorado Hills, CA 95762
Phone: 916-941-6896
(web) www.savasbeatie.com
(E-mail) sales@savasbeatie.com

Our titles are available at special discounts for bulk purchases. For more details, contact us us at sales@savasbeatie.com.

Proudly printed in the United States of America.

To the descendants of Capt. Riddick Gatling, Jr., 33rd North Carolina Troops, and to the thousands of other descendants of the men of the Branch-Lane brigade. After 150 years, "The Bravest of the Brave" finally have a history.

Thank you for letting me tell their story.

Table of Contents

Table of Contents (continued)

Maps and Photos have been placed throughout the book
for the convenience of the reader.

Preface

"**Who** has written up the war history of the glorious dead of Lane's brigade?" lamented former captain Riddick Gatling, Jr., of the 33rd North Carolina Troops, in 1887. "Who has ever written a line to tell of the sacrifices, the suffering and the ending of these more than immortal men? Who has ever told of the heroic death of General Branch at Sharpsburg? . . . Why has the history of that brigade not been written?" Gatling would likely be stunned that 150 years later, no complete history of the Branch-Lane brigade has appeared in print. In fact, 138 years passed before the history of just one regiment in the Branch-Lane brigade saw print.[1]

To understand the war in-depth, one must understand how a brigade worked in camp and in combat, how regiments were organized, and how the men reacted to battle, to being away from home, and to inter- and intra-unit politics. The men of the Branch-Lane brigade served in the Army of Northern Virginia from May 1862 through Appomattox, enduring cold and hungry

---

1 *Raleigh News and Observer*, March 10, 1887.

winters, long and hot marches, and the deadly chaos of more than 35 battles and skirmishes. Theirs is a truly remarkable story.

It seems much of my writing has been focused, in one way or another, around the extraordinary Branch-Lane brigade. My first book, a history of the 37th Regiment, was released in 2003. Other books and articles have followed, including studies on the battle of Hanover Court House, the breakthrough at Petersburg, and Gettysburg. Other authors have undertaken books on the brigade's regiments, specifically the 18th and 28th Regiments. On many occasions, I have been honored to stand in a cemetery, presenting the history of this fine group of Tar Heels during a dedication of a stone for someone's ancestor who served in the brigade. It has also been an honor to speak about the brigade at Pamplin Historical Park and at the North Carolina Museum of History in Raleigh, and to participate in tours at Chancellorsville, Fredericksburg, and Hanover Court House.

In 2008, I stood on stage beside the flag of the 37th Regiment, speaking of its past as it went on display in the state history museum. On the same stage in 2014, I was privileged to speak about the recently conserved state flag of the 33rd Regiment. Then, in 2016, I joined an honor company, firing a volley when a monument to the brigade was dedicated near Petersburg. This book grew from my desire to tell the story of this incredible brigade, a story that has been a part of my own life for the past 20 years. It is a story largely told in the words of these men themselves, a rich and complex history of their experience that also demonstrates how a Civil War brigade worked, moved, and fought.

It is my hope Riddick Gatling, Jr., would be pleased with this long-overdue history of the Branch-Lane brigade.[2]

2 Michael Hardy, *The Thirty-seventh North Carolina Troops* (Jefferson, NC, 2003); Michael Hardy, *The Battle of Hanover Court House* (Jefferson, NC, 2006); Michael Hardy, "The 37th North Carolina Troops," *America's Civil War* (May 2003), 16:115-17; Michael Hardy, "The Gettysburg Experiences of Lt. Iowa Michigan Royster," *Gettysburg Magazine* (July 2003), 29:121-24; Michael Hardy, "A Day of Carnage & Blood," *America's Civil War* (March 2005), 18:98-104; Michael Hardy, "McClellan's Missed Opportunity," *America's Civil War* (March 2007), 20:154-61; Frances Casstevens, *The 28th North Carolina Infantry* (Jefferson, NC, 2008); James Gillispie, *Cape Fear Confederates: The 18th North Carolina Regiment in the Civil War* (Jefferson, NC, 2012).

Guide to Abbreviations Used in Footnotes

Depositories

AU: Auburn University Library, Auburn, AL

CMSR/NA: Compiled Military Service Records, National Archives, Washington, D.C.

DU: Perkins Library, Duke University, Raleigh, NC

EU: Emory University Library, Atlanta, GA

KMHS: Kings Mountain Historical Society, King's Mountatin, NC

NA: National Archives, Washington, D.C.

NCDAH: North Carolina Division of Archives and History. Raleigh, NC

NCMH: North Carolina Museum of History, Raleigh, NC

SHC/UNC: Southern Historical Collection, University of North Carolina, Chapel Hill, NC

UNC/C: Atkins Library, University of North Carolina–Charlotte Library, Charlotte, NC

UVA: University of Virginia Library, Charlottesville, VA

VHS: Virginia Historical Society, Richmond, VA

Other Abbreviations:

JL: James Henry Lane
LB: Lawrence O'Bryan Branch
NBP: National Battlefield Park
NMP: National Military Park
OR: *The Official Records of the War of the Rebellion*
SHSP: Southern Historical Society Papers
UDC: United Daughters of the Confederacy
VMI: Virginia Military Institute

Chapter 1

"I do not see how the union is to be saved."

Lawrence O'Bryan Branch

SMOKE DRIFTED FROM THE nearly deserted town of New Bern, North Carolina. Confederate forces under Brig. Gen. Lawrence Branch had set fire to the bridge over the Trent River and to military stores before retreating farther north. Federal soldiers hotly pursued the Confederates, but upon reaching the town, they stopped to extinguish the conflagration before it engulfed the entire city. For Branch, it was an inglorious beginning to a brief military career.

Lawrence O'Bryan Branch was not a military man. He was just the opposite: college educated, railroad president, and a politician, all attainments "true" military men despised in superiors. However, a later biographer praised Branch's "sense of honesty, firmness and common sense men of greater renown did not have." Lawrence Branch was born near Enfield, in Halifax County, North Carolina, November 28, 1820, the son of Joseph and Susan Simpson Branch. After the death of both his parents, the future Confederate general was adopted by an uncle, John Branch, a former governor and sitting United States senator. Lawrence traveled to Washington, D. C., where his private tutors included future secretary of the treasury Salmon P. Chase. The

Lawrence O'Bryan Branch was a college graduate, lawyer, railroad president, and, when this image was taken, a member of Congress. No genuine portrait of him in Confederate uniform has been located.

McClees' Gallery of Photographic Portraits of the Senators,
Representatives, & Delegates of the Thirty-fifth Congress.

Branch family returned to North Carolina, and Lawrence entered the University of North Carolina in 1835, eventually graduating from the College of New Jersey (now Princeton University) at the age of 18 in 1837. Branch studied law in Tennessee before being admitted to the bar in 1841 to practice in Florida. For six weeks he served as an aide-de-camp to General Leigh Reid in the Seminole Wars, his only pre-war military experience.

On a return trip from New York in 1843, Branch met Ann (Nancy) Haywood Blount, at a resort in Warren County, North Carolina, and they married the next year. At first, the newlyweds made their home in Florida. Soon thereafter, Branch purchased property in Raleigh and was admitted to practice law in North Carolina. In 1852, Branch was appointed a director for the Raleigh & Gaston Railroad Company, becoming president of the line a few months later. The railroad prospered under Branch. Nevertheless, he chose to resign in 1855 when nominated by the Democratic party to run, successfully, for the U.S. Congress.[1]

Washington was raucous as Branch took up his new responsibilities. A civil war in the Kansas Territory had spilled its violence over into the house and senate chambers. Discussion regarding Kansas continued to foster discord and, "Late night sessions were frequent, and wild, free-for-all shouting matches a daily occurrence."[2] A dinner companion of President James Pierce and friend of Mississippi senator Jefferson Davis, Branch twice won re-election. When President James Buchanan attended the commencement exercises at the university in Chapel Hill in 1856, he and his party stayed at the Branch home in Raleigh.[3]

Like much of the South, North Carolina was in a state of turmoil in 1860. The dominant Democratic party had been completely torn asunder. The presidential election presented four different candidates, three of whom Southerners could support. Branch stumped for the election of Vice President John Breckinridge, the southern rights Democrat from Kentucky. Breckinridge, however, lost the election to Republican Abraham Lincoln, an

1   James S. Brawley, "The Public and Military Career of Lawrence O'Bryan Branch," UNC, (MA Thesis), 1951, 1-29.

2   Robert V. Remini, *The House: The History of the House of Representatives* (New York, 2006), 155.

3   Brawley, "Branch," 49, 58, 77; Jefferson Davis, *The Papers of Jefferson Davis*, 14 vols., Lynda L Crist, Mary Dix, and Kenneth H. Williams, eds. (Baton Rouge, 1995), Vol. 8 (1862), 207n12.

Illinois lawyer of limited political experience. Lincoln's name didn't even appear on the ballots in the South.[4]

A states' rights man, Branch believed in secession, though he failed to see Lincoln's election as adequate reason to quit the Union. On November 28, he left for Washington for the second session of the 36th Congress, although he confessed to Nancy he did not expect to stay long. Everyone admitted "that the Union will be dissolved, and the only question is how many states will go off," he wrote on December 3. Three days later he added, "I do not see how the union is to be saved from dissolution. Some of the Black Republicans are anxious to conciliate, but others will not consent, on the other hand South Carolina will not be conciliated." When Howell Cobb resigned from President Buchanan's cabinet, Branch was offered the position of secretary of the treasury. He declined, reasoning he could best serve North Carolina during this grave time by staying in the House. One of the state's leading newspapers, Raleigh's *The Standard,* applauded Branch and former governor Thomas Bragg for standing with the Union. Its Washington correspondent noted:

> In taking this position, they are neither submissionist or enemies of the South. They will demand for the South what she ought to claim and will not yield an inch, but will labor with the conservative men of the country to prevent dissolution. If it must come they will go as North Carolina goes. These gentlemen are known to be sound Democrats, but we honor them nevertheless for the manly and conservative position they take.[5]

North Carolina was torn asunder. With pro-Union and pro-secession meetings occurring across the state, neighboring South Carolina left the Union on December 20, 1860, followed by Mississippi, Florida, Alabama, Georgia, Louisiana, and Texas, all by February 1. Branch planned to stay at his post in Washington until brought home by his constituents, or until Congress adjourned. He also advised that the state should prepare to defend itself. On January 24, the General Assembly passed an act initiating a vote on calling for a secession convention and providing it with delegates should the people agree to call a convention. The balloting took place February 28 and was defeated by

---

4   Brawley, "Branch," 96, 102.

5   Lawrence Branch to Nancy Branch, December 3, 6, 1860, BP/UVA; ibid. 73, 113. Branch was offered the Postmaster General's position, but declined this post also. *The* [Raleigh] *Weekly Standard*, December 25, 1860.

merely 650 votes. Branch apparently came out in favor of the convention in a letter read during a rally in Green Level, Alamance County, the day before the balloting. Influential Raleigh newspaperman William W. Holden promptly labeled Branch a disunionist, and the two became bitter rivals.[6]

Branch remained in Congress, and on several occasions made strong appeals both in committee and on the House floor for the preservation of the Union. However, the North Carolinian recognized reconciliation was unattainable. "[L]et us separate in peace, and form other and more satisfactory arrangements. . . . It would be a crime against our fathers to marshal armies for the purpose of holding them in subjugation," he beseeched from the floor of the House. Branch continued to serve until March 4 when Congress adjourned, and he was back in Raleigh by March 6.[7]

April 1861 was a crucial month in North Carolina. Branch actively supported secession for the first time in a meeting on April 3 in Raleigh, telling listeners he had given up on the Union. On April 12, Confederate forces in Charleston, South Carolina, opened fire on Fort Sumter, which capitulated on April 13. Lincoln then issued a call for 75,000 troops, including a portion from North Carolina. "I can be no party to this violation of the laws of the country and to this war upon liberties of a free people," Governor Ellis promptly telegraphed Lincoln. "You can get no troops from North Carolina." Ellis moved quickly, ordering seizure of the forts along the coast, along with the arsenal in Fayetteville and the U.S. Mint in Charlotte. On April 20, the governor called the General Assembly into a special session. On May 1, legislators called for a May 13 election of 120 delegates, to meet in a May 20 convention in Raleigh. One historian considered the group meeting in Raleigh "one of the ablest political bodies ever assembled in North Carolina." By that afternoon, the delegates had adopted an ordinance of secession, which was signed the following day.[8]

Branch got caught up in the excitement of the moment. He enlisted as a private in the Raleigh Rifles, although Holden complained that Branch attended but one drill, and even then had to be summoned by a sergeant. On May 20,

6 The [Raleigh] *Weekly Standard*, March 6, 13, 1861; The [Raleigh] *State Journal*, April 3, 1861.

7 Brawley, "Branch," 124.

8 The [Raleigh] *State Journal*, April 10, 1861; John Barrett, *The Civil War in North Carolina* (Chapel Hill, NC, 1963), 11; Joseph Sitterson, *The Secession Movement in North Carolina* (Chapel Hill, NC, 1939), 245.

Ellis appointed Branch quartermaster and paymaster for the state's troops, with the rank of colonel. Considering how many men were enlisting, the total lack of supplies, and the paucity of weapons and uniforms, Branch's task was difficult. Nonetheless, another member of the department later claimed it "was ably and well managed, as was everything else that Colonel Branch . . . had anything to do with." When Branch's department was re-organized in September 1861, he resigned. Meanwhile Governor Ellis died in July and was replaced by Henry T. Clark, president of the Senate. Clark sent Branch and George Davis, soon-to-be a Confederate senator, as envoys to Richmond to confer with the Confederate president regarding North Carolina's perilous position, as its coast was being assailed by the Federal navy. Four coastal fortifications along the Outer Banks had fallen, closing the Pamlico Sound. Clark wanted some of the North Carolina regiments stationed in Virginia re-assigned to the state's coastal area. Jefferson Davis demurred, believing such a drain on Confederate forces assembled in Virginia from other states would doom the fledgling Confederacy.[9]

Returning from Virginia, Branch was appointed on September 20 as colonel of the 33rd North Carolina Troops. For the next two months, Branch oversaw the organization, armament, and drilling of his regiment, primarily stationed in the Raleigh area.

In early 1861, the Confederate government created a Department of North Carolina. The department was divided into two districts: the Wilmington area under the command of Brig. Gen. Joseph Anderson, and the area between the Albemarle and Pamlico Sounds under Brig. Gen. Daniel H. Hill. Unhappy with the lack of support along the coast, Hill requested a transfer to the army in Virginia. The day his request was approved, November 16, the Confederate Congress approved the nomination of Branch to the rank of brigadier general. Branch was just shy of his forty-first birthday. *The Daily Register* in Raleigh was delighted with Branch's promotion: "Should the opportunity offer, we predict

---

9   *The* [Raleigh] *Weekly Standard*, April 17, 1861; The Raleigh Rifles became Company K, 14th North Carolina Troops. Branch's name does not appear in the roster. Weymouth Jordan, et. al., eds., *North Carolina Troops, 1861-1865: A Roster*, 19 vols. (Raleigh, NC 1961-present), 5:484, hereafter cited as Jordan, *NC Troops*. Branch's name does appear in a list of volunteers in a "home guard" company organized April 16, 1861, with former governor and U.S. senator Thomas Bragg as captain. See *North Carolina Standard*, April 16, 1861; Brawley, "Branch," 130; A. Gordon, "Quartermaster-Generals Department," in Walter Clark, *Histories of the Several Regiments and Battalions from North Carolina in the Great War, 1861-'65*, 5 vols. (Raleigh, NC, 1901), 1:24. Hereafter cited as Clark, *Histories*.

that [Branch] will demonstrate the fitness" of his appointment. The officers of the 33rd regiment even drafted a series of resolutions regretting the loss of "so acceptable a commander," who "had endeared himself to his command by a strict, impartial and able attention to his duties." The officers wished him "success in his new field" and recognized Branch as an "accomplished gentleman and good scholar." Branch thanked the men for their kind words, agreeing with their sentiments, and promising his men they would never be disappointed in their first commander.[10]

Not everyone was pleased with Branch's promotion. Holden believed it the responsibility of the general public to "disapprove of and condemn any . . . appointments made . . . by the authorities . . . which puts at hazard the vital interest of North Carolina." Branch was no military man, and had been promoted over older and more experienced men because of his political connections. Through his newspaper, Holden continued to snipe at Branch for the next few months.[11]

About the time Branch was promoted, the Department of North Carolina was divided into a third section. Branch retained command of the District of Pamlico, strengthening existing fortifications below New Bern or building new ones. After the loss of Roanoke Island, Branch's superiors consolidated the widely scattered regiments into a unified force charged with the protection of New Bern. Under his command were the 7th, 26th, 27th, 33rd, 35th, and 37th NC Infantry, six companies of the 2nd NC Cavalry, and five companies of artillery, somewhere around 4,000 men.

Federal soldiers under Ambrose Burnside arrived at the mouth of the Neuse River in mid-March 1862 and slowly began working their way toward New Bern and the Confederate defenses. On March 13, Federal gunboats began shelling the area at Slocum's Creek; with Federal soldiers disembarking later that day. As they advanced up the river, the gunboats kept pace, showering the riverbanks with shrapnel. After spending the night in the rain, Federals resumed their advance. Branch divided his force into two wings. The 27th and 37th Regiments, composing the left wing under Lee's command, stretched west from Fort Thompson on the Neuse River. The right wing was composed of the

10 *Journals of Congress of the Confederate States of America*, 7 vols. (Washington D.C., 1904-1905), 1:474; *The Daily Register*, November 20, 1861, December 11, 1861; *The* [Raleigh] *Weekly Register*, December 4, 1861.

11 *The* [Raleigh] *Weekly Register*, November 23, 1861.

Lawrence Branch commanded the Confederate forces at the battle of New Bern, North Carolina, in March 1862, as depicted here in a *Harper's Weekly* woodcut. Three of the five regiments in his future brigade fought along with him. *Harper's Weekly, April 5, 1862.*

7th and 38th NC Regiments, with a company of militia on their left, all under the command of Col. Reuben Campbell. The militia was posted at a brick yard on the Atlantic & North Carolina Railroad Road. The 26th NC and part of the 2nd NC Cavalry stood farther to the right in redoubts, with an independent infantry company securing the far right flank. The 33rd NC was held in reserve, with the rest of the 2nd Cavalry posted to the rear.

On the morning of March 14, Burnside divided his force into three columns, and advanced toward the Confederate position several miles below New Bern. The Federal right, moving along the river, made contact first, but the attack stalled. Confederates also beat back a reinforced second assault. With the

battle quieted on the Confederate left, the third column of Federals attacked at the center of the line, and the militia fled, opening a gap in Branch's line. The 35th NC attempted to turn to meet the attack, but in the confusion withdrew from the field. Branch called upon the 33rd NC to plug the gap, and for a short time the Federal attack stalled once again.

A fresh Federal brigade arrived, further exploiting the yawning gap in the Confederate line. The reinforcements flanked the 7th North Carolina, and eventually, the 37th regiment as well. When he saw his left collapsing, Branch called for an orderly withdrawal. It turned out to be anything but. The remaining Confederates on the left bolted, making for the bridge over the Trent River. Confederates on the right sloshed off into a swamp. Branch intended to hold New Bern, but as his soldiers reached its outskirts, a Federal gunboat arrived and began shelling the town. Setting the bridge over the river on fire along with various buildings, and the Confederates made their way toward Kinston.[12]

In his official report, Branch placed his losses at 578 killed, wounded, and captured. Burnside's losses were listed as 483 killed and wounded. Newspaper opinion of the loss varied. Branch's critics jumped to capitalize on the defeat. Naturally W. W. Holden blamed Branch, while Governor Clark blamed others. *The Register* defended Branch, while the *Hillsborough Recorder* wrote that General Branch "bore himself bravely and firmly as any man could, preserving his coolness and presence of mind." Wilmington's *Daily Journal* lamented the quarrel between the papers. Regardless of who was to blame, the Confederacy had suffered another defeat, just one of several in the late winter and early spring months of 1862. As spring crept over the countryside, the future of the Confederacy looked bleak.[13]

12 Barrett, *The Civil War in North Carolina*, 100-106.

13 *The War of the Rebellion: A Compilation of the Official Records of the Union and Confederate Armies*, 128 vols. (Washington, D.C., 1880-1901), Series 1, vol., 9, 211, 247, hereafter cited as *OR*. All references are to Series 1 unless otherwise noted. See also *Register*, March 22, 1862; *Daily Journal*, March 31, 1862; *Hillsborough Recorder*, April 2, 1862.

Chapter 2

"We are drilling very hard every day"

The Formation of Branch's Brigade

Initially, the first six months of the war went well for the fledgling nation. From April- October 1861, the Confederacy won two major battles and had advanced into the border states, attempting to "liberate" areas held by the U.S. government. Then the Confederacy hit some snags: enlistments decreased, and leaders allowed their early advantage to slip away. The war entered a second phase in November 1861. Union forces began to embark on major campaigns, and the blockade of Southern ports began to take its toll. By the time the battle of New Bern began, Kentucky and much of Tennessee had been lost. Missouri was in Union hands, as was Port Royal on the South Carolina coast. By the beginning of May 1862, the New Mexico Territory was under Union control, and northern Virginia had been abandoned; Fort Pulaski outside Savannah had fallen to the Union navy, as had the Confederacy's largest city, New Orleans.

Only three days after the battle of New Bern, the War Department created the 2nd North Carolina Brigade, placing Branch in charge. Initially, the brigade comprised the 18th, 25th, 28th, 33rd, and 37th North Carolina regiments. In April, the 25th NC was transferred to Brig. Gen. Robert Ransom's new brigade,

William H. Rockwell enlisted in the Columbus Guards No. 1 in April of 1861. His photograph records white or buff straps holding his cartridge box and possibly bayonet scabbard. His company was assigned to the 18th North Carolina. He was killed at Frayser's Farm on June 30, 1862.

Library of Congress

and the 7th NC transferred from Brig. Gen. Samuel French's brigade to Branch's brigade.[1]

Of the five regiments under Branch's command, the 18th regiment was the oldest. Three of the companies had been pre-war private militia companies, the most colorful being the German Volunteers, three dozen of whom came from Germany. Ten others were from Prussia, nine from Bavaria, two from Luxemburg, and one each from France, England, and Denmark, plus a great many native-born North Carolinians. These three companies had all been ordered to capture Fort Caswell on Oak Island when North Carolina's secession looked certain. All of the companies in the 18th NC came from the coastal counties of New Hanover, Bladen, Columbus, Robeson, and Richmond. In July 1861, the regiment was mustered into state service at Camp Wyatt, near Wilmington, as a 12-month regiment designated as the 8th North Carolina Volunteers.[2]

Elected to command the regiment was 28-year-old James D. Radcliff, a Charleston native and graduate of the South Carolina Military Academy. Radcliffe was serving as the dean of a military school in Wilmington before the

1 *OR* 9:447-48.

2 The 18th Regiment was composed of: Company A, "German Volunteers" (New Hanover County); Company B, "Bladen Light Infantry"; Company C, "Columbus Guards No. 3"; Company D, "Robeson Rifle Guard"; Company E, "Moore's Creek Rifle Guard" (New Hanover County); Company F, "Scotch Boys" (Richmond County); Company G, "Wilmington Light Infantry"; Company H, "Columbus Guards No. 1"; Company I, "Wilmington Rifle Guards"; and Company K, "Bladen Guards." Jordan, *NC Troops*, 6:308-412.

war and as the engineer officer at Fort Caswell since the secession crisis. He was considered "an excellent drillmaster and disciplinarian." [3]

Following the formation of the 18th regiment, the men were detailed south of Wilmington to work on the Fort Fisher defenses. In early November, they, along with the 25th North Carolina Troops, were transferred to South Carolina in an attempt to block the Union thrust at Port Royal. Arriving too late to fulfill their mission, they were detailed to guard the railroad running through the Grahamville area. During this time, a special order arrived from the adjutant and inspector general's office in Richmond. In the early days of the war, the general assembly in North Carolina had authorized the formation of 10 regiments of state troops and 14 regiments of volunteers. Both organizations had regiments numbering from 1st to 10th, a system causing a good deal of confusion. To remedy this problem, Radcliffe's 8th North Carolina Volunteers was re-designated the 18th North Carolina Troops.[4]

As early as December 1861, enacting a conscription bill, to swell the ranks of a shrinking Confederate army, became a matter of serious discussion in Richmond. By the spring of 1862, the Confederate government faced the expiration of the one-year terms of enlistments for men in more than 150 regiments. Legally, these men could simply chose to go home. To address this problem, the Confederate Congress passed the Furlough and Bounty Act in December 1861. This new law granted all enlisted men who had enlisted for one year a $50 bounty and up to a 60-day furlough if they re-enlisted for three years or the duration of the war. Many 18th Regiment troops chaffed under their backwoods assignment and lack of action. Some believed they should simply allow their terms of enlistment to expire, and then make their way to Virginia and enlist in front-line regiments. Officers often disapproved. Most of Company H met on February 25 to elect new officers for a proposed company of cavalry, and to the ire of many, Colonel Radcliffe broke up the meeting. "It is a pretty come off that a Col. of a Reg't," wrote William Bellamy testily, "should assume the authority of repealing what the Confederate Congress of America enacts." On a cold, early March day, when the regiment assembled to re-enlist for three years or the war, only 16 of the 900-plus men in the ranks answered the

---

3 Bruce Allardice, *Confederate Colonels: A Biographical Register* (Columbia, MO, 2008), 315; James Sprunt, *Chronicles of the Cape Fear River, 1660-1916* (Raleigh, NC, 1916), 307.

4 Graham Dozier, "The 18th North Carolina Infantry Regiment, C. S. A.," Virginia Polytechnic Institute and State University (Master's Thesis, 1992), 4-13.

Captain John Hughes served as quartermaster of the 7th Regiment from May 1, 1862, until his transfer to Robert Hoke's brigade in November 1863.

Histories of the Several Regiments and Battalions from North Carolina

call. Radcliffe had some reason for hope just a few days later when both the 18th and 25th regiments were ordered back to North Carolina to reinforce Branch's command preparing to battle Burnside's Federals. The 18th failed to arrive in time to participate in the battle and went into camp near Kinston.[5]

Branch's second oldest regiment was the 7th North Carolina State Troops, organized (for three years or the war) at Camp Mason, near Graham, Alamance County, in August 1861, and composed of men primarily from the counties of Alexander, Iredell, Cabarrus, New Hanover, Mecklenburg, Nash, Johnson, Rowan, and Davidson. In the 7th Regiment, the new colonel more than compensated for Branch's lack of military experience. Reuben Campbell was born in 1818 in Iredell County. He was a graduate of both the University of North Carolina, and, in 1840, West Point. Following graduation, Campbell was assigned as a lieutenant in Company E, 2nd US Dragoons. Brevetted to the rank of captain for distinguished service during the battle of Buena Vista, he then served in California and the New Mexico territory. In 1857, Capt. Campbell led soldiers into the Mountain Meadows area of southern Utah in order to re-bury the bones of those killed in the massacre earlier that year. On May 11, 1861, he

---

5 James M. Matthews, ed., *The Statutes at Large of the Provisional Government of the Confederate States of America* (Richmond, VA, 1864), 223; W. J. H. Bellamy Diary, March 3-9, 1862, Southern Historical Collection, University of North Carolina-Chapel Hill, hereafter SHC/UNC; OR 9:443.

resigned his commission in the United States Army, and on May 16, was appointed a colonel of the 7th Regiment. [6]

The commands had an international flavor. While Company A of the 18th Regiment had a large German contingent, Company D of the 7th boasted a number of men from Ireland. According to one officer, once the regiment was mustered into service and given a $13 bounty, "some two dozen" from Company D "went to Graham and gratified their native fondness for whiskey to excess." Upon their return they came across their regiment on the drill field. The Irishmen "acted in [such] a boisterous manner . . . it was necessary to arrest the entire party." The new soldiers presumably slept off their bounty in the guardhouse.[7]

At the end of August, the 7th regiment found itself constructing fortifications near New Bern. One week later it was transferred to Carolina City; two companies went to Hyde County and the remainder deployed on Bogue Island. That December, the 7th regiment relocated to Newport for the balance of the winter months. On March 5, 1862, the 7th Regiment was transferred via rail to New Bern. Fighting in the battle a few days later, it lost six of its members killed, 15 wounded, and 30 missing, along with, according to one officer, "the best lot of camp equipment it ever had." The brave men of the 7th, said Branch, "met them with the bayonet and drove them head-long over the parapet, inflicting heavy loss on them as they fled." New Bern was merely the first of more than 30 battles and skirmishes in which the bayonets of the 7th met the foe.[8]

The next regiment assigned to Branch's brigade was the 28th North Carolina, organized on September 21, 1861, for 12 months at Camp Fisher, near High Point. Most of companies that made up the 28th Regiment came

---

6 The 7th Regiment was composed of Company A, Iredell and Alexander Counties; Company B, Cabarrus County; Company C, New Hanover County; Company D, Mecklenburg County; Company E, Nash County; Company F, Rowan County; Company G, "Wake Rangers"; Company H, Cabarrus County; Company I, Iredell County; and, Company K, Alexander County. Jordan, *NC Troops*, 4:407-503. Allardice, *Confederate Colonels*, 88-89. In early September 1857, Mormon militia members, masquerading as Piute Indians, attacked and killed 120 members of a wagon train, sparing only a few children, and hastily buried the bodies in shallow graves.

7 J. S. Harris, *Historical Sketches, 7th Regiment North Carolina Troops* (Mooresville, NC, 1893), 4.

8 *Charlotte Observer*, May 5, 1895; Harris, *Historical Sketches*, 9.

from the Piedmont and foothills sections of North Carolina, including the counties of Gaston, Stanley, Montgomery, Yadkin, Orange, and Cleveland.[9]

Elected to command the 28th Regiment was Virginia native James Henry Lane. Born July 28, 1833, Lane was a graduate of the "West Point of the South," the Virginia Military Institute. Among Lane's professors was Thomas J. Jackson. Upon his graduation, on July 4, 1854, second in his class, Lane served as a private tutor before enrolling in the University of Virginia, where he received a master's degree in 1857. Lane was an assistant professor of mathematics at VMI during the 1857-58 term, then served in a few different academic positions until the fall of 1860, when he became professor of natural philosophy and instructor in military tactics at the North Carolina Military Institute in Charlotte. With the coming of the war in April 1861, Lane, with the other professors and cadets at the Institute, reported to a camp of instruction near Raleigh. Charged with drilling the hundreds of men in camp, Lane soon learned he had been appointed a major in the 1st North Carolina Volunteers which was soon in Virginia. On June 10, 1861, he helped lead the regiment at the battle of Big Bethel. Promoted to lieutenant colonel soon thereafter, Lane was notified about two weeks later of his election as colonel of the 28th North Carolina, which came as a shock to Lane, since he was relatively unknown in the state. Lane resigned from the 1st Regiment, accepted the proffered position as colonel of the 28th Regiment, and set off to High Point to meet his new command.[10]

Once the regiment was mustered into service, it was quickly transferred to a camp near Wilmington. According to Lane, the *Wilmington Journal* ran the following article about his regiment:

On a recent visit to the camp of the 28th Regiment we were pleased to see that a complete town of neat wooden tenements has taken the place of the canvas village of the latter part of the summer and fall, affording convenient and comfortable quarters with chimneys, for the men, houses for the stores and other purposes. We found

9   The 28th Regiment was composed of Company A, "Surry Regulators"; Company B, "Gaston Invincibles"; Company C, "South Fork Farmers" (Catawba County); Company D, "Stanley Yankee Hunters"; Company E, "Montgomery Grays"; Company F, "Yadkin Boys"; Company G, "Guards of Independence" (Orange County); Company H, "Cleveland Regulators"; Company I, "Yadkin Stars"; and, Company K, "Stanley Guards." Jordan, *NC Troops*, 8:113-220.

10 Kenneth Phillips, "James Henry Lane and the War for Southern Independence," Auburn University (Master's Thesis, 1982), 1-41.

nearly all finished, with the exception of some of the officers' quarters, Colonel Lane's among the number, these being left to the last, as, being less crowded, the necessity was not so pressing.

Almost as we go to press the 28th moves down Second street, with steady tramp, the long line of their bayonets gleaming in the sun, and the firm bearing of the men indicative of determination and giving promise of gallant service when called upon. The drill and marching of the regiment are, to our feeble notions, as good as could be desired by regulars. If there is less of the pomp and circumstance of war with our plainly arrayed troops than with the fancy corps raised in Northern cities, experience has shown that there is more pride that will stand and will not run unless it be forward. Colonel Lane may well be proud of his regiment.[11]

In March, orders arrived for the 28th regiment to move toward New Bern to reinforce Branch's command. It proved to be a fruitless endeavor. The regiment arrived in time to support their retreating fellow Tar Heels. Lane's command trudged through the rain and mud back to Kinston and went into camp.

The fourth regiment in Branch's new brigade was his old command: the 33rd North Carolina Troops. Part of the regiment came from the Piedmont and foothill counties of Iredell, Cabarrus, Forsyth, and Wilkes, while the others were out of the eastern counties of Edgecombe, Gates, Hyde, Cumberland, and Greene.[12]

Assuming command after the promotion of Branch, Clark Avery was born in December 1828 at "Swan Ponds" in Burke County, a member of one of the most prominent families in western North Carolina. His grandfather, Waightstill Avery, served as the first attorney general of the state. Clark attended the University of North Carolina and farmed in Yancey and Burke counties before the war. On April 25, 1861, he was appointed captain of a Burke County group that became Company G, 1st North Carolina Volunteers. In

11 Clark, *Histories*, 2:467.

12 The 33rd Regiment was composed of Company A, Iredell County; Company B, Clark's Guard" (Edgecombe County); Company C, "Cabarrus Hornets"; Company D, "Wilkes Regulators"; Company E, Gaston County; Company F, "Dixie Invincibles" (Hyde County); Company G, "Cumberland Rangers"; Company H, Hyde County; Company I, "Confederate Stars" (Forsyth County); and, Company K, Gaston County. Jordan, *NC Troops*, 9:123-234.

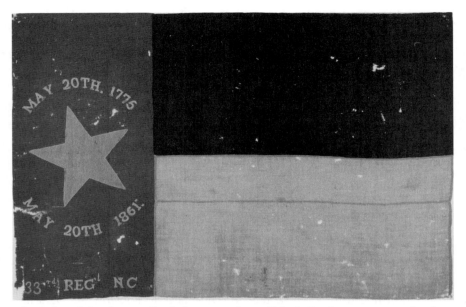

It is believed that this state flag, belonging to the 33rd North Carolina, was captured at the battle of New Bern, North Carolina on March 14, 1862. *North Carolina Museum of History*

November, he was mustered out of service and elected lieutenant colonel of the 33rd Regiment.[13]

In January 1862, the 33rd NC was transferred from a training camp near Raleigh to New Bern. For the next few weeks, part of the regiment patrolled the countryside, while the remaining men constructed defensive works south of town. Life was hard on these new soldiers. Lieutenant Joseph Saunders wrote home to his mother in January 1862 that he had awoken one morning to find "my tent was covered all over with ice a half inch thick." [14]

The battle of New Bern was the regiment's first taste of combat. During the battle, Colonel Avery had just ordered his out-flanked regiment to retreat when he, 150 of his men, and the regimental flag, were captured. When Avery surrendered his sword and pistol to a Federal officer, a nearby soldier recalled him exhibiting "a bullet hole through his cap, which had just cleared his head,

13 Allardice, *Confederate Colonels*, 47; Jordan, *NC Troops*, 9:118.

14 Joseph Saunders to "Dear Mother," January 23, 1862, Joseph Saunders Letters, SHC /UNC.

Officers in the 37th North Carolina (left to right): Jordan Cook, Andrew J. Critcher, and Thomas D. Cook. All three were elected as lieutenants in the Watauga Marksmen on September 14, 1861. The sword and pistol are probably photographer's props. *Terry Harmon*

and remarked he had rather it had gone through his head than to have surrendered." Avery was sent first to Fort Columbus in New York harbor, and then transferred to Johnson's Island, Ohio. In September he was transferred again, this time to Vicksburg, where he was paroled. On November 10, 1862, he was declared exchanged at Aiken's Landing, James River, Virginia.[15]

Officially created on November 20, 1861, the 37th North Carolina was the final regiment assigned to Branch's command. Sixty percent of the regiment came from the western counties of Ashe, Alleghany, Alexander, Wilkes, and Watauga. The rest of the regiment hailed from the southern Piedmont counties of Union, Mecklenburg, and Gaston. Company officers selected Charles Cochrane Lee as colonel to command the regiment. Born in Charleston in February 1834, the son of Stephen and Caroline Lee, as a youngster Charles moved with his family to Asheville, NC, where his father opened a boys' school. Charles secured an appointment to West Point and graduated fourth in his class in 1856. He was assigned to the ordnance department and stationed at the Waterlivet Arsenal in New York. In 1859, Lee resigned from the army and accepted a professorship at the North Carolina Military Institute teaching mineralogy, geology, chemistry, infantry tactics, and serving as commandant of cadets. In 1861, Governor Ellis sent Lee north, hoping to secure military munitions for the state. Two months later, Lee served as an aide under General

15 Joseph Denny, *Wearing the Blue in the Twenty-fifth Mass. Volunteer Infantry* (Worchester, MA, 1879), 102; Jordan, *NC Troops*, 9:118.

P. G. T. Beauregard in the ordnance department in Charleston, and might well have witnessed the bombardment of Fort Sumter. Lee went on to be elected lieutenant colonel of the 1st NC, fighting at the battle of Big Bethel. Upon the promotion of D. H. Hill to the rank of brigadier general, Lee accepted command of the 1st and was promoted to colonel. The 1st Volunteers, a six-month regiment, had just mustered out of service eight days before Lee's election as colonel of the 37th Regiment.[16]

On December 27, the 37th NC moved from High Point to Camp Mangum near Raleigh. Orders on January 9 directed the regiment to move via rail and join the other regiments near New Bern. Colonel Lee had misgivings about serving under Branch. He scoffed at Branch's lack of military knowledge and his "being fond[er] of his own position than the best interest of the service." From the camp at the fairgrounds, the regiment moved to Camp Tadpole, three miles east of New Bern, and then on February 20, to Camp Lee, one mile south of its previous location. Bennett Smith, serving in one of the Watauga County companies, groused about the new site, writing to his family back home, "The water is bad hear I had rather drink out of them mud holes thare on Brushy Fork." For the next few weeks, the regiment busied itself with drill and working on fortifications.[17]

Each regiment in Branch's brigade contained 10 companies. Contemporary military manuals prescribed that each company be composed of approximately 100 men, with three to four officers: a captain in command, a first and second lieutenant, and occasionally a third or junior lieutenant. The rank and file elected men to fill each of these positions. Often the officers were local lawyers, merchants, political figures, even ministers. Of the 10 original captains in the 18th NC, there were three lawyers, three merchants, a farmer, and a planter. Election did not mean the most qualified man was in the position of captain, only the most liked or influential. Company commanders were responsible for the day-to-day operations of their respective units: drill, overseeing commissary

16 The 37th Regiment was composed of Company A, "Ashe Beauregard Riflemen"; Company B, "Watauga Marksmen"; Company C, "Mecklenburg's Wide Awakes"; Company D, "North Carolina Defenders" (Union County); Company E, "Watauga Minute Men"; Company F, "Western Carolina Stars" (Wilkes County); Company G, "Alexander Soldiers"; Company H, "Gaston Blues"; Company I, "Mecklenburg Rifles"; and, Company K, "Alleghany Tigers"; Jordan, *NC Troops*, 9:471-591; William Stevens, "Charles C. Lee." William Powell, ed., *Dictionary of North Carolina Biography*. 6 vols. (Chapel Hill, NC, 1979), 4:43.

17 Charles Lee to James Lane, March 3, 1862, James Lane Papers, Auburn University, hereafter cited as Lane Papers, AU; Bennett Smith to Wife, February 24, 1862, private collection.

and quartermaster requisitions and issues, dispensing military justice for minor offenses, work details, and guard-mounting details. Company-grade officers appointed the non-commissioned officers from the enlisted personnel. The first sergeant, or orderly sergeant, carried the lion's share of the workload. He called the roll, filled out the morning reports, oversaw punishments, designated the men for guard and fatigue duty details, and kept detailed records regarding the issue and condition of military equipment, such as weapons, accouterments, and clothing. The first sergeants also oversaw each company's other non-commissioned officers: four other sergeants and eight corporals.[18]

Companies were typically recruited from the same geographical areas. While each company might have been from a certain county, usually one or two districts within those counties provided the majority of the men. Watauga County, for example, provided two companies to the 37th NC. Company B, under Capt. Jonathan Horton, was primarily composed of men from the Boone and Blue Ridge districts, while members of Company E, Capt. William Farthing commanding, hailed mostly from the Beaver Dams, Valle Crucis, and Cove Creek districts. Since companies came from the same close-knit geographical areas, the men were often all related to one other. Thirty-seven percent of Company A of the 33rd NC had a surname appearing at least twice in the muster roll. Of the original 67 volunteers from Iredell County, 34 were somehow related—fathers, sons, brothers, uncles, nephews, cousins. Captain Robert Cowan's younger brother, Thomas, enlisted a year after he did. Adolphus Summers enlisted in July 1862, while his father Basil enlisted in March the next year. Brothers Archibald and William Montgomery served with their first cousin George Montgomery.[19]

Word of mouth was the chief recruiting tool, especially in areas without a local newspaper. A man often received permission from the governor or adjutant general to recruit a company which usually elected him captain. In larger areas, advertisements might run in a local newspaper. According to an advertisement in the *Carolina Watchman* on July 15, 1861, William Lord sought 35 more men to complete his company. "Lincoln is determined to conquer us if he can," read the article. "Shall he whip us? If not, then rally to the ranks. I want

18 Jordan, *NC Troops*, 6:308-412.

19 Hardy, *Thirty-seventh*, 12; ibid., 9:123, 133; William Alexander, "Fought them like Tigers: The Life and Times of the 33rd North Carolina Infantry Regiment," Western Carolina University, (Master's Thesis, 2003), 59.

Many brothers, sons and fathers, uncles, and cousins fought together in the brigade during the war. Lawrence Stewart (left) and John Walter Stewart (right) were brothers serving in the 18th North Carolina. Lawrence was killed at the battle of Ox Hill, Virginia, on September 1, 1862, and John was mortally wounded at Gettysburg and died on July 19, 1863. *Histories of the Several Regiments and Battalions from North Carolina*

THIRTY-FIVE MORE MEN. FIFTEEN DOLLARS BOUNTY paid to each man. Regular pay from $11 to $20 per month. Board, clothing, everything free. We will be in the 7th Regiment under Col. Campbell, with one or two companies from Rowan." Eventually the men failed to elect Lord captain of the company, and he later transferred to a different regiment. [20]

The men and boys who made up these companies came in every conceivable size and shape, educational background, and economic demographic. While most Civil War era men would be considered slight in stature by today's standards, some were quite tall. Almost two out of three of Richmond County's Scotch Boys, members of the 18th Regiment, stood over six feet tall. Jackson Gibbs, of Mecklenburg County (37th NC), at six feet, seven inches, was probably the tallest man in the brigade. Ages also varied widely. Scores of teenagers 16 and younger joined these regiments. The youngest appears to have been Phineas Dicksey, a mere 12 when he enlisted in Company C, 18th Regiment on August 12, 1861. A couple of months later, Dicksey was promoted to a musician and carried a drum for several months before being

20 Jordan, *NC Troops*, 4:473.

discharged as underaged in July 1862. The 18th discharged many underaged recruits, but others continued to serve in the Brigade's other regiments. A few men were over 50 years of age. Jonathan Horton was 55 years old when he was elected a captain in the 37th Regiment. He served until July 15, 1862, resigning by reason of "old age and feeble health." Yet even more senior was 63-year-old Joseph Williford (33rd NC). Though some of the records are inconclusive, the vast majority of these men were self-sufficient, non-slave owning yeoman farmers before the war.[21]

Age and place of residence, along with class, were just a few parameters separating the men in the ranks. Thirty-one counties stretching from the mountains to the sea were represented in the 50 companies in the brigade. Five alone came from New Hanover County, with three from Alexander, Cabarrus, Iredell, and Mecklenburg Counties. Of course, over the life of a company, more men could be added from different areas. Company F of the 7th Regiment was originally composed of men from Rowan County. However, men from at least 11 other North Carolina counties were in this company, including 41 from Davidson County. Of the 50 men elected to command companies, six of them weren't even from North Carolina. One was from Germany, two from Scotland, two from Virginia, and one from Washington, D.C.[22]

Once the 10 companies of a regiment were together in a training camp, the company-grade officers assembled and elected a colonel, lieutenant colonel, and major. At times, these were men from the pool of company-grade officers. In the 28th regiment, Thomas Lowe was serving as Captain of Company C before being elected lieutenant colonel, and Richard Reeves was Captain of Company A before being elected to the rank of major. Seven of the 15 field and staff commanders came from the ranks of company commanders. The colonel was the regimental commander, responsible for leading the regiment on the battlefield and at regimental drills. His other duties included appointing staff, overseeing distribution of supplies, and instructing both officers and men. The lieutenant colonel was the next in command and responsible for the right half of the regiment, while the major was third in command and responsible for the left half of the regiment. Any time the colonel was away, the lieutenant colonel stepped into the role. The colonel appointed the regimental staff: the adjutant,

21 Dozier, "18th North Carolina Infantry," 6; Hardy, *Thirty-seventh*, 11; Jordan, *NC Troops*, 6:336; 9:208, 485.

22 Jordan, *NC Troops*, 4:452-61.

assistant quartermaster, and assistant commissary of subsistence. The adjutant of a regiment was responsible for communicating the orders of the regimental commander to the companies. He also kept up with the regiment's copious paperwork and copied general and special orders from higher headquarters into the regimental order book. An assistant quartermaster received, documented, and issued stores, while the assistant commissary of subsistence requisitioned provisions, drew rations for the regiment, and superintended their distribution and preparation. Others on the regimental staff included a surgeon and assistant surgeon, who oversaw the overall health and well-being of the men, and a chaplain.

It took time and a great deal of patience to transform these raw companies into a cohesive fighting unit. While the vast majority of the men in these new regiments had been required to serve in the pre-war militia, only a few men, like colonels Lee and Campbell, had any concept of the work required to shape volunteers into soldiers. New recruits had to be taught respect and discipline, as well as the required distance between officers and enlisted men, this last a difficult task considering that many, especially from the rural areas, were at least distantly related. Officers, while learning their new responsibilities, had to remember their men were volunteers sacrificing much for their new country. Moreover, companies had to be supplied with everything. Early regiments, like the 18th, received uniforms and serviceable weapons. Samuel Harding (28th NC) reported in January 1862: "I got one pare of pants and, one shirt, and one pare of drawers, one pair of shoes, and one pare of socks and one over coat and drawed one good blanket that I wouldn't take ten dollars for." Supplies the 37th NC received at the end of 1861 may be regarded as fairly representative: 157 caps, 621 private's coats, 630 pairs of trousers, 76 shirts, 126 pairs of drawers, 64 pairs of gloves, 770 overcoats, 166 knapsacks, 826 knapsack straps, 34 wall tents, 111 wall tent flies, and 2 iron pots, along with other items such as chairs and a desk. Of course, many of these items, like the tents, were lost after the retreat from New Bern. [23]

The weapons issued to the regiment were an odd assortment. Possibly due to Branch's former work in the quartermaster's department, the 33rd Regiment was issued rifles, reportedly .577 Enfields from Great Britain. James Harris of the 7th NC, however, wrote after the war that only Companies A and F were

23 Samuel Harding to "Dear Father," January 23, 1862, in Frances Casstevens, *The Civil War in Yadkin County, North Carolina* (Jefferson, NC, 1997), 127-28; Hardy, *Thirty-seventh*, 27.

armed with rifles, while the remaining eight companies were issued smoothbore muskets. Both the 28th and 37th Regiments were originally armed with antiquated flintlock muskets. Colonel Lane of the 28th refused to accept the arms, and informed the adjutant general it would be better to disband his regiment than issue the men "such useless masses of wood and metal." Governor Clark also read the note and found Lane's words "disrespectful and highly unbecoming of an officer." If the regiment were disbanded, Clark wrote, it would reflect negatively on the officers under his command. John Conrad (28th NC) believed the flintlocks strictly temporary and good "only for . . . learning manuvers of arms." The governor then complained to Lane's then-superior, Brig. Gen. Joseph Anderson, about Lane's aiding in the disaffection (and insubordination) within the 28th. Things were little better in the 37th Regiment, which had also received flintlocks. "[Colonel] Lee says he will not Leed his Men in to battle without Number One arms," reported William Morris. At that very moment, Lee was traveling to Fayetteville to look into the matter personally. Not long thereafter, the 37th Regiment received converted smoothbore muskets. Later, companies D and F of the regiment were armed with rifles. Flank companies like these often served as sharpshooters or skirmishers for the regiment.[24]

"We are drilling very hard every day," reported an officer in the 28th. Anybody would have reported the same thing, because companies and regiments drilled almost continuously: keeping men occupied, preparing them for the battlefield, and creating esprit within the ranks. Soldiers learned how to march in a column of fours, to wheel by company and battalion, and to form a line of battle. When weapons arrived, they repeatedly practiced the motions of loading and firing by files, ranks, at will, and to the right or left oblique.[25]

Of course, disgruntlement with various officers was endemic. John Kinyoun (28th NC) noted in October 1861 that one "Gibbon of Charlotte" had been appointed surgeon, and the men were "not favorable impressed. . . . [H]e

24 Clark, *Histories*, 1:362; James Lane to J. G. Martin, October 18, 1861; Henry Clark to James H. Lane, October 24, 1861, Governor's Letter Book 155, 175-76, North Carolina Division of Archives and History, hereafter cited as NCDAH; Julia O'Daniel, *Kinfolk of Jacob Conrad* (n.p., 1970), 285; Henry Clark to J. R. Anderson, October 25, 1861, Governor's Letter Book, 177, NCDAH: William Morris to "Deare Companion," January 10, 1862, William Morris Letters, SHC/UNC.

25 John Kinyoun to "beloved Wife," April 4, 1862, John Kinyoun Papers, Duke University, hereafter cited as DU.

says that he is going to ride round to see the sick of the regiment [, and] that talk has lowered him very much in the estimation of the officers." Kinyoun considered Gibbon "very aristocratic," because he had lived "in the town of Charlotte" before the war. Likewise, William Lee Davidson of the 7th NC was unhappy with the promotion of Branch to brigadier general, instead of his own commander, Col. Campbell. "You have doubtless heard" wrote Davidson,

> of the political General Branch recently appointed to take charge of the Coast of N. Ca., L. O'B. Branch! If we don't get licked repeatedly before the war ends, it won't be for the want of just such appointments. . . . Campbell should have been the first man in the state promoted. In his stead, miserable jackasses who scarcely knew their right hand from their left, and certainly not our military evaluation, were the first to receive military preferment. Truly has our state been ungrateful to him.

Intermingling of classes presented another hurdle for new soldiers to overcome. "I am tird of so many masters & Sutch tite rules," Bennet Smith wrote home. The mingling of the elite class with other classes seldom happened before the war. Most soldiers fell into the emerging Southern middle class—small slaveholders, prosperous self-sufficient non-slaveholding farmers, and professionals like doctors and merchants—or the poorer yeoman class. Having all social classes thrown together undoubtedly created tension. Of course, Kinyoun's sniping at Gibbon could merely have been envy. Kinyoun himself, with a law degree from Columbia University and a medical one from the Bellievue Medical School, hardly qualified as a plebian.[26]

Besides adjusting to the brigade organizational schema, every regiment in Branch's command was internally re-organizing. In April 1862, the Confederate Congress passed a conscription act, requiring all able-bodied white men ages 18-35 to be drafted into military service. The law later exempted government employees; workers in heavy industry, mining, and transportation; and various

---

26 Ibid., October 4, 1861, Kinyoun Papers, DU; Bennett Smith to "Dear Wife," April 16, 1863; William Davidson to Alexander McPheeters, December 1861, Alexander McPheeters's Papers, DU; Casstevens, *Civil War in Yadkin County*, 235. Based upon Joseph Glatthaar's definition of net worth—(poor class = $0-$799, middle class = $800-$3,999, and upper class = $4,000+)—the two Watauga County companies in the 37th NC broke down like this: poor: 62 enlisted men; middle: 9 officers, 72 enlisted men; upper: 2 officers and 9 enlisted men. Real estate and personal property amounts were not listed for 21 other 37th NC soldiers identified in the 1860 US Watauga County census. Glatthaar, *General Lee's Army: From Victory to Collapse* (New York, 2008), 474.

other occupations, such as teachers, ministers, and druggists. Conscripted men were allowed to hire substitutes. Fifty-six year old Michael Goowdin (37th NC), for instance, entered the army as a "sub[stitute] for his own son." William Taylor, however, was just 16 when he enlisted as a substitute in the 28th Regiment. Substitutes were often paid large sums, sometimes more than $500, to join the army in someone's place.[27]

According to the law, soldiers who had signed up to serve one year now had to serve three years, or for the duration of the war. Regiments were also allowed to reorganize and elect new company and field-grade officers. Individual soldiers could re-enlist in their original companies or join new ones. William Morris (37th NC) confessed that the act's provision for a bounty and furlough to 12-month re-enlistees motivated his entire company to re-enlist. Men who waited to be conscripted were forced into regiments with vacancies, while volunteers selected their own companies. John Alexander, also of the 37th, plainly stated that "willingly or unwillingly. . . . I would rather go in of my own accord than to be forced in." Many men already in the ranks advised loved ones to spread the word that established companies sought new recruits. "if you heare of any person that wants to come to this co[mpany] tell them to come on as soon as possible," Morris wrote.[28]

Some companies took advantage of the chance to dispense with unpopular officers. Competition for officer slots could be fierce. John Kinyoun submitted his resignation as captain of his company in the 28th Regiment on March 28 to apply to the medical examination board for a department position. Although ineligible, Kinyoun maintained a keen interest in his replacement. He disliked Thomas Apperson deeply, a man "as low as any negro that you can find in his words or truthful feelings . . . there is too much free negro about him for me." Nonetheless, Apperson won the election on April 12. [29]

Little discernible change within the officer corps of the 7th and 33rd Regiments happened after the voting. In the 37th, William Rankin, appointed

27 Jordan, *NC Troops*, 8:184; 9:529. Goodwin died of disease in a hospital in Rockingham County, Virginia, in November 1862. Taylor deserted from a hospital in October 1862. A search of Jordan reveals at least 17 men who were discharged from the various regiments in the brigade after providing substitutes.

28 William Morris to "Deare Companion," April 18, 1862, Morris Papers, SHC/UNC; John Alexander to Wife, April 27, 1862, John Alexander Papers, UNC-Charlotte.

29 John Kinyoun to "beloved Wife," March 28, 1862, Kinyoun Papers, DU; Jordan, *NC Troops*, 8:174.

Major William Rufus Rankin in the 37th North Carolina lost his bid for re-election in April 1862. He went on to serve as sergeant-major of the 28th North Carolina, and surrendered at Appomattox.

David Rankin, Jr.

major for only two weeks, lost his office to Capt. Charles Hickerson. Four other company-grade officers lost, and four others chose to resign a day or two before the voting in the face of probable defeat. The 28th experienced greater upheaval. Samuel Lowe replaced Maj. Richard Reeves. Fourteen company-grade officers also lost re-election. Two others resigned, while Capt. William Martin, appointed major in the 11th Regiment, transferred; a general courts-marital cashiered Lt. William Gilbert for an unknown offense. The officer corps of the 18th NC was completely remade. Colonel James D. Radcliffe lost, replaced by Robert Cowan, a Wilmington native and UNC graduate. Cowan had been serving as a lieutenant colonel in the 3rd NC before his election as commander of the 18th. Lieutenant Colonel Oliver Mears was likewise defeated. Regimental adjutant Charles D. Myers refused to serve under the colonel and resigned. In all, seven of the 10 company captains were replaced. In some companies, all the officers lost. Of the 26 officers who lost the election, 14 were replaced by privates from the ranks. For example, in Company I, Pvt. John D. Barry replaced Capt. Robert Williams. For a regiment soon to be tested in combat, a complete changeup in leadership could prove devastating.[30]

---

30 Jordan, *NC Troops*, vols. 4, 6, 8, and 9, were used to conduct this survey. One card in Myers's compiled service record states he was defeated for re-election. Yet another card states he "Declined appt. at reorganization." Since adjutants were appointed, not elected, the latter is probably true. Jordan, *NC Troops*, 6:306; Charles D. Myers, Roll 0265, M270, Compiled Military Service Records, National Archives, hereafter cited as CSR/NA.

While the regiments were learning their roles within the new brigade, Branch reorganized his staff. Several men helped a brigade commander run the unit. Lieutenant James Bryan, likely already serving before Branch's appointment, was the ordnance officer. Captain Daniel Carraway held the assistant commissary of subsistence post. One of Branch's kinsmen, William Blount Rodman, a lawyer from Washington, NC, served for a month as Branch's quartermaster before resigning and later becoming a cavalry colonel. Mississippi native Maj. Joseph Engelhard, who attended both UNC and Harvard Law School, began as assistant quartermaster in the 33rd Regiment before transferring to brigade staff in June 1862 as Rodman's replacement. Francis Hawks, an assistant engineer during construction of New York's Central Park before the war, became Branch's engineer officer in March 1862. Branch nominated his brother-in-law, William A. Blount, Jr., as his aide-de camp, with the rank of lieutenant. Aides-de-camp held rather undefined positions as a general's personal staff. During battle, they frequently conveyed messages. At other times, they could fill in wherever necessary. Branch's other aide-de-camp was Lt. William Cannady, a former West Point cadet. [31]

On March 27, Branch's superior, Maj. Gen. Theopholus Holmes, advised Gen. Robert E. Lee that after inspection and review of Branch's command, the regimental commanders had assured him "that there was no demoralization . . . the men were tolerably well supplied and most anxious to advance." According to John Conrad (28th NC), Holmes complimented the men's patriotism: they should, he said, be "held up as a bright example and be rewarded for [their] valor."

Amidst all this organizational tumult, Branch remained unsure about exactly how many Federals remained nearby. He estimated three or four regiments, with five or six steamers. However, he did know the enemy were camped beyond the Trent River, and the bridge was gone.[32]

Despite Holmes's assertions, Branch's regiments that fought at New Bern were in rough shape. One officer noted in early April 1862, the regiments which lost their baggage had been reduced to living in demoralizing "brush houses."

---

31 Robert E. L. Krick, *Staff Officers in Gray: A Biographical Register of the Staff Officers in the Army of Northern Virginia* (Chapel Hill, NC, 2003), 2-35, 76, 86, 90, 122, 137, 154, 160, 256, 369. Robert Hill briefly served as Branch's assistant adjutant general in March and early April 1862. On April 9, he was appointed colonel of the 48th NC and transferred.

32 *OR* 9:453; O'Daniel, *Kinfolk of Jacob Conrad*, 292.

Captain Morris luckily kept his money, but he had lost his uniform, sword, trunk, and other items during the retreat. Others noted loss of blankets and clothes. With state supplies running low, Governor Clark generated some relief by appealing to the people of the state to help resupply the destitute regiments with clothes and blankets. Local newspapers published resolutions of thanks from two companies in the 37th.[33]

From time to time, regiments undertook various missions. Picket duty towards New Bern was common. William Bellamy (18th NC) found the 24-mile trip a "long & tedious walk" but thought "an attack will be made on Newbern soon." Jackson Bost (37th NC) recalled in mid-April, the men marched 16 miles toward New Bern, dismantling the railroad and returning with the rails. Iron rails were in scarce supply across the Confederacy, and they could be reused elsewhere. James Harris reported on May 1, that half of the 7th Regiment had been sent beyond the Trent River to gather provisions, and had scarcely been in the area a few hours when word reached Colonel Campbell to recall his pickets and return to Kinston. Branch's Tar Heel brigade had been ordered to Virginia.[34]

33 William Barber to Branch, April 1862, Branch Papers, UVA; William Morris to "Dear Companion," April 13, 1862, Morris Papers, SHC/UNC; Noah Collins, Reminiscences, 15, Noah Collins Papers, NCDAH; *Charlotte Daily Bulletin*, March 25, 1862; *Western Democrat*, April 8, 1862.

34 Bellamy, "A Journal or Diary of Events," 35-36, SHC/UNC; Jackson Bost to Rev. E. S. Davis, April 26, 1862, Jackson Bost Letters, DU; Harris, *Historical Sketches*, 10.

Chapter 3

"Boys, you have stern work before you."

The Battle of Hanover Court House

After the disastrous battle of Manassas in July 1861, Federal forces retreated into Washington's defenses. Abraham Lincoln, seeking a new army commander, selected Maj. Gen. George B. McClellan, who strengthened the capital's defenses while building a 100,000-man command he christened the Army of the Potomac.

The new commander was charged with two tasks: protecting Washington and crushing the rebellion while capturing the Confederate capital at Richmond. At first, he wanted to take his army along the same route used in July 1861, an attempt to outflank the Confederates dug in around Manassas. Lincoln favored this plan. It kept the Federal army between the Confederates and Washington. However, McClellan, citing strong Confederate defenses and exposure of his own flanks and supply lines, came up with his own plan. McClellan wanted to sail down the Chesapeake Bay, disembark at Urbanna on one of the peninsulas east of Richmond, and quickly move against the city before the Confederates could respond. Lincoln eventually acquiesced, providing McClellan left enough men to protect the Federal capital.

Alfred Waud made a sketch of the opening of the battle of Hanover Court House that appeared in *Harper's Weekly* on June 21, 1862. Branch's brigade, particularly the 18th North Carolina, can be seen on the hill in the background. *Harper's Weekly*

Since Manassas in July 1861, Confederate forces under General Joseph E. Johnston had labored to fortify their position. Johnston, a 55-year-old West Point graduate, commanded the Confederate forces in northern Virginia along a 50-mile front from Dumfries in the east to Leesburg. However, he could only muster 36,207 officers and men to cover this area. So in late February, he chose to abandon northern Virginia, consolidating his forces behind the Rappahannock River. With the Confederates around Fredericksburg too close to Urbanna, McClellan was forced to adapt, landing instead at Fort Monroe on a different peninsula east of Richmond. Lincoln once again approved the plan, only asking that "adequate" forces be left behind to defend Washington. On March 17, the lead elements of the Army of the Potomac got underway. Confederate forces scrambled as McClellan's soldiers landed on the peninsula and began moving inland. Yet the Confederate bluff had been so convincing McClellan believed he faced superior numbers and called for a siege of the city of Yorktown. It took weeks for McClellan's soldiers to dig embrasures and haul heavy cannon to the line. All the while, Johnston was transferring his army from the Fredericksburg area to Yorktown to oppose the Federals.[1]

1   OR 5:1086. Including the Valley and Aquia Districts, Johnston had 47,617 men present for duty.

While Federal soldiers labored in the swamps southeast of Richmond, Confederate authorities began transferring troops from other states to stymie McClellan's advance. Seven brigades containing 30 infantry regiments, two infantry battalions, and three artillery batteries were sent to Virginia in the space of just a few weeks.[2]

Orders arrived in early May 1862 for the transfer of Branch's brigade. Robert E. Lee wrote Branch's superior of the necessity to concentrate forces. Each regiment was issued three days' rations for the move. The regiments boarded a train in Kinston, which took them to Goldsboro, where they boarded the Weldon Railroad and made their way north. They moved in this order: 37th Regiment, 903 officers and men; Latham's Battery, 80 horses and 99 men; 33rd Regiment, 644 officers and men; 28th Regiment, 1,217 officers and men; Brem's Battery, 51 horses and 97 men; 18th Regiment, 816 officers and men; 7th Regiment, 876 officers and men, and Bunting's Battery, 70 horses and 91 men. The brigade's sick were to be transported to a general hospital, and the number of available surgeons increased.[3]

It took time to gather enough rail transportation. The 28th NC departed on May 2, The 7th NC left on May 4 and arrived in Richmond on the evening of May 6 after a "very disagreeable" trip, according to John Johnston, "in open flat cars." William McLaurin wrote that his regiment, the 18th, departed on May 7 and arrived in Richmond the next day. The trip proved fatal for some men and dangerous for others. According to Bennett Smith, Hugh Icehower of the 37th, "was a drinking he had un cupled the cars 3 times and them a running he was on top of the train and would cimbe down between them and pull the cupling pin out and on the 4th time he fell between and the wheels cut him in 3 pieces." Near the Virginia-North Carolina line, the train carrying the 37th Regiment derailed, injuring several men who were transported to a field hospital in Petersburg.[4]

2 Steven Newton, *The Battle of Seven Pines, May 31 – June 1, 1862* (Lynchburg, VA, 1993), 104, 109-10; According to Freeman, there were no exact figures for Branch's brigade, but it "was one of the largest in the Army." Douglas Freeman, *Lee's Lieutenants: A Study in Command,* 3 vols. (New York, 1942), 1:201n3.

3 OR 9:471; Order from Branch's headquarters, April 30, 1862, Lawrence Branch (LB) Letterbook, NCDAH.

4 Clark, *Histories,* 2:21, 545; J. H. Johnston, Diary, Civil War Collection, NCDAH; Bennett Smith to Wife, May 8, 1862, private collection. At least four were reported injured: Clarence Carter, Fielden Asher, George Norris, and William Helms. Jordan, *NC Troops,* 9:474, 486, 494,

Richmond was the largest city most brigade members had ever seen. Since becoming the Confederate capital in May 1861, its original population of almost 40,000 more than doubled. Richmond was a center of the war industry as well: scores of businesses, both private and government, produced necessary munitions and accouterments of war. Marching between railroad stations to swap trains was about the only experience the Tar Heels had in Richmond proper, unless ill or wounded in battle, when they required treatment in one of the numerous hospitals that sprang up in the city during the war. Richmond "is a big place" wrote one brigade member. "I saw the Statute of Washington he was sitting on a horse Jest like [a] man drest in military clothes . . . ; the nigurs was drest finer than the white people." The 37th NC's chaplain, Albert Stough, recalled the cheering ladies "waiving white handkerchiefs from every cottage. . . . Southern flags waving [and] . . . many bouquets thrown to our boys as we passed by."[5]

As the 28th Regiment passed through Richmond, Col. Lane visited Gen. Robert E. Lee personally to request better weapons for his command. The general promised to send rifles to Gordonsville, and then, following up on current matters, inquired about Lane's flank companies. On May 10, Lane had written Branch about trying to get at least 130 rifles for his command. Branch responded that "400 Enfield Rifles" had been ordered for the flank companies of the 28th and 37th Regiments.[6]

Strategically important Gordonsville sat at the intersection of the Virginia Central RR, running from Richmond to the Shenandoah Valley, and the Orange & Alexander RR, which ran north, all the way to the outskirts of Washington, D. C. The connection to the Shenandoah Valley was crucial, a lifeline funneling both soldiers and supplies from the "Breadbasket of the Confederacy" to the Eastern theater of war. Branch's brigade was placed under the command of Maj. Gen. Richard Ewell, whose division was located in the Shenandoah Valley. Confederate forces spread out in a huge front across central Virginia. Joe Johnston, with the principal Confederate army of 60,000 men, confronted McClellan's 100,000-man host east of Richmond,. At

---

515. Branch reported on May 10 the 18th Regiment was delayed "by a break down on the R. R." LB to Richard Ewell, May 10, 1862, Branch Papers, UVA.

5   Bennett Smith to Wife, May 8, 1862, private collection; *Biblical Recorder*, May 14, 1862.

6   JL to LB, May 10, 1862, LB to Lane, May 11, 1862, Branch Papers, UVA; Hardy, *Thirty-seventh*, 55.

Fredericksburg, Confederate forces under Brig. Gen. Charles Field with 2,500 soldiers, faced a Federal force of 30,000 men. There were an additional 6,500 Federals in the upper Rappahannock River area. Ewell and Jackson, with 8,000 men in the Shenandoah Valley, watched 20,000 Federals. Beyond the Shenandoah Valley were an additional 20,000 Federal soldiers. General Lee, on assigning Branch to Ewell's division, wrote that Branch was to remain east of the Blue Ridge, not to be called upon unless absolutely necessary. [7]

On May 10, Branch's movement toward Madison Court House was interrupted by a note arriving from Ewell that the Federals were breaking camp, possibly heading toward Fredericksburg. Branch was ordered to Orange Court House. Word then arrived the Federals had merely changed camps. On May 14, Ewell directed Branch to take the troops in and around Gordonsville "into the valley . . . to Lurary." Ewell believed Branch's men should have at least five days' rations, but needed to travel light. "The road to glory cannot be followed with much baggage," explained Ewell.[8]

Branch's men set out on the evening on May 16 in torrential rain and managed to cover 12 miles before orders came from Ewell to halt. At noon on May 17, Ewell told Branch to continue, but after covering three miles, he was again ordered to halt and return to Gordonsville. The next day, Ewell ordered Branch simply to remain where he was. This constant stream of conflicting instructions frustrated everyone. Branch believed it originated "from rivalry between Gens. Jackson and Ewell," and declared it "very unfortunate" that so many junior officers "of the old army" had been transformed "into Brigadiers and Major Generals." Sergeant John Alexander (37th NC) confided to his wife that he had never been "so completely worn out in my life as when we halted Saturday night. . . . you know that I was always opposed to walking." Colonel James Lane told a fellow former Confederate officer after the war that Ewell's order

> to the Valley, as was publically understood, to join Ewell; but really, as it afterward turned out, to deceive the enemy & make him believe that reinforcements were being sent to Jackson. After passing through a little town or village called Criglersville, not far

7   Richard Ewell to Robert E. Lee, May 13, 1862, Heartt-Wilson Papers, SHC.

8   LB to Richard Ewell, May 10, 13, 1862; Richard Ewell to LB, May 11, 12, 1862, all in Brawley, "Branch," 161; Richard Ewell to LB, 12 May 1862, Branch Papers, UVA; OR 12/3:890-91.

from the eastern base of the Blue Ridge, we were kept moving slowly forward during the day in full view of a Yankee signal station & at night we were marched back & ordered into bivouac . . . . None of us went over the mountain.[9]

George Johnston (28th NC) recalled the brigade received orders on the afternoon of May 19 to proceed toward Ewell and Jackson. "In high spirits, with many a shout and song, we pressed manfully on." They marched into early evening before stopping, and watched a thunderstorm break upon the mountaintop. Up early the next morning, the brigade began to ascend the mountain, enjoying the scenery as they climbed. After three miles, Johnston's regiment was resting by the roadside, when a "courier came dashing through our ranks" with urgent orders from General Johnston himself sending Branch's brigade to Hanover Court House. At Madison Court House, Branch informed Ewell about the new orders, and even while marching in the opposite direction, told Ewell he hoped to "soon have the opportunity to report to you in person." Branch obviously wanted to join in the action in the Valley and possibly restore what reputation he had lost at New Bern.[10]

Down the mountain went the brigade, covering the first eight miles in three hours. From the end of the column George Johnston witnessed "poor fellows . . . dropping out by scores, and lining the road-side with their woebegone faces." Johnston recalled leaving a fellow officer in the 28th who had completely given up "stretched on his back in a thicket." The brigade covered 22 miles before going into camp. The next day, they arrived in Gordonsville and began to transfer via rail to Hanover Court House, arriving on May 22.[11]

Like Gordonsville, Hanover had an important railroad junction. The Virginia Central ran through Hanover County and intersected with the Richmond, Fredericksburg, & Potomac RR at Hanover Junction. It was a crucial line for men and supplies coming to Richmond. Branch's redeployment

9   LB to Mrs. Branch, May 18, 1862, Brawley, "Branch,"163 (quoted); John Alexander to "Dear Wife," May 14, 1862, Alexander Papers, UNC/C; JL to Thomas Mumford, January 4, 1893, Mumford-Ellis Papers, DU. Branch never mentioned the idea that his brigade was being used as a distraction, only his frustration about the indecisiveness of Ewell and Jackson.

10 George Johnston diary, June 8, 1862, NCDAH; Joseph E. Johnston to LB, May 19, 1862, Branch Papers, UVA; *OR* 12/3:898. There is an annotation on the bottom of the note from Johnston that the telegram was sent the day before, but Branch apparently had not received the telegram.

11 Johnston, Diary, June 8, 1862.

This First National flag, made of silk and presented to the 33rd North Carolina in September 1861, was the banner the regiment most likely carried during the battle of Hanover Court House. *North Carolina Museum of History*

from the Gordonsville area to Hanover placed him between two large Federal forces. General Johnston ordered Branch both to protect the railroads, and, if a battle commenced, to attack the enemy's flank.[12]

When McClellan personally left Washington, D.C., he forwarded a memo to the war department outlining the 74,000-plus soldiers he left behind to protect the capital. However, upon recalculation by Federal officials, it appeared McClellan had left a scant 26,761 men, too few for Lincoln's definition of "adequate" defenders. The president ordered Maj. Gen. Irvin McDowell's I Corps to remain behind. and over time, augmented McDowell's force with additional troops, including some from the Shenandoah Valley. About the time Branch arrived at Hanover Court House, McDowell's force numbered around 40,000 men. These men were posted just north of him, at Fredericksburg, while southeast sat McClellan's Army of the Potomac. McClellan, always believing he was outnumbered, repeatedly requested McDowell's men. Lincoln eventually conceded, but required McDowell to stay between Washington and the Confederate army. McClellan thus had to extend

12 OR 11/3:537.

his right flank to link up with McDowell's men. This required eliminating the Confederates in Hanover County.

The arrival of Branch's brigade did not escape notice. A party of Pennsylvania cavalry reported on May 24 a Confederate force composed of "not less than 3,000 infantry, six pieces of cannon, and 300 cavalry, four regiments having arrived day before yesterday." Confederate pickets spotted the Federal soldiers who were as close as Taliaferro's Mill, reconnoitering the Confederate position. George Johnston recalled being at Colonel Lane's tent on May 24 when the drummers beat the "Long Roll." Soldiers scrambled into ranks, marched to a large field, and formed a line of battle where they stood "in a drenching rain," before being allowed to return to camp. The enemy had been only 30 Federal cavalrymen instead of an entire regiment as originally reported. The next day the brigade repeated the drill, marching two miles to meet an illusory enemy force. Branch ordered his regimental commanders to ship some 309 sick men and the excess baggage via rail to Richmond, while he abandoned camp near Hanover Court House and moved toward Ashland. On the evening of May 26, Branch established his headquarters at Slash Church. His command now contained not only his five regiments, but Latham's Battery of four guns, the 12th NC, the 45th GA, and an undisclosed number of Virginia cavalry.[13]

Cavalry pickets were positioned at the intersection of local roads. Around midnight, two companies of the 37th were dispatched toward Taliaferro's Mill to reinforce the Confederate pickets. Branch bedded down at the church for the evening, sleeping in his clothes in one of the pews. He was joined by his staff, as well as by Lt. Col. Edward Haywood (7th NC) who was suffering from a toothache. An increasingly active Federal presence undoubtedly worried Branch. He hoped for the arrival of Brig. Gen. Richard Anderson he had told his wife earlier. "He ranks me and I would rather be relived of the responsibility of chief command."[14]

Stonewall Jackson's activities in the Shenandoah Valley postponed the planned conjunction of McDowell and McClellan, with some of the troops sent from the Shenandoah Valley ordered to return and try to trap Jackson's force.

13 Eric Wittenberg, *"We Have it Damn Hard Out Here:" The Civil War Letters of Sergeant Thomas W. Smith, 6th Pennsylvania Cavalry* (Kent, OH, 1999), 34; Johnston, Diary, June 8, 1862; LB to Joseph Johnston, May 24, 1862, Branch Papers, UVA; B. B. Douglas to LB, May 25, 1862, Branch Papers, UVA. Latham's Battery arrived on May 26 with only "half enough men for the efficient service of the guns and with horses entirely untrained." Clark, *Histories*, 2:469.

14 LB to Nancy Branch, May 24, 1862, May 26, 1862, Branch Papers, UVA.

The others were ordered to remain in place near Fredericksburg. McClellan still believed that at some point McDowell would join him and decided to clear the Confederates between his force and McDowell. He assigned the task to Brig. Gen. Fitz John Porter and the V Corps. Porter's men set out early on the morning of May 27, but the incessant rains turned the roads into quagmires, slowing the march to a crawl. The Confederates fared little better. One officer in the 28th NC complained that "all suffered much that night as we had no tents neither had we slept in tents one night in five weeks, traveling all the time in the mud & rain." Porter divided his force into two columns. The first was composed of a division of infantry, with artillery and cavalry support. This force advanced northwards along the New Bridge Road. A single brigade of infantry, with cavalry, composed the second column, and it advanced along a road running next to the Pamunkey River. Porter assumed that Branch's small force was still near Hanover Court House, and this second column was ordered to strike Branch's flank and rear.[15]

As the Federals struggled through the mud, they encountered Confederate cavalry at every intersection. At times, the Federals had to deploy infantry and artillery to assist the cavalry. Branch received reports of a small body of Federals moving toward the picket post belonging to the two companies the 37th NC sent out the previous evening. He ordered Lane to take the entire 28th Regiment, along with a section of Latham's battery, to reinforce the pickets. At the same time, he sent the 45th GA down the Ashcake Road toward Ashland to repair the railroad and to keep open the Confederate line of retreat. Lane led the 28th past the rest of the brigade, across the railroad tracks, and to the farmhouse of Dr. Kinney. Ten men from each company were detailed to fill their companies' canteens at a nearby well. From the Kinney farm, Lane marched his regiment down toward the Pamunkey River. However, when he reached the picket post, he found it abandoned. Lane searched for the pickets until a courier informed him of Federals troops advancing in his rear. Then he quickly turned his column back toward the Kinney farm.[16]

---

15   Allen Speer. *Voices from Cemetery Hill: The Civil War Diary, Reports, and Letters of Colonel William Henry Asbury Speer, 1861-1864* (Johnston City, TN, 1997), 46; OR 11/1:682, 702.

16 Ibid., 741; Speer, *Voices From Cemetery Hill*, 46. William Mauney (28th NC) writes they moved a half mile down the road but halted before reaching the mill. William Mauney, Diary, May 27, 1862, Kings Mountain Historical Society, Cleveland County, NC.

Captain George Johnston and Company A were now in the lead. "I had the privilege of heading the noble column," he recalled in his diary,

> marching by the side of our gallant Col. Every moment we expected to fall upon them. I was as cool and collected as ever in my life, and, though busily engaged in cheering up my men, thought often of my beloved Nannie wife, and asked God to cover my head in the hour of battle, for her precious sake. . . . We were looking for the foe upon our right; a thick wood lay in that direction; in this the Col. feared an ambush, and ordered me to deploy my 1st platoon as skirmishers through it, to look out for the enemy, and to hold them in check until he could form the regiment. I obeyed and soon had my men beautifully deployed for nearly quarter of a mile to the right of the head of the column. Half of my 2nd platoon was deployed in like manner upon the left, under command of 2nd Sergt. Martin. . . . At every step we knew not but that the next would throw us in their midst—but my brave boys pressed on unfalteringly. . . . Suddenly I heard the report of several rifles; I listened and in the distance heard the clear voice of Col Lane, 'Halt, Front- By Co. left wheel, march.'[17]

Lane had stumbled upon Federal skirmishers from the 25th New York Infantry. After properly aligning his Tar Heels on the road to his front, Lane bellowed, "Charge—charge them, brave boys!" The 28th Regiment, some 900-men strong, crashed through the woods, through a ditch, and over a fence, chasing the New Yorkers on the east side of the New Bridge Road to the south. Lane led the 28th into the yard of the Kinney House, and the fighting quickly turned into a hand-to-hand struggle with the Federals on the west side of the road, often with bayonets, swords, and knives. A New Yorker reported one of his officers lay dead near the house, "and all through the yard and around the house the dead of both sides covered the ground." What was left of the four Federal companies on the west side of the road quickly retreated. During the attack, the reserve of the 25th New York tried to advance toward the fighting, but portions of the 28th redeployed and opened fire, driving them back.[18]

Lane quickly re-formed his men to confront other enemy troops forming to his south. Lane ordered his men to drop their rain-soaked knapsacks and to lie down behind a fence. He then deployed the two guns of Latham's battery, while sending word to Branch that he needed reinforcements. Prisoners the

17 Johnston, Diary, June 8, 1862.

18 OR 11/1:743; *Rochester Democrat and American*, June 10, 1862; Speer, *Voices of Cemetery Hill,* 50-52.

28th captured were passed on to a detachment of the 4th VA Cavalry, while with the infantry coming up in support, the artillery pulled back behind the Kinney farmhouse structures. William Speer recalled the deadly Federal artillery fire. While the regiment redeployed, "a shell passed so near my head I dodged to one side & came near to falling, the shell striking the flagbearer & a private in Company C." In another instance, he saw "a shell strike a young Mr. Roberts of Co. A injuring him badly fracturing both of his thighs from which he died. Also I seen two more men of Co. A killed with shells, taking the top of one of their heads & cutting the other" in two. At the advance of a Federal brigade, despite Lane's attempts at extending his flank and redeploying his men, he couldn't withstand the onslaught until reinforcements arrived. In their hasty withdrawal, the Confederates had to leave their dead, seriously wounded, knapsacks, an ambulance, wagon, and one of the artillery pieces. The bulk of the regiment headed back toward Hanover Court House, with the Federals in pursuit. The remaining Confederate artillery piece stopped at least once and opened fire at the pursuers. Under the impression they had finally found the main Confederate line, the Federals deployed their infantry and artillery; all the while the Confederate infantry continued to retreat beyond the court house.[19]

Lane's requests for reinforcements had not gone ignored. Unbeknownst to Lane, Branch was contending with a fight of his own. As enemy forces pursued Lane, two other Federal regiments and a section of artillery headed down the Ashcake Road, intent upon cutting the telegraph and wrecking the railroad. A Confederate cavalry picket spotted and reported the advance. Colonel Lee of the 37th NC ordered Lt. Col. William Barber to deploy two companies into the woods beyond Lebanon Church while Lee rode to Slash Church to report this movement. Barber withdrew his two companies, falling back and reforming on the rest of the regiment. Latham's other section of artillery arrived and soon commenced returning fire. Lee realized upon returning that the enemy force was much larger than his own and called for the 12th NC to come to his aid.

Federal artillery fire soon found the range on the Confederate guns and destroyed one caisson, whereupon Latham redeployed his artillery. The Federal brigade commander, Brig. Gen. John Martindale, requested Porter send reinforcements. Porter's answer flabbergasted him: he was ordered to send one regiment up the railroad tracks to destroy bridges and structures, while the other regiment and artillery moved off to the right toward Hanover Court

---

19 Speer, *Voices*, 52-53; OR 11/1:744.

House. Martindale dashed off another note, reiterating a large body of Confederates to his front and left, not his right. But he obeyed his orders and broke off the engagement. Mud and a broken caisson caused a delay, and Martindale used his remaining regiment, the 2nd Maine Infantry, as a rear guard. Porter's second reply again informed Martindale there were no Confederates in his front. Disgusted, Martindale sent a third courier to Porter, while gaining permission from his division commander to assume responsibility for his own actions. A Federal cavalry picket soon reported that the Confederates were advancing, and Martindale ordered the 2nd ME back to the intersection of the New Bridge and Ashcake Roads.[20]

About the time the long-range artillery duel ceased, Branch arrived on the field from his Slash Church headquarters. Lane's request came shortly thereafter, and Branch chose to send the 18th, 33rd, and 37th regiments to the 28th's assistance, but discovered the road blocked. As Martindale was posting the 2nd Maine, he spied the 44th NY Infantry, with a section of Martin's Massachusetts Battery in tow. When Martindale explained his plight, the commanders of the infantry and artillery agreed to place themselves under his command. Martindale also sent for the fought-out 25th New York. He positioned his men with the 2nd Maine on his right, masked by a thick timber, then two artillery pieces, the 25th and 44th NY on his left. Meanwhile Branch quickly developed a plan of attack. He ordered the 33rd NC toward the Federal left and the 37th to attack the Federal right, both regiments through the woods. The 18th NC would move across an open field and attack the center. The 12th NC was held in support.

From the start, Branch's plan fell apart. The 33rd entered the woods on the right and promptly got confused. Companies A and B were deployed as skirmishers, and as they advanced, a courier arrived, directing the regiment to fall back. However, regimental commander Lt. Col. Robert Hoke couldn't recall his skirmishers who continued to advance toward the New Bridge Road. At the edge of the woods, they discovered a small group of Federal soldiers in a clearing. Captain Joseph Saunders wanted to capture them and ordered a detachment to circle around to their rear. Once in position however, the detachment fired and charged, driving off the bluecoats. Saunders then

---

20 Janet Hewett, et. al., eds., *Supplement to the Army Official Records,* 100 vols. (Wilmington, NC, 1994-2001), 2:367; OR 11/1:703-704; the 37th Regiment only had seven companies. Two companies had been sent out on picket, while a third was detailed to guard the regimental baggage.

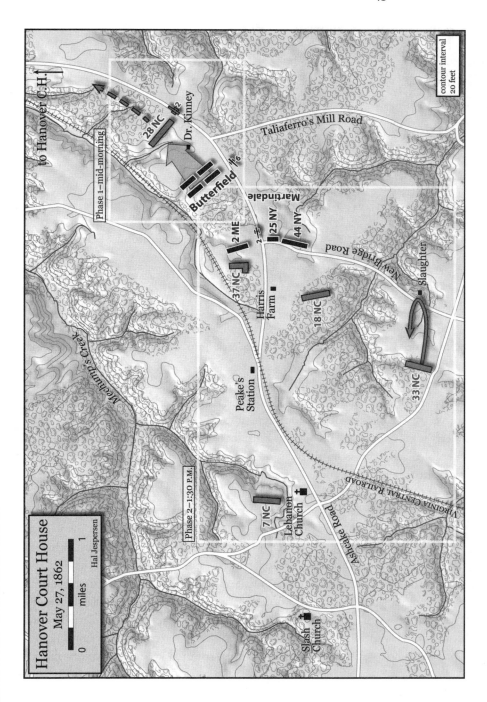

Hanover Court House
May 27, 1862
Hal Jespersen

0   miles   1

contour interval
20 feet

to Hanover C.H.

Phase 1–mid-morning

Mechump's Creek

28 NC

Dr. Kinney

#2

Taliaferro's Mill Road

Butterfield

#6

Martindale

2 ME

2 #

25 NY

44 NY

New Bridge Road

Slaughter

37 NC

Harris
Farm

18 NC

33 NC

Peake's
Station

Phase 2–1:30 P.M.

Lebanon
Church

7 NC

Ashcake Road

VIRGINIA CENTRAL RAILROAD

Slash
Church

Colonel Robert H. Cowan advanced the 18th North Carolina across an open field during the battle of Hanover Court House.

Histories of the Several Regiments and Battalions from North Carolina

proceeded to capture a Union field hospital, rounding up a couple of mobile prisoners and releasing some members of the 28th NC captured earlier that day. Some of the escaping Federals alerted Martindale, who sent half of the 44th NY back toward the area. Saunders beat a hasty retreat. At some point, the Federals abandoned their task and fell back to their original position.[21]

As the 33rd dithered about in the woods, the 18th and the 37th Regiments launched their attacks. Colonel Cowan ordered the 18th to fix bayonets and move forward at the double quick. One of the participants said the men had been "told to hold our fire, charge with loaded guns, and capture the battery, if possible." After passing through a small belt of timber, they entered a large cultivated field. The enemy was reportedly just 200-250 yards beyond the timber. Yet the Confederates soon learned the Federals lay some 600 yards away. Cowan ordered the regiment "forward at charge bayonets" and the 18th started to move across the field. "The artillery was playing upon our men all the while,—throwing shrapnel principally; and soon the Minnie rifles began to assist." Federal artillery and infantry had no other targets on the field at this point. An officer from the 2nd ME recalled "The enemy . . . appeared boldly in our front, advancing in perfect order, . . . the Stars and Bars defiantly flying." Despite the severity of the fire, the 18th got to within 75 yards of the Federal position. Cowan, with an unaided advance or a retreat equally unthinkable, "halted his line—gave the command to fire—poured in four or five destructive

21 Joseph Saunders to mother, June 6, 1862, Saunders Papers, SHC.

volleys; and under the cover of the smoke threw the regiment into the piece of woods" to his right. There Cowan reformed his lines and continued to fire away.[22]

"Boys, you have stern work before you. It is no child's play—do your duty," admonished Colonel Lee. It had taken the 37th NC much longer to get into position. Undergrowth choked the woods; the adjutant estimated visibility at not more than 30 steps. About the time the Carolinians should have been able to wheel to the right and capture the battery, up rose the 2nd ME, delivering a volley that stopped their advance. Moses Hart attested that he and his comrades had gotten to "within 30 yards of the enemy before we discovered them." And while the conflict lasted, it "was as fierce as any during the war." And losses were heavy. "I went into the fight with 60 men and came out with 36 . . . . When we met the enemy we thought there was 1500, but I don't suppose there were much less than 15,000." Stalled in the thick woods, the 37th Regiment rose to fire, then dropped to the ground to reload. Federal artillery began to enfilade their right, and the four companies there bent back at roughly right angles to the troops on their left, a maneuver called refusing the flank. Part of the regiment fired toward the artillery, while the rest engaged the 2nd ME. One Tar Heel in the 37th Regiment recalled exploding shells knocking both Colonel Lee and Major Hickerson from their horses. Both Lieutenant Colonel Barber's and adjutant William Nicholson's horses were killed.[23]

Caught in a crossfire, both the 25th NY and the Federal artillerymen began to give way, and soon portions of the 44th NY as well. Had the 33rd NC been able to get into position to sweep down the New Bridge Road, the battle of Hanover Court House might have concluded differently. However, both the 18th and 37th Regiments ran low on ammunition. Moreover, the noise of the battle alerted Fitz John Porter to his blunder. Confederates were in his rear, and Martindale was engaged with them. Porter quickly dispatched several regiments back to Martindale's position, and these five regiments outflanked both the 18th and 37th and forced them to retreat. Branch had kept the 7th Regiment as a reserve, despite Colonel Campbell's appeals otherwise. In the gathering

22 Philadelphia *Times*, October 20, 1883; *Wilmington Journal*, June 12, 1862; OR 11/1:741.

23 Wilmington *Journal Weekly*, June 12, 1862; *Weekly Catawba Journal*, June 19, 1862; *Spirit of the Age*, June 9, 1862; Raleigh *Register*, June 7, 1862. One account says Hickerson gave his horse to Barber.

darkness the 7th was finally ordered in and delivered several volleys ending the pursuit for the day. Branch's brigade fell back to Ashland that evening.[24]

While the 7th and 33rd Regiments sustained few losses, Branch's three other regiments did not. Total Confederate losses are estimated at 798, including 59 killed, and 210 wounded, 59 fatally. Losses in some community-based companies were tragic. Company G of the 37th Regiment lost James, Joel, John, and William Robnett, possibly brothers from Alexander County. Marvin and James Key, along with their cousin R. J. Key, of the 28th NC were all killed in the fighting around the Kinney farm.[25]

Doctor Robert Gibbon, the 28th NC's surgeon, established his field hospital during the battle near a stream, about 200 yards from Kinney's home. The rest of the surgical team established the brigade hospital at Lebanon Methodist Church. As the Confederates retreated, Branch ordered John Shaffner, the 33rd's surgeon to move all his ambulatory patients to Ashland. When Shaffner relayed this order to the brigade surgeon at the hospital, three surgeons "disgracefully" mounted up and "left the wounded, ambulances, instruments and supplies lying unprotected in the yard." Shaffner dismounted, loaded the wagons with medical supplies and "whatever was of value," along with 30 of the wounded soldiers, and sent them toward Ashland. Overall, 105 of Branch's wounded fell into enemy hands, including Shaffner while attending to "some of our wounded men, who had been necessarily left behind." Assistant surgeon W. R. Barham and hospital steward John Abernathy of the 28th Regiment were also captured. Barham apparently escaped while Abernathy was imprisoned at Fort Delaware. The Kinney farm grounds were used later as a hospital. A member of the 28th NC, captured late on May 27, passed by the Kinney farm the next morning. "I beheld an awful sight," he remembered,"the houses, corncrib, shuck pen, wagon & yard full of wounded,

---

24 Schenck wrote Branch's brigade "so hurt the Northern division opposing them that there was no immediate pursuit." Martin Schenck. *Up Came Hill: The Story of the Light Division and its Leaders* (Harrisburg, PA, 1958), 37; *Weekly State Journal*, October 1, 1862. According to an article on Branch after his death, Campbell sought out the general the next day and "magnanimously told him that he had done the right in holding him in reserve."

25 The story of the Robnett brothers being killed is often repeated. Some family members believe William and James Robnett were brothers, as were cousins Joel and John C. Robnett. Email, Bill Robinette to author, October 20, 2010, in my possession; Casstevens, *The 28th North Carolina Infantry*, 239.

Lane was forced to abandon a cannon and caisson during the fight between the 28th North Carolina and Butterfield's brigade. They were later photographed in the camp of the 17th New York Infantry. *Library of Congress*

with their cries & moanings from the affect of wounds & the surgeon's knife & here & there lay a poor soldier who had expired during the night."[26]

The loathsome task of burying the Confederate dead fell upon the Federals. One member of the 5th NY recalled seeing a young Confederate frozen in the act of loading his musket, "his hand was still on the ramrod having rammed the charge about half home." This same New Yorker recalled burying "a fine looking young fellow about 18 years old, his Bible was in his shirt bosom and we left it there. It was a pity but we had not even an old blanket to wrap around him." Captain Speer (28th NC) complained he saw members of the 5th NY pillaging Confederate dead taking "money, pocket knives and other little tricks. I felt sorry for these poor men far from home and friends." Members of the

26 *The Catawba Weekly Journal,* June 10, 1862; Louis Shaffner, "A Civil War Surgeon's Diary," *North Carolina Medical Journal* (September 1966), 23:410; Jordan, *NC Troops,* 8:111, 112, 9:120; Speer, *Voices from Cemetery Hill,* 57.

14th NY dug a trench and buried 25 Confederates together, placing an "orderly sergeant at their head, the post he occupied when alive; at each corner of the plot they placed stakes, and at one end of it, cut on a tree, '25 N.C. X killed.'" The Federal dead buried on the field were reinterred not long after the war. The final disposition of Branch's dead remains a mystery.[27]

Branch's biggest loss came from men unable to evade the enemy. Federal forces captured 609 of them, including the 105 wounded. Many of the captured came from the 28th NC, elements of which had been left to fend for themselves after Colonel Lane's position collapsed. Capt. George Johnston ran into the two companies of the 37th during the retreat. Johnston wanted to turn around and try to cut his way to the main Confederate lines but was persuaded otherwise. His ad hoc command spent the night huddled together, without fires, "the most cheerless, comfortless night" he ever passed, he said. The next morning, Johnston was determined to cross the Pamunkey River. The men made a raft to float their weapons over and strung rifle slings together to combat the current. After several trips, Johnston discovered the majority of his men couldn't swim, and "dreaded the water more than the Yankees." Already crossed over, Johnston implored them to cross. Instead they tried to find a boat and were discovered by Federal cavalry in the process. Now Johnston's men from the opposite bank beseeched him to return, which he did. He was captured with his soldiers. Captain Speer recalled seeing men broken down in every direction as they neared the Pamunkey River. Like Johnston, Speer could have made it over the river, but many of his men could not. Speer remained with them and was captured about dusk on May 27. On May 28 the prisoners marched 18 miles, and another eight miles the next day Numerous groups of Federal soldiers aside the road along the way cussed and berated them "as G. D. dirty rebels, Rebel cut throats, you ought to be hung, have your throats cut, burnt, etc. No one would give us the credit of being humans; [we] did not have horns nor tails but, damn them, they are Rebels." From White House landing, the prisoners were loaded aboard a steamer, chugged past the wreckage of the USS *Congress*, and transferred at Fortress Monroe to the *Star of the West* for a voyage to New York. Confined at Fort Columbus, most were paroled in August.[28]

27 Stevens [to unknown], June 11, 1862, quoted in Brian Pohanka, *Vortex of Hell: History of the 5th New York Volunteer Infantry* (Lynchburg, VA, 2012), 230-31; Speer, *Voices*, 59; *Oneida Weekly Herald*, June 17, 1862.

28 Johnston, Diary, June 8, 1862, NCDAH; Speer, *Voices*, 56, 61.

James Atkinson of the 33rd North Carolina was captured at Hanover Court House, but managed to escape that evening. He would be wounded at Sharpsburg, Chancellorsville, Reams Station, and Jones Farm, but made it to Appomattox, where he was paroled.

Histories of the Several Regiments and Battalions from North Carolina

---

Many North Carolinians avoided capture and eventually returned to their commands. Captain Nicholas Gibbon (28th NC) led 70 men through the swamp, evading Federal cavalry, only to be accused of abandoning his regiment when he reported to Branch, who apologized to Gibbon a few days later. Lane led other remnants of his regiment through Taylorsville and on to Ashland. He not only discovered Branch gone but also little food to feed his famished men. Several barrels of whiskey were uncovered, though, and Lane ordered one of them rolled out into the street. "I did not have to repeat the order," Lane wrote, "and you can imagine the effects upon empty stomachs." Suitably fortified, Lane's men, "with songs, old rebel yells and a general waving of caps," struck out for Branch's main force. Lane asked Branch to send Dr. Gibbon with wagons to transport the sick and broken-down men back. Henry Bennett (37th NC) "managed to slip about till he got seven miles from the battle field, and finally reached our lines in safety," reporting to his captain, John Ashcraft. Confederates continued to trickle in over the next few days. Portions of the 37th's Company D who had been sent out on picket and then cut off, arrived back on May 31, many so fatigued wagons were sent to retrieve them.[29]

---

29 Nicholas Gibbon, May 1862, Diary, Nicholas Gibbon Papers, UNC/C; *Charlotte Democrat*, July 1, 1862; *Biblical Recorder*, June 11, 1862; JL to Thomas Munford, January 4, 1893, Lane Papers, AU; JL to WB, May 29, 1862, Branch Papers, UVA.

Jubilant Union soldiers swept through the former Confederate camp, capturing two company-level flags. On hearing of the battle, McClellan informed his superiors in Washington, D.C. of the victory and claimed the Confederate force completely destroyed. McClellan himself visited the battlefield, calling it "a glorious victory." McDowell crossed a portion of his command over the Rappahannock River on May 25, and moved towards the Federals at Hanover. Richmond was aware of McDowell's movement, and of course, Branch's defeat at Hanover, and on May 28, the papers from the various departments were boxed and ordered to the railroad depot for transport south. But nothing came of McDowell's move: he never joined the main Federal army, and after their victory at Hanover, Porter's troops returned to their former position. The pressure from the north was mitigated.[30]

While his soldiers rested and refitted, Branch was fighting a new battle. An article appeared under the pseudonym "Hanover," giving a detailed account of the fighting and criticizing Branch's generalship. Branch's headquarters were more than a mile from his command, "Hanover" claimed, and the general had missed the entire first part of the battle and failed to reinforce the 18th and 37th which were engaged. So for "the men, company and regimental officers" the battle below Hanover was "a brilliant affair for North Carolinians. Of the rest the public must judge." Several newspapers in North Carolina did just that. The *Spirit of the Age* concluded if just half of the reports about Branch's conduct as a commander were true, "he is very incompetent and so obtuse or excessively vain that" he didn't even know it. "[H]e ought to be immediately cashiered."[31]

The "grossly slandering" letter infuriated the general, and his search for "Hanover" soon succeeded. The newspaper article bore similarities to the official battle report Colonel Lee of the 37th NC had filed, and it wasn't long before Lee was pressured to reveal his adjutant, William T. Nicholson, had penned the letter, possibly with the help of an officer from the 33rd. When confronted, Nicholson confessed. Branch preferred charges against him, citing his "monstrous and abominable slanders." Nicholson now felt moved to write a follow-up letter, stating he had subsequently discovered "some facts had been unintentionally misstated, and that certain expressions had been used which

30 Stephen Sears, ed. *The Civil War Papers of George B. McClellan: Selected Correspondence, 1860-1865* (New York, 1992), 279; for more information, see Hardy, *The Battle of Hanover Court House.* The captured flags belonged to Company E, 12th NC State Troops, and Company D, 45th GA.

31 *The Spirit of the Age,* June 9, 1862.

might, if unexplained, be constructed to reflect upon the personal bravery or generalship of General L. O'B. Branch." He went on to add that he now believed Branch had been on the field before the first gun was fired, directing each of his regiments during the battle, and that no less a person than General Lee had sent congratulatory orders to Branch afterwards.[32]

On June 3, after receiving Branch's after-action report, Lee wrote approvingly of Branch's activities at the battle below Hanover Court House. Lee realized Branch had faced superior numbers and asked the North Carolinian to convey to his men "my hearty approval of their conduct, and hope that on future occasions they will evince a like heroism and patriotic devotion." Undoubtedly, Branch needed the praise. He had fought in two battles as commander of all of the Confederate forces engaged, and had lost both. The press, some of which was already hostile to him, was having a heyday over the accusations of one of his junior officers.[33]

Dissatisfaction also ran throughout the brigade. Captain Morris (37th NC) wrote home: "we was Defeated through General Branches Bad Management." Colonel Cowan received so many letters that he submitted his own to the Wilmington *Journal*, stating he had not been arrested "for using abusive language of Genl. Branch." His relationship with Branch was "pleasant and friendly," Cowan said, and he found all the rumors "excessively annoying, but well calculated to impair the efficiency of our Brigade at a time when all our strength is wanted." But greater events would soon transpire to take the focus off of Branch and his brigade.[34]

---

32 Clark, *Histories*, 1:24; "Charges and Specifications against William T. Nicholson . . ." n.d., Branch Papers, UVA; *The Weekly Catawba Journal*, June 19, 1862. Apparently, the charges against Nicholson were dropped.

33 OR 11/1:743.

34 William Morris to "Deare Companion," May 30 1862, Morris Papers, SHC/UNC; *Wilmington Journal*, June 26, 1862.

Chapter 4

"Literally shot to pieces."

The Seven Days' Campaign

W hile General Branch was busy fighting at Hanover Court House, his brigade was being folded into a new infantry division.

For some time, Gen. Joseph E. Johnston had been attempting to form a larger organization from some of the brigades flowing from around the Confederacy into the Confederate capital in Richmond. The names of Brigadier Generals Ambrose Powell Hill and Lafayette McLaws were proposed to the Confederate Senate as commanders, and both were promoted to major general within days of one another in late May 1862. On May 27, Hill sent a note to Branch communicating Johnston's order that assigned Branch's brigade to Hill's command. Hill also ordered Branch to collect and prepare his men to move. Apparently, Hill didn't know of Branch's recent engagement, and early on May 28, he told Branch to remain where he was, as Hill was planning to advance the following morning and "fight or fall back together as circumstances may require." Nicholas Gibbon (28th NC) remembered seeing General Hill in Ashland conferring with Branch on May 28. After sending his wounded off via railroad, Branch was ordered to fall back to Brook Church later that same day.[1]

"Powell" Hill, as his intimates called him, was a Virginia native and 1847 West Point graduate who served in Mexico and battled Seminoles in Florida. Resigning from the US Army in March 1861, Hill was appointed colonel of the 13th VA Infantry, and on February 20, 1862, a brigadier general. Just 90 days later, he went from commanding a regiment with several hundred men to an appointment as a major general in command of 20,000. At 36, he was the youngest major general in the Confederate army. "I am Glad to Say that we are thrown under General Hills command," wrote William Morris of the 37th NC.[2]

Realizing that a merger of McClellan's and McDowell's forces would likely doom the Confederate capital, Johnston chose to attack. On May 31, he launched an assault against two Federal corps seemingly isolated south of the Chickahominy River. Though poorly synchronized, the attack did drive back the Federals and inflict serious casualties. With the arrival of enemy reinforcements the Confederates fed more men into the battle. Eventually, the Federal lines were stabilized. The Confederates renewed the attack on June 1, but made little headway. "The cannonading was distinctly heard in our camp," recalled James Harris (7th Regiment). Branch himself wrote home of "a heavy fight" lasting a day and a half not far from his position. He saw "little prospect of my being in the main battle," although whether this relieved or frustrated him isn't entirely clear. Several other members of the brigade reported hearing the engagement, but the Tar Heels were never ordered to the front.[3]

Although the outcome on the field was inconclusive, the serious wound Gen. Johnston sustained on May 31 changed the course of the war because Davis assigned Robert E. Lee to replace him as commander of the Confederate forces in Virginia. Born in Virginia in 1807, son of a Revolutionary War hero and early Virginia governor, Lee grew up in Alexandria, just across the Potomac River from Washington. After graduating from West Point in 1829, he

---

1   James Robertson, *General A. P. Hill: The Story of a Confederate Warrior* (New York, 1987), 58; Gibbon, "Diary," Gibbon Papers, SHC/UNC 30; A. P. Hill to Branch, May 28, 1862, Branch Papers, UVA; *OR* 11/ 3:554; Branch left Ashland and met Hill at Stony Point. Schenck, *Up Came Hill*, 37.

2   Ezra Warner, *Generals in Gray: Lives of the Confederate Commanders* (Baton Rouge, LA, 1959), 134-35; Robertson, *Hill*, 58; William Morris to "Deare Companion," May 30, 1862, Morris Papers, SHC/UN.

3   Harris, *Historical Sketches*, 12; LB to "My Dear Nannie," June 1, 1862, Branch Papers, UVA.

Ambrose Powell Hill served as the Branch-Lane brigade's division commander until late May 1863, when he was elevated to lieutenant general and given a new corps in the Army of Northern Virginia. Hill was killed during the final hours of the Petersburg Campaign on April 2, 1865, not far from the brigade's position. *Library of Congress*

embarked on his career as an Army officer assigned to the engineering corps. Lee traveled frequently, working on the Mississippi River and on various coastal fortifications. In 1831, he married Mary Ann Randolph Custis, a granddaughter of Martha Washington.

After service in the war with Mexico, Lee served as superintendent of West Point from 1852-55. In 1861, Lee was a cavalry colonel on garrison duty in Texas. On April 20, 1861, Lee resigned his commission, three days after Virginia seceded from the Union. He soon was appointed commander of Virginia's state forces, and within a month was commissioned a Confederate general. Lee served in western Virginia and as a departmental commander along the coasts of Florida, Georgia, and South Carolina before being re-assigned to Richmond as Davis's military advisor.[4]

"Headquarters Light Division" was scribbled across the top of a dispatch from Hill to Branch, on June 1, 1862, the first use of Hill's designation for his new command. Hill's division now contained six brigades: Branch's North Carolinians, known as the Fourth Brigade, Light Division, and Joseph Anderson's brigade of Georgia regiments, plus a Louisiana Battalion, formed the original core of the division. Joining them were four Virginia regiments under the command of Charles W. Field; five South Carolina Infantry regiments under Maxcy Gregg; James J. Archer's five-regiment brigade of men from Alabama, Georgia, and Tennessee; and William D. Pender's six-regiment brigade of Arkansas, North Carolina, and Virginia soldiers. Lieutenant Colonel Lewis Coleman commanded Hill's artillery, nine batteries. Only Anderson outranked Branch among the brigadiers.[5]

Hill ordered Branch on June 1 to send out two regiments from Brook Church toward Mechanicsville. For the next three weeks, groups of soldiers from the brigade did picket duty along the Chickahominy River, while the remainder of the brigade worked on fortifications. Their camp consisted of "rude shelters," made of old carpets, blankets, boughs, and whatever else was on hand. John Conrad (28th NC) reported that his company only had one tent with a pair of flies sheltering them at night. He and another soldier shared their two blankets. Branch told his wife that between May 27 and June 1, he had slept in his clothes. Many brigade members had lost their knapsacks, including blankets, at Hanover. Federal cavalry and infantry were just a short distance across the river, and at night the two sides could speak to each other. In the

4 Warner, *Generals in Gray*, 80-81.

5 OR 11/3:555, 567-68. It is unclear why Hill chose the name. One of Hill's biographers wrote that he "wanted his men to have a reputation for alacrity and agility; or the name may have been nothing more than an antonym for the largest division in the Confederates armies." Robertson, *Hill*, 63.

absence of large movements or actions, small skirmishes broke out regularly. Bellamy recalled one skirmish that "waxed warmly," where he "did my best to drop a dirty villain on a large grey or white horse, who rashly & boldly rode out in an open field & apparently requested us to do him the honor of introducing to his ears the report of our muskets." Eventually the rider was unhorsed, and while it is unclear just who was responsible, Bellamy believed he was.[6]

As soon as Lee assumed command, he began improving his army, which he re-christened as the Army of Northern Virginia—whose "ancient fame" he felt sure "every man has resolved to maintain"—in the order announcing his promotion. Commanders were ordered to have their men ready to move, to keep the troops fresh, and to ship all surplus baggage and broken-down equipment to depots. Lee strove to ensure better regular provisions to his troops, and even authorized a whiskey ration, with the permission of division commanders. Work surged forward on the fortifications around Richmond as well. Lee also had the regimental commanders create a provost guard "to prevent straggling." Lee's troops noticed: a member of the 33rd Regiment reported everyone's health and well-being "rapidly improved of late, and the measures taken by our regimental and brigade commanders to supply us with nutritious and healthy food are eliciting the heartfelt thanks." This was the general feeling throughout the army.[7]

Tactically, Lee developed a plan to drive McClellan from the gates of Richmond. First, Lee reorganized the army, eliminating the two wings plus reserve concept, and broke up one division. At the same time, he added troops brought in from other states. By the end of June, Lee commanded the largest field army in Confederate history. Next, Lee set his troops, despite their grumbles, working on field fortifications, which could be held by fewer men. Lee also sent his cavalry commander, J. E. B. Stuart, with 1,200 troopers, on his now-celebrated ride around McClellan's army. The ride began June 12 and took four days to navigate completely around McClellan's 100,000-man plus force. Stuart's ride provided Lee with critical information: The enemy's right flank was "in the air," unprotected by any natural topographical feature like a river or high ground. Stuart's ride had also disrupted McClellan's supply lines. Lee's plan was

6   OR 11/3:567-68; Bellamy, Diary, 40-41; LB to "My Dear Nannie," June 1, 1862; O'Daniel, *Kinfolk of Jacob Conrad*, 303.

7   OR 11/3:569, 576-77; *Weekly State Journal*, July 1, 1862. See also Joseph Glatthaar, *General Lee's Army: From Victory to Collapse* (New York, 2008), 123-34.

set: He would pull Stonewall Jackson's command out of the Shenandoah Valley and turn McClellan's flank, trying to force a decisive battle between the two armies. The operations were scheduled to begin on June 26, with Branch's brigade playing a crucial role in the opening salvos of the battle to save Richmond.[8]

According to Lee's overall plan, Branch's brigade would simultaneously serve as a liaison between Jackson's force, arriving to Branch's north, and protection for their right flank, and Hill's division to the east. Hill's orders on June 24 instructed Branch and the other commanders to have all brigades "draw two days' rations (hard bread) to be issued cooked." Each regiment was allowed only a single wagon for ammunition. Soldiers would carry but one blanket and leave their knapsacks behind. Anyone who could "be possibly spared must take their place in the ranks." And of course, "[b]rigade commanders are urged to see that their men are in good fighting condition." Captain Marmaduke Johnson's Virginia battery was attached to Branch's brigade, and except for five companies of the 33rd NC left on picket duty under the command of Lt. Col. Robert Hoke, the brigade broke camp on the afternoon of June 25. Upon making camp at Half Sink that evening, the 18th assumed picket duty.[9]

Reveille came at 3:30 the next morning. Jackson had orders to move out a little earlier, and as soon as he sent word to Branch, his brigade was ordered to cross the Chickahominy River. Branch expected this word around 4:00 a.m., but it did not come. Stonewall was running late. A little after 8:00 a.m., Hill cautioned Branch to wait. Branch had posted his men in an open field, in full view of Federal pickets. Branch, trying to deceive them, pulled his men back a half mile to the rear into some woods and continued to wait. Word from Jackson finally arrived a little after 10:00 a.m. Although Jackson was six hours behind, and not even close to being in the right position, Branch had his men formed and fording the river within ten minutes. The 7th Regiment, along with a section of artillery in tow, took the lead. Three companies of the regiment, under Lt. Col. Edward Haywood, were thrown out a good distance as

---

8   Sears places the number of men Lee had on hand at the start of the Seven Days' Battles at 92,400. See Stephen Sears. *To the Gates of Richmond: The Peninsula Campaign* (New York, 1992), 156.

9   A. P. Hill to LB, June 24, 1862, Branch Papers UVA; OR 11/2:894.

skirmishers in front of the column, to sound the alarm if they approached a large body of the enemy.[10]

Just before reaching Atlee's Station, Haywood encountered some 200 Federal troopers, possibly of the 8th IL Cavalry. Haywood's skirmishers attacked, apparently near the Crenshaw farm, and quickly ran them off. He reported capturing a flag, "their company books and memoranda," with just a few wounded of his own. Once the Federals withdrew, five companies of the 33rd Regiment crossed the river and joined the main column. Sometime between 3:30-4:00 p.m., Branch made contact with a portion of Jackson's command under Richard Ewell, with whom he spoke shortly, and then, Branch wrote, "we proceeded on our respective routes." Haywood continued pressing on his skirmishers, and just beyond Atlee's Station, the Federals made another stand and were again driven back. Branch recalled that the Federals contested his advance at several points, but he pressed on anyway. On reaching the Meadow Bridge Road, Branch learned from stragglers that Hill's division had already crossed over and was engaged in battle along Beaver Dam Creek. Branch didn't reach the battlefield until 6:00 p.m. After fruitlessly searching for Hill, he returned to his brigade about the time Hill found them. Branch was ordered to support a battery, and then his men slept on their arms in a line of battle. The brigade's losses for the day were slim.[11]

Everything had gone wrong for Lee on June 26. Jackson was late, and A. P. Hill, growing impatient, had crossed the river and launched several frontal assaults that failed to dislodge the enemy. The day was a tactical defeat but a strategic success. Jackson's position thwarted McClellan's lines of communication and supply, and he had to retreat.[12]

Once again Branch's brigade arose early. The artillery began dueling just before dawn, producing scattered casualties. Men of the 7th NC were ordered into a stretch of woods; several hours later, they reformed on the road. "While awaiting orders," the Carolinians "learned the enemy had abandoned his position and was in full flight, and they set out immediately in pursuit. Leaving a

---

10 Ibid., 881-82. Robertson writes Branch never sent Hill the note from Jackson announcing Branch's movement or Jackson's tardiness. Freeman wrote Jackson's note "doubtless was relayed to A. P. Hill and by him sent to Lee on the Mechanicsville Pike, but of this there is no record." Robertson, *Hill*, 68; Freeman, *Lee's Lieutenants*, 1:509.

11 *OR* 11/2:881-82, 886-87.

12 Joseph Harsh, *Taken at the Flood: Robert E. Lee and Confederate Strategy in the Maryland Campaign of 1862* (Kent, OH, 1999), 94.

thin line of troops and artillery, the majority of Federal forces had pulled out under the cover of darkness, to a naturally strong position on the other side of Gaines' Mill, a slope beyond Boatswain's Swamp. Lee devised a second flanking maneuver, again using Jackson's command, augmented by D. H. Hill's division. Gregg's brigade of the Light Division had first uncovered the Federal position, driving in their skirmishers. Hill waited until his other brigades came up before launching an assault. Branch was positioned to the right of Gregg's brigade, and as he neared the field, his lead regiment, the 7th NC, encountered the enemy. Hill told Branch to move in two regiments, and hold the balance in reserve. Branch sent the 28th forward with the 7th. Part of the 7th Regiment gave way, just as the 28th was set to hook up with its left flank. Colonel Campbell ordered the regiment to fall back and reform, and, during this attempt, someone ordered the regiment to another portion of the field. So Campbell, with seven companies, marched away to the right. According to Haywood, a quarter of mile later these troops were ordered to "advance across a swamp and over an abatis of felled trees up a hill upon an intrenched position of the enemy." and during this charge, "our patriotic colonel lost that life which was so dear to his whole regiment."[13]

The colonel had been carrying the regimental flag at his death. At the beginning of the war, the ladies at home presented many companies with flags. Once a regiment was mustered, it usually packed away its company-level flags or sent them home for safe-keeping. North Carolina issued state flags to many regiments. The 7th Regiment's was silk, the 33rd's wool bunting. Later, Confederate battle flags replaced these state flags. The brigade was issued new battle flags on June 26, 1862, but more information about these banners is lacking. The flags were entrusted to the color guard: a color sergeant and a set of corporals. The center company of each regiment was designated the color company, and carrying the flag was a great honor, as was capturing an opponent's flag. Regiments dressed to the flag during various formations and rallied on the colors during battle. Carrying the flag was also the most dangerous position on the battlefield: flags, and the men who bore them, were prized targets. Wounding or killing a color bearer could disorganize a regiment during an attack.[14]

13 Harris, *Historical Sketches*, 13; OR 11/2:888.

14 Company-level flags exist for the original Company A, 7th Regiment; Company A, 28th Regiment; and Company H, 37th Regiment. The first two are in the North Carolina Museum of

Against a seemingly impregnable Federal position, the 7th Regiment surged ahead. Cpl. Henry Fight was carrying the regimental flag and "was instantly shot down," recalled James G. Harris after the war. Harris seized the colors next, and likewise, was wounded. "Col. Campbell himself seized the colors, and advancing some 20 paces in front of his regiment, ordered them not to fire, but to follow him." His men obeyed and rushed forward, Campbell leading with the flag in one hand and his sword in the other. "When within less than a stone's throw of the deadly guns, the heroic Col. Campbell was pierced by an enemy bullet and instantly killed," reported one of his soldiers. After the war, another recalled that, as Campbell fell, the flag of the 7th "covered his body as perfectly as if it had been placed there by deft and designing hands." Lieutenant Duncan Haywood seized the colors next, the staff of the flag having been shot in two, and likewise was killed, "staining with his life's blood the battle flag." The rent and bloodied banner next passed to Cpl. Lazarus Pearny, who bore it aloft for the remainder of the battle. These seven companies were finished fighting for the day, and later reported the bloodstained regimental banner "was literally shot to pieces and bore upon its field the marks of thirty-two balls." The other three companies, under Haywood's command, had been ordered to support Jackson's troops, but they did not become seriously engaged.[15]

Likewise, the 18th Regiment became separated from the brigade. Cowan wrote that the swampy, ravine-cut terrain forced his regiment farther to the right. Robert Holliday was entrusted to carry the regiment's flag that day. After the war, he recalled advancing

> through a pine thicket, marching by the right flank. The order was then given "by the left flank, guide center." You know that meant dress on the flag. . . . Everything was still in front of us but the first thing we knew we got it heavy from both the right and left flank, the fire being very severe. We were ordered to fall back. We obeyed it and

---

History, the latter at the Gettysburg National Military Park. All of these flags are variants of the First National. The Watauga *Democrat* reported the post-war existence of the flag of Company B, 37th North Carolina Troops, but its whereabouts are unknown. The silk state flag of the 7th Regiment and the wool-bunting state flag of the 33rd Regiment survive at the North Carolina Museum of History. Glenn Dedmondt, *The Flags of Civil War North Carolina* (Gretna, LA, 2003) 73, 103, 133, 142; Watauga *Democrat,* January 27, 1898, February 3, 1898; Gibbon, Diary, 15, Gibbon Papers, UNC/C.

15 *Mooresville Tribune,* May 13, 1992; Harris, *Historical Sketches,* 14; OR 11/2:888; *Statesville Landmark,* May 12, 1899; R. W. York to Mrs. B. R. Lacy, Ben Lacy Papers, NCDAH; *Daily Confederate,* June 7, 1864.

that rapidly. The wind was blowing quite strongly, and as I was on the run with the flag it caught in a scrub oak. The harder I pulled the faster it stuck. By this time the regiment being some distance to the rear, I remember that Colonel Cowan said, when he gave me the colors into my hand, "Never give up the flag" so I gave another hard tug with the staff and the latter pulled away from the flag, leaving it in the tree. I threw the staff down, seized the flag, got it, stuck it into the breast of my coat, and left in a hurry, stooping to avoid the very heavy fire. When I regained the regiment I cut a pine sapling, tied the flag to it and so I bore the flag until I was wounded.

After numerous assaults on the enemy position, at last the men made their way through the abatis, securing a somewhat protected position at the base of the Federal works. There, the regiment stalled, unable to go farther.[16]

The 28th NC was attempting to form on the left of the 7th when a concentrated infantry and artillery fire drove that regiment back. Colonel Lane attempted to lead his regiment out when Branch ordered him right back into the woods. Enemy fire caused portions of the 28th NC to give way. One company reformed and joined the rest, but three companies became separated and fought with other commands. "I cannot describe the incessant roar of musketry mixed with the loud boom of the cannon," wrote John Conrad, "and I dont think any thing ever equaled it." At some point during the battle, a staff officer from one of Jackson's brigades, Brig. Gen. Arnold Elzey's, came asking for help. Lane responded with his regiment while "exposed to a front and right enfilade infantry fire" and assumed a new position on the Confederate left, which helped drive the Federals from the field.[17]

Officers from the 33rd Regiment reported their role in the battle of Gaines' Mill more ambiguously. Hoke simply wrote of arriving on the field about 4:00 p.m. amidst heavy fighting. The regiment stayed till dark, "by which time the enemy had been driven back a distance of 2 miles." Nothing in Branch's report clarified the 33rd's role. Perhaps Hoke hoped to conceal the fact that the 33rd regiment had been the victims of friendly fire during the battle. The 37th Regiment formed behind the 33rd, and once into position, opened fire. "when discovering all was not right, we fell back a few yards," one private in the 37th recalled,

16 Clark, *Histories*, 1:26; *The Semi-Weekly Messenger*, April 7, 1905.

17 OR 11/2:893; O'Daniels, *Kinfolk of Jacob Conrad*, 309.

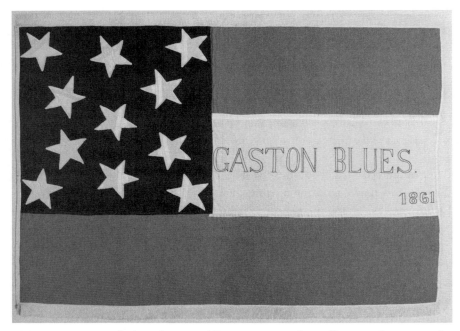

Many companies in the brigade received flags prior to marching off to war. This variant of a First National flag belonged to the Gaston Blues, which became Company H, 37th North Carolina. *Gettysburg National Military Park*

reloaded, rallied and fired again. . . .When becoming better satisfied that all was not right, we fell back about two hundred yards to a branch, reloaded and rallied a second time, when a majority fired a third time. . . . Major Cowan of the 33rd North Carolina Regiment came down with out-stretched arms, screaming at the top of his voice "Cease firing, cease firing gentlemen, cease firing" for we were . . . killing our own men.

It took Cowan and Col. Lee several minutes to gain control of their troops. Lee stormed about "looking more like a maniac or mad-man . . . , than the Honorable Colonel of the regiment."[18]

William Barber, lieutenant colonel of the 37th, offered few clues in his report about his regiment's role during the battle. The heavy enemy fire, combined with the nature of the terrain, threw the regiment "into considerable confusion," he wrote, "thereby rendering it inefficient for a short time until order could be restored." George Cochran provided more detail in his post-war

18 OR 11/2:895; Collins, "Reminisces," 22.

Private Robert Choplin of the 28th North Carolina (right), was mortally wounded at the battle of Gaines' Mill. His brother, Sgt. Joseph Choplin (below), serving in the same regiment, was reported missing in action after the battle.

Cheryl I. Martin

memoirs. The regiment was advancing in a column of fours down the road when first fired upon, throwing the column into confusion. Once the men were formed in a line of battle, the Federals "opened with a heavy fire." Several Tar Heels had begun to return fire when stopped by Col. Lee. "Brave men will not stand up and be shot down if they can't return fire. So the men began to waver." Lee advanced to the front and ordered the men to follow him, but no one moved. Eventually Lee got his men re-formed and headed in the right direction, advancing to within a short distance of the Union lines.[19]

Combat was intense. Firing the musket or rifled musket required a man to retrieve a cartridge from his cartridge box, tear off the end, and pour the black powder down the barrel, followed by the lead projectile. Then he used the

19 OR 11/2:895, 896; Cochran, *A Brief Sketch*, 23-26.

ramrod to push the projectile all the way down the length of the barrel. Improperly seated rounds could rupture barrels. Once a soldier selected a percussion cap from his cap box and placed it on the cone or nipple of the rifle, he then pulled back the hammer, aimed, and pulled the trigger. Black powder quickly fouled weapons, particularly rifles, and they became harder to load. All the while, the cacophony of the cannon and thousands of small arms was deafening. Often, the choking smoke hung thickly on the battlefield. Then came the thud of a bullet hitting a soldier and the cries of the wounded. John Alexander (37th NC), recalled after the war, while fighting at Gaines' Mill that "Gus Monteith, a good man, was shot on my left. He fell against a large limb that had just fallen behind him, that propped him up in a sitting posture, although he was quite dead. John Beard, a mere boy, was shot through the lungs and the ball dropped in his vest pocket."[20]

The chaos of the battle often made hearing and following orders difficult, if not impossible. Peter Turnmire (37th NC) recalled that while in line of battle at Gaines' Mills, he

> was standing between Thos. Hodge on the right and Vincent Greer on the left, a minnie ball struck Hodge about the heart and I eased him down on the right and Vincent Greer was struck in the temple and I eased him down on my left. When the order was given for us to fall back for reinforcements, I did not hear the orders and Captain Horton came and slapped me on my back with a sword and said we were ordered to fall back. As we went down the hill where we formed in the morning . . . . Calvin [Triplett] went down the hill with us and a stray ball struck him in the heart and he pulled his shirt bosom open and said, 'Look here! Capt. Horton, I'm killed,' and fell back dead.

As on many of the fields where the brigade fought, the thunderous roar of small arms and cannon was deafening at Gaines' Mill.[21]

Late in the day, Stonewall Jackson finally got his men into the fight, and about 7:00 p.m., the entire Confederate army on the field moved toward the Federal fieldworks. Jackson's position on the Federal flank and rear rendered their situation untenable. From the 28th NC reports, it was part of this flanking maneuver. As the men advanced, they spotted a Union officer 100 yards ahead

---

20 *Charlotte Observer*, July 1, 1903.

21 *Lenoir Topic*, August 14, 1908.

trying to rally his broken ranks. Lane wanted to capture him, but Sgt. Maj. Milton Lowe volunteered, explaining that "my life is of little importance; yours is of immense value, for on it depends the fate of our regiment." Lowe soon returned, the reins of the horse in his hand and his sword at the breast of the Federal officer, who was presented to Lane. Soon Lane was off again, waving his sword and encouraging his men. Not long thereafter, he was wounded. . . . Lane was struck on the head by a minnie ball. "Coolly stopping, he turned to Sergeant Milton A. Lowe . . . and, bending down his head, said with the utmost sang froid, 'Sergeant, is my scalp cut?' Sergeant Lowe, as brave and as cool as . . . Lane himself, examined his head carefully, and said: 'No, Colonel, it is only scorched a little.'" The day ended with the Federal forces in retreat.[22]

Branch's brigade rested on the field that night, and spent June 28 transporting the wounded off the field, burying the dead, and gathering up the spoils of battle. Noah Collins (37th NC) upon surveying the battlefield, discovered all the vegetation at a certain height mangled by the small arms and artillery fire. He found "a pine stump . . . about . . . eight inches in circumference . . . struck by seventeen small arms balls and grape shot, which had cut it off at the height of six feet." Collins recalled the "pools of blood being so very thickly scattered about that a person could scarcely set his feet clear of them," and found the job of burying the dead "odious or hateful and [a] offensive task." His comrades doubtless agreed. The temperature reached the upper 80s on June 27 and 28, and bodies, of friend or foe, quickly putrefied.[23]

The order to prepare two days' worth of rations became further complicated by rain on the evening of June 28. General Lee concluded that he had achieved part of his strategic goal: the Federal army was in the open and on the move. McClellan had chosen to change the location of his supply base from the York to the James River. It presented the Confederates with a tempting opportunity. If Lee could coordinate the different divisions of his army, and get them to attack in unison, there was a chance to destroy the Army of the Potomac before it reached the James River. Lee planned to strike a different portion of the Federal column with each of his divisions. Hill's division, now combined with Longstreet's division and under Longstreet's command, would attack the head of the column. Branch's brigade and the rest of the force set out

22 *Western Democrat*, July 27, 1862; Clark, *Histories*, 2:547-48.

23 Harris, *Historical Sketches*, 14; Collins, Reminisces, 25; Robert K. Krick, *Civil War Weather in Virginia* (Tuscaloosa, AL, 2007), 62.

on June 29, crossing the Chickahominy River. On June 30, they arrived near the village of Glendale early in the afternoon. Hill's division was held in reserve for some time. According to James Harris (7th NC), about 5:00 p.m., the brigade filed into a strip of woods, stacked arms, and began cooking dinner. The brigade began taking artillery fire in the woods, and the men, deprived of their supper, were ordered to fall back into ranks. Federal troops pressed Longstreet hard, and Hill's division moved toward the front. "[W]ith springing steps" Branch's brigade pressed forward. In his official report, Branch said he had no guide, but simply advanced toward the origin of the shells. On the way Branch encountered parts of Kemper's brigade streaming toward the rear, and Kemper himself soon rode up and gave Branch the Federal artillery's location.[24]

Confederate artillery blocked the road, and it took a while for the Tar Heels to pass, all the while exposed to "a hot fire from the enemy's guns." Upon reaching a hill, the brigade moved by the right flank "for several hundred yards, and . . . formed in an open field on the right of the road." The men took up the cry "Stonewall," and began advancing across two open fields, Col. Cowan wrote, "in the face of a perfect shower of grape and musketry." Echoing Cowan, the 28th's Col. Lane, recalled his men "were exposed to a murderous fire of shell, grape and small arms." Lane was wounded in the face during the attack and likely replaced by Maj. William Montgomery. Lieutenant Colonel Haywood of the 7th was also wounded during the attack. Perhaps it was at this point portions of the 7th Regiment began faltering. As the possibly apocryphal story goes, A. P. Hill, upon seeing the wavering 7th, rode forward and seized the regiment's colors, trying to rally the men breaking for the rear. "Damn you," he yelled, "if you will not follow me, I'll die alone!" Shortly thereafter, the 7th rallied, and Maj. Junius Hill assumed command.[25]

With men dropping at every step, Branch's brigade pressed on toward the Federal line. About 100 yards from one of the enemy batteries, Col. Lee was exhorting the 37th with "On, my brave boys!" when he was struck by an artillery

24 Harris, *Historical Sketches*, 15; OR 11/ 2:759, 765, 838, 883. Longstreet writes in his official report that Branch was ordered to protect Longstreet's line's right flank, and goes on to criticize him for not supporting the attack. Yet neither Hill nor Branch writes anything about the order. By contrast, Hill reports that Gregg's brigade was sent to support Longstreet's left, which Longstreet fails to mention in his official report. Both Sears and Robertson write Branch was a part of the original attack by Longstreet, while Schenck says the brigades were fed in piecemeal. See Robertson, *Hill*, 88; Sears, *To the Gates of Richmond*, 293; Schenck, *Up Came Hill*, 87.

25 Harris, *Historical Sketches*, 15; OR 11/2:889, 891, 893; *Richmond-Times Dispatch*, October 28, 1934.

projectile. Adjutant William Nicholson rushed over to Lee, raising him up in his arms, "and asking him if he was hurt—'Yes' was his reply. Colonel are you hurt much? . . . He was unable to answer this question, and almost instantly died in the arms of his Adjutant, who brought his body from the field, with such of his personal effects as were not blown away." When told of Col. Lee's death, "his men wept as if they had lost a father." A private in the 37th claimed Lee "as gallant an officer as ever trod the battle field of Virginia . . . as brave as a lion and gentle as a lamb and thought it not inconsistent with his profession as a soldier, to acknowledge Jesus Christ as the Captain of his Salvation." The brigade continued pushing on, capturing two Federal cannon. Branch drove his men even farther. Nevertheless, nightfall, along with the discovery that the Federals overlapped his right flank, forced Branch to call a halt. The brigade camped on the edge of the battlefield, and Branch sent a staff officer to Hill for orders, which were to remain in place overnight, and to fall back the next morning to the area where the attack had started.[26]

Confederate forces called this engagement Frayser's Farm, where they had succeeded in driving. the Federals off the field, capturing more than a dozen cannon, and even a division commander. Yet they had failed to cut the critical intersection at Glendale, and the remainder of the Federals slipped away into the darkness.

McClellan's army took a new position on Malvern Hill. While the hill was not an imposing imminence, it offered a marked tactical advantage in terrain. Attacking Confederates would have to traverse open farmland to assault the Federal position. McClellan packed all the artillery he could muster on three sides of Malvern Hill, in addition to 70,000 infantry. Moreover, artillery on Federal gunboats on the James, two and a half miles away, could reach the Confederate lines. Robert E. Lee chose to bombard the Federal position with artillery before ordering an infantry assault. Both failed miserably.

Branch's brigade moved toward Malvern Hill on the afternoon of July 1, and, around evening, was ordered to a supporting position on the field. An unnamed staff officer directed the brigade to a new location, and, after two of its regiments had been posted, Branch determined it to be the wrong position. The general took the remaining three regiments and moved to his left, but as he

---

26 Jordan, *NC Troops*, 9:468; John Alexander, *Reminiscences of the Past Sixty Years* (Charlotte, NC, 1908), 73; *The Charlotte Democrat*, August 5, 1862; OR 11/2:883. Branch most likely captured two 20-pounder Parrott Rifles belonging to Battery C, 1st Battalion, NY Light Artillery.

Col. Charles C. Lee, the commander of the 37th North Carolina, was mortally wounded by an artillery shell at Frayser's Farm on June 30, 1862, and died that same day. He father led the 16th North Carolina, and his cousin, Stephen Dill Lee, would end the war as a lieutenant general.

Porter Crane Figg

later reported, "I proceeded toward the left and reached a position near to the enemys batteries, but still too far for my short-range guns, and in full range of their artillery. Making my men lie on the ground," he continued, "they remained in the position until the firing from our side had ceased; then collecting my brigade, I returned to my camp of the morning."[27]

The week of fighting was at an end, and Branch's brigade had taken a severe beating. Two of its most experienced regimental commanders were dead. Branch regarded Reuben Campbell (7th NC), killed with the colors of his regiment in his hand, "the bravest of the brave," and considered "his loss . . . irreparable." Campbell's replacement, Lt. Col. Haywood, wrote, "The country and our State too painfully appreciate the loss of our most capable colonel for me to say aught in his praise." Campbell's remains were interred in the Snow Creek Cemetery in his native Iredell County, NC. Colonel Charles C. Lee (37th NC) was killed at Frayser's Farm. Branch mourned the loss of a "thoroughly educated soldier and an exemplary gentleman, whose whole life had been devoted to the profession of arms." Lee's remains were also returned to North Carolina. "Thus has died upon the altar of our country one of nature's noblemen, none who knew him but to love him, a gentleman, a scholar and a true soldier fallen. May his memory ever remain fresh in our hearts, his

27 OR 11/2:884. During the repositioning at Malvern Hill, the brigade suffered several wounded to shrapnel.

monument a nations gratitude. Peace to his ashes," eulogized the *The North Carolina Whig*. All the businesses in Charlotte were closed on the day of Lee's funeral; he was buried in Elmwood Cemetery.[28]

While the Federal army had retreated down the Peninsula, Lee's army was battered. Many believed further operations impossible. Furloughs were cancelled for healthy soldiers, and Lee sought new troops to offset the losses of the Seven Days Campaign. According to various regimental reports, Branch's brigade lost 87 men killed and 596 wounded, with 28 missing. Three of the regiments reported an average of 443 men present on June 26. If the other two regiments' losses were comparable, then Branch's brigade lost 32 percent of those engaged.[29]

Serious upheaval rent the ranks of the officers corps at both regimental and brigade level. Numerous officers and men were wounded, and several never returned to fight with their regiments. Captain William Morris was the highest ranking officer on the field and had to assume regimental command following the death of Col. Lee. Major Cowan (33rd NC) wrote Branch from Richmond, that he was more seriously wounded than he thought, requiring more time to recover.

Several officers had proven themselves unworthy of the important positions they held. Regimental commanders singled out six such men for having absented themselves from their commands on the eve of battle. Two officers came from the 7th Regiment. One, Lt. William Green, was not present during the campaign, while the other, Lt. Melmoth Hill, disappeared after the fight on June 27. Both were allowed to resign. In approving Lt. Green's resignation, Col. Campbell found him incompetent as well. The problem was worse in the 37th Regiment. Lieutenant Colonel Barber singled out four company-grade officers; three claimed sickness and were allowed to resign. The fourth, Lt. John J. Owen, "behaved badly"—and not only during the Seven Days' Battles. He had also shown "cowardice at the battle of New Bern." Owen was dropped in August 1862 and forced to re-enlist in the company as a private. Gen. Branch also lost three staff officers: Capt. William E Canady died of typhoid fever the first of July; William A Blount was wounded at Gaines' Mill

---

28 Ibid., 883, 888; Allardice, *Confederate Colonels*, 89, 235; *North Carolina Whig*, July 8, 1862.

29 The 7th regiment reported 450 men present; the 18th Regiment reported 400; the 28th regiment, 480. Jordan, *NC Troops*, 4:397; 6: 297, 8:101.

and resigned; and while Lt. Francis Hawks was also wounded, but eventually returned.[30]

Branch was concerned about the loss of leadership in his brigade. On July 28, he wrote Gov. Henry Clark, that his command was "very weak in officers," and he had ordered his regimental commanders to recommend men for promotion. Branch specifically asked the governor to see that William Barber, the 37th's lieutenant colonel, and Major Junius Hill of the 7th, both advanced to the next grade. (Hill's promotion to lieutenant colonel was dated June 27, and Barber's June 30, the dates of death for their predecessors.) Branch also sought to refit his brigade. On July 24, Maj. Robert Cowan, commanding the 33rd NC, formally requested Branch a second time to allow an officer to go to Raleigh and procure clothing for his regiment. Many were without shoes and had been for weeks. He was worried about the combat effectiveness of his regiment: if the regiment were ordered away, many of his men would be left behind due to the lack of serviceable footwear.[31]

General Lee had accomplished part of his goal: McClellan's army no longer threatened Richmond. After the fight at Malvern Hill, McClellan moved his soldiers even farther down the Peninsula, positioning them around Harrison's Landing. Lee chose not to attack, considering this part of his operation complete. However, Lee failed in his overall goal of crushing the Federals. And his victory had come at an enormous cost. Confederate casualties were estimated at more than 20,000 men. Yet Lee was proclaimed the savior of Richmond, and the hopes of the Confederacy's future now rested on his shoulders. No criticisms came for Branch's brigade, with minor roles in the fighting at Mechanicsville and Malvern Hill, and at the forefront at Gaines' Mill and Frayser's Farm. Branch was undoubtedly relieved that someone else was in command. He simply received orders and followed them.

---

30 William Morris to "Deare Companion," July 21, 1862, Morris Papers, SHC/UNC; Robert Cowan to LB, July 4, 1862, Branch Papers, UVA; William Green, M270, Roll 173, RG 109, CMSR, NA; OR 11/2:897; Jordan, *NC Troops*, 9:234, 502.

31 LB to Henry Clark, July 28, 1862, Branch Papers, UVA; Robert Cowan to LB, July 24, 1862, Branch Papers, UVA. Pender, now commanding an all-North Carolina brigade in the Light Division, likewise wrote his "men were dissatisfied and deserting" and his regiments "were without officers." William Hassler, ed. *One of Lee's Best Men: The Civil War Letters of General William Dorsey Pender* (Chapel Hill, NC, 1999), 164.

Chapter 5

"I fear if we get under Jackson we will get hard times."

Cedar Run—Second Manassas—Ox Hill

Once McClellan was beaten, pushed away from Richmond, and camped with his back to the James River, President Lincoln appointed Maj. Gen. John Pope to command a new Union army, the Army of Virginia, composed of several different organizations, some of which had already tangled with Jackson in the Shenandoah Valley. Pope's was a twofold mission: to protect Washington, D. C., and to threaten Lee's army, thereby relieving pressure on the Army of the Potomac. The Federals sought to capture Gordonsville, Virginia, severing one of Lee's vital rail connections. Pope issued a set of hard-war guidelines designed to punish Southern civilians. Pope's men would live off the country, and civilians would be held responsible for damages inflicted by guerrillas. Forced to take action, on July 13 Lee sent Jackson and his troops to meet Pope's advance and "restrain, as far as possible, the atrocities which he threatened to perpetrate upon our defenseless citizens." Lee considered Pope a "miscreant."[1]

1   OR 12/2:176.

Branch's brigade spent a few days near Malvern Hill following the battle, then moved back to a camp on the Charles Court House Road. During the hot and humid days of July, a different battle broke out between the brigade's division commander, A. P. Hill, and his superior, James Longstreet. A newspaper editor attached as a volunteer aide-de-camp to Hill's command during the Seven Days wrote a glowing report of the fighting at Frayser's Farm, slighting Longstreet and others and elevating Hill's role. Firing back in a different newspaper, Longstreet tried to correct the record, only to infuriate Hill, who had nothing to do with the first letter. On July 12, Hill asked Lee to "be relieved from the command of Major-General Longstreet." Longstreet endorsed and forwarded Hill's request, adding: "If it is convenient to exchange troops, or to exchange the commander, I see no particular reason why Maj. Gen. Hill should not be gratified." That same day, when Longstreet, through his staff officer, Maj. Moxley Sorrel, asked Hill for a routine report, Hill declined "to hold further communication with Maj. Sorrel." This prompted several other letters from Longstreet, which Hill ignored. Longstreet then placed Hill under arrest, with command of the division passing to Brig. Gen. Joseph Anderson. Hill subsequently challenged Longstreet to a duel.[2]

In the face of impending violence, General Lee quickly intervened and calmed his subordinates. On July 26, Longstreet released Hill from arrest, and the following day, orders arrived transferring Hill to Jackson's command. Branch's brigade started to Gordonsville soon thereafter. While the public lauded Jackson, at least one member of the brigade did not celebrate the transfer. "I fear if we get under Jackson we will get hard times," William Cloninger (28th NC) wrote just before the march began.[3]

During this time, Branch was authorized to have new battle flags inscribed with the regiments' battle honors. The general took the opportunity to review the different engagements, noting that while he could have withdrawn before "superior forces at both New Bern and Slash Church," he had chosen to stay. On "assuming command," he wrote, "he resolved never to retreat before any hostile force without fighting it, [because] he did not place too high an estimate on the valor and discipline of the brave men it is his pleasure to command. . . .

---

2 Robertson, *Hill*, 97.

3 G. Moxley Sorrel. *Recollections of a Confederate Staff Officer* (Jackson, TN, 1958), 89; *OR* 12/3:919; Harris, *Historical Sketches*, 15; W. W. Cloninger to "Dear Mother," July 29, 1862, Bell Wiley Collection, Emory University.

Whilst making this bloody but brilliant record . . . you have been, as the soldiers of freedom should always be, modest, uncomplaining, and regardful of what is due others." The quartermaster was responsible for furnishing flags to the brigade. The flags of the 7th, 33rd, and 37th regiments were all emblazoned: "New Berne, Slash Church, Mechanicsville, Gaines Mill, Fraziers [sic] Farm, [and] Malvern Hill," while the flags of the 18th and 28th regiments carried all the same names, except "New Berne." The flags arrived later that year.[4]

During this period, soldiers in the field went to the polls to elect the next North Carolina governor. Governor Ellis, who had denied troops to Lincoln, died of illness in July 1861. Henry T. Clark, president of the state senate, replaced him, but chose not to run in the election. William Johnston of Mecklenburg County, president of the Charlotte & South Carolina Railroad, had served as a delegate to the secession convention, but had no prior political experience before choosing to run for governor. Johnston represented the pro-Davis administration faction in the Confederacy, which advocated prosecution of the war until "the last extremity with no compromise with enemies, traitors, and tories." His opponent was Buncombe County native Zebulon Baird Vance, who had served in the state General Assembly and the U.S. House before the war. Possibly more importantly, he was colonel of the 26th NC, which had fought under Branch at New Bern. Vance represented another strain of Confederate political thought that supported the war effort, but believed protection of civil liberties should be preeminent at all costs. Soldiers cast their ballots on July 31. Three brigade regiments—the 7th, 18th, and 33rd—cast a majority for Johnston; the 28th and 37th voted for Vance. Overall, the soldier vote in the army overwhelmingly favored Vance, 6,843 to 3,339. Back in North Carolina, the tally was 54,423 to 20,448 in Vance's favor.[5]

Near month's end the Light Division encamped about five miles southeast of Gordonsville. For a few days, the men rested and participated in brigade drills which undoubtedly improved the fighting qualities of both Branch's brigade and the Light Division.[6]

Their preparation wasn't in vain. Ascertaining that a portion of Pope's Federal army was advancing, Jackson chose to attack it. Orders went out to

---

4 Harris, *Historical Sketches*, 16. Harris records he copied the order from the order book of the 7th Regiment.

5 Charlotte *Daily Bulletin*, August 9, 1862; *Semi-Weekly Standard*, August 9, 1862.

6 Reminiscences of Samuel A. Ashe, Box 70, Folder 6, Military Collection, NCDAH.

commanders in the early morning hours on August 4 to fix rations and prepare to move. Doctor John Shaffner (33rd NC) complained that the men had been "drummed out of our tents" about daybreak on August 6, with everything packed, but then failed to move. Further orders directed preparation of three days' additional rations, "which bodes work." The division did not step off until late afternoon, marching northward until midnight, and closing up with Jackson's two other divisions.

Up early the next morning, the Confederate veterans trudged along in oppressive heat until about midnight when Jackson called for a halt near Orange Court House. That night Hill received orders to have his men up and ready to fall in behind Ewell's division as it moved north in the morning. Hill did as ordered, but unbeknownst to him, Jackson had changed his orders again. Ewell was proceeding on a different road, and Hill was following troops of Charles Winder's division, not Ewell's. At least a brigade and a half had passed before Hill discovered he had been ordered to be in front of these troops. Hill chose to wait instead of cutting into line. An angry Jackson soon arrived, demanding to know why the Light Division had not moved. "Hill explained why, in as few words as possible, for he was seething," and Jackson rode off, convinced Hill was dragging his feet. Thereafter relationships between Jackson and Hill were strained. By the time the heat forced a halt in the movement, Hill's command had marched about one mile.[7]

The regiments had barely bedded down when distant skirmishing roused the troops. It was August 9, and it took few moments for the men, sleeping without tents, to rouse themselves, fall into ranks, and take up their arms. Branch claimed the brigade was on the march a few minutes later. With mid-afternoon temperatures approaching 100 degrees, the men trudged on through another blistering day. "Oppressively hot," was how one officer in the 7th Regiment described the weather, "and many men not sufficiently recovered from wounds and disease were unable to keep in the ranks." Stragglers lined the roadsides. Britton South of the 37th NC "[f]ell out of ranks" that day and later died of "phthisis." A member of the 7th wrote that his regiment only took 100

---

7 John Shaffner to "My Dear Friend," August 6, 1862, John Shaffner Papers, NCDAH; Robertson, *Hill*, 101. Jackson "later conceded that Hill was unaware of the new marching schedule." see James Robertson, Jr. *Stonewall Jackson: The Man, the Soldier, the Legend* (New York, 1997), 524.

men into the pending battle. Typhoid brought Branch himself so low he was forced to ride in an ambulance.[8]

Near Cedar Run, seven miles south of the town of Culpeper, Jackson encountered a Federal corps under the command of Nathaniel Banks. Confederate artillery took the lead and, for two hours, opposing batteries dueled. Jackson's two foremost divisions positioned themselves in a line from Cedar Mountain northwards across the Culpepper Road. Around 5:00 p.m., Banks launched two attacks, driving back large portions of the Confederate line. Jackson attempted on several occasions to rally his men, nervously casting an expectant eye toward the rear for the Light Division's arrival. One of Hill's brigades had already been posted on the Confederate right when Hill, with Branch's brigade in the lead, appeared on the road. Jackson rode to Hill who was walking at the head of the column, and ordered him to deploy his brigades along the road.

By this time Branch had emerged from his ambulance and took command of the brigade, although he was so weak he required frequent rest. Branch later wrote that Jackson wanted him to advance, proclaiming his "left . . . beaten and broken, and the enemy was turning him." Hill ordered Branch to the left of the Culpepper Road, and Branch formed his regiments: the 7th on the left, followed by the 18th, 33rd, 28th, and the 37th, its right resting on the road. The brigade dropped knapsacks and prepared to advance. One of Jackson's staff officers observed that Branch:

> while waiting orders . . . took occasion to give his troops . . . a speech. . . . General Jackson hearing of this delay and the cause of it, started with an unfathomable smile and galloped to the spot. As he reached the right of the brigade he took off his hat, rode rapidly along the line looking the men steadily in their faces as he passed along. When he reached their commander, he said curtly, "Push forward, General, push forward!"[9]

---

8   OR 12/2:222; Thomas Hickerson, *Echoes of Happy Valley* (Chapel Hill, 1962), 84; Robertson, *Stonewall Jackson*, 529; Harris, *Historical Sketches*, 17; William McDaid, "Four Years of Arduous Service: The History of the Branch-Lane Brigade in the Civil War." Michigan State University (Ph. D. dissertation, 1987), 92, 94; Jordan, *NC Troops*, 9:535. "Phthisis" was pulmonary tuberculosis or a similar progressive systemic disease.

9   LB to Mrs. Branch, August 15, 1862, Branch Papers, UVA; *OR* 12/ 2:22-23; Robert Krick. *Stonewall Jackson at Cedar Mountain* (Chapel Hill, NC, 1990), 226; Henry Kyd Douglas, *I Rode with Stonewall: Being chiefly the war experiences of the youngest member of Jackson's staff from the John Brown raid to the hanging of Mrs. Surratt* (Chapel Hill, NC 1940), 124.

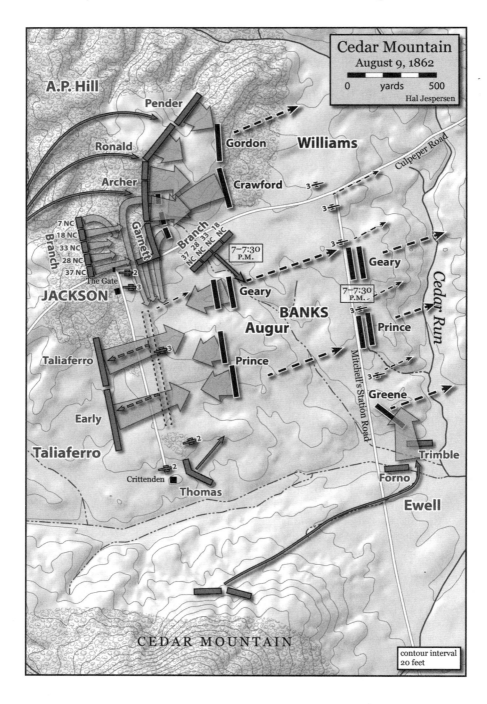

Cedar Mountain
August 9, 1862

0   yards   500

Hal Jespersen

A.P. Hill

Pender

Gordon

Williams

Ronald

Crawford

Culpeper Road

Archer

Branch
37 28 33 18
NC NC NC NC

7 NC
18 NC
33 NC
28 NC
37 NC

Garnett

Branch

The Gate

7–7:30
P.M.

Geary

JACKSON

Geary

BANKS

Augur

7–7:30
P.M.

Prince

Cedar Run

Taliaferro

Prince

Mitchell's Station Road

Greene

Early

Taliaferro

Trimble

Crittenden

Thomas

Forno

Ewell

CEDAR MOUNTAIN

contour interval
20 feet

Branch's brigade thereby stepped off into the woods toward their front. But for some unknown reason, the 7th NC did not. Quite possibly, this regiment, having the furthest to go when Branch formed up the brigade, was not in position, or, maybe failed to hear the command in the thick woods. After "one or two ineffectual attempts to advance," Col. Haywood rode off looking for Branch. He returned with orders from Jackson to move to the right of the Culpepper Road. Branch later attributed the 7th's problems to the loss of Col. Campbell during the Seven Days, implying Haywood was either unready or unqualified.[10]

With Branch out in front, the brigade advanced about 200 yards before encountering a demoralized group of Confederate soldiers streaming toward the rear. These were members of the 27th Virginia, a part of the famed Stonewall Brigade. Other soldiers were probably mingled in, possibly Virginians from Col. Thomas Garnett's brigade. The sheer number of men fleeing was enough for Branch to conclude the entire Stonewall Brigade had been broken, even though portions of it still held the far Confederate left. The "brigade coolly opened ranks to allow the fugitives to pass," reported a member of the 33rd NC, "then closing up in compact lines pressed gallantly on, in nowise disturbed by the terror-stricken cries of the runaways." Captain Walter Lenoir (37th NC) wrote the Virginians produced "considerable disorder" within the Tar Heel ranks; however, he did notice that within his own company, Virginians actually filled the gaps they created, swelling, in places, the thin ranks of Branch's brigade. Branch's men had to pull him behind the lines more than once as they charged toward the enemy, and he didn't go unscratched. "I was struck by a spent ball but it did no injury," Branch wrote home.[11]

A. P. Hill was also attempting to rally the broken ranks in the woods, according to a letter written by Dr. John B. Alexander (37th NC) long after the war. Alexander and Dr. Shaffner were trying to find a place for their field hospital when Hill rode up and pointed his pistol at Shaffner, demanding to know why he had left his post. "I am at my post," Shaffner quickly responded.

---

10 Harris, *Historical Sketches*, 17; Clark, *Histories*, 1:370; OR 12/2:221; LB to Nancy Branch, August 15, 1862. Haywood was cashiered on December 28, 1863, for drunkenness. Possibly this was connected to his behavior on a battlefield. See Allardice, *Confederate Colonels*, 189.

11 Clark, *Histories*, 2:55; Hickerson, *Happy Valley*, 84; LB to Nancy Branch, August 15, 1862. In his journal, Branch states the entire Stonewall Brigade was "utterly routed and fleeing as fast as they could run." *Confederate Veteran* (September 1917), 25:9, 415 (quoted).

"I am not a major, but a surgeon." Hill "begged his pardon" and went after actual stragglers, whom he organized and got moving back toward the fight.[12]

Once the straggling Confederates on his front cleared, Branch ordered his men to open fire. The volley drove the remaining enemy soldiers out of the woods and back across the field. Branch's brigade advanced to a fence bordering a recently harvested wheat field. He posted the 18th, 33rd, and 28th along this fence, with the 37th forming the brigade's right along another fence bordering the Culpepper Road. Noah Collins (37th NC) found the Federals "within sixty yards" of his position along the Culpepper Road and "gave the Union troops seven well-directed rounds, taking rest on a lane fence every time." Branch's brigade had just helped repulse an attack across the wheat field by a solitarily Union infantry regiment, when up the road trotted a battalion of enemy cavalry. "Just then the Federal cavalry made one of the most brilliant and gallant charges during the entire war," wrote a member of the 37th NC. The "whole brigade reserved its fire until the column came in point blank range, when it poured a withering volley into it, sending it back in 'confusion worse confounded.'" Of the 164 cavalrymen who charged, 92 became casualties.[13]

Shortly after the cavalry charge was repulsed, Branch advanced about 100 yards into the wheat field, near Cedar Run, halting in a slightly protected area. The brigades to Branch's left charged about the same time, driving the remaining organized Federal brigade on the field from the woods to Branch's left. "I halted near the middle" of the field, Branch wrote in his journal, "in doubt which direction to take." At this point, the color-bearer of the 18th NC advanced to the crest of the hill to his front, and boldly stood with his flag visible to the retreating Federals. Jackson rode into the field, and Branch's men "recognized him and raised a terrific shout as he rode along the line with his hat off." Jackson ordered the brigade to "incline to the right" while advancing. Walter Lenoir recalled the utter exhaustion plaguing his company in the 37th, such that he had to help them continue in the pursuit of the enemy. Noah Collins, also of the 37th, wrote that he dropped out and "could not . . . take part," in the final charge "in consequence of an almost intollerable . . . thirst." The entire Federal corps that had attacked Jackson, breaking portions of the Confederate line, was now retreating. The Confederates maintained the pursuit even as darkness descended. Jackson remained with the brigade, directing its

12 Charlotte *Observer*, November 16, 1903.

13 Collins, *Reminisces*, 27; Clark, *Histories*, 2:655; Krick, *Cedar Mountain*, 235.

movements, until the advance was called off. Then the men fell back "and slept on the battlefield among the dead and wounded." August 9 had been a long day for them.[14]

After falling out from dire thirst, Collins stumbled around the battlefield, until joining a portion of the 28th NC but then fell out again. Once rested, he passed "over the battle field; partly in quest or search for water and my command, and partly for the purpose of rambling among the dead and wounded." Collins soon found a group belonging to his brigade. "[A]fter passing several of the dead and wounded," he wrote,

> we came upon an old Welchman, who was wounded in the hip, with two or, three Union soldiers lying close to him, one of whom was too ill to be turned over, and while conversing with the Welchman . . . we looked down between two rows of corn . . . and saw a dark figure coming up between the rows of corn towards us. . . . it being so very dark that we could not distinguish a Union soldier from a rebel, more than a rod from us; we let it approach within about fifteen paces of us, closely watching it, with regard to combative signs, with our rifles at a charge and ready, when the other cried out, who comes there? Have you got arms? When I added, not giving the Union soldier time to reply; if you have any side arms about you, you had better not raise a hand, for if you do you are a dead man that very instant; to which the poor wounded man replied, falling down at the same time; No my God, I have not got any arms, neither do I want any; after which we invited him up and introduced him to some of his wounded comrades.[15]

An anonymous member of the 33rd Regiment recalled standing by the corpse of Sgt. Hance Hayes. "With a sweet smile upon his face and his hands quietly clasped upon his breast," described the man, "he had quietly and peacefully breathed out his life in defence of his native land. The very moon-beams that, from a . . . cloudless sky shone brightly down upon the face of battle, seemed to quiver, as if in pain at the scene before them." The correspondent went on to discuss the cries of the wounded for water and how

14 *OR* 12/2:222-23; Krick, *Cedar Mountain*, 265; Hickerson, *Happy Valley*, 84; Collins, Reminisces, 27. Thomas Sutton (18th NC) wrote "by special order from corps headquarters a handsome compliment was paid to the 'gallant soldiers of Branch's brigade.'" No such order can be found, and Jackson barely mentions Branch's brigade in his official report. *OR* 12/2:183-85.

15 Collins, Reminiscences, 27-28.

"the Queen of the night shown more sweetly down upon the cold and pallid faces of the dead."[16]

During the night, a staff officer stopped to confer and, oddly, asked Branch "how he felt." The general replied that "he was delighted with the result of the day and . . . proud of [how] his brigade had acted." Jackson himself spoke similarly. Branch's after-action report said the brigade drove the Federals "back with terrible slaughter through the wood" at the critical moment of the battle. "The conduct of officers and men during the battle merits great praise." Branch's troops honored their commander on the day following the battle. Captain William Davidson (7th NC) presented him a sword captured from the adjutant of the 28th New York. "No honor which the brigade could confer, would be too great to manifest the unqualified terms of approbation cherished by it, for the manner in which you had so nobly discharged your whole duty," Branch reported Davidson declaring as he presented the trophy. The brigade suffered 15 killed and 84 wounded in the action late on August 9. Overall, the Confederates lost 231 killed and 1,107 wounded.[17]

Caring for the wounded and burying the dead occupied most of the following day. That evening, the brigade camped in the woods through which it had charged. On August 11, the Federals offered an official truce for burying their own dead. At mid-afternoon, Jackson set his army in motion, retiring toward Gordonsville. With two additional Federal corps converging just to his north, Jackson planned to fall back and await reinforcements, hoping a portion of Pope's army would venture forth. Jackson's own division led, followed by Ewell's, then Hill's. On the morning of August 12, Nicholas Gibbon, temporary brigade quartermaster, met Branch's Tar Heels on the road and distributed rations of fresh beef. After the battle, Gibbon complained, fires were forbidden, and the men had to live on hard bread and whatever could be scavenged from the field. The hungry soldiers took their rations, filed off the road into the shade, and commenced cooking.[18]

Hill's division settled near the Crenshaw Farm, about halfway between Gordonsville and Orange Court House. Jackson suspended the customary

16 *The Semi-Weekly Standard*, September 20, 1862.

17 Clark, *Histories*, 2:472; OR 12/2:185; Brawley, "Branch," 189. Some controversy attended the role of the brigade in the battle. Freeman notes members of Jackson's staff felt Branch overstated its role, taking credit actually belonging to Winder's brigade. *Lee's Lieutenants*, 2:502.

18 Gibbon, typescript "Diary," 17, in Nicholas Gibbon Papers, UNC/C.

Nicholas Gibbon was a quartermaster in the 28th North Carolina and, in the summer of 1862, was temporarily assigned to brigade staff.

Histories of the Several Regiments and Battalions from North Carolina

drills on Thursday, August 14, calling instead for "divine services." Chaplin Stough (37th NC) preached in the 7th NC's camp with General Branch and his staff present. The brigade did get a few days of rest, but the men had to keep three days' rations on hand and stay ready to move at a moment's notice. Branch complained on August 15 about just ordering his men to pitch their tents when orders came to fix rations and be ready to move.[19]

Still confronting McClellan below Richmond, Lee realized he needed to crush Pope before McClellan or troops under Burnside coming from North Carolina could reinforce him. Lee therefore put elements of his army in motion on August 10, using his interior railroad lines to transport 30,000 soldiers under Longstreet from the environs of Richmond to Gordonsville. Lee planned his attack on Pope to start on August 16, the day Jackson's command left its camps, but delays forced him to postpone. Furthermore, Pope wasn't where Lee thought; the original plan would have been a disaster. Before Lee could get his army into position, Pope, who had captured dispatches outlining Confederate strengths, fell back behind the Rappahannock River. Lee began moving his army across the Rapidan River on August 20, and soon, only the Rappahannock stood between the two armies.[20]

On August 22, Jackson's three divisions were at Warrenton Springs. Ewell's division crossed the river on an old milldam, but night fell before the

19 Harris, *Historical Sketches*, 17; Lawrence Branch to Nancy Branch, August 15, 1862.

20 Harsh, *Confederate Tide Rising*, 119; OR 12/2:675.

other divisions could cross. Overnight, the heavens opened, and the resulting deluge swelled the river, washing away the dam, trapping Ewell's division on the opposite side. Jackson ordered a bridge built over some old pylons while Ewell's men dug in. Pope, believing Jackson's entire command had been trapped on his side of the river, began moving swiftly to deliver a crushing blow. Union artillery appeared and opened fire. Hill deployed his artillery and ordered various regiments to support the big guns. The 18th NC fell in behind McIntosh's battery, while the 28th and 33rd NC, under Col. Lane's command, supported Braxton's and Davidson's batteries. Lane ordered a portion of the 28th out "into an open field, as far as practicable to act as sharpshooters," while the rest of his two regiments sheltered behind a hill. Confederate artillery waited until the Federal infantry arrived before opening a "severe and protracted" cannonade, recalled one eyewitness. Ewell's division soon moved back across the river, when the temporary bridge was finished.[21]

Lee recognized his predicament. All of his efforts to slip around Pope's flank had floundered, and enemy numbers were swelling, with reinforcements from both Burnside's and McClellan's commands. Given the situation's gravity, Lee chose to gamble. Defying military logic of the time, Lee split his army, sending Jackson on a wide-flanking maneuver to cut the railroad line between Pope and Washington, D. C. As a diversionary measure for Pope, Longstreet's divisions held fast to their line along the Rappahannock. Once the railroad was cut, Longstreet would march hard to join Jackson, a movement, Lee hoped, that would force Pope back toward the U.S. capital.[22]

Branch's brigade moved out at four in the morning of August 25. On crossing Hazel Run, one 18th NC soldier recalled wading into the stream and using it as a roadbed, trying to stifle the dust generated by the feet of thousands of men. Given the region's record-breaking summer heat, any cool stream was welcome relief. At Amissville, five miles west, Jackson turned north and moved behind the Bull Run Mountains. By 11:00 p.m., Hill's division reached the community of Salem. Jackson had moved 23,000 men 25 miles, in just 14 hours. "[We] had nothing to eat but roasting ears," remembered one Carolinian, "and we marched so fast that . . . an artillerist [claimed] that if we went much further, the battery would be left behind." After reveille at four the following morning,

21 Mauney, "Diary," May 1862; Clark, *Histories*, 2:551.

22 John Hennessy, *Return to Bull Run: The Campaign and Battle of Second Manassas* (New York, 1993), 93.

James Weston complained of the lack of rations while on campaign in the summer of 1862. He would rise to the rank of major of the 33rd North Carolina and end the war with a parole at Appomattox.

Histories of the Several Regiments and Battalions from North Carolina

the footsore soldiers again took to the road. At Salem, the column turned not toward the Valley, but east, and during the day, the men passed through Thoroughfare Gap, Gainesville, and toward Manassas Gap. "Every man was pressed to the utmost of his walking capacity," recorded James Harris (7th NC). After another day-long hike, the men halted and procured green corn from the surrounding fields. The lead elements of Jackson's command reached Bristoe Station, capturing it after a short fight. Next, two infantry regiments and some cavalry turned north, and after a rare night attack, captured Manassas Junction and its wealth of quartermaster and commissary stores.[23]

Jackson left Ewell's division at Bristoe Station and moved his other two divisions to Manassas Junction. Branch's brigade most likely led the column. Upon arriving around 8 a.m. on August 27, the 18th Regiment was detailed to join the two infantry regiments already guarding the immense Federal stores. The rest of Branch's brigade filed off into a field near some old earthworks, awaiting issue of "yankee rations." Apparently, Federal soldiers appeared to the north before those rations could be issued. Branch quickly formed his four remaining regiments, posting them near a battery of guns. Other brigades of Hill's command deployed to Branch's right. The Federals were on the attack, and a relatively green brigade of New Jersey troops got to within a couple

23 Shaffner to "My dear Friend," September 7, 1862, Shaffner Papers, NDAH; Clark, *Histories*, 1:29, 2:552; Harris, *Historical Sketches*, 19.

hundred yards of the Confederate line before the Confederates fired and shredded a ragged bayonet charge. The Federals withdrew in considerable disorder. Infantry tried to close on the disorganized Federals, but Confederate artillery, moving swiftly, beat them to it, pouring "charge after charge of canister into their disordered ranks." Branch had to be content with capturing wounded and straggling Federals, including one Irishman dragged out of a culvert by a 28th NC trooper. The captive clapped "the Tar Heel on the shoulder, remarking: 'You got us badly this time. Come, let's take a drink.' Both of them 'smiled' out of the same canteen," Lane recalled after the war.[24]

Eventually, Hill returned his command to the captured depots. John Alexander (37th NC) reveled in the bounty they had seized:

> The depot was an immense building, filled with unlimited supplies of flour, crackers, bacon, mollasses, sugar, coffee, whiskey, clothing, harness for wagons and artillery, fixed ammunition for small arms and for cannon. We tarried here all day, got out whatever we needed that we could carry of rations; swapped our old harness for new, replenished our cartridge boxes and filled our caissons with shells and shrapnel.

Doctor Shaffner gloried in the food his fellow famished Tar Heels "found [in] abundance—including many delicacies. Our men supplied themselves with all they could carry,—all captured wagons were loaded." A member of the 18th NC wrote of finding "a very fine saddle . . . intended for the Dutch General Siegel, sent to him by his friends and admirers." The saddle ended up instead a trophy they presented to their commander Col. Purdie. John Frink, another 18th NC member, fondly recalled decades later "some of the best French brandy I ever drank."[25]

Jackson, however, grew more apprehensive as the day wore on. Enemy forces were approaching his position from different directions and in great numbers—about three times his own strength. After setting ablaze stores that could not be transported, Jackson ordered his command to move out at 1:00 a.m. During a "night . . . made hideous by the explosion of shells," the guide Stonewall had furnished the Light Division led it astray. Hill's division was

---

24 OR 12/2:675; Hennessy, *Return to Bull Run*, 125-26; Lane, "28th North Carolina Infantry," *Charlotte Observer*, February 17, 1895.

25 Alexander, *Reminiscences*, 78-79; John Shaffner to "My dear Friend," September 7, 1862; Clark, *Histories*, 2:69; *The San Angelo Daily*, April 20, 1926.

supposed to march north on Sudley Road to a position near Groveton. Instead, it was led to Centerville, some four miles out of the way. Around 10:00 a.m., orders written two hours earlier arrived from Jackson. In them he ordered Hill to move toward the fords on Bull Road and cut off the Federals, whom he believed in retreat. Hill, though, had captured documents showing Pope's forces not at all retreating. So he chose to disregard Jackson's orders and link up with the rest of Jackson's command.[26]

While his troops could have withdrawn westward toward the mountains, joining forces there under Longstreet, Stonewall Jackson decided instead to stay and await the arrival of the balance army—and in the meantime, if given the opportunity, strike a blow against the enemy. When Hill's division arrived, Jackson placed the command on the far left of his line, covering his escape route to the north, across Catharpin Run. Jackson's troops occupied a low-lying ridge near Groveton, fronted by an unfinished railroad. Hidden in the woods, most of the men slept. Late on August 28, Jackson spied a Federal division moving up the Warrenton Turnpike toward Manassas. Seeing an opportunity, Jackson ordered his men to attack, but their attacks weren't coordinated, and the Federals mounted a stiff resistance. Branch's brigade advanced into the open field in front of the railroad, and at some point, while the 28th Regiment continued ahead, the rest of the brigade angled to the left, all the while exposed to a galling enfilading artillery fire. When Union cavalry appeared on the brigade's left that afternoon, Branch dispatched four companies from the 37th NC to contest them. Later, Branch sent the 18th Regiment in for support, but darkness ended the battle. The Federals withdrew, and the brigade bivouacked on the field.[27]

"The early dawn reverberated with the thunder of artillery and the strange hissing and shrieking of shells as they passed in mid air, and what fitting prelude to the coming storm," James Harris (7th NC) recalled. Hill placed the Light Division in two lines along a half-mile front. The brigades of Field, Thomas, and Gregg formed the front line, with Pender, Archer, and Branch in reserve. Gregg, with Branch and some artillery behind him, constituted the left of Jackson's line. Convinced he could crush an isolated Jackson, Pope launched

26 Charlotte *News*, August 30, 1909; OR 12/2:670.

27 James Lane, "History of Lane's North Carolina Brigade," *SHSP*, 8:152-53; Harris, *Historical Sketches*, 19.

numerous attacks against different portions of the Confederate line. Many of those attacks fell upon the Confederate left.[28]

Save for sending one company (from the 7th NC under John Turner) to support a battery, Branch was not involved in the first attack. Turner led his men to the left of Crenshaw's battery. Lane chronicled what happened next:

> Turner was sent with his company to the extreme left, to deploy as skirmishers in front of Crenshaw's Battery. Turner had a white tent fly rolled and swung across his shoulder. He was advised to take it off, as it made him conspicuous, but he would not do it. Soon after he had formed his line, a yankee mounted officer rode to the front. Turner seized a gun from one of his] men and fired, the horse fell and the yankee "skedaddled" to the rear. Just then a yankee private fired from behind a large tree and wounded Turner severely on the head. This exasperated Turners men: two of them rushed from the line and advanced on the tree from different directions. The yankee having more faith in his heels than in the tree, broke to the rear in a run, but soon fell dead before the unswerving aim of those ragged rebels amid the cheers of the whole skirmish line.[29]

Soon after, Branch told Lane to take the 28th and 33rd Regiments to reinforce Turner's skirmishers and drive the Federals in the woods beyond the cornfield. Lane moved to the left of Crenshaw's battery, but before he could engage the enemy, he observed them falling back before Turner's men. On his right, Lane saw Gregg's brigade and so halted his own command, but sent out three additional companies of skirmishers to link up with Turner's men farther to the left.[30]

Around 3:00 p.m., the Federals renewed their attacks on Jackson's left. With Gregg's brigade running dangerously low on ammunition, Branch rushed the 37th Regiment into the fight. Portions of the 37th Regiment began collapsing under the intense fire. Walter Lenoir recalled that within a few minutes, "two thirds of my company had been struck. It required my utmost efforts to keep the others from giving way. I more than once seized men by the shoulders . . . and forced them back into the ranks." Companies on both his

---

28 Harris, *Historical Sketches*, 19

29 James Lane, "Reminiscences of Gallant Men in the Brigade," Box 71, Folder 49, Military Collection, NCDAH.

30 *OR* 12/2:676.

right and left gave way, according to Lenoir. Some men fell back approximately 50 yards, where he was able to rally them to return to the fight.[31]

Branch rushed back for more support. He found the 7th Regiment first, but in some disorder. A spent ball had just struck Col. Haywood in the left eye, and command fell to the next ranking officer, Capt. Robert McRae. Amid the storm of shell and shot, Branch personally led the 7th Regiment forward, and ordered the 18th to follow. The smoke on the battlefield masked the approach of his regiment, James Harris recalled, and the Carolinians poured several "buck and ball" volleys into the Union flank, driving them past the railroad and into the woods beyond. "These regiments swept the enemy back in almost the twinkling of an eye," Branch added, "regaining the ground lost by General Gregg and re-establishing our line. " Ammunition was running dangerously low all along the left of the Confederate line, so with their front momentarily secured, Branch set his men to scouring among friend and foe alike for cartridges. Hill informed Jackson of their situation, and Stonewall replied that the lines must be held.[32]

Again the Federals charged the Confederate left. Many of the muskets became fouled with the prolonged firing. Branch, seeing a soldier struggling to load a cartridge, grabbed the weapon, rammed the round home, and handed it back. In another instance, William Haywood (7th Regiment), the colonel's teenage brother, with his right arm wounded and unable to fire his musket, found Branch and offered to carry messages for him. Branch sent him to the rear for medical aid. Both Branch and Hill were spotted dismounted and encouraging the men to hold the line at the point of the bayonet. The fighting in many cases was hand-to-hand, and many Federals "were killed by having their skulls broken with rocks." Branch called for the 28th Regiment to move from its position on the far Confederate left to support his present line; the 33rd would now hold the left. However, in the shock of battle, the orders were misunderstood, and the relatively fresh 28th redeployed farther to the right than Branch had envisioned. Once in their new position, the 28th charged the Federals twice, driving them back beyond the railroad cut and out of the woods to the front. "Never have I witnessed greater bravery and desperation," Col. Lane marveled in his official report. Jackson observantly dispatched Early's

---

31 Hickerson, *Happy Valley*, 85.

32 LB to Nancy Branch, September 8, 1862, *Our Living and Our Dead* (September 1874), 1:41-42; Harris, *Historical Sketches*, 19.

Robert F. Hoke started the war in the 1st North Carolina Volunteers. He was appointed major of the 33rd North Carolina in November 1861. In August 1862, he became colonel of the 21st North Carolina Troops. Hoke finished the war as a major general.

North Carolina Museum of History

brigade of Ewell's division to shore up his beleaguered left, and the fresh 2,500 men forced back the Federals.[33]

On the far left, the 33rd still held the flank of Jackson's entire line. Lane reported that Lt. Col. Hoke led the regiment forward into an open field, driving back the Federals in disorder. Once Lane redeployed, however, the role of Hoke and the 33rd Regiment is unknown.[34]

After dark descended, Branch consolidated his command. His brigade had lost 30 killed, 185 wounded, and one missing. Harris attributed the light casualties to fighting from the woods and from behind the railroad embankment. The men did their best to find sleep behind the bank of the unfinished railroad. Many undoubtedly thought about the same thing running through Dr. Shaffner's mind: "Longstreet should have arrived Friday morning, but where was he? Would he come in time? Could we hold out until then?" Unbeknownst to the men, Longstreet had indeed arrived and the tide of the battle was about to change. That evening, when examining the cartridge boxes of his men, Branch discovered to his dismay they held a total of just two dozen cartridges. When he sent a regiment out on picket duty, he had the 12 pickets

---

33 *Weekly State Journal*, October 8, 1862; Clark, *Histories*, 2:552, 656; George Hahn, *The Catawba Soldiers of the Civil War* (Hickory, NC, 1911), 167; Lane, "History of Lane's Brigade," *SHSP*, 8:154.

34 Lane, "History of Lane's Brigade," *SHSP*, 8:153.

issued with the 24 cartridges; the remainder of his men stood guard with nothing more than fixed bayonets.[35]

August 30 dawned with the Federal army still confronting Jackson's divisions. Pope had convinced himself that the Confederates were retreating, ignoring some few who reported Longstreet's fresh divisions on the field as well as the Federal left flank. Pope tried a couple of times to break Jackson's line, only to be stymied by massed Confederate artillery. Then Longstreet, guided by Lee, launched a massive counter assault. With nearly 30,000 soldiers, Longstreet slammed into Pope's flank. Only a tenacious defense on Chinn Ridge saved the Federal army from the complete disaster Lee so often sought. Unlike yesterday when Branch's brigade witnessed firsthand the attempts to turn the Confederate flank, this time it stayed out of the fight. One 7th NC officer recalled the men rotating to the rear to draw rations and a fresh supply of ammunition. Though some skirmishing occurred throughout the day, and one officer recalled his men of the 33rd being "under a furious artillery fire," Branch's men were spared more bloodletting.[36]

About 6:00 p.m., Hill advanced his command across the railroad tracks toward the Federals under Longstreet's pounding. Branch maintained his position on the Confederate left; to his right were the brigades of Archer, Thomas, Pender, and Brockenbrough, with Gregg in support. Hill maintained the Confederates "drove everything before them." Thomas Sutton (18th NC) recalled "a most disastrous and complete route [sic]" of the Union army. Branch, though failing to engage any large groups of enemy soldiers, led the brigade forward until well after dark, around 10:00 p.m., and captured a large field hospital. The brigade slept in the field that evening, tent-less and under heavy rains.[37]

The following morning, Branch led his brigade back toward the rear, re-crossing the "truly appalling" battlefield. "Dead men and horses in a state of putrefaction met the eye in every direction," a shaken James Harris (7th NC) wrote. "[P]oints of attack and repulse were marked by groups of slain, intermingled with the blue and gray . . . The stench was well nigh intolerable, and the site one at which the heart sickened." Much of the morning was spent

35 John Shaffner to "My dear Friend," September 7, 1862; McDaid, "Four Years" 109; Harris, *Historical Sketches*, 20; Lane, "Brigade Commanders," *SHSP*, 10:245.

36 Harris, *Historical Sketches*, 20-21; Clark, *Histories*, 2:552.

37 OR 12/2:672, 677; Clark, *Histories*, 2:69.

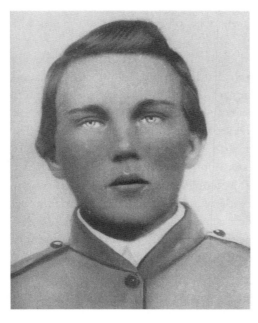

Emberry Walters, a private in the 37th North Carolina, survived a head wound at the battle of Second Manassas.

Carol Bullins

burying the dead and tending to the wounded. Many of Hill's wounded were taken to the Buckner Farm. One regimental surgeon recalled they had no bread for the men, but plenty of mutton. Lenoir of the 37th returned to the wood line where his regiment had fought and dug out a minie ball that had struck a tree near his head. Lenoir believed the slug had already passed through the head of Pvt. William Weaver, before hitting the tree. At another spot, he counted a white oak tree about 18 inches in diameter that had been struck 20 times. He marveled that any of his men had escaped the battle. Much to general dismay, noon brought orders to fall in. The commissary wagons had not arrived: the brigade had to march off without eating.[38]

Beaten, the Federals fell back a few miles to Centerville and occupied earthworks Confederates had built the previous year. After surveying the position, Lee decided against attacking. Instead, he orchestrated yet another flanking movement. Although they were in poor shape, Lee chose Jackson's three divisions to spearhead the attack, since they were closer than Longstreet's men. Jackson would try to get between the Federals and Washington, forcing Pope to abandon his works at Centerville. About 2:00 in the afternoon of August 31, Branch's men set out. Hill's division led the march, behind a screen of cavalry. Under a grueling pace, numerous men fell out of the ranks, and eventually Jackson told Hill to slow the pace. At the halt that evening, the Light

---

38 Harris, *Historical Sketches*, 21; *Charlotte Observer*, August 29, 1903; Hickerson, *Happy Valley*, 85. Robert Gibbon (28th Regiment) was left in charge of a portion of the Division's wounded, about 300 men, at the Buckner farm. See Gibbon to Samuel Moore, November 17, 1862, M331, Roll 105, RG 109, CMSR, NA.

Division had advanced just 10 miles. It was a long, cold night, with no rations except what the men could forage locally.

Jackson's other two divisions took the lead the next morning on a "cloudy, cold and dreary" day. Hill's command brought up the rear. A heavy line of skirmishers, likely including some men of the 7th NC, covered the right of the column. William Howard wrote that around 2:00 in the afternoon, portions of the brigade had skirmished with Federal cavalry, killing "some three or four [and taking] six or seven prisoners." The advance slowed to a crawl: Jackson's command covered only three or four miles. Around 4:00 p.m., Jackson detected Federals advancing along the Ox Road on his right flank. Jackson ordered the Branch and Brockenbrough brigades to move off and reconnoiter in that direction. Branch moved his brigade forward around 5 p.m. The troops crossed through an open field, entered a piece of woods before making contact with the enemy as "a heavy rain" opened.[39]

In a torrential rain, the battle raged between the two forces. A cornfield in front of the Tar Heel's position masked the Federals, and in "the smoke of battle and growing darkness," wrote Harris, the enemy's line "could be outlined by the flashes of his guns . . . reminding one of myriads of fire flies in a peaceful summer evening." As the Federals tried to flank Branch, the general withdrew the 18th Regiment from his center and sent it to shore up that section. Brockenbrough's Virginians fell back, and it briefly appeared that Branch's brigade likewise would be forced to give way. Captain Robert MacRae, commanding the 7th Regiment, was struck in the neck, and command passed to Capt. John G. Knox. Lieutenant Octavius Wiggins (37th NC) remembered years later that the cold rain not only drenched the men, but also fouled the muskets as well. It was simply too wet to load the paper cartridges. When Branch informed Hill that he was almost out of ammunition, he was ordered to hold his position "at the point of the bayonet." Hill then sent the brigades of Gregg and Thomas to Branch's aid.[40]

Darkness and the downpour eventually halted the battle of Ox Hill, or Chantilly. The Confederates held the field, and their enemies continued their retreat toward Washington. Once in the rear, Branch's men commenced foraging for corn and building fires. The 28th Regiment, to its disgust, was sent out on picket duty and denied the luxury of fire to dry out both themselves and

39 Harris, *Historical Sketches*, 21; Howard, Diary; OR 12/ 2:677.

40 Harris, *Historical Sketches*, 21; Clark, *Histories*, 2:656; OR 12/2:667; Jordan, *NC Troops*, 4:405.

their clothes. Lane considered the battle "one of our severest." It cost the brigade 14 killed, 92 wounded, and 2 missing.[41]

The brigade did not move on September 2, but instead drew rations and rested. General Branch took time to pen a letter to his wife, reflecting on the campaign thus far. "Since I wrote you last," he told her,

> we have been almost constantly in the rear of the enemy . . . We have performed the most remarkable marches recorded in history. If we had not the actual experience it would not be credited that human nature could endure what we have endured. Fighting all day and marching night not for one day only, but for a whole week. The little sleep we have had had been generally on the battle field surrounded by the dead and wounded. Some of the soundest sleep I have ever had has been on the naked ground without cover and with rain pouring down in torrents. The only rations we have had for a week are fresh beef without salt or bread.

"Washington and all Maryland including Baltimore," he continued, "and all Pennsylvania up to the Susquehanna are at our mercy." He hoped the war would soon draw to a close so that he could return home, a hope all his men shared. Captain Morris (37th NC) assured his family that he was "Stout and Hearty," despite being struck with several spent balls and shells. He wrote briefly, because the army was "advancing towards Alexandra," and he thought he was only 20 or so miles from the Federal capital.[42]

Morris was mistaken. Lee was aiming for neither Alexandria nor Washington, both targets too heavily defended, even for the highly vaunted Army of Northern Virginia. Lee had other plans, a campaign that would forever alter Branch's stalwart Carolinians. Over the course of the past month, Branch's men had fought three pitched battles, playing significant roles at both Cedar Mountain and Second Manassas, and holding fast at Ox Hill under wretched conditions. As the brigade marched away from the Washington outskirts, a newspaper back in the Old North State branded Branch and his men, "the Bravest of the Brave."[43]

41 *OR*, 12/2:667; McDaid, "Four Years," 111.

42 LB to Nancy Branch, September 2, 1862; Brawley, "Branch," 196 (quoted); William Morris to "Deare companion," September 2, 1862, Morris Papers, SHC.

43 *North Carolina Whig*, July 8, 1862.

Chapter 6

"The brave, lamented General Branch."

Harpers Ferry—Antietam—Shepherdstown

In just three months, the Army of Northern Virginia had gone from a bottled-up fighting force within sight of Richmond's church spires to one of the most storied armies in military history. The Confederate capital had been saved, two major Federal armies defeated, and most of Virginia swept clean of the enemy. Lee's army was up early and under arms on September 2, ready to renew the conflict with Pope. Yet the enemy had slipped away overnight, first to a better defensive position, and then about noon to the capital's stout fortifications. Laying siege to Washington was beyond the ability of Lee's army, and he spent much of the day studying his maps and consulting with Longstreet and Jackson to craft a new strategy.

Several options were available. He could keep his troops right where they were as a constant menace that dared the Federals to leave the safety of their defenses and fight out in the open. While tempting, the plot was unworkable. The surrounding countryside had been ravaged by both armies for over a year, and the Confederate supply lines were poor. Staying near Chantilly was impossible. Plus, there were two Federal armies in Washington, D. C., and it was only a matter of time before, rested and refitted, they could again take the offensive. Lee was loathe to surrender the initiative. He could move south, toward central Virginia, but that meant surrendering much of the territory so recently gained by so much blood. Or, he could move to the west, maybe even as far as the Shenandoah Valley, seizing the isolated Federal post there. Or, he could move north into Maryland, and maybe as far as Pennsylvania, disrupting Federal transportation routes and destroying war industries. In the end, Lee opted to take the Army of Northern Virginia to Leesburg, in Loudoun County. Largely untouched by the war, the area provided plenty of foodstuffs for the army, and while there, Lee would threaten the Federal garrisons, and be poised to cross the Potomac River into Maryland.

Upon learning the Federals had retreated closer to Washington, D. C., Lee ordered his army to stack arms and rest. Like Morris of the 37th NC, who believed the army within 20-25 miles of Washington, James Harris (7th NC) reported being only "25 miles to Washington City" and only "11 miles" from the Maryland state line. Harris recalled cooking two days' worth of rations—boiled beef and roasting ears—under orders to march the following day. As the army set out, Lee paced his men, wanting his infantry to move no more than 10 miles on the first day. Harris recorded that the brigade moved out early on the morning of September 3, not toward the Federal capital, but west, and passed through Dranesville and Leesburg before stopping for the evening.[1]

By the time Lee arrived in Leesburg on September 4, he had decided to cross the Potomac into Maryland. By moving north, the army could live off land untouched by the war. It would also allow Virginia farmers time to harvest their crops, or at least recover somewhat from occupation. A Confederate army on Maryland soil might stimulate recruitment and allow local citizens to join the Southern army. Federal infrastructure, such as canals and railroads, could be ravaged. More importantly, a Southern victory on Northern soil might lead to recognition of the Confederate states by England or France.[2]

Lee issued General Order No. 102 from Leesburg. Commanders were instructed to reduce their baggage to "cooking utensils and the absolute necessaries of a regiment." Surplus animals were left behind with the army's

---

1 William Morris to "Deare companion," September 2, 1862, Morris Papers, SHC/UNC; D. Scott Hartwig, *To Antietam Creek: The Maryland Campaign of September 1862* (Baltimore, MD, 2012), 91; Harris, *Historical Sketches*, 22; Harsh, *Taken at the Flood*, 51.

2 For an exended discussion of Lee's reasons for invading the North, see Harsh, *Taken at the Flood*, 47-51.

chief quartermaster. Soldiers were warned that they were "about to engage in most important operations, where any excess committed will exasperate the people, lead to disastrous results, and enlist the populace on the side of the Federal forces in hostility to our own." Only quartermasters and commissaries were authorized to purchase supplies for the army. Further, Lee established a special provost guard to follow the army, charged with keeping the men with their commands, arresting stragglers, and punishing "all depredators." Guards were placed at the rear of the brigades "to prevent the men from leaving the ranks, right, left, front, or rear." Other orders sent all shoeless men in Leesburg toward Winchester.[3]

Jackson met with his division commanders that evening and specified a 4:00 a.m. start to the march the next day. When Jackson rode into Hill's camp at the prescribed time next morning, half the division wasn't even on line, earning Hill a mild reprimand from Stonewall. The Light Division set out soon thereafter at a blistering pace. Hill was not going to be chastised again for foot-dragging. But the hurry soon dispersed the column and created stragglers. Around noon Jackson observed the faltering Light Division plodding along, rode to the head of the column and ordered it to halt for rest. Hill and his staff, who had ridden ahead, wondered why the column had not appeared, returned, and queried the lead brigade. When Hill heard the explanation, he rode up to Jackson, dismounted, took out his sword and presented it hilt-first to Jackson. "If you take command of my troops in my presence, take my sword also." Jackson told Hill to put away his sword and consider himself under arrest. Then as the senior brigade officer present, Branch had to assume command of the Light Division, and command of the brigade fell to the senior colonel, James Lane. "I found that under . . . Gen. Branch, my orders were much better carried out," Jackson later wrote.[4]

On September 5, Jackson started crossing his three divisions over the Potomac River at White's Ford. James Harris (7th NC) recalled going over at 4:00 p.m., in "water . . . waist deep, and the channel covered with rocks varying in size from large to small." Nicholas Gibbon, still with the wagon train, observed some men "with their shoes and pants hanging on their guns, others with theirs rolled up above their knees and others wading through the clear

---

3 OR 19/2:592-93. On barefoot soldiers, see Hartwig, *To Antietam Creek*, 97. Evidence indicates some 5,000 soldiers of Lee's army were left behind due to infirmity or lack of shoes.

4 Robertson, *Hill*, 130-31; Freeman, *Lee's Lieutenants*, 2:149.

Then-private John D. Duncan, 18th North Carolina, was captured in Frederick, Maryland, on September 12, 1862. He was probably left there sick or was a straggler. He survived the war.

Histories of the Several Regiments and Battalions from North Carolina

stream without seeming to care whether they got wet or not." Branch doubtless basked in his new role as commander of the Light Division, writing home on September 7 that he had "crossed the Potomac at the head of six brigades, comprising about half of General Jackson's Army." The Light Division and the rest of Jackson's command continued on toward Frederick, eventually taking a position guarding the intersection of the Baltimore & Ohio Railroad bridge and the Georgetown Pike. At some point during the march Jackson ordered Branch to prepare two days' rations, and, upon learning that the men had no food, ordered them to procure roasting ears from a nearby cornfield.[5]

Nicholas Gibbon recalled a close encounter in a local store. "On approaching Boonesboro," Gibbon wrote after the war:

I found that the stores were open and I resolved to ride ahead of the Army. . . and see what was to be had. So when the foremost troops neared the town, a Lieut., Sergt. and myself galloped ahead while the troops stopped for the night about a half mile back.

Leaving our horses with some boys at the hotel we went at once into the stores and looked around. I had just bought a hat. . . . when there seemed to be a general excitement all around and at the same time a boy ran past the door exclaiming "the

---

5 Harris, *Historical Sketches*, 22; Gibbon, Diary, 19; LB to Nancy Branch, September 7, 1862, Branch Papers, UVA; Lane, "Brigade Commanders," *SHSP*, 10:243. The timeframe of the Potomac River crossing is unclear. According to Hartwig, the Light Division was the last to cross, and did not do so until the evening. In a note to Branch dated September 5, at 3:00 p.m., however, Jackson implied at least a portion of the division was already across the river. Hartwig, *To Antietam Creek*, 100, 107; OR 12/2:594.

Union Cavalry are coming, they are shooting the men." I heard several pistols crack at the same time and as I jumped out into the street I saw a body of cavalry charging by where I had left my horse. I jumped back in the store and ran through into a back yard and into a garden where I concealed myself among the bushes and vines expecting that the Yankees would dismount and search for us.

A thousand thoughts entered my brain at once for I did not know what force they had and how long before our troops would drive them back, or they might find and carry me off. But I was soon relieved for a body of our Cavalry charged upon the Yankees and made them fly from the town in more haste than they had entered. On going into the street to look after my horse, he was not to be found nor could I find the boy I had left him with, but the other two horses we found in a lot where they had gone, as we thought, when the boys let them loose.

Next morning I was glad to find my horse had retired in good order to where he had left the troops and was taken up by a man who delivered him to me.[6]

Many Confederate troops rested from September 7-9. They had opportunities to bathe in the Monocacy River, shop in surrounding stores when passes could be procured, and write letters home. Morris (37th NC) wrote twice, telling his loved ones of the recent battles he had fought and his close calls, including being hit with several spent musket balls and a piece of shrapnel that knocked him down. Morris believed that Jackson had the "yankees rather by the horns," and that the "Enemy [is] Terible Frightened" and refused to fight any more. Somewhere around 600 Marylanders had joined the Confederate army since they had arrived, and coffee, sugar, milk, and butter were all cheap. While he listed the names of the dead and seriously wounded from his former company, his morale remained high. By one estimate Branch's brigade marched 272 miles in a single month. But at a cost: "Stonewall get the good of his men to soon," Charles Mills (7th NC) wrote. "[H]e marches them so hard that they are nerly broke down before they get to the battle field."[7]

A couple of Branch's regiments received new men during the lull. The conscription law passed earlier that year funneled 2,000 into the Army of Northern Virginia as the Maryland campaign unfolded. Ninety went to the 18th Regiment, while 130 were sent to the 7th Regiment. One of the new men to join

---

6   Gibbon, Diary, 19, Gibbon Papers, UNC-Charlotte.

7   William Morris to "Dear Companion," September 8, 1862, Morris Papers, SHC/UNC; McDaid, "Four Years," 113; C. F. Mills to "Dear Sister," August 26, 1862, C. F. Mills Papers, DU.

the 18th Regiment, William Barlow, wrote home on September 8, complaining it had taken eight days of hard marching to join the army and "we are all most tired out. . . . I never knew what hard times were till now." With Jackson's command, Barlow found himself in a place where he knew "we must fight." These new recruits lacked weapons and accoutrements. While the 220 new men helped fill out depleted ranks, they were a mixed blessing: untrained, unaccustomed to the hard marches that made Stonewall Jackson famous, and vulnerable to numerous diseases that ran rampant throughout the army. Barlow had been in the army just under three weeks and now faced active campaigning. And he was already complaining of not feeling well and being underfed.[8]

Lee needed to open lines of communication and supply through the Shenandoah Valley. His advance should have forced the Federal garrisons at Martinsburg and Harpers Ferry to evacuate, but they held fast. To move his army to Hagerstown, Lee first needed to either capture the towns or force out the Federals. Therefore he, Jackson, and Longstreet devised a plan which divided the army into four parts. Following the conference, Lee issued the now-famous Special Order No. 191, sending copies to five different generals, outlining the movements of the army's various divisions. Both Lee and Jackson sent a copy of the order to D. H. Hill, since Hill's division was temporarily attached to Jackson's command. Federal soldiers found a copy, wrapped in three cigars and lying beside a fence, and forwarded it to McClellan. Lee's battle plan ordered 38,000 men, or 58 percent of the army under Jackson, to invest Harpers Ferry; the remaining 28,000 men, under Longstreet and D. H. Hill, would occupy Hagerstown and Boonsboro, protecting the rear of the force attacking Harpers Ferry.

According to the plan, Confederate forces would fall on Harpers Ferry from three different directions. Jackson's three divisions, including the Light Division, were to follow the National Road, crossing South Mountain at Turner's Gap. Once past Boonsboro, they would cross the Potomac River and enter the Shenandoah Valley. After capturing or destroying the Federal garrison at Martinsburg, Jackson's three divisions could then seal off the area from the west by occupying School House Ridge opposite Bolivar Heights. Two other commands, under Maj. Gen. Lafayette McLaws and Brig. Gen. John G. Walker,

---

8 Harsh, *Taken at the Flood*, 40; Locke W. Smith, Jr., ed., "'God Save Us All In Heaven.' The William Rufus Barlow Letter Collection." *Company Front* (2013) 27:2,20; Clark, *Histories*, 2:32. Barlow writes, "We had orders to write as soon as we got hear."

occupied Loudoun Heights and Maryland Heights, respectively, encircling Harpers Ferry.

Jackson's troops had the longest route. They set off early on September 10, passing over the Catoctin Mountain via Hagan's Gap, and then over South Mountain via Turner's Gap. The Light Division camped that evening between South Mountain and the village of Boonsboro. At Hill's request, one of Jackson's staff officers intervened that evening on his behalf. Jackson acquiesced, returning Hill to command of the Light Division and Branch to his brigade. On the eve of battle, Jackson clearly wanted his most experienced division commander with his men, instead of brooding at the rear of the column. The troops rose at 3:00 a.m. the next morning and marched an hour later, crossing the Potomac at Light's Ferry. Two miles below the ferry, the column reached Harmony Church where the road split. Jackson aimed to capture the Federal garrison at Martinsburg. So, while the Light Division took the main road toward the town, Jackson's two other divisions took the left fork. Upon learning of Jackson's advance, the Federals evacuated the town and retreated to Harpers Ferry, abandoning numerous quartermaster stores to the men of the Light Division. That evening, Hill's men stopped five or six miles below Martinsburg. They were on the road at 4:30 a.m. on September 13, bivouacking south of Halltown that evening.[9]

With some difficulty, since rivers separated the three commands, Jackson learned that the encirclement of Harpers Ferry was almost complete. Late on the afternoon on September 14, Jackson sent the Light Division to turn the enemy's left flank and enter Harpers Ferry. Hill ordered Pender's, Archer's, and Brockenbrough's brigades, with Thomas in reserve, to occupy Bull's Hill. Branch's and Gregg's brigades proceeded along the Shenandoah River, following the railroad until they reached a point they believed to be in the rear of Bolivar Heights. The brigade then began scaling the side of the mountain in the darkness. "We had literally to pull ourselves up by bushes, roots or anything projecting from the mountainside, some of us actually having to brace ourselves against trees, so as to hold our guns in position and ready to fire at the word given," wrote a member of the 18th Regiment. At some point during the ascent, the 7th NC's skirmishers chased away Federal pickets. Between 3:00 and 4:00

---

9 Hartwig, *To Antietam Creek*, 222-28, 521; Stephen Sears, *Landscape Turned Red: The Battle of Antietam* (New York, 1983), 103-37.

a.m., Branch's and Gregg's brigades were in position, just 400 yards from the Federal lines.[10]

Heavy fog shrouded troops' positions around Harpers Ferry early on September 15. Confederate artillery commenced bombarding Federal defenses as the fog lifted. After an hour, the artillery duel ceased, and as Confederate infantry prepared to charge, white flags appeared along the Federal lines. The depth of the their enemies' preparations convinced the Federals that further resistance was pointless, and they surrendered the town and its garrison and booty: 12,500 Federal prisoners of war, 13,000 small arms, around 200 wagons, and 73 pieces of artillery. Branch marched his brigade into town, noting that the Federals were "the best-dressed and best-provided soldiers I ever expect to see. . . . there is not a private amongst them who is not better dressed than I am . . . [yet] they don't fight like our men." The men in his various regiments were able to pick up many supplies. "We boys were turned loose on these good things and you may be sure we availed ourselves of them," wrote Austin Jones (7th NC). "One more time in our lives we ate as much sugar as we wanted. . . . we bore off a good quantity, and were so refreshed and elated that we scarcely knew ourselves." Major Morris (37th NC) wrote of obtaining sugar, too, and coffee, as well as "clothes plenty to Doo Me all winter as we all Got what we wanted at Harpers Fery." Several Carolinians wrote of swapping their smoothbore muskets for rifles, either British Enfields or U.S.-made Springfields. Obviously, not everybody received new weapons; some members of the 18th NC were still carrying smoothbore muskets as late as May 1863.[11]

Walker's and McLaw's Divisions did not partake in the captured bounty. They were rushed off not long after the Federals surrendered. The Light Division remained behind, overseeing the parole of prisoners and the captured supplies. Some supplies headed toward Lee's army, others toward Virginia. Jackson's two other divisions were also quickly on the march.

While Harpers Ferry was being reduced, Confederate forces north of the town struggled to hold off Federals attempting to relieve the forlorn garrison. D. H. Hill's division redeployed to the three passes through South Mountain

---

10 Clark, *Histories*, 1:372; 2:70; Hartwig, *To Antietam Creek*, 533-35. Harris goes on to state his regiment lost one killed and three wounded during the nighttime skirmishing.

11 LB to Nancy Branch, September 16, 1862, Mrs. Lawrence O'Bryan Branch Papers, NCDAH; Austin Jones. *The Capture of Harpers Ferry* (n.p., 1922), 2; William Morris to "Deare Companion," September 23, 1862, September 24, 1862, Morris Papers, SHC/UNC; Clark, *Histories*, 2:33, 70; James Harris to Erza Carman, February 1, 1900, Ezra Carman Papers, NA.

and bore Federal attacks all day on September 14. After stubborn resistance, the Confederates fell back that evening. Their sacrifice, however, bought their comrades time to capture Harpers Ferry. Once Lee learned of the defeat at South Mountain, he began consolidating his forces near the strategically situated village of Sharpsburg. From there Lee could flank the Federals if they attempted to attack McLaws. Moreover, Sharpsburg was close to the Potomac, on roads being used by Jackson's command, and had useful defensive terrain.[12]

Fighting began early on the morning of September 17 with artillery and then a Federal attack on the Confederate left. The attack fell on Jackson's two divisions and swirled through the West Woods and the cornfield, near the Dunker Church. Hood's Division likewise clashed with Federals over much of the same ground. Eventually the fighting died out on that end of the line, with the Confederates barely holding, and shifted to the center of the line. D. H. Hill's brigades, posted in a sunken road, withstood numerous assaults before being outflanked on their right. After three hours of intense fighting, the Confederate center gave way. Two counterattacks failed to dislodge the Federals now occupying the sunken road. Only Confederate artillery and the Federals' own confusion halted the attack. Eventually, the Federals dropped back a short distance to the top of a hill. Fighting now shifted to the Confederate right. The enemy troops there were under the command of Maj. Gen. Ambrose Burnside, whom Branch and some of his brigade had fought at New Bern six months earlier. Burnside spent a portion of the day waiting for McClellan's orders.

The terrain along Antietam Creek, located in a valley between two steep hills, provided some of the best natural defensive works on the battlefield. A single stone bridge crossed the creek here. Confederates on the west side of it used the natural cover and improvised breastworks of fallen trees and fence rails to strengthen their position. Lee had originally positioned two divisions on his right. All of one and part of the other left during the day to bolster Confederate defenses in other sectors. Union forces began assaults to take the bridge shortly after 10:00 a.m. The nature of the ground forced the attacking Federals to bottleneck at the bridge, easy targets for Confederate rifles. After a third attempt, around 1:00 p.m., the bluecoats captured the bridge. As additional Federal infantry and artillery arrived, they met resistance only from Confederate artillery and a handful of infantrymen. A little after 3:00 p.m.,

12 Freeman, *Lee's Lieutenants*, 2:203.

about 8,500 Federals began advancing toward David R. Jones's division of 2,800 men, the few Confederate defenders deployed around Cemetery Hill. If this small force collapsed, Lee would lose the only road to the ford over the Potomac, his only line of retreat. Eventually, all but one Confederate brigade gave way, and a few Federal soldiers began entering Sharpsburg.

The entire Army of Northern Virginia was on the verge of annihilation. Watching all of this transpire, Lee could see two columns approaching and asked a staff officer to identify them. One column was Federal infantry. The other was his army's salvation: the Light Division.

Around 6:30 that morning, Hill had been ordered to move with all due haste toward Sharpsburg. By 7:00 a.m., Gregg's brigade was marching, followed by Branch and three other brigades. Thomas's brigade stayed behind to finish the work at Harpers Ferry. Disregarding Jackson's mandate of stopping for 10 minutes to rest every hour, Hill pushed his men fiercely—"a rapid and fatiguing march," Lane said—stopping only once or twice. Around 2:00 p.m., the column began crossing the Potomac River, with the men forbidden to slow down or remove clothing. "[O]ur clothing was saturated with water from the hips down," recalled one, and the "up-hill foot-race from the river to the battle-field, caused none but those of unquestioned endurance to be there to go into action." Lieutenant Iowa Michigan Royster said his regiment, the 37th, had only 50 men when they gained the fields above Antietam Creek; the same was true for other regiments in Branch's brigade, in other words, leaving somewhere between 250 and 300 men, not even half a regular regiment.[13]

Branch halted his brigade as he drew near the battlefield and rode off in search of Gen. Hill for orders. While Branch was gone, Hill arrived and stopped his mount in front of the 28th Regiment, asking, "Who commands this regiment?" When James Lane stepped forward, Hill ordered him to take the 28th down the road toward Sharpsburg to support a battery (McIntosh's). He was to "drive the enemy's sharpshooters advancing" through a cornfield fronting the battery. Lane thereupon moved his regiment down the road, halting in a cut, but his skirmishers encountered no Federals. Lane sent his

13 Clark, *Histories*, 2:33; *OR* 19/1:985; Iowa Royster to Mary Royster, June 29, 1863, SHC/UNC. Harsh criticizes the time it took A. P. Hill to cover the 17 miles. Not only was his division not ready to march that morning, writes Harsh, but Hill took the longer route to Sharpsburg. Franklin's corps of Federals covered almost the same distance and arrived fresh, "while Hill shed 40 percent of his troops along the route." Harsh, *Taken at the Flood,* 418.

brother to find Branch and report the regiment's position. While supporting the guns, the 28th missed the fighting that developed.[14]

Despite direct evidence of it, Hill and Branch doubtless connected. Hill ordered Branch to assail the Federals assaulting Cemetery Hill. The 7th Regiment moved ahead, followed by the 37th through a cornfield in front of the North Carolinians. Believing their reinforcements were near at hand, the 8th Connecticut continued to surge ahead toward the approaching Carolinians. Although the left of the 7th NC was thrown into momentary confusion by Federal artillery, it soon recovered and continued its advance. James Harris recalled that "a cannon shot, or two, sped across the brow of the hill," as they crested it; they ducked back behind the hill and continued forward. The two Tar Heel regiments hit the 8th CT on the flank and rear, delivered several volleys, and forced its withdrawal. A different enemy regiment, possibly the 23rd OH, opened its own enfilading fire on the right of the Tar Heels, who fell back about 100 yards and re-formed. Before they could advance again, Gregg's brigade flanked the Ohio regiments along the stone wall to the Tar Heels' right. The 7th and 37th advanced once again, wheeling to the right and stopping at the wall, with Branch personally guiding and encouraging his men. For the second time, enemy artillery may have caused havoc in the the 7th NC's ranks. As they came on line, wrote Harris,

> a shell was exploded in its ranks with destructive effect and some confusion ensued. Company commanders at once exerted themselves to prevent further disorder and First Sergeant Thos. P. Mallory. . . who had borne the colors with conspicuous courage throughout the campaign, placed himself in front and appealed to the men to align themselves on the colors which they did under fire, then moving forward, the regiment occupied the stone wall.

Archer's brigade now stood to the right. Captain Morris, commanding the 37th, didn't stop his men at the wall. They went over it and into a corn field, but meeting "a warm fire," fell back to the stone wall. At this point the 7th NC rose

---

14 Ezra Carman, *The Maryland Campaign of September 1862*, 2 vols., Thomas Clemens, ed. (El Dorado Hills, CA, 2012), 2:478; JL to Ezra Carman, March 22, 1895, February 10, 1900, Ezra Carman Papers, NA. No one seems to know the exact order of Hill's brigades. Major William Montgomery wrote Erza Carman that his regiment and Branch's brigade were in the lead, while Montgomery's commanding officer, James Lane, said Branch's brigade was last out of Harpers Ferry, with the 28th last in line. Montgomery to Carman, October 8, 1897, JL to James Harris, June 5, 1896, Lane Papers, AU.

General Branch's headquarters flag was left in a farmhouse in Virginia as the General's remains were transported farther south. *North Carolina Museum of History*

from its reserve position in a grassy field and joined the fight behind Archer's brigade. The 37th NC, returning from its own attack, soon joined them. Morris fell in behind the 7th, and the two regiments deployed a little farther down the line, possibly to the left of the remnants of Brig. Gen. Robert Toombs's Georgia brigade.[15]

With the sun setting, Lane could see the Federals retreating toward the bridge over Antietam Creek. Hill's march from Harpers Ferry had saved the day, and Lane told his regiment to give the "Rebel Yell." Orders from Branch soon directed the 28th Regiment to rejoin the rest of the brigade. The 18th NC stayed at the stone wall as a reserve behind Archer's brigade. Lane didn't have a guide through the darkness, so his men went too far to the right and had to countermarch back toward the correct position. From the shadows, Lane heard the voice of Maj. Joseph Engelhard, the brigade quartermaster. Stopping his regiment, he asked Engelhard about Branch. "[H]e has just been shot," came

15 William Montgomery, James Harris, Spier Whitaker, Jr. to Ezra Carman, Feb. 10, Feb.1, Feb. 16, 1900, respectively, in Ezra Carman Papers, NA; Harris, *Historical Sketches*, 23; Carman, *The Maryland Campaign*, 2:479; *Weekly State Journal*, October 1, 1862. The 37th NC captured two Federal flags left behind at the stone wall. William Morris to Ezra Carman, June 1, 1896, Carman Papers, NA.

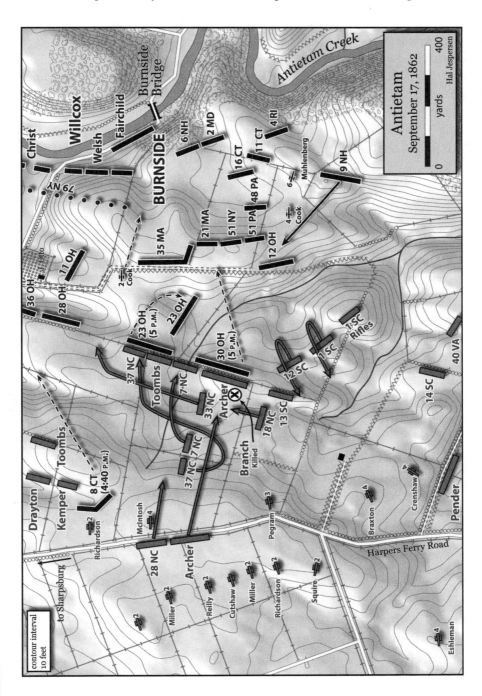

Antietam
September 17, 1862

Hal Jespersen

0   yards   400

contour interval
10 feet

the stunning response. "[T]here he goes on that stretcher dead [and] you are in charge of the brigade."[16]

Branch's exact movements on that late September afternoon are unclear. If his command numbered only 300 men, Hill should have seen him easily when the 28th was ordered away. It appears the 37th went into the fight without orders. Accounts of Branch's death vary. The traditional account is that he was conferring with fellow generals Gregg and Archer, when he

> stepped forward and formed with these Generals a little group, which evidently attracted the attention of some sharpshooter on the other side. For, just as he was raising his glasses to his eyes, a single shot was fired, and a bullet was sent to do its deadly work, which, striking him in the right cheek, passed out back of his left ear, and he fell dying into the arms of the faithful and gallant Major Engelhard, of his staff.[17]

Ezra Carman wrote in his history of the Maryland campaign that Branch was killed while consulting with Col. Edwards and Maj. McCorkle of Gregg's South Carolina brigade. Another account claims Branch was in a cornfield and unable to see exactly where the enemy was:

> [Gregg] sent him word that from the position he held on the hill they [Federals] could be plainly seen. Gen. Branch immediately repaired thither with part of his staff. He was much pleased with the severe punishment his two regiments were inflicting upon the enemy, and his ammunition being short, he sent Lieut. J. A. Bryan of his staff, to order [his regiments] to cease firing. . . . At this moment Capt. Lemmons of Gen. Archer's staff, called General Branch's attention to a body of troops moving on the left. This threw his right side to the line of battle and grouped several together. Gen. Branch had just taken out his field-glass and was adjusting it to his eye, when a rifle ball entered his right cheek and passed out behind his left ear. Without a murmur, without a word, seemingly without a pain, the noble spirit of that gallant officer, in the heat of battle, amidst the victorious shouts of his beloved brigade, passed from earth to eternity.[18]

Colonel Lane, writing to Carman after the war, mentioned more than once that Engelhard told him Branch had been killed by a stray bullet. Stephen Sears

---

16 JL to Ezra Carman, March 22, 1895, February 10, 1900, Carman Papers, NA.

17 Clark, *Histories*, 2:554. Captain John Hughes, the 7th Regiment's quartermaster, actually wrote the account.

18 Carman, *The Maryland Campaign*, 2:479; *Weekly State Journal*, October 1, 1862.

believes that Branch was riding to the front to press the attack when he was fatally struck. The most likely explanation is that a Federal soldier, spotting a clump of enemy officers in the dusk, took a timely shot at the group and hit Branch.[19]

Engelhard took responsibility for Branch's remains as Lane set off to the wall where most of the brigade was clustered. An order directing the the 28th to join him found the 18th instead. Throughout the action, the 18th had been held in reserve behind Archer's brigade. In the darkness Lane discovered Georgia troops from Toombs's brigade intermixed with his Tar Heel regiments. It took some time to reorganize the men, and the dead Federal soldiers on his side of the stone wall—"too close to where I wished to spread my oilcloth [and] blankets"—had to be moved away from a spring and on down the hill. Overall, Branch's brigade had lost 20 killed, 79 wounded, and four missing, for a total of 103 men including Branch. Lane claimed that he tried to keep the news from the men, for morale's sake. Yet word of the general's death filtered swiftly through the ranks.[20]

The brigade spent much of the next day crouched behind the wall, awaiting another attack that would never come. The Carolinians did not venture forth, but had to contend with sharpshooters' bullets whizzing by with uncomfortable regularity. A late-day rain shower further dampened their spirits, but it did help Confederate strategy. Lee chose to move his army back across the Potomac and into Virginia that evening, and the weather helped mask the sounds of the thousands of war-weary feet, and the seemingly innumerable army wagons, guns and caissons, ambulances, officers' horses, and cavalry. Longstreet's men began retiring first, followed by the others. Several recorded Branch's former brigade as the last infantry to withdraw, not fording the Potomac until 10:00 a.m., September 19. The "rear of the column [had been] shelled as it disappeared over the hills on the Virginia side," according to a 7th NC soldier.

19 JL to Ezra Carman, March 22, 1895; Sears, *Landscape Turned Red*, 320.

20 JL to Ezra Carman, February 10, 1900; McDaid, "Four Years," 128; *Weekly State Journal*, October 1, 1862. William McLaurin, in his history of the 18th, relates how Branch, before he was killed, ordered the regiment out, beyond the Confederate line, where the "lines met in this corn-covered valley, and the conflict was terrific, decisive. Burnside was hurled back and a rout prevented." Clark, *Histories*, 2:32. However, Andy Proffitt of the 18th, wrote on September 22, 1862: "We did not get to fire but was exposed to the fire of the enemy in an open field... Several of our Reg. were killed and wounded." M. A. Hancock, ed., *Four Brothers in Gray* (Sparta, NC, 2013), 149-50.

The Light Division stopped about five miles beyond the town of Shepherdstown and went into camp.[21]

Forty-four guns and two undersized infantry brigades under Brig Gen. William Pendleton, the Army of Northern Virginia's artillery commander, guarded the army's vulnerable rear at Boteler's Ford. Pendleton held on to the ford until nightfall, when under some pressure he was forced to abandon his important position and fall back, losing four guns in the process. Word eventually reached Stonewall Jackson that the Federals had managed to gain a foothold on the Virginia side, and by 6:30 the next morning the Light Division was heading back toward the river.[22]

Around 8:30 a.m., Hill deployed his division in two lines in a cornfield out of the sight of the enemy. The brigades of Pender, Gregg, and Thomas, all under Pender, comprised the first line, while the second line contained Archer, Lane, and Brockenbrough, with Archer in command. The enemy had several regiments on the Virginia side of the river, but learning of a sizeable force of Confederates just beyond sight, their commanders began ordering them back across the river. Since the bridge was long destroyed, only two suitable places to cross were possible in this area: an old mill dam and Boteler's Ford. Needless to say, the Federals on the Virginia side of the river struggled to cross at both these points.[23]

Pender ordered his three brigades to step off. Federal artillery quickly found the range and poured forth a murderous fire against the advancing Confederate soldiers. While on the move, Pender's brigade became separated from the other two commands. Believing he was being flanked by Federal infantry, Pender called for assistance. The request brought forth three reserve brigades that stepped off into the same withering artillery fire. "We never forgot the feeling that ran through us about the time we got the order to go forward," recalled an officer in the 33rd NC. "We had hardly started before the bullets began to whiz about our heads, which did not help to soften the first feeling." The Confederates advanced "exposed the hole way to the heaviest bombing

21 Harris, *Historical Sketches,* 23. Both Harris and A. P. Hill in his official report say the brigade did not cross over till 10 a.m. OR 19/1:981.

22 OR 19/1: 982. See also Thomas McGrath. *Shepherdstown: Last Clash of the Antietam Campaign, September 19-20, 1862* (Lynchburg, VA, 2007), 30-87.

23 McGrath, *Shepherdstown,* 107-17.

said to be by old soldiers that they ever saw," wrote one of the fresh conscripts from the 18th.[24]

For various reasons, one Pennsylvania regiment (the 118th) failed to retire. In service for just three weeks, and in the heat of combat with Hill's veterans, the Pennsylvanians found many of their rifles defective. All the other Federal regiments were back across the river as Pender's men surrounded them. Under a devastating fire from the Confederates above, the Federal regiment was doomed. Proffitt recalled that "the Yankees lay on the field in heaps and piles." He and his brother Alfred, also in the 18th, "shot as long as we could see a blue coat. . . . The bombs burst around our heads with terrific fury and showers of grape canister fell mingled with limbs of trees thick around us." For the rest of this hot September day, the Confederates lay on the river bank, exposed to Federal artillery, gathering their dead and wounded into a hollow to protect them from shrapnel. Lane reported brigade losses at three killed and 71 wounded. For the time being at least, McClellan's pursuit was thwarted. That evening, the Light Division pulled back and moved to Martinsburg, remaining there until September 25, when it moved to Bunkersville.[25]

Lee had actually entertained hopes of continuing the Maryland campaign. He had wanted to re-cross into Maryland on September 20 or 21 at Williamsport, and sent his cavalry to occupy the town and its ford over the Potomac. However, McClellan's troops drove back the Confederate cavalry. With the fords near Shepherdstown and Williamsport blocked, Lee realized that his campaign was at an end. Furthermore, Lee knew his army was spent. It did not "exhibit its former temper. . . . [The] condition of our troops now demanded repose." Thus, the Army of Northern Virginia rested.[26]

Lane remained in command of Branch's brigade, as Maj. Engelhard began the arduous task of transporting Branch's remains back to North Carolina. Delivering the news to the family in Raleigh proved difficult. A "dispatch" on September 21, as the family was heading to church, reported Branch dead. "All day Sunday we endured the suspense, not knowing whether it was a idle rumor

24 Survivors' Association. *History of the 118th Pennsylvania Volunteers* (Philadelphia, PA, 1905), 94; Hancock, *Four Brothers in Gray*, 149-50.

25 Hancock, *Four Brothers in Gray*, 149-50; OR 19/1:986; Harris, *Historical Sketches*, 24. Apparently, no reports for the various regiments in Branch's brigade and the Maryland Campaign survive.

26 OR 19/1:152.

General Branch was memorialized by many after his death. *The Southern Illustrated News* featured his image on its front page in June 1863.

The Southern Illustrated News

coming from a straggler from the battle field," Branch's oldest daughter Susan, wrote, "or whether it was a sad reality." That evening, a second dispatch came, stating that the General was safe, at least according to a gentleman who had spoken with one of A. P. Hill's aides. The conflicting notes continued through the next day, until Monday evening, when a dispatch arrived from Engelhard, relating the facts of the General's death and that he was escorting the remains back to North Carolina. William Blount and William Rodman, both relatives and former staff officers under Branch, along with Robert Haywood and John Spelman met Engelhard when he arrived in Richmond. Engelhard expected to be in Raleigh on September 24. "[I]t is terrible news to bear," Susan wrote. "What is home with out him, or what will it ever be?"[27]

On September 24 Raleigh officials met at the courthouse. As was customary, a resolution expressing the city's grief was passed and a committee appointed to work out the details of Branch's funeral. When his body arrived Thursday evening, military forces met the train, escorted the casket to the Capitol rotunda, and posted an all-night guard. All businesses closed on Friday morning, and the number of mourners on hand was said to rival crowds at the visit of Henry Clay in 1840. Episcopal clergyman Rev. Dr. Mason conducted

27 *Weekly State Journal*, October 1, 1862; Susan Branch to "dear Aunt," September 23, 1862, Mrs. Branch Papers, NCDAH. According to an article in the *Winchester Evening Star*, September 16, 1920, Branch's headquarters flag accompied the General's remains as far as Winchester, VA. In 1920, the flag was donated to the Hall of History, now the North Carolina Museum of History.

funeral services the next morning inside the Capitol. "Every clergyman in the city" accompanied him. Then "the body was borne on a bier by eight soldiers" through the ranks of soldiers presenting arms to a waiting hearse, "decked with regimental colors, and wreaths and evergreens." The military escort, portions of the 8th and 31st Regiments, with 600 conscripts, set off with the hearse "to the mournful sound of the muffled drum." At the City Cemetery, the Episcopal service for the dead concluded, ceremonial volleys were fired, and the "earth closed over all that was mortal of a devoted husband, a fond and affectionate father, a most estimable and useful citizen and a brave and skilful soldier." Branch left behind his wife Nancy and four children.[28]

Many lamented Branch's death. "The Confederacy has to mourn the loss of a gallant soldier and accomplished gentlemen, who fell in battle at the head of his brigade," A.P. Hill wrote. "He was my senior brigade commander, and one to whom I could have entrusted the command of the division with all confidence." Robert E. Lee referred to "the brave, lamented General Branch" in his report. Even Raleigh editor W. W. Holden softened a little on his views of the dead officer. He had hammered Branch's appointment as brigadier general a few months earlier. Although he did not directly praise Branch for the position he had attained, he came close. His death, wrote Holden, "will be deeply and widely deplored. The fall of the humblest private in the ranks of our noble soldiers sends sorrow to the heart of every true North Carolinian, but when one occupying the position of a leader like Gen. Branch falls, its effects are more widely felt. . . . He falls in a just cause, and leaves a reputation of which his family and friends may justly be proud."[29]

And what of Branch's reputation? Douglas Southall Freeman wrote that "[i]n a Division where brigade command was above average, he had learned rapidly and had won distinction, though he had received no professional training in arms before the war." Martin Schenck, in his history of the Light Division, appraises Branch as "a good soldier, respected by his men and superiors alike." James Robertson, in his biography of A. P. Hill, describes Branch as a "hard-hitting brigadier as well as a good follower." While not a military man, Branch did have the capacity to manage an organization, a skill he learned as a railroad president. Obviously intelligent, a graduate of Princeton, lawyer, and member of the U.S. Congress, Branch also had connections, such as

---

28 Raleigh *Register*, September 27, October 1, 1862; *Weekly State Journal*, October 1, 1862.

29 OR 19/1:150, 981; *The Weekly Standard*, October 1, 1862.

his friendship with Jefferson Davis before the war. Varina Davis told Nancy Branch in September, "I scarcely know how to believe the news," on learning of the General's death, a testament to the family's closeness.[30]

Branch's first two battles, New Bern and Hanover Court House, were both losses. New Bern had opened much of eastern North Carolina to Federal raids. Hanover might have allowed Federal forces under McClellan and McDowell to link up, almost certainly spelling the end to the Confederate capital in Richmond. To Branch's credit, he faced vastly superior odds at both engagements. Once Branch's brigade was folded into the Light Division, his performance was solid. On a couple of occasions, such as during Jackson's advance to Harpers Ferry, Branch temporarily commanded the Light Division, but never in combat. Lawrence O'Bryan Branch's war was at an end, but it was far from over for his brigade.

---

30 Freeman, *Lee's Lieutenants*, 2:251; Schenck, *Up Came Hill, 224;* Robertson, *Hill*, 60; Christ, ed., *The Papers of Jefferson Davis*, 8:207n12.

Chapter 7

"Oh! How fearful the scenes around a 'Field Hospital'"

Brigade Medical Care

Walter Lenoir was a 39-year-old widowed lawyer living in Caldwell County at the start of the war. He spent time in his brother's company in the 25th NC, recruiting for Vance's Legion, and in an unattached company that became a part of the 58th NC before he was elected captain of Company A, 37th NC. He had been in Virginia only six weeks before entering his third battle. At Ox Hill, Lenoir was lying on the ground behind his men while the battle and rain raged. As Lenoir turned to encourage his men, he "felt an awful pain in my leg. . . . A musket ball had passed through my right leg . . . from side to side, about the middle of the leg, and as the surgeon afterwards informed me breaking both bones." Not long thereafter, Lenoir was struck again; this time, a ball glanced off his shin and took off the big toe on his already injured leg. Lenoir's ensuing battlefield struggle, which he documented in January 1863, provides a unique glimpse into the plight of the wounded. After being struck,

I determined to try to crawl to the rear in search of some of the infirmiry corps to bear me off the field, as I was utterly disabled, and feared that an artery might have been severed which would require prompt surgical aid. I managed to drag myself about ten steps when I stopped from exhaustion, finding myself in an open place caused by a little road . . . more exposed to the fire. . . . While lying there I had sand thrown on my cheek twice by musket balls which struck the ground by my head. And the shells from a Yankee battery which was enfilading our line . . . seemed to pass in fearfully close proximity to my body. . . . It had rained hard during the night, and I was chilled and thoroughly wet when I was found a little after dark by one of my men. As none of the infirmiry corps seemed to be near I was bourne off by four men on my blanket stretched between two fence rails. . . . On that night . . . I was carried about a quarter of a mile to a house where I was laid upon a narrow porch already so crowded with wounded men that there was only room for me at the entry, where my wounded leg was struck occasionally during the night to my great torture by the feet of persons passing in and out. On the next morning I was carried on stretchers about three quarters of a mile, and deposited on the ground in an old field where some wounded men had been brought together. Here I lay without receiving any surgical aid till about ten o'clock on the morning of the 3rd, when to my great relief I found that several surgeons were in attendance and ready to proceed with the amputation of my leg. I was placed under the influence of chloroform, and my leg soon taken off by Dr. Shaeffner surgeon of the 33rd NC, and the stump dressed. I waked up just as the dressing was completed without retaining the slightest consciousness of any part of the operation.

Lenoir, with other wounded, was transported via wagon to Middleburg, VA. He eventually made his way back to Caldwell County, regretting the loss of his leg.[1]

Months of active campaigning for Branch's former brigade produced hundreds of wounded men just like Lenoir. Tending to them, to those who contracted diseases, and to the remains of the dead exceeded the resources of both the regimental medical staffs of the brigade, and of the hospitals to which the men were eventually sent.

Each regiment was supposed to have a surgeon, assistant surgeon, and a hospital steward—theoretically three men per 1,000 soldiers. After battle and disease took their toll, though, only 13 men were available as surgeons in the entire brigade. The original five, appointed as the regiments were mustered, came from individual communities providing regiments. All five were medical school graduates and practicing physicians before the war. However, a private practice anywhere in North Carolina could not have prepared anyone for the

---

1 Hickerson, *Happy Valley*, 85-86.

Surgeon Robert Gibbon had a brother in the 28th North Carolina, and another brother, John Gibbon, was a prominent general in the Union army.

Histories of the Several Regiments and Battalions from North Carolina

mass trauma the war generated. A young man wishing to become a doctor attended one of the few medical colleges in America. Classes involved purchasing an attendance card for the seven standard lectures, without any classroom laboratories or any hands-on clinical instruction required. The second year repeated the lectures of the first year. Usually, a student wrote a thesis and thus became eligible to receive his degree.

Thirty-year old James Miller (18th NC) graduated from the medical department of the University of the City of New York and was practicing in Wilmington at the start of the war. He was appointed on June 15, 1861. Robert Gibbon (28th NC), a 38-year-old Pennsylvania native and graduate of Philadelphia's Jefferson Medical College, had a brother serving as assistant commissary of subsistence in the same regiment and was appointed surgeon in September 1861. Richard B. Baker (33rd NC) was a native of Gates County and graduate of both the University of Virginia and the University of Maryland. He started his practice in 1846 and was 40 years old when he joined the Confederate army. The 7th Regiment had been without a surgeon for several months when Wesley Campbell was appointed on November 6, 1861. Campbell, 31, was also a graduate of the Jefferson Medical College. James Hickerson, another Jefferson Medical College alumnus, lived in Wilkes County and was only 27 when he became surgeon of the 37th.[2]

2   Jordan, *NC Regiments*, 4:406, 6:307, 8:111, 9:119, 469.

Army regulations were adopted in 1862 requiring an examination of medical applicants before their promotion and appointment. Thomas Wood worked for an apothecary in Wilmington before the war. He enlisted in the 18th NC in October 1861 and served as first sergeant for a short time before becoming ill. Wood regained his health in a hospital in Richmond and was detailed there as ward master and apothecary. All the while, he was permitted to attend lectures at the Virginia Medical College. After completing his first year of studies, Wood was allowed to appear before the "Board of Medical Examiners," in Richmond and on examination day, was asked to write on "Typhoid Fever." Oral examinations next quizzed him on the diseases of the chest, anatomy, the arteries, and surgery. A few days later, Wood received an official note announcing he had been appointed assistant surgeon. He transferred out of the 18th and served with the 3rd NC Regiment.[3]

Some applicants shuddered at the mere thought of undergoing the examination. James Hickerson of the 37th NC submitted his resignation on December 10, 1862, informing the war department he had "been appointed by North Carolina" and declined to be examined. Colonel Barber regretfully endorsed Hickerson's resignation, observing that for the past 14 months, Hickerson had "discharged the duties of his office."[4]

Not all regiments had the required medical staff at all times. Wesley Campbell served as surgeon for the 7th Regiment for the duration of the war. Yet the 33rd appears to have had no surgeon after John Shaffner left the regiment to serve in the 4th NC in early 1863. Edward Higgenbothom, a hospital surgeon in Richmond, was appointed to the post, but existing records don't indicate he was ever actually present with the regiment. Most of the men who replaced the original surgeons in the regiment were younger.[5]

---

3   H. H. Cunningham. *Doctors in Gray: The Confederate Medical Service* (Baton Rouge, LA, 1958), 32-35; *Regulations for the Army of the Confederate States, 1863* (Richmond, VA, 1863), 238; Donald Koonce, ed. *Doctor to the Front: The Recollections of Confederate Surgeon Thomas Fanning Wood, 1861-1865* (Knoxville, TN, 2000), 32-42; Jordan, *NC Regiments*, 6:412.

4   The Chief Surgeon of Hill's Division added Hickerson had appeared before the board and received an "unfavorable report." His resignation was obviously rejected, for Hickerson submitted a second letter on December 28, resigning due to bad health. This was accepted on January 3, 1863. James Hickerson Roll 402, M270, RG109, CMSR, NA.

5   Lyon Tyler, ed. *Encyclopedia of Virginia Biography*, 3 vols. (New York, 1915), 2:777; Thomas Wood. "James Fergus McRee, M.D." North Carolina Medical Journal (January 1892), 29/1:10-20. Other surgeons in the brigade include 18th Regiment: Tazwell Tyler, son of former U.S. President John Tyler, and Thomas Lane, brother of Col. James Lane; 28th Regiment:

A regimental surgeon had many duties in camp, including responsibility for the cleanliness of both of the men and the grounds, the provision of good food and clean water, and recommending improvements through the chain of command. Surgeons filed daily reports of the sick and compiled monthly returns reporting the numbers of sick, wounded, and deceased. Senior regimental surgeons also filed requests for hospital and medical stores. On being appointed surgeon of the 28th NC in 1861, Robert Gibbon requisitioned 34 medicines including chloroform, calomel, quinine, and morphine.[6]

Each surgeon had a couple of assigned assistants who were likewise trained medical personnel and commissioned officers, either lieutenants or captains. The surgeon and assistant surgeon(s) divided the patient load. According to an 1861 manual, the assistant was responsible for a raft of duties: "making up medicines, seeing that the patients get them at the proper time, apply dressings, bandage fractured limbs, keep the register, diet and prescription books, and assist in compiling the monthly and quarterly returns." When the surgeon was absent or ill, the assistant substituted. Likewise, when a portion of the regiment was detached, the assistant surgeon accompanied the detachment. Twenty-one men served as assistant surgeons of the brigade. At least 10 were college-educated. Benjamin Brookshire (7th NC) was appointed, but failed to appear for duty. Others were transferred to different regiments. Alexander Gordon appears as assistant surgeon of the 18th Regiment in March 1863. "F. Cox" served the 28th "but a short time," and W. R. Barham, who joined the same regiment in April 1862, was captured during the battle of Hanover, escaped, and disappeared.[7]

Robert Gibbon, who was replaced by James McGee in 1864, and a few months later, by William Gaither, assistant surgeon of the 26th Regiment; 37th Regiment: James Hickerson, who resigned on December 28, 1862, by reason of "indigestion and general debility," and was replaced by assistant surgeon John Alexander on January 7, 1863. Alexander served until May 15, 1863, when he resigned by reason of "a bilious attack" and "acute dysentery." George Trescott, an established South Carolina physician, replaced Alexander. Trescott served the regiment until the surrender in April 1865. One other doctor, George Moffitt, was assigned to the 37th Regiment, but failed to report for duty. Jordan, NC Troops, 6:307, 8:111, 9:120, 469-70.

6 J. Julian Chisolm, A Manual of Military Surgery for the use of Surgeons in the Confederate Army (Richmond, VA, 1861), 102-106; Robert Gibbon, Requisitions for Medicines and Hospital Stores, October 16, 1861, Roll105, M331, RG109, CMSR, NA.

7 Chisolm, A Manual for Military Surgery, 107. Those who disappear from the records include the 18th NC's Charles Lesesne, who transferred to the 39th VA, and Hugh Gardner, who transferred to the 33rd NC. Jordan, NC Troops, 4:406, 6:307, 8:111, 9:120, 470.

Each regiment was also allowed a hospital steward. Wiley Cornish was appointed the 18th Regiment's only steward in March 1864, and Thomas Sparrow served as the 37th NC's sole steward from March-May 1862. The other three regiments had stewards for the duration of the war. There may have been others whose records do not survive, or the post might have been filled by men detailed from the various regiments. Hospital stewards oversaw the hospital stores and supplies as well as the nurses and cooks. "Often," according to regulations, "he acts as medical dispenser and apothecary" and if "intelligent" can "be instructed in the preparation of prescriptions for the sick."[8]

Sick call took place soon after the men were drummed out of quarters for roll call, and before breakfast. Soldiers with a medical complaint gave their names to the orderly sergeant, who then escorted them to the surgeon. One company officer noted in January 1862 he had "about 30 Men on the Sick Roll." The surgeon decided which cases went to hospital, and which returned to quarters for rest. He then sent a report to the commanding officer. Hospital tents were preferred, but local buildings were often used. Hospitals were something of a novelty for soldiers; few existed in the country before the war. Usually mothers, wives, or sisters of the sick or injured treated them in homes. Occasionally, a doctor might be called. Hospitals that did exist served slaves, the poor, insane, or travelers. At the beginning of the war, most people viewed hospitals with trepidation. William Morris (37th NC) wrote home in January 1862 that one of his men, on hearing the regiment was getting ready to move, "slipped off," adding the solider "has a poore opinion of the hospital." A few months later, Morris reported another of his men, Amos Morris, was sick in town. "I think they Doo better than to Go to the Hospital," he said.[9]

Regimental commanders were reluctant to transfer troops from regimental or brigade field hospitals to the general hospital system in places like Richmond, Charlottesville, or Lynchburg, because men might feign illness for the comforts of a clean bed and decent food instead of camp-life rigors. In early June 1862, Col. Lee ordered John Alexander, a physician in the 37th NC, to sweep through

---

8   Jordan, *NC Troops*, 4:407, 6:308, 8:112, 9:121, 471; Chisolm, *A Manual for Military Surgery*, 65-66.

9   Margaret Humphreys, *Marrow of Tragedy: The Health Crisis of the American Civil War* (Baltimore, MD, 2013), 6-7; William Morris to "Deare Companion," January 7, 10, July 21, 1862, Morris Papers, SHC/UNC.

Thomas Lane, brother to James H. Lane, began as an assistant surgeon in the 28th North Carolina. In March 1863, Thomas transferred to the 18th North Carolina as a surgeon, a position he held until his parole at Appomattox on April 9, 1865.

College of William and Mary

three hospitals in Virginia, and one in Goldsboro, NC, "to gather up all of our men who have been in the Hospital, and are fit for duty," and send them back to the regiment. Likely other regimental commanders also sent someone to round up shirkers. Although men in hospital were guarded, they did evade the guards and take off for home on occasion. Furloughed soldiers were beyond the reach of the army. A truly sick soldier could be furloughed home, typically for 30 days, relieving the army from its responsibility to feed and care for him. If a soldier were sick or his wounds not properly healed, then he could appear before a doctor who could grant an extension of his furlough.[10]

The vast majority of the sick and wounded went to hospitals in Richmond. Not long after First Manassas in July 1861, the Confederate government recognized the need for better hospital facilities. Construction on Chimborazo Hospital thus began in October 1861, and when it was finished, there was room for 3,000 patients. In March 1862, about the time Branch's brigade was created, construction began in the western outskirts of Richmond on Winder Hospital, which was situated on 125 acres and could accommodate 4,300 patients.

Private homes, tobacco warehouses, and, in emergencies, churches also furnished hospital spaces in Richmond. The North Carolina hospital there, also known as General Hospital #24, occupied a three-story tobacco factory on the corner of 26th and Main Streets. Enlisted men arriving via railroad had no say

---

10 John Alexander to "Dear Wife," June 5, 1862, Alexander Papers, UNC-Charlotte.

about their hospital assignments. Rufus Carson (28th NC) was wounded at Fredericksburg in December 1862, transported to Richmond by train, and initially taken to General Hospital #25 ("the Texas Hospital"), where he arrived five days after being wounding. He convalesced at Winder Hospital until February, when he rejoined his regiment.[11]

Confederate hospitals sought to care for their patients despite shortages of almost everything: food, personnel, facilities, medicines, and equipment. Most of the large general hospitals had extensive staffs including stewards, matrons, nurses, cooks, laundresses, gardeners, and bakers. In many cases, slaves or free persons of color filled these roles to free needed men for the ranks. In some instances, white women were hired as matrons or ward matrons, responsible for keeping the wards clean and supervising delivery of food and administration of medicine. According to Margaret Humphreys, these women could create a sense of an extended family at a hospital. At home, female family members provided medical care. In the general hospitals, women often came to look upon the soldiers as they would their own sons. They in turn often regarded these compassionate women as surrogate family members. John Carson (28th NC) was wounded in 1863 and transported to the Florida Hospital in Richmond. The hospital's matron, Mary Reid, the former Florida governor's wife, "played the role of a mother to the sick and dying soldiers," Carson recalled.[12]

Carson enjoyed the food at the Florida Hospital. Providing nutritious food, it was widely recognized, helped speed recovery for convalescing soldiers. Yet hospitals struggled with this throughout the war. Chimborazo Hospital was undoubtedly the model for the rest with its own bakery, brewery, icehouses, and a nearby farm providing a vegetable garden and a pasture for hundreds of cows and goats. Plus, the hospital operated a boat on the James River between Richmond and Lynchburg, bartering cotton for provisions.[13]

Sick officers could afford the luxury of seeking quarters in private houses for recuperation. Lieutenant John Conrad (28th NC), for example, stayed at a home in Lynchburg in September 1862, while suffering from "Intermitten

---

11 Rebecca Calcutt, *Richmond's Wartime Hospitals* (Gretna, LA, 2005), 25, 139; R. W. Carson, "Reminiscence of Civil War by Mr. R. W. Carson," [unidentified clipping], June 5, 1908, NCDAH.

12 Humphreys, *Marrow of Tragedy*, 50-51; Carson, "Reminisces," in NCDAH.

13 Carson, "Reminisces"; Calcutt, *Richmond's Wartime Hospitals*, 153.

John Abernethy served as a hospital steward in the 28th North Carolina in 1862. He later transferred back to Company H as a lieutenant, but died before the year ended.

Histories of the Several Regiments and Battalions from North Carolina

Fever," he wrote. "I like my boarding house very well." In October, he recorded that he was "fattening every day. . . if you could only see me eat once, especially dinners; as we have Cabbage, tomatoes, Corn, potatoes, (Irish and Sweet) mutton, beef, and occasionally fried chicken."[14]

During late summer and early fall of 1862, Noah Collins (37th NC) bounced between several hospitals. As the army began moving toward Federal forces near Manassas, an "almost intolerable, or unindurable flux Diarrhea" struck him. He and another soldier received a pass to remain "behind and take the best care of ourselves that we could." For the last part of August, the pair stayed with some local farmers. On September 9, Collins appeared before "old Doctor Cross," in Leesburg, who advised him to rest: "be as quiet as possible for a while." The following morning, the "Invalid Examining Board," examined and later admitted him to the Episcopal Church Hospital in Leesburg. He left Leesburg on September 17 and walked to Charlestown. Learning that Union soldiers might be near, he moved on to the Jordan White Sulphur Springs Hospital, where he was admitted on September 24. Collins stayed until October 17, "suffering to an alarming extent, in consequence of being too sick to eat." He walked thence to Winchester and was admitted to the Academy Hospital. The following day he set out on foot again toward Staunton, arriving on October 25 and admitted to the Presbyterian Church Hospital. Two days later

14 Conrad, "Civil War Letters," 313-15.

Private Archibald Council, 18th North Carolina, photographed here wrapped in a blanket. He was severely wounded at Chancellorsville and died three weeks later on May 25, 1863.

Library of Congress

Collins was loaded onto a train and transported to Chimbarazo Hospital in Richmond. Five days later, he had been moved via rail to Danville, Virginia, and admitted to the White House Hospital. He was not discharged until December 12, when he started on his way back to rejoin his regiment.[15]

Collins's ailment, chronic diarrhea, was "the number-one disease of the war" and, coupled with dysentery, "the number-one cause of nonbattlefield morbidity and mortality." Diarrhea itself was not a specific disease, but a symptom of many diseases. Contaminated food and water, food poisoning, and a general breakdown of the body fostered other ailments. Acute diarrhea was "loose and frequent bowel movements over the course of several days." Chronic diarrhea was worse: it lasted for longer periods of time, leading to weight loss, emaciation, and overall weakness. William Morris noted Lt. William Glenn (37th NC) "has Been sick for the past 2 months past with Feaver & Cronick Diareare. he Looks Like A Dead Man." Glenn resigned from the company, heading home to recover. W. B. Morton (28th NC) was discharged on January 27, 1862, by reason of "a prolonged attack of pneumonia followed by a chronic cough and diarrhoea." He died three days later. According to records, fellow 28th member William T. Blanton, hospitalized in Richmond with typhoid fever and diarrhea, died on June 30, 1862, after he "drank cold water to great excess." Andrew J. Teague (37th NC) wrote in June 1863: "my bowls has bin runing off sum for the last few days." Teague's problem might

15 Collins, Reminiscences, 29-33.

Typhoid fever and diarrhea killed many, including Pvt. William T. Blanton, 28th North Carolina, on June 30, 1862.

Greg Mast

have been persistent. He was captured in May 1864 and died of chronic diarrhea at Elmira on April 25, 1865.[16]

One of the leading causes of chronic diarrhea and dysentery was typhoid fever, also known as "camp fever." Typhoid, believed to be the cause of one-fourth of all disease-related deaths in the Confederate army, entered the body through food and water contaminated by excrement. A soldier would begin to feel fatigue and depression, often followed by diarrhea. Then came body aches, loss of appetite, chills, delirium, and possibly bronchitis leading to pneumonia. No definitive test existed to diagnose the disease. One surgeon calculated 25 percent of all deaths in the Confederate army in the 19-month period between January 1, 1862, and August 1, 1863, came from typhoid.[17]

The most common treatments for typhoid were opiates. Some doctors prescribed calomel, caster oil, or quinine, believing these medicines would cleanse the body and rid it of the disease. All they actually did was exacerbate the problem. Doctors administered quinine, while treating the diarrhea and pain with opiates. Turpentine was also given, along with calomel. Typhoid, or typhoid pneumonia, seems to have seriously stricken the brigade from late

16 Humphreys, *Marrow of Tragedy*, 27, 67; Glenna Schroeder-Lein, *The Encyclopedia of Civil War Medicine* (Armock, NY, 2008), 87; William Morris to "Deare Companion," July 21, 1862, Morris Papers, SHC/UNC; Jordan, *NC Troops*, 8:160, 197, 9:470, 536, 551, 566. William Glenn re-enlisted in the 37th two months later as a private. He was promoted to sergeant major and later, a lieutenant in Company G.

17 Bell Wiley, *The Life of Johnny Reb: The Common Soldier of the Confederacy* (Baton Rouge, LA, 1943), 252; Schroeder-Lein, *The Encyclopedia of Civil War Medicine*, 309-10. Alexander, *Reminiscences*, 73.

Diseases affected officers just as they did enlisted men. Lieutenant Colonel Thomas L. Lowe, 28th North Carolina, died of a "fever" on June 10, 1862.

Catawba Soldiers in the Civil War

summer 1862 through January 1863. A survey of five companies, one from each regiment and from different parts of the state, reveals 12 men who died of typhoid fever between August 1862 and January 1863. Since the hospitals in Richmond were full, most of those ill with typhoid fever in 1862 were treated in camp.[18]

Many other diseases ran rampant through the camps at various times. Men died of pneumonia, often as a complication of a cold, the measles, or typhoid fever. Between January 1862 and August 1863, about 18 percent of Confederate soldiers contracted pneumonia, with 3.15 percent succumbing. Pneumonia ravaged the regiments in the winter of 1862-63. Thirteen men in the five surveyed companies died between November and February. Childhood diseases coursed wildly through the camps as well. Men from the country, while hardened from lives working outside on their farms, were susceptible to ailments that most children contracted through contact with others. Measles, mumps, and jaundice were common. Captain Morris (37th NC) wrote in January 1862 he had 30 men on the sick roll: one bad case of pneumonia, with the balance being "Yellow Janders following the mealses." In April he himself

18 The five companies surveyed were Company A, 7th Regiment (Iredell and Alexander Counties), Company E, 18th Regiment (New Hanover County), Company G, 28th Regiment (Orange County), Company E, 33rd Regiment (Gates County), and Company K, 37th Regiment (Alleghany County).

William Green, a private in the 37th North Carolina, died of disease in January 1863.

Sheree Sloop

had the mumps. Doctor Alexander noted in October 1862 that all the new conscripts had the measles and mumps.[19]

Close conditions in which the men lived led to the spread of these diseases. The brigade had at least three fatal cases of measles. Robert Bunn (33rd NC) died of the disease in February 1862; David Eldridge (37th NC) in July that year of "pneumonia and diarrhea following measles"; and William Brewer (7th NC) in October 1862. George Cochran (37th Regiment) noted he and his brother deliberately went into a tent set aside for measles patients, trying to contract the disease. He believed "it would better to have it in camp where we could be better . . . cared for." The Cochran brothers developed "blooming cases," but both survived. At least one soldier, Joel Green (28th NC), died of tuberculosis. Joseph Powell contracted and died of spinal meningitis. Several in the brigade, such as Davis Riggs (18th NC), died of scurvy.[20]

Smallpox, a dreaded disease, appeared in the army largely after the Maryland campaign and again in the fall of 1862. Symptoms included fever, aches and pains, and small, red, pus-filled blisters that, after scabbing over, would drop off and leave pitted scars. One brigade officer noted several cases of smallpox in the brigade in October 1862. Many believed recently released

19 Schroeder-Lein, *The Encyclopedia of Civil War Medicine*, 247; William Morris to "Deare Companion," January 7, April 25, 1862, Morris Papers, SHC/UNC; John Alexander to "My Dear Wife," October 11, 1862, Alexander Papers, UNC-Charlotte.

20 Cochran, *A Brief Sketch*, 7; Jordan, *NC Troops*, 4:747, 6:409, 8:167, 9:144, 236, 475.

Confederate prisoners had brought them the disease. John Green (28th NC), captured during the battle of Hanover Court House, noted that all returning prisoners were placed in a smallpox camp two miles from Richmond for observation. Confederate medical officials were quick to vaccinate soldiers by taking a scab from an active case, making a small incision in the arm of the soldier, and inserting the scab. This induced a mild form of smallpox. At times, though, the inoculation knocked out entire companies from duty. Smallpox killed at least five members of the brigade during September-December 1862, another four in the spring, and three additional men in December.[21]

Of course, opportunities to contract venereal diseases were never lacking. One writer estimated Richmond had more prostitutes during the war years than Paris and New Orleans combined. Except in severe cases, most men were treated in camp, leaving few surviving records. The symptoms usually abated, only to reappear years later, because no reliable treatments were then available. Only two brigade soldiers are documented as contracting STDs that forced them out of the service. Lieutenant James W. Hayes, Jr., resigned in January 1863, because of gonorrhea, and James Hilliard was discharged six months later because of syphilis. Both were members of the 33rd NC.[22]

Undoubtedly the weather—numerous reports of snow and cold temperatures—wreaked a great deal of havoc on the men's health. Late winter and early spring 1863 seem to have been the most unhealthy for the brigade during the war. Captain Jackson Bost (37th NC) noted in March 1863 more sickness and death in camp than at any point previously. That same month Dr. Alexander (37th NC) reported 62 men on the sick list, "a great deal of pneumonia and typhoid fever." On April 1, he wrote that in the past three months, he had treated 600 cases of sickness. Right after the battle of Chancellorsville, Lt. Col. William Speer lamented as many as 175 sick men a day in the 28th Regiment.[23]

---

21 Schroeder-Lein, *The Encyclopedia of Civil War Medicine*, 278-79; William Morris to "Deare Companion," October 24, 1862, Morris Papers, SHC/UNC; John L. Green, Civil War Collection, Box 70, File 57, NCDAH. Smallpox incapacitated 5,000 members of the Army of Northern Virginia during the battle of Chancellorsville. Wiley, *The Life of Johnny Reb*, 254.

22 Clifford Dowdey, *Experiment in Rebellion* (Garden City, NY, 1946), 114; Jordan, *NC Troops*, 9:202, 209.

23 Jackson Bost to Rev. E. L. Davis, March 27, 1863, Bost Papers, DU; John Alexander to "Dear Wife," March 7, April 1, 1863, Alexander Papers, UNC/C; Speer, *Voices from Cemetery Hill*, 101.

Scores of men were so wrecked by service-connected disease or injury they had to be discharged. Lieutenant Joseph Todd's (37th NC) arm failed to heal after a smallpox inoculation, and he was sent home in December 1863. Major William Montgomery (28th NC) left the service in September 1862 after "a severe and long continued attack of spermatorrhoea." William Smith (37th NC) was discharged in March 1863 by reason of "both physical and mental inability which renders him entirely unfit" for duty. Gunshot wounds resulting in the loss of fingers or the inability to use limbs usually necessitated a discharge. Watson Holyfield (28th NC) was shot in the right shoulder, rendering his arm useless. Columbus Stroup (37th NC) lost the use of his right hand due to a wound. In at least two cases, soldiers actually maimed themselves to avoid duty. Alexander Lanier (28th NC) was discharged after "cutting off three of his fingers" in October 1861, while Jeremiah Blackburn (37th NC) "shot his own finger off." Blackburn's injury did not warrant a discharge. He was detailed to the hospital as a nurse.[24]

"Oh! How fearful the scenes around a 'Field Hospital' during a bloody battle," Chaplain Francis M. Kennedy (28th NC) wrote in May 1863. Many soldiers' perspective on general hospitals gradually changed during the war. Visions of the horrors associated with field hospitals, which tended to combat trauma, nevertheless haunted some for the remainder of their lives. Surgeons, their assistants, the hospital stewards, even members of the brigade band all had various assignments during battle. Regimental surgeons collectively established a brigade hospital at a location in the rear. Buildings or level fields near water, a stream or well, close enough to the front lines to be accessible, but out of range from small arms and artillery fire served best. The designated building flew a hospital flag. General Branch's hospital at the battle of Hanover Court House was established in a house, "on which the hospital flag was conspicuously displayed."[25]

Assistant surgeons on or near the front lines supervised the infirmary corps, which offered aid to the wounded and assisted those unable to walk off the battlefield. The assistant surgeon was supposed "to equip himself with a

24 Jordan, *NC Troops*, 8:110, 113, 119; 9:473, 486, 520, 577.

25 Francis Kennedy, Diary, May 1863; *OR* 11/ 1:742; Cunningham, *Doctors in Gray*, 113-14. Schroeder-Lein writes "tents were often kept away from the battle, in the baggage train, and were not available during the battle itself." See Schroeder-Lein, *The Encyclopedia of Civil War Medicine*, 152.

pocket case of instruments, ligatures, needles, pins, chloroform, morphine, alcoholic stimulants, bandages, lint, and splints." Of course, the Confederacy often ran short of supplies, so the assistant surgeon was able to do little more than try to stop the flow of blood, or administer a shot of whiskey before sending a man to the rear. Members of the brigade who served in the infirmary corps are hard to identify. Orders stated the infirmary corps should have about 30 men from each regiment, but no one appears in the records as being thus detailed. Several were detailed to drive ambulances, and in the case of James Fry (7th NC), detailed to the ambulance corps. Doctor John Alexander (37th NC) wrote that four stretchers were first issued to the regiment on the eve of the Seven Days battles on June 25, 1862, but he didn't identify who carried them. "They were made of two poles, well fastened to the sides of strong duck cloth, and were about six feet long." One possibility is that the band members of the 33rd NC were the only infirmary corps for the entire brigade.[26]

Traditionally, members of the band or the regiment's field musicians served as stretcher-bearers during battle, after safely stowing their instruments. Oliver Lehman, a member of the 33rd's brass band, remembered he and his fellow bandmates "caring for the wounded and taking them to the field hospital just behind the line of battle. . . . often under severe shelling and small arms fire but we escaped almost miraculously." However, even if the drummers and fifers joined the band members, the number of men helping the wounded off the field was far below the 130 men established by regulations.[27]

The weapons used during the war produced ghastly wounds. Artillery fired solid round shot; hollow spherical balls filled with black powder; case shot, which contained small lead balls packed in sawdust; and canister, which held many small balls packed in sawdust. Solid shot simply sailed through the air or bounced along the ground, taking out troops as it went. Spherical and case shot were designed to explode in the ranks, killing and maiming men with the sharp iron fragments or the lead balls within. Artillerists switched to grape shot and, later in the war, canister, as opposing infantry formations closed in. A cannon loaded with canister was like a large shotgun, devastating at close range. Artillery was used to soften up a target, or in defensive situations. To a large degree, it was a more psychological weapon than a strategic one. David Dugger

---

26 Cunningham, *Doctors in Gray*, 114; Jordan, *NC Troops*, 4: 466; Alexander, *Reminiscences*, 71.

27 O. J. Lehman. "Reminiscences of the War Between the States," Civil War Collection, Box 71, Folder 19, NCDAH.

(37th NC) recalled the first time he came under artillery fire. He and another soldier had been detailed back to camp to cook for the regiment during the battle of New Bern. "On the return [to the company]," he explained,

> we had about a half dozen camp kettles full of peas. The kettles were strung on a pole, with George [Lawrance] at one end and I at the other. We had to go through a pine grove, and while going through there, we heard our first bomb shells, and we did not know what they were, and there we stood looking and wondering what on earth they could be as they went whizzing through the air. Presently one cut the top out of a pine, and then we found out what they were and forthwith proceeded to hug the earth without getting our arms around it. As soon as the sound of the shell died away we gathered our pole and started to the Fort. When we got there we had peas all over us, so that we could hardly be told from the peas.[28]

According to a family story, Joel Fairchild (37th NC) saw a nearly spent artillery round rolling toward him at Gettysburg. He attempted to stop it with his foot. The ball was moving a little faster than Fairchild anticipated, resulting in a broken ankle and a furlough home. William Barlow (18th NC) wrote that during the battle of Sharpsburg, he was struck in the wrist by a "bomb shell" and was able to walk back to the hospital. These two were lucky.[29]

Early in the war, many on both sides carried smoothbore muskets. These .69 caliber weapons commonly fired a buck-and-ball load, composed of one .64 caliber lead "ball," and three small "buck." Effective range was only 80 yards. According to one historian, "Musket balls generally entered and exited the body more cleanly." As the war progressed, many on both sides were issued rifled-muskets in .577 caliber (British Enfield) and .58 caliber (Springfield). These rifles fired a minie ball, an elongated piece of soft lead with grooves cut into the sides to help it obtain greater distances and accuracy. A rifled Enfield or Springfield was effective at 400 yards, and still deadly at 1,000 yards. "Minie balls usually flattened or deformed in other ways upon contact, tearing tissue, shattering bone, and leaving a larger exit than entrance wound if they went all

---

28 *Watauga Democrat*, June 18, 1891.

29 Email, Paul Fairchild to author, February 13, 2002, in author's possession; Barlow to "My dear wife," September 25, 1862, *Company Front*, 21. These descriptions are for smoothbore artillery, like 12-pound Napoleons. Rifled artillery, like Parrott and Ordnance Rifles fired many of the same types of projectiles.

the way through the body." Dirt, bits of clothing, and, at times, parts of the gear the soldiers wore were carried into the wounds.[30]

For the Tar Heels in the Branch-Lane brigade, the minie balls caused the most injury on the battlefield. A soldier often rummaged through his clothing to see where he was hit. When Calvin Triplett of the 37th was struck near the heart at Gaines Mill, he opened his shirt to show Capt. Horton, declared, "I'm killed," and fell dead. Others were killed outright. Michael Tally (37th NC) wrote home about the death of his uncle, John Tally, telling how he "was shot through forrade wright above the right eye his brains were all shot out."[31]

If a wounded soldier could stand, he often trudged to the field hospital. Those unable to walk had to await friends or stretcher-bearers. It was an imperfect system, and often, men waited some time for attendance. At Chancellorsville, William McLaurin (18th NC) was shot in the left thigh. As he worked his way to the rear to escape capture, McLaurin used "two muskets as crutches" to support himself. Others had friends to help them. Allen Bumgardner was slightly wounded during a battle in July 1864. As he started toward the rear, he came across fellow 28th member Adley Holler. Bumgardner picked up Holler and "carried him to a secure place, and went and found a litter-bearer to care for his friend." Some struggled on their own before help found them. Captain J. McLeod Turner was wounded during the fight at Fredericksburg in December 1862, "the ball entering his right breast passing through the lung and out behind the shoulder. . . . After receiving the wound he started to the rear, the blood spouting from his mouth, when he was again struck, this time in the head." Turner arose and walked a half mile before his brother found him and procured an ambulance and medical aid.[32]

As if the battlefield horrors were not gruesome enough, the field hospitals surpassed them. Men were wounded in every conceivable location, and surgery was primitive. If there were no obvious exit wound, the surgeon searched for one, often with his finger, and maybe with a Nelaton probe. If possible, he'd remove the bullet. Peter Turnmire was escorting a prisoner to the rear at Chancellorsville when he was wounded in the right hip by "a stray ball." At the division hospital, he was placed "on the ground under the shade of tree" until

---

30 Schroeder-Lein, *The Encyclopedia of Civil War Medicine*, 152.

31 *Lenoir Topic*, August 14, 1905; Michael Tally to Susan Tally, June 7, 1864, private collection.

32 Clark, *Histories*, 2:40; Hahn, *The Catawba Soldier*, 177, 185; *Western Democrat*, January 20, 1862.

the doctor had time to examine him. The doctor wanted to place Turnmire under chloroform, arguing that he could not otherwise stand the removal of the ball. "Dr. you do not know what I can stand," Turnmire retorted. "I stood for it to go in there and I can stand for it to be taken out." Turnmire survived the operation, and the war. In many cases, the soft lead projectiles destroyed the bones they struck. John Green (33rd NC) was traveling through Richmond when he stopped to see fellow soldiers. He recalled visiting with "Farranton Furr" who had a ball pass through his right arm and enter "his side about his right tit & went through his side and come out close to his back bone. I seed the ball he was shot with they was a piece of bone sticking to it about half inch long."[33]

On a few occasions, the wounded were not as damaged as they thought. Doctor Alexander remembered a soldier brought in from the Chancellorsville battlefield, who was refusing to allow the stretcher-bearers to move him. As Alexander tried to move the man, he began to "kick like a steer, saying that his whole back was shot off, and if he was moved he would die." When Alexander cut off the soldier's clothing and started to examine him, he found a place on the man's back badly bruised by a piece of shell, yet the skin was not broken. "Get up, old man. . . you're not hurt," Alexander told him. The soldier moved a little, "found out he was not going to die, got out, got his gun, and went back to the firing line." The slightly wounded frequently went unreported in official records.[34]

For wounds involving mangled flesh and shattered bones, amputation was deemed the best possible way to save a soldier's life. Chisolm's surgical manual required that amputation be performed within 24 hours. Most patients, like Walter Lenoir and Peter Turnmire, were sedated with chloroform during surgery if it were available. Some soldiers did not survive the operation or the subsequent infection. The five-company survey of the brigade produced 12 examples of amputation. Henry Baker (37th NC) was wounded and captured at Gettysburg, dying August 1, 1863, at Chester, PA, of "mortification of stump after amputation." Once removed, limbs were tossed into a pile or out a

---

33 *Lenoir Topic*, August 14, 1905; John Green to "Dear Wife," n.d., in *Stanley County Heritage* (Waynesville, NC, 2002), 313. There was no "Farranton Furr" in the 33rd Regiment. There was a John C. Furr in Green's same company who was discharged on September 12, 1862, for "fracture of humerus." Jordan, *NC Troops*, 9:152.

34 *The Gastonia Gazette*, May 8, 1906.

Some soldiers who were wounded and unable to stand the rigors of campaign duty were transferred to serve in the Invalid Corps. One of these men was Caleb Boomer, who served in the 33rd North Carolina, was wounded at Fredericksburg, and transferred in November 1864.

North Carolina Division
of Archives and History

window. John Green (28th NC) recalled that following his slight wound at Chancellorsville, the surgeon at his hospital employed him as assistant, burying amputated limbs.[35]

Gangrene was probably the most feared condition a wounded soldier could develop. The fast-moving putrefaction of the tissue often proved fatal. Gangrene clogged arteries, creating blood clots, which caused tissue to die. Once gangrene was diagnosed, stricken patients were isolated in separate wards and given chloroform; the infected area was then cleaned with nitric acid, iodine, or carbonic acid. In some cases, a second amputation was necessary. At least four brigade members died of gangrene, while two others were discharged.[36]

Once a wounded soldier was deemed well enough to travel from the battlefield, he was taken to a staging area and forwarded to a general hospital. For many, the trip was tortuous. George Cochran (37th NC) was struck in the leg at Chancellorsville and eventually carried off the battlefield. A day after

---

35 Chisolm, *A Manual for Military Surgery*, 140; Jordan, *NC Troops*, 9: 525. Green, "Reminiscences," NCDAH. Those companies surveyed were Company C, 7th Regiment; Company F, 18th Regiment; Company B, 28th Regiment; Company I, 33rd Regiment; and, Company E, 37th Regiment. According to Ansley Wegner, 155 men from the brigade applied for prosthetics, or compensation, after the war. *Phantom Pain: North Carolina's Artificial-Limbs Program for Confederate Veterans* (Raleigh, NC, 2004).

36 Schroeder-Lein, *The Encyclopedia of Civil War Medicine*, 115.

being wounded he was loaded into a wagon, whose bed was covered with "cedar brush," and the long journey toward Richmond began about sundown. "My wound was now so sore that any jar was torture," recalled Cochran after the war. He continued:

It was a ten-mile, night trip and every pebble a wheel hit caused pain to the sufferers. Gullies, rocks and stumps brought forth groans, wails and entreaties from every wagon in the train, to all of which I contributed my full share. . . Bad as it was at its best, the drivers seemed to think that there might be some improvement and they added a little more hell from time to time, though I wouldn't accuse them of being willful or neglectful. The night was dark as pitch and the imp of perverse got into the game and turned over the wagon in front of mine, filled with maimed soldiers. Cries, groans and bitter curses supplemented by the finest efforts of our gifted quartermaster in the line of eloquent and lurid profanity, set in the background of funeral woods, amid midnight silence and gloom, it made a picture more realistic of the Inferno than ever Dante dreamed. . . . But the worst had yet to come. The long street over which we must travel on reaching Richmond was paved with round river rocks. When we entered the street, it was a continual series of bounces. I was in so much pain that I could not refrain from crying out, and I did, though sometimes I clenched my teeth in effort to stifle a groan. Nearly every other wounded man in the train was doing the same thing. . . . Truth is, I was as nearly dead when I reached the hospital as I ever expect to be not to be actually dead.[37]

Cochran was not the only one to suffer during transport from a battlefield to a general hospital. The journey often took a long time. Thomas Lane (33rd NC) was wounded on May 12, 1864, at Spotsylvania Court House. A minie ball pierced his thigh, fracturing his femur. A field hospital doctor or assistant bound his broken leg to a "rough plank," and Lane appears to have been in this state until he arrived at the Jackson Hospital in Richmond on May 18. Chaplain Kennedy wrote immediately after the battle of Chancellorsville, describing removal of the wounded. The slightly wounded were sent off on May 4. Those left had to endure bad weather. Kennedy mentioned prying the planks from houses, gathering pine tops, and placing the wounded on them. They were elevated out of the mud, but not out of the rain. By May 9, all of the men with Kennedy, presumably at the brigade or divisional hospital, had been loaded in

37 Cochran, *A Brief Sketch*, 28-29.

the division wagon and ambulance train and transported to Hamilton's Cross Roads, to await a train to Richmond.[38]

Not all of the wounded and sick survived the hospitals. Wounds and subsequent diseases in general hospitals, camps, and on battlefields claimed many a soldier. In mid-nineteenth century America, almost all soldiers hoped to die a "Good Death," by having the opportunity to make preparations for the world to come. Dying a "Good Death" eased the burden on people back home. Historian Mark Schantz observes: "Americans came to fight the Civil War in the midst of a wider cultural world that sent them messages about death that made it easier to kill and be killed. They understood that death awaited all who were born and prized the ability to face death with a spirit of calm resignation." Lieutenant Wiley Cloninger (28th NC) was struck down during the battle of Fredericksburg. When told he must die, Cloninger folded his arms across his chest and stated, "If I must die, then I will let you all see that I can die like a man." He passed a day later, and the message of his death was related to his loved ones. Colonel William Speer was struck in the back of the head by a piece of shrapnel at the battle of Reams Station in August 1864. He lingered for a few days, telling friends "he should soon be where there was no war, that he had given his body to his country and his soul to God." This idea did not always ease the pain of the loved ones back at home. "My poor heart bleeds when I think of my poor child being murdered," Elizabeth Speer, Col. Speer's mother, wrote after learning of her son's death.[39]

If a soldier was killed in battle, and his army victorious, then friends might be able to bury him and mark the grave. John Carpenter (28th NC) wrote to the mother of his friend, D. A. Fronberger, after the latter's death at Fredericksburg. After the battle, Carpenter and others from Company B "dug a lone grave and buried all that was killed out of our company the[y] were all put in side and side." The head of each grave was marked and Carpenter described who was buried where. Lieutenant Daniel Boger (7th NC) told of the burial of William Bost at the battle of Reams Station in August 1864. While Boger could not attend to it personally, he had a couple of men bury Bost near a house near

38 *Confederate State Medical and Surgical Journal* (September 1864), Vol 1, Issue 9,136; Kennedy, Diary, May 4-9, 1863, SHC/UNC-CH.

39 Clark, *Histories*, 2:475; Speer, *Voices from Cemetery Hill*, 151. See Drew Gilpin Faust, *This Republic of Suffering: Death and the American Civil War* (New York, NY, 2008), 8-17; Mark Schantz, *Awaiting the Heavenly Country:The Civil War and America's Culture of Death* (Ithaca, NY, 2008), 2.

the station, and had his grave marked. A few days later, Lt. Brantley Saunders of the 4th NC Cavalry set out to retrieve the remains. With some difficulty, Saunders procured a "rough coffin" and found Bost's grave. "[H]e had not been buried deep as he should have been and he was swollen bad and smelled so bad we could scarcely manage to handle him," wrote Saunders. "I just put him in his coffin and nailed him up tight in his coffin and brought him up to Petersburg . . . and buried him and he (remained) until Rush came after (him)." Bost's case is unusual. In almost all cases, unless the deceased soldier were an officer, he was buried on the field and not sent home. On a few occasions, the dead of the Branch-Lane brigade fell into the hands of the enemy. Colonel Speer noted after his capture at Hanover Court House, he was taken back to the battlefield. Speer observed Union soldiers burying Confederate dead, 50 in one space. One Federal, writing about this same battle, chronicled:

> The work of collecting and burying the dead soon commenced. The woods were full of dead rebels who lay, as they fell, in all shapes. They were all carried out and laid in a ghastly row on the grass. One fine looking young man was shot through the heart as he was loading his gun. His hands had not changed their position, one extended above his head drawing his rammer and the other grasping his gun by his side. His eyes were open and the expression of his countenance as calm as though he was sleeping, but the fearful wound in his breast told that he would never wake on earth again. We buried over one hundred of them.[40]

The thought that a fellow soldier's remains might fall into the hands of the enemy plagued many a Southern soldier. "[I]t is a hard thing to see friend fall by My Side wilter & Die in there own Blood," wrote Capt. Morris (37th NC) "But what is more painful yet is to see them Dye in that Manner & have to be Left to Bury themselves for I feare they will Not Be by the Enemy." With the success rate of Lee's army through much of the first half of the war, Confederate dead were frequently buried by their messmates, or at least other Confederate soldiers.[41]

40 J. T. Carpenter to Mrs. Katie Froneberger, Jan. 13, 1862[3], Fredericksburg National Military Park; Dan Boger to "Dear Sister," August 27, 1864, private collection; B. H. Saunders to Abigail Smith, September 12, 1864, private collection; Speer, *Voices*, 59; Oliver Norton, *Army Letters, 1861-1865* (Dayton, OH, 1990), 85.

41 William Morris to "Dear Wife," May 5, 1862, Morris Letters, SHC/UNC.

Some soldiers died in camp. Early in the war, especially when the regiments were in North Carolina, there was always an effort to send these remains home. John Conrad (28th NC) noted in November 1861, when his regiment was stationed near Wilmington, a soldier had died from Capt. Speer's company, probably Wilson Pendry. Conrad wrote two companies of the 28th escorted the remains "in solem procession," most likely to the train depot. As the war progressed, the men grew more calloused to the sight of the dead. Bennett Smith (37th NC) complained in a letter home in April 1863 of the little attention paid to the sick and dead. Deceased soldiers were often buried without a coffin, and if one could be procured, it was, according to Smith, roughly constructed of fence planks.[42]

Soldiers sent to one of the general hospitals in Virginia frequently died without even a friendly face nearby, their bodies taken to the closest cemetery and interred. Approximately 295 members of the brigade are buried at Hollywood Cemetery in Richmond. After the war ended, some efforts were made to retrieve Confederate soldiers buried at Gettysburg and in Arlington National Cemetery and re-inter them in their native soil. In North Carolina, Oakwood Cemetery in Raleigh has sections for these soldiers. The Confederate Section there contains the graves of 41 brigade members, although 20 of them died after the war, most likely in the Old Soldiers home.[43]

Commanding officers, family members, and friends took it upon themselves to write condolence letters to the loved ones back at home. These letters assured families about the state of their lost loved ones. William Rose (7th NC) wrote to Joseph Lipe's wife Margaret in 1862, that her husband had died after being wounded during the Seven Days battles. Rose wrote they often went "to the woods . . . to offer up praise to God to guide us through this troublesome world. He was always reading his Bible and trying to prepare himself for a better world which I surely hope he is now resting." Private Ambrose Stearns (37th NC) died of unknown cause on August 2, 1862. Lieutenant Lawson Potts told his widow he had buried Stearns "very descant moore so than a great many poore soldiers." At times, it was the enemy writing

---

42 *Kinfolk of Jacob Conrad*, 288; Bennett Smith to "Dear Wife," April 16, 1863, private collection.

43 Of the 295 brigade members buried at Hollywood, 17 were brought back from Gettysburg. Chris Furguson, *Southerners at Rest: Confederate Dead at Hollywood Cemetery* (Winchester, VA, 2008); Charles Purser and Frank Powell, III, *A Story Behind Every Stone: The Confederate Section of Oakwood Cemetery, Raleigh, North Carolina* (Wake Forest, NC, 2005).

to loved ones in North Carolina. Iowa Michigan Royster (37th NC) was wounded on July 3 at Gettysburg and found by a chaplain from a Maine regiment. Royster summoned the chaplain, gave him his parents' address, asking him to write them, telling of his "Good Death," and he "died trusting in Jesus without a doubt of his acceptance." The chaplain believed Royster would recover, and, for a few days, he did improve, but died suddenly of a "hemorrhage." The Maine chaplain was able to assure the family he had "never seen so exultant a death-bed experience in his ministry."[44]

At times, letters of condolence arrived after the close of the war. Colonel William Barber of the 37th NC was mortally wounded on September 30, 1864, and died on October 3. On August 15, 1866, Robert E. Lee wrote to Barber's son, Edward:

Master Edward A. Barbour[sic]

The grief which I experienced at your father's death, is greatly relieved on learning that you possess a large share of his mental vigour; and bid fair at a future day to fill the place he held in the love and estimation of his fellow citizens. That you may the more certainly do this permit me to urge upon you to study in your youth the holy precepts of the Bible, to practice virtue in preference to all things; and to avoid falsehood and deception of every kind, which will be sure to debase the mind and lead to every vice and misery.

In contemplating the virtues and achievements of the good and great men of whom history presents so many examples, keep constantly in mind the conduct of your father, and endeavor to equal him in goodness, tho you may fall short his greatness. Wishing you every happiness and success in life, I am very truly your friend,

R. E. Lee
Lexington, Va.[45]

Many within the ranks suffered the invisible wounds of war. Post-traumatic stress disorder was not defined until 1980, yet Civil War soldiers undoubtedly

44 *Morresville Tribune,* May 13, 1992; L. A. Potts to Mrs. Stearns, August 21, 1862, A. L. Stearns Letters, DU; Iowa Michigan Royster to "Mother," June 29, 1863, Royster Papers, SHC/UNC.

45 Robert E. Lee to Edward Barbour, August 15, 1866, private collection.

suffered from the condition because of the trauma they witnessed. Insomnia, depression, excessive anxiety, emotional detachment, irritability, nightmares, and flashbacks are all ways in which PTSD can manifest. When James Lipe (7th NC) was killed at the battle of New Bern in March 1862, his brother Joseph was nearby and wrote of seeing James die. Joseph wanted desperately to help his brother, "but there was no chance for the yankees was a swarming an we had to retreat." A day later, Joseph wrote he "wished I had not sean him fall for I can't get it out of my mind." Likewise, Dr. Alexander wrote about a mortally wounded soldier at Chancellorsville, whose eyes followed him around the hospital. "I will never forget those eyes, the way they stared at me," he wrote 43 years later.

Exhibiting signs of possible shell shock, William H. A. Speer (28th NC) penned a letter home concerning his poor health and "shaky" condition two weeks after the close of the fighting at Chancellorsville. Some historians have stressed that PTSD led to desertion in soldiers unable to cope with the war's multitudes of horrors.

While the precise circumstances are unclear, one case might be that of Capt. John Elms (37th NC). Elms, an 18-year-old student from Mecklenburg County, was mustered into service as a first sergeant in October 1861. Early that December he was promoted to sergeant major and transferred to the field and staff. Nothing in his records indicates his absence from the battles of New Bern and Hanover Court House. On June 28, Elms was appointed captain and transferred back to his former company. According to his colonel, however, he missed all of the engagements in which his regiment was engaged. During the Seven Days' Battles and Cedar Mountain, for example, Elms accompanied his men for a time but became "exhausted" and fell out before the fighting commenced. He wasn't with his men at Second Manassas, Ox Hill, Harpers Ferry, Sharpsburg, or Shepherdstown. Barber described Elms as "a good officer in camp." Because he did not want to damage the "character of a young man," Barber gave him an additional chance. Elms was with his company on the morning of the battle of Fredericksburg, but before the battle began he received permission to return to camp to get a pair of shoes. Barber ordered the quartermaster to give Elms shoes and send him back, but a day later Elms was still behind the lines in camp. An order issued for Elms to rejoin the men, but he responded that "he did not intend to go—he had his reasons for his course which he did not intend to make known to [the quartermaster or Col. Barber]." Elms was sent to the surgeon, who testified that "there is nothing the matter with him as far as health is concerned." Elms was allowed to resign and, a few months later, joined the 56th NC.[46]

Exact numbers of those who were killed, wounded, or contracted diseases within the brigade will never be known. A conservative estimate is that of the 8,975 men who saw service in the brigade, 3,154 of them died during the war. Regardless of what killed these men, the effects of the war were devastating. All of the soldiers who served under Branch and Lane carried the scars of the war, both physical and mental, for the rest of their lives.

46 *Mooresville Tribune*, April 22, 1992; *The Gastonia Gazette*, May 8, 1906; Speer, *Voices*, 103; John Elms, Roll 0401, M270, RG109, CMSR, NA. For an interesting discussion on North Carolina soldiers and PSTD, see David Silkenat, *Moments of Despair: Suicide, Divorce, and Debt in Civil War Era North Carolina* (Chapel Hill, NC, 2011), 53-60.

Chapter 8

"I Doo Not Like to Beare old abes Mark."

The Fredericksburg Campaign

Branch's brigade was wrecked. Having a dangerous reputation was taking its toll on officers and men alike. Since arriving in Virginia in May 1862, the brigade had experienced three major campaigns, plus the battle of Hanover Court House, and had suffered somewhere around 219 killed, 1,166 wounded, and 741 missing or captured. Branch was dead, killed on the field near Sharpsburg. Only the 37th NC had a colonel present and in command. One colonel was a prisoner of war, one was wounded, and the other one was sick. It was a small, bedraggled group Lane led into camp at Bunker Hill, near Winchester. Rest and abundant rations, along with a flush of new conscripts and return of sick, wounded, and stragglers, eventually swelled the depleted ranks.[1]

---

1 McDaid, "Four Years," 81,109, 128; Hardy, *Hanover Court House*, 119. Haywood (7th NC) was wounded at Second Manassas, Cowan (18th NC) resigned on November 1, 1862; Lane (28th NC) commanded the brigade; Avery (33rd NC) was captured during the battle of New Bern; only Barber (37th NC) retained command of his regiment.

James H. Lane learned of his promotion to command the brigade
immediately before the start of the Fredericksburg Campaign.

Virginia Military Institute

Many now wondered about Branch's permanent replacement as commander of the brigade. Lane was the senior surviving colonel, and by custom, entitled to the command. Not only did Lane deserve it; he wanted it. On September 19, within 24 hours of Branch's death, near Shepherdstown, Lane asked former Brig. Gen. Joseph Anderson "to use your influence to have me appointed to the vacancy." Anderson forwarded the note along with a personal letter to Jefferson Davis, describing Lane as "an intelligent and accomplished officer." Lane next wrote on September 23 to Henry Wise, Virginia's former governor, U.S. congressman, and a family friend, with the same plea. Wise endorsed Lane's missive and forwarded the note to Secretary of War George Randolph, who likewise passed along a favorable recommendation. At the same time, Lane himself wrote Randolph, touting his qualifications. The officers in the brigade circulated a petition supporting Lane's promotion. Apparently, the only other officer considered for the position was Thomas L. Clingman, then commanding a brigade in North Carolina. Yet Lee, writing to Maj. Gen. Gustavus Smith in Richmond, stated he "considered it just and proper that the colonel of Branch's brigade, who had been recommended for promotion, be assigned to the command." Lane not only had Lee's support, but also Jackson's and Hill's.[2]

As Lane waited for the decision, the brigade began rebuilding. The wagon train finally arrived, with baggage. Teamsters and wagon-masters had not seen the rest of the brigade since mid-August. The men were ordered by squads and companies to the Opequan River for bathing. Sick men were sent to the hospital, and men who had fallen out of the ranks during the prolonged marches returned to their regiments. Additional conscripts also arrived. The 18th NC received 90 men during the battle of Sharpsburg. An additional 384 augmented the ranks of the regiment. The 33rd NC received 404 men, while 385 joined the 37th NC. Only 31 joined the 28th NC, perhaps because scores of men captured at Hanover Court House had returned.[3]

No clear explanation exists for exactly why the conscripts chose to avoid the army until compelled to join by law. "Age, camaraderie, Christian duty, and

2   JL to Joseph Anderson, September 19, 1862; Joseph Anderson to Jefferson Davis, JL to Henry Wise, JL to George Randolph, September 23, 1862, all in M331, Roll 0125, Roll 109, CMSR, NA; OR 19/2:689; *Fayetteville Observer*, March 22, 1894. James J. Pettigrew was authorized by Lee to replace Branch, but Pettigrew's "superiors felt he could not be spared." Earl Hess, *Lee's Tar Heels: The Pettigrew-Kirkland-MacRae Brigade* (Chapel Hill, NC, 2002), 41.

3   Based on a survey of volumes 4, 6, 8, and 9 of Jordan, *NC Troops*.

the greater demands of home . . . were at least some of the motivating factors that inoculated men against the war fever of 1861." The Light Division reported 4,700 men present in late September. By mid-October, that number had almost doubled to 9,400 men. A special act of the Confederate Congress the following month allowed Lee to formally organize the army into two corps. The reorganization did not directly affect Branch's former brigade, which was still in the Light Division. On paper, it was now in the Second Corps and still under Stonewall Jackson's command.[4]

Considerable friction developed between the brigade veterans and the new conscripts. The veterans viewed the conscripts as less dedicated to the cause or suspected their unknown fighting abilities likely to reflect badly on the regiment. In early October 1862, Capt. Morris (37th NC) wrote the new men were "in fine Sperrits Generally but they have not Seen the Elaphant yet. I Don't Know how they will Stand the Shells and Shot." The conscription act allowed men go into a company of their choosing if they came in before the grace period ended. Many of the conscripts from Gaston County had requested to join his company in the 37th, Morris reported. William Barlow of Caldwell County wrote with an air of disappointment that his fellow enlistees "don't get to go to the regiment we wanted to go to." Instead, they were assigned to the 18th NC. This influx of conscripts from the foothill counties of North Carolina into a regiment primarily from the coastal regions, led to further problems in quite possibly the most problematic regiment in the brigade. According to the *Fayetteville Observer*, 100 men from Rutherford County in Camp Hill near Statesville, bound for the 18th, opposed "going to that Reg't. as they had no acquaintances or friends there." In the end, they did agree to go, but hoped to be transferred to a regiment with more Rutherford County men.[5]

It took time for conscripts to become accepted members of their new regiments. Possibly to help the men adjust, or to give its commander further experience in his post, Lane's brigade was selected for a small mission in October. Hill told Lane to report to Jackson, who had been one of Lane's professors in the early 1850s, at VMI. After the war, Lane recalled Jackson "did

4   Gibbon, Diary, 20; McDaid, "Four Years," 139-40; Kenneth Noe, *Reluctant Rebels: The Confederates Who Joined the Army after 1861* (Chapel Hill, NC, 2010), 9; Robertson, *Hill*, 155.

5   William Morris to wife, October 4, 1862, August 8, 1862, Morris Papers, SHC; William Bartow to "Dear Wife," August 28, 1862, *Company Front*, 17-18; *Fayetteville Observer*, September 1, 1862.

not impress the cadets as being a very handsome man, nor as strikingly military in his bearing." However, "Jackson soon impressed the cadets as being a man of great bravery, conscientious and fearless in the discharge of every duty, strictly honest and just in his intentions." When Lane reported to Jackson's headquarters, he expected to be "received in the stiff, formal manner of old which I so well remember, be given orders, and instantly dismissed." Yet Lane was surprised:

> [O]n entering the General's tent, he at once rose with a smile on his face, took my hand in both of his in the warmest manner, expressing his pleasure at seeing me, and asking why I had not been to see him before, at the same time handing me a camp stool and pressing me to take a seat beside him. His kind words, the tones of his voice, his familiarly calling me Lane—whereas it had always been Mr. Lane at the Institute put me completely at my ease. I felt I was in the presence of a warm hearted friend, and then, (I think it was, for the first time,) I began to feel that magnetism, which, with his record as a successful fighter in the Valley, had so endeared him to his troops. After a long and pleasant conversation, he gave me my orders. [6]

Lane's orders were to advance towards Hedgesville and the North Mountain Depot, tear up the tracks of the Baltimore & Ohio Railroad, and establish contact with Confederate cavalry operating in the area. Most of the Light Division went along. The brigade set out on October 21, and possibly returned on October 23. According to Morris, the march was some 30 miles. A recent conscript in the 37th NC complained the march was hard and the men not properly fed. Confederate forces destroyed more than 20 miles of track and moved to within four miles of Harper's Ferry, recently reoccupied by the Federals, who had not contested the destruction of the railroad. Lane's brigade went into camp near Berryville following the raid.[7]

On returning to camp, Lane was called back to Jackson's headquarters. Jackson "received me in the same cordial, warm hearted manner," and complimented the brigade on its work:

6 James Lane, "Reminiscences of Gen. Thomas Stonewall Jackson," 1, 3, 25-27, Lane Papers, AU.

7 Lane, "Reminiscences of Jackson," 26; Harris, *Historical Sketches*, 24; William Morris to "Deare Companion," October 24, 1862, Morris Letters, SHC; Andrew Teague to "Dear wife," October 25, 1862, *Kinfolk* (February 1997), 1:16; Robertson, *Hill*, 156.

When I rose to go, he took my hand in both of his, looked me steadily in the eye, and in words and tones of friendly warmth which I can never forget, again expressed his confidence in my promotion, and bade me a good-bye with a 'God bless you Lane.' From that time forth I felt the very warmest attachment to him and never failed to pay him my respects whenever I was near him; and he invariably received me with the most friendly interests and talked to me as a father would to a son—I was then just twenty nine years of age.[8]

Union soldiers crossed the Potomac into Loudoun County on October 26. A week later, a small group of them attempted to capture Castleman's Ford. Two brigades of the Light Division, with two batteries of artillery, drove them away. Lane's brigade was apparently not involved. William McLaurin noted that the 18th Regiment was engaged at Snickers Gap in mid-November, possibly when Hill captured the gap on November 9, although fellow 18th soldier Thomas Sutton wrote of the regiment being called out several times, but never engaged. The brigade settled down into an uneasy lull in the action, dealing instead with promotions and the weather. Some soldiers wrote home of warm temperatures one day, with snow a few days later.[9]

On November 7, while snow fell on Lee's Army, President Lincoln removed McClellan as commander of the Army of the Potomac. He had tired of McClellan's sluggishness in pursuit and replaced him with Maj. Gen. Ambrose Burnside. Many in Lane's brigade would remember Burnside, who had handed them their first battlefield defeat back in March. Burnside's plan, partially inherited from McClellan, was to steal a march on Lee and move to Fredericksburg. If they moved quickly enough, his forces could be across the Rappahannock River and on their way to Richmond before Lee had time to intercept them. Burnside's troops arrived across the river from Fredericksburg on November 17. They discovered the requested pontoon boats were days behind schedule. Two days later, the weather seriously deteriorated. Longstreet's forces had taken up the line of march on November 18. Believing Burnside would cross the Rappahannock and move toward Richmond, Lee ordered most of Longstreet's corps to the North Anna River. When Lee learned the Federals were still north of Fredericksburg, he chose to consolidate his army there to contest Burnside's advance. "The longer we can delay him and throw

8   Lane, "Reminiscences of Jackson," 27.

9   OR 29/1:983; Jordan, NC Troops, 2:34, 71.

him into winter, the more difficult will be his undertaking. It is for this reason that I have determined to resist him at the outset and to throw every obstacle in the way of his advance," Lee wrote to Jefferson Davis. Longstreet's men began arriving in Fredericksburg on November 20.[10]

Lee originally wanted Jackson's corps to fall upon the rear of Burnside's column, but chose to reunite the two wings of his army when Burnside failed to advance farther. The Light Division broke camp around 2:30 a.m. on November 22. It took almost two weeks for Jackson's men to make the 175-mile march to Fredericksburg. Lack of shoes among the troops only made the journey more miserable in the cold and occasional sleet. James Harris (7th NC) wrote of men having "to wear moccasins made of raw hide" in place of brogans. William Perry related that during the march, he "got barefooted on the rout and marched 2 days without Shoes, which completely ruined my feet, as it was cold & Snowing part of the time." William Howard (7th NC) chronicled in his dairy the day-to-day marches, most of which, at least on the west side of Blue Ridge, were in the snow. On November 28, Howard recalled setting out early and

winding around an back an round around until I got nearly to the top when I stopt an looked back and could see our Long lines of infantry winding around side the mountain an our Long Train of artilery in front an Long train of wagons an ambulances in the rare it was abutyful sight to Look back on an more espeseley to look on the butiful valey behine and several butyful towns too so this was a grand sight to one that never saw such her the hills stood above us most as high as the eye could see an great rocks hangin out lik they had as soon fall as to stay when they was.[11]

Records reported two members of the 18th Regiment had trouble as the brigade moved southeast. W. B. Norman died "on the road," and Lawson Harwood "dropped out on the march." The Light Division arrived in the Fredericksburg area on December 4 and encamped at Thomas Yerby's plantation, "Belvoir."[12]

10 Robert E. Lee to Jefferson Davis, November 25, 1862, quoted in Clifford Dowdy and Louis Manarin, *The Wartime Papers of R. E. Lee* (New York, 1961), 345.

11 Harris, *Historical Sketches*, 25; W. J. Perry to "Dear father," December 12, 1862, FSNMP; William Howard, Diary, November 28, 1862, NCDAH.

12 Jordan, *NC Troops*, 6:370, 396.

Lane learned of his promotion while on the march through Snickers Gap. Hill notified him of his promotion to brigadier general, commanding what had been Branch's brigade. Hill "doffed his hat and publicly congratulated him on his promotion and assignment, the brigade went wild with delight." Lane's promotion was dated November 1, 1862. At 29, he was, at the time, the youngest Confederate general in service.[13]

The brigade spent about a week on the Yerby farm. One member of the 18th Regiment recalled getting too little to eat, and walking six or seven miles to a mill to get half of a bushel of meal to make cornbread. An officer in the 28th reported the issue of new uniforms for the men, including desperately needed shoes, but complained of absent socks and scarce blankets. Various regiments received new clothes and new battle flags. The flags Branch ordered months earlier came on December 4, bearing battle honors painted in a distinctive white.[14]

Federal pontoon boats arrived on November 25. After nightfall on December 10, engineers commenced spanning the Rappahannock with pontoon bridges. Confederate pickets allowed the bridge building to proceed until their targets were within easy range. A Union artillery bombardment of the town began early on December 11. When the Confederate pickets forced the enemy engineers from their unfinished bridge, Federal artillery opened upon the Confederates in Fredericksburg, shelling the town. Throughout the day, Union guns pulverized Fredericksburg. Once Confederate artillery fire slackened, the engineers began their work again, only to be greeted by intense small arms fire. Eventually, Federal infantry ferried across the river and established a beachhead. Intense street fighting ensued between the infantry and Confederate sharpshooters. Not until a Federal division crossed the river on the pontoons were the Confederates chased out of the city. The Federals then sacked the town.

Lee thought the main Federal attack would be launched against Marye's Heights, to the west of the town, and picked Longstreet's corps to hold this position. To bolster Longstreet's right, Lee ordered in one of Jackson's

13 *Fayetteville Observer*, March 22, 1894.

14 William Barlow to Elizabeth Barlow, December 9, 1862, *Company Front*, 24; Speer, *Voices from Cemetery Hill*, 85. Captain George Thompson, 28th NC quartermaster, signed for his regiment's flag on December 4, 1862. The statement reads "One Battle Flag with inscription." The flag was obviously painted with the battle honors before it arrived. Thompson, Roll 0351, M270, RG109, CMSR, NA.

divisions, aligning it along the railroad. Hill's division was the closest, and at 6:30 a.m., Jackson ordered the men out of their camp. "We were put in position about 7 o'clock a.m. on the R.R. and waited all day for the attack," Lt. Evander Robeson (18th NC) wrote. Lane recalled watching refugees from Fredericksburg streaming to the rear, "delicate women with infants in their arms and helpless little children clinging to their mothers' dresses, all thinly clad." One of his men called out "Look at that, fellows. If that will not make a Southern man fight, what will?" Hill arranged the Light Division in two lines. On the left he posted Pender's brigade, with Lane's brigade to his right. Lane's Carolinians were positioned 150 yards in front of Pender to take advantage of some timber "jutting out into the low ground, some distance from the main body." A 200-yard-wide patch of swampy ground lay 150 yards from the end of Lane's right. The next Confederate brigade, Archer's, was 150 yards beyond the other side of the low ground. This left a 500-yard gap in the Confederate line. Two regiments of Brockenbrough's command stood beyond Archer. Hill's second line comprised Thomas, Gregg, and the rest of Brockenbrough's brigade.

Many of the men used the time to strengthen their defenses, while Hill ordered several buildings in his front burned, and a company of the 7th NC complied. Skirmishers kept up a steady fire at each other all day. Eventually the small-arms fire ceased, and soon thereafter, the artillery. That evening, the pickets "got quite intimate . . . proposing to swap whiskey or coffee for tobacco." Whether this swap ever happened is not known, "We had to sleep at our lines with very small fires," wrote a member of the 28th.[15]

The gap to the right of his brigade concerned Lane greatly. He initially discussed the matter with Brig. Gen. Gregg, positioned with his brigade to his rear, and then went to Gen. Hill about "our relative positions." Hill believed the area was well defended and did not make any changes. Jackson personally inspected the lines and, rumor has it, announced the open area was the spot where the Federals would attack. Others also noticed the defect in the Light Division's position. Heros von Borke, a Prussian cavalry officer serving as one of Jeb Stuart's aides, was riding with Stuart when his trained military eye observed the vulnerable area. "On the left wing of A. P. Hill's division,"

---

15 *The Bladen Journal*, December 7, 1961; Jordan, *NC Troops*, 2:476; OR 21:645; Harris, *Historical Sketches*, 25; *Semi-Weekly Standard*, January 13, 1863. George Cochran (37th NC) wrote fires were not allowed the night of December 12. Maybe his regiment was out on picket, although no evidence confirms this. Cochran, *A Brief Sketch*, 32.

explained von Borke, "we had to pass a small piece of wood, extending in a triangular shape about six or eight hundred yards outside of our lines, with a base of about half a mile, offering, in my opinion, a great advantage to the enemy, and I remarked to Stuart that I thought it ought to be cut down." His general disagreed, believing instead that Confederate artillery on the flanks would sweep the field, creating a crossfire that would keep the Federals in check. Despite the many misgivings, the gap on Lane's right was not repaired.[16]

Following a pre-dawn reveille, Jackson appeared before the brigade left the woods with his "cap pulled down over his forehead, almost hiding his eyes," wrote a member of the 33rd. "The troops cheered him wildly. He gave us a sharp, searching, but not unkindly look, raised his cap, and rode rapidly on. His eyes seemed to be on fire, so eager was he for the fray." One Carolinian wrote of taking position in a ditch that had ice and snow in it, which melted and became mud as the temperatures warmed. Lane positioned his brigade along the railroad embankment, left to right: 7th, 18th, 33rd, 28th, and 37th. A slight rise in the landscape fronting the brigade extended almost 100 yards and blocked view of the enemy, save for the two regiments on the brigade's right. Early on, Confederate artillery passed to the front of Lane's brigade, going into position on a small rise to his left.[17]

Not long after daybreak on December 13, the 7th NC, together with the 1st TN of James Archer's brigade (and possibly the 18th NC) deployed as skirmishers across the Light Division's front, while also supporting the artillery deployed in advance of the main Confederate line. One hundred yards beyond the railroad, the 7th NC tore down a fence and placed the rails along a shallow ditch, creating what one man described as a "hastily improvised breast work." At 9:00 a.m., the Federals advanced two strong lines of skirmishers. The enemy artillery also opened fire. The 7th regiment, save for one company, fell back. A short time later portions of the Confederate artillery also limbered up its guns and withdrew, an officer informing Lane their tubes "were choked." Junius Hill, commanding the 7th NC, moved his entire regiment to the crest of the hill and fired at the Federal skirmishers. They soon withdrew, as did the rest of the

---

16 OR 21:654; Heros von Borke, *Memoirs of the Confederate War of Independence,* 2 vols. (New York, 1938), 2:106. Robert L. Dabney says Jackson saw the gap, and remarked "The enemy will attack here." Yet his biographer contends had Jackson noticed the gap, "he would have closed it promptly." Robertson, *Stonewall Jackson,* 652.

17 *The Bladen Journal,* December 7, 1961; Jordan, *NC Troops,* 2:35, 556.

Confederate artillery. Federal guns were raining fire on the Confederates. Shrapnel from just one shell wounded Capt. Turner and nine others. The 7th NC fell back to the railroad.[18]

Credit for forestalling the early Federal advance did not rest solely with the 7th. Artillerist John Pelham positioned a lone 12-pounder Napoleon in a natural depression that concealed his location on the flank of the Federal lines. Pelham gave the order to open fire when long lines of blue coats halted just 400 yards from the Confederate position. The Confederate gunners loaded as fast as they could, but eventually, they ran low on ammunition and were forced to retire. Yet his stand had held the Federal advance for an hour, and developed their position and point of attack. A Federal artillery bombardment, "a heavy fire," followed, attempting to soften up the Confederate lines. While much of the Federal shot and shell passed over the brigade, wrecking havoc in Jackson's reserve, a few rounds found their mark. John Blackwell (18th NC) lost his hearing, "caused by nervous shock from bursting of [a] shell." John Lusk of the 37th NC had his "head bruised," while James Munday, of the same regiment, was "bruised badly in the thigh" by pieces of bombs. The members of the brigade not involved in the skirmish spent their time hugging the railroad embankment.[19]

About mid-morning, the fog from the river, mixed with smoke from the fires in Fredericksburg, began to lift. Spread out before the Confederate defenses, poised to attack, were division after division of Union troops. They moved to within 800 yards, until Confederate artillery, up to then deceptively silent, began gouging the massed Federal ranks. Their advance stalled in the relentless fire, men all going prone or falling back behind their own artillery. Once again Federal artillery blanketed the Confederate position. "The artillery fighting by this time had become general on both sides on our right and left," wrote a Carolinian. "The roar of artillery, the bursting of shell, and crashing of timber was terrific to the sight and ears of mortal man." After an hour,

18 James Lane, writing 10 days after the battle, and James Harris, 31 years later using his wartime diaries, provided differing accounts of the battle's beginning. Lane says the 7th and 18th advanced beyond the railroad to skirmish with the Federals; Harris says they never moved beyond the railroad. No sources other than Lane's, stating he ordered out the 18th, describe their involvement. A third source, a letter simply signed "A Sergeant," states the brigade aligned on the railroad. *Semi-Weekly Standard*, January 13, 1863; OR 21:654; Harris, *Historical Sketches*, 26-27.

19 Clark, *Histories*, 2:35; Jordan, *NC Troops*, 6:323; 9:531-32; *Semi-Weekly Standard*, January 13, 1863.

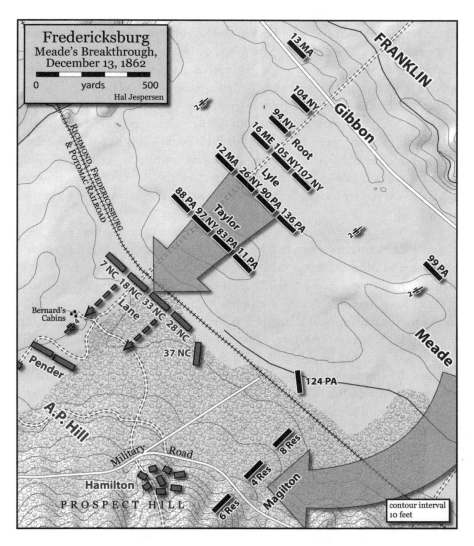

Confederate artillery fire slackened and the Union infantry resumed their advance. The Federals struck Archer's position first, and then moved into the woods to Lane's right.[20]

Colonel Barber sent the regiment's adjutant back to get Gen. Lane's instructions should the 37th NC be outflanked. Lane told Barber to hold his position for as long as possible, regardless of the circumstances. In an effort to

---

20 *Semi-Weekly Standard,* January 13, 1863.

minimize his exposed flank, Barber refused his three right companies to create something approaching an L-shaped line. A member of A. P. Hill's staff reassured Barber that the area was impassable. At the same time, Lane sent a second note to Hill, advising him of Federals passing around the brigade's right flank. Possibly the first Federal force to test Lane's position was the 142nd PA. The 37th NC hit this new regiment with deadly volleys, and it retreated quickly behind the railroad's protection. The 8th PA Reserves moved past their fellow Pennsylvanians, only to fall under Lane's infantry fire as well. These were veteran soldiers, however, and wheeled to face the 37th's three companies head-on. Yet Barber and part of the 37th stalled two enemy regiments, and then a third.[21]

Lane officially reported that nine Federal regiments passed his right, into the area many thought impenetrable. The Federals ran into Gregg's brigade and were largely drawn in that direction. Lane's attention was drawn from his right to his front. Colonel Avery (33rd NC) called his men to attention, a lieutenant adding "Look out—the Yanks are coming!" Noah Lewis, a recent conscript, heard the lieutenant, and thinking the Federals were close at hand, loudly exclaimed ""Oh, Lorddy!" lowered his musket and fired. The entire regiment "broke out in a big laugh—and I could not contain myself," Dr. Shaffner confessed. Lane recalled seeing William Martin (28th NC), sitting on top of the railroad embankment, calling "to his comrades to watch the Yankee colors, then fired and down they went. This was done repeatedly as other soldiers passed loaded rifles to Martin." Simultaneously, Capt. Edward Lovell stood on the tracks waving his hat, cheering on his men."[S]trange to say," Lane wrote, "neither he nor Martin was struck." As the Federals approached, Avery asked Lane if he could advance to the brow of the hill and meet the enemy. Lane refused: "[H]old your position at all hazards." The first advancing enemy brigade stalled, went prone in the mud, and then partially broke, with about half of the men fleeing towards the rear. A second Federal brigade fared little better.[22]

<hr>

21 OR 21:654; Barber's official report, 37th North Carolina Troops, CSA Collection, DU. The 142nd PA suffered the highest number of casualties in the Third Division, I Corps. Francis O'Reilly. "Busted up and Gone to Hell: The Assault of the Pennsylvania Reserves at Fredericksburg," *Civil War Regiments: A Journal of the American Civil War* (2006) 4/4:20.

22 Francis O'Reilly, *The Fredericksburg Campaign* (Baton Rouge, LA, 2006), 188; John Shaffner to "My Dearest Friend," December 21, 1862, Shaffner Papers, NCDAH; Clark, *Histories*, 2:475, 556.

Captain Edward Lovell stood on the railroad embankment and cheered his men on at the beginning of the Fredericksburg battle.

Histories of the Several Regiments and Battalions from North Carolina

Once the Federals were within 150 yards, the 28th and rest of the 37th opened fire. The hill in front of the brigade's other regiments obstructed their sight to just 40 yards. And it was a sight "awful to behold," a 28th NC vet remembered. "[I]n less than fifteen minutes there were long gaps of fifteen or twenty feet in their lines . . . you could see the men fall in every direction; but on they came, and still our boys give it to them." Increasing pressure on the right spurred Lane to request help from Gregg's brigade, but Gregg had dropped mortally wounded, his brigade driven back in disorder, while the threat to Lane's right continued. Colonel Barber was struck in the neck and forced from the field, whereupon command of the 37th fell upon Maj. Morris, who was soon wounded himself. One round slammed through his canteen and into his haversack, before being stopped by a piece of hardtack. A second round struck his left ear, drenching his uniform in blood. Some tried to get him to go to the rear, but he considered the wound slight and did not want to turn his back to the enemy. "I Doo Not Like to Beare old abes Mark but am thankfull to God that it is no worse," Morris wrote home five days after the battle. George Cochran (37th NC) recalled crouching behind the lines with his men. One soldier, David Meadows, "would stand upright to shoot, taking careful aim each time, and although cautioned, paid no attention. Presently a ball struck him in the forehead and he fell across my knee." Alexander Campbell "was badly wounded in the neck, and a man named Smith was shot in the eye. . . . A load of 'buck and ball' passed through my coat, three of the buck shot lodging in the coat lining."

Beginning to run low on ammunition, troops of the 37th NC scavenged among the cartridge boxes of the dead and wounded for additional rounds. This was not enough. Federal soldiers pressed in, and hand-to-hand fighting occurred at times. "[W]e had to use the bayonet & buts of our Guns," Morris recorded. One member of the regiment, Peter Smith, was in fact killed by the butt of an enemy's rifle. Another Federal soldier from Maine saw his brother fall wounded, then charged and bayonetted the Tar Heel. "Curse you, you killed my brother!" he cried. As their line collapsed, many members of the brigade were captured. Lieutenant John Pettus was struck in the head and leg, and then dragged off by the feet by the "Yankee wretches," Lane related, but Pettus obviously escaped, as there is no record of his capture.[23]

Out of ammunition, and with the Federals pushing in from three directions, the 37th NC broke for the rear, thus exposing the 28th NC, also with scant ammunition. The Federals gained the railroad, firing into the Carolinians below them. Some attempted to fling their rifles with attached bayonets at the Federals, successfully in a few instances. A few of the Federals found their mark as well. William Mauney, recorded fellow 28th member Michael Kiser, "was stricken through with a bayonet," as was Julius Neagle. Kiser survived. Neagle did not. The 28th broke not long after the 37th, as did the 33rd. The 18th NC attempted to refuse their flank, but likewise was forced back. Only the 7th Regiment still manned the line. They tried to hold the Federals to their front, and on their right along the railroad embankment, but also had to give way. Out of ammunition, the 37th and 28th Regiments headed rearwards, while the remaining regiments fell back around 100 yards. Colonel Avery ordered the 33rd to charge the Federals to stem their advance. They struck the 16th Maine, stopping them at the railroad. The arrival of additional Federal regiments rendered the 33rd's position untenable, but did buy Lane time to reform portions of his brigade, before ordering the 33rd to disengage and rejoin him. Lane's new line had the 7th on the left, the 18th in the center, and the 33rd on the right. Pender's brigade, which Lane requested to help, stretched out its skirmishers to cover Lane's front while he repositioned his men.[24]

---

23 *Semi-Weekly Standard*, January 13, 1863; OR 21:654-55; Cochran, *A Brief Sketch*, 33; O'Reilly, *The Fredericksburg Campaign*, 194; William Morris to "Dear Companion," December 18, 1862. It is unclear who Peter Smith was. No one by this name appears in the roster of the 37th Regiment, nor in a listing of killed and wounded from Gaston County in the *Charlotte Democrat*, December 30, 1862. Morris says Barber's wound was slight and Lieutenant Colonel Ashcraft was absent. Lane writes, however, Barber's neck wound paralyzed his arm. OR 21:655.

24 OR 21:654-55; Mauney, Diary, 6, 7; Clark, *Histories*, 1:375; 2:557.

The line was pieced together just in time. Elements of several different Federal regiments, flushed with success but hopelessly intermingled, came crashing through the woods. A volley or two forced them back toward the railroad. The Federals had accomplished their objective. They had captured not only the Confederate defensive line along the railroad, but the military road as well. Pleas for reinforcements soon reached the Confederate reserve. Jubal Early sent Atkinson's brigade of Georgians to help stabilize Archer's line and his other brigades to steady the far Confederate right.

Walker's brigade of Jubal Early's division plugged the gap in the center of Hill's line—the yawning area between Lane's right and Archer's left. Thomas's brigade of Hill's division also surged to the front. The brigade of Georgians fell in on Lane's reorganizing troops and fired into the Federals. On four occasions, the Federals attempted to punch through the line held by parts of Lane's and Thomas's brigades, and each time, they were turned back. Slowly but steadily, all the Federals in the gap within Confederate lines staggered back across the railroad. Thomas, Lane's 7th and 18th Regiments, and Pender's brigade all surged ahead, driving the enemy in front of them. Dwindling ammunition supplies prevented the Confederates from moving except briefly past the railroad. The breech in Confederate lines had been sealed. By 2:30 that afternoon, large-scale fighting on the Confederate right dwindled, and the fighting shifted to the Confederate left. The area in front of Lane's brigade became known as the Slaughter Pen.

Longstreet's corps held the Confederate left, largely perched behind a stone fence on Marye's Heights. As the attacks of the Confederate right abated, four Federal divisions moved up the slope in front of Marye's Heights. For two hours, they fruitlessly hurled themselves at the Confederate defenders. Later in the afternoon, fresh divisions tried again, followed by one more attempt near dusk. At no time did the enemy assailing Longstreet achieve the level of success they achieved on Jackson's front. The unrelenting attacks cost Burnside around 12,500 casualties as opposed to Lee's of around 4,600. Lane's brigade lost 60 men killed, 315 wounded, and 188 captured. The captured Carolinians startled one Northern journalist:

It was pathetic to see their home-made outfits, their knap-sacks of worn carpets—carpets used as blankets and coverlets and patchwork quilts that had seen home service, the butternut jackets and ragged hats. . . Those North Carolina boys were lank, yellow, weather-beaten, rough haired with bony limbs, and wore ragged jackets. They had plenty of teeth and eyes and many of them would be called . . . 'greenhorns,' but they were terrible soldiers.[25]

In the tree line behind their original position, Lane found the 37th and 28th Regiments, which had made their way back to the ammunition trains and then reformed their depleted ranks. Lane led them back to their original position. "We slept on the battlefield," wrote a member of the 28th, who proceeded to describe:

> the awefulness of the scene, in about 20 steps from me lay all night one of my county men, a conscript, shot through the head, and yet not dead, mourning and struggling all night for life; close to me lay one of my own company dead, and about one hundred and fifty yards of us lay hundreds of dead and wounded Yankees, making all the lamentations, mourning, praying and crying for help, for water and for death.

Orders came to prepare for a rare night attack, but Jackson later suspended the operation, and the Confederates spent the night sleeping on the frozen ground, without any fires to draw enemy fire. At least part of the time, portions of the 7th NC were out on picket in front of the brigade. The brigade stayed in this position through Sunday, and heavy skirmishing throughout the day produced several killed and wounded. On December 15, D. H. Hill's division replaced the Light Division, and Lane's brigade retired to a secondary line where they built "very good" breastworks out of "logs, bush, and dirt. [26]

Lane performed admirably in his first battle as a brigade commander. He had established his headquarters about 50 yards behind the line, but was "much exposed" throughout the battle. A member of the 28th NC reported he had "three gun-shot holes through his clothes." Lee admired the brigade's "brave and obstinate resistance," the same terms Jackson used in his official report. Surprisingly, while Hill singled out Pender in his report, he had scant words for Lane and his brigade. Lane readily praised his men. Colonels commanded four of his regiments, while Lt. Col. Junius Hill commanded the 7th Regiment. They all performed gallantly, "with bravery, and to my entire satisfaction," Lane wrote. The 28th and 37th Regiments "fought like brave men, long and well." He also had accolades for his staff, the ambulance corps, and Lt. James A. Bryan,

25 McDaid, "Four Years," 160; *The Charlotte Observer*, December 3, 1893.

26 *Semi-Weekly Standard*, January 13, 1863; Harris, *Historical Sketches*, 27; OR 21:655-56.

brigade ordnance officer, as well as special praise for the new conscripts, "many
. . . under fire for the first time. They proved themselves worthy accessions to a
brigade which has borne itself well in all of the battles of the last eight
months."[27]

Burnside pulled his army back across the river on the night of December
15. Lane's brigade remained in position until December 17, when it moved to
Moss Neck, going into winter quarters at Camp Gregg, named for fellow Light
Division brigade commander Maxcy Gregg, who succumbed to his wounds on
that same day. After months of marching, fighting, battling disease and poor
food, the brigade needed rest. For the next few months, the Carolinians settled
down into the staid routines of camp life.

Chapter 9

"It is so terrible dull here."

Daily Camp Life

Soldiers spent more time in camp than on campaign. In all of 1863, Branch-Lane brigade members were involved in combat for just over a week. The regiments actively campaigned perhaps an additional month. For the rest of the time, the Carolinians contended with the drudgery of daily camp life. They spent more time in 1862 and 1864 under fire or on active campaign, but the soldiers still spent much more time in camp than on the way to fight some battle or another.

Highly regulated, camp life for soldiers bristled with many rules. Their daily lives were organized in ways that seldom seemed rational. The rat-a-tat of a drum or shrill notes of a bugle awakened them almost every morning. Sleepy soldiers crawled out of their blankets, tents, or cabins to stand in formation while an orderly sergeant called the roll. The men then washed and tended to breakfast, followed by sick call. As the orderly sergeant escorted the sick to the surgeon, the men had time to police the company streets. Next came guard mounting, at times, just a few men from each company. At others, the entire regiment marched out to picket some post. Other soldiers were detailed to fatigue duty or duties such as company cooks or clerks. Those not assigned

Calvin Miller served as a musician in the 37th North Carolina from March 1862 until December 1864, when he was reduced to the ranks. He was captured twice and deserted in February 1865.

John Hawkins

extra duties didn't escape either company or platoon morning drill. Orderly call came at noon, with dinner call a half hour later, followed by regiment or brigade drill for the rest of the afternoon. Dress parades were held in the late afternoon or early evening. The men then had some free time after supper, which most spent playing music and games, attending theatrical performances or religious services, or reading and writing letters home. Regulations required the men were to turn out for a final roll call at retreat, usually at 8:00 p.m., and turn in at tattoo at 8:30 p.m. Frequently, officers worked well into the night, after the enlisted men were sent back to their tents or shanties. Inspections and church services occupied Sundays. Cold weather with snow, or orders to be ready to move quickly, could throw the daily schedule into confusion.[1]

Each regiment in the brigade had its own drum and fife corps. Soldiers detailed from the ranks served as drummers or fifers. Some were actual drummer boys. A survey of the 18th showed 11 musicians. The youngest was 12. Four of the 11 were dismissed from the service for being too young. The oldest brigade drummer was 32 when he enlisted. Terrell Bledsoe, 28th NC, was mustered in as a fifer at age 38 and was discharged in May 1862 for being too old. William Lisk was 29 when he was mustered in as a musician in August 1861, and he served as such for the entire war. The musicians had to be up half an hour before the camp. They woke up the men, signaled them when to eat, kept

1 *Regulations for the Army of the Confederate States,* 24; Greg Mast, *State Troops and Volunteers* (Raleigh, NC, 1995), 24.

them in step during drill, and often told them when to retire at night. Three of the regiments, the 7th, 28th, and 33rd, listed no drum major. The 7th NC did list P. H. Welsh as a musician attached to the field and staff, but he disappears from the records in May 1863, only to be captured in Gates County, VA, and imprisoned in Maryland in March 1865. Two men served as drum majors in the 18th NC: Howard Williams, then Henry Woodcock. John Carlton was leader of the field music in the 37th NC from March 1862 until he deserted in February 1865. Musicians were not always safely behind the lines. Drummer Jones Smyer (28th NC) was wounded in battle, captured, and died of his wounds in a prisoner camp in New York.[2]

One regiment in the brigade, the 33rd, also had a brass band. It had been organized in February 1862, and largely consisted of men from Bethania in Forsyth County. Oliver Lehman, a cornet player and leader of the band at the Bethania Moravian Church, arrived to instruct the band following the battle of New Bern. In February 1863, he officially joined the regiment, and a couple of weeks later, transferred to the band. Edwin Dull, a 28-year-old farmer and the band's oldest member, was given the position of chief musician. The band's two dozen members were 20 years old on average. Also known as Lane's Brigade Band, they played for guard duty at nine every morning, at dress parade about sunset, and for reviews. Lehman later wrote that:

> Every night that the weather was favorable the Brigade Band was ordered to play one hour and the cheer of the soldiers could be heard for miles. Our lines and the enemy's were often so close together that frequently when our band played a popular air, a Yankee band in our front would play the same air we played, followed by yells from their men.

Being in the brass band did not provide immunity from the horrors of the war. The musicians followed the battle, bearing wounded off the field "often under severe shelling, and small arms fire." On occasion, the musicians were given weapons and stood guard around the brigade's baggage wagons. Band members William Anderson and James Conrad were both wounded at New

2 Jordan, *NC Troops*, 4:407, 6:308, 8:115, 151, 169, 9:471.

Bern. Anderson died, and Conrad eventually joined the Invalid Corps. William Ketner, Lewis Kimbrough, and Julius Stauber all died of disease.[3]

Depending on the season, the soldiers in the Army of Northern Virginia stayed in a variety of shelters. While on active campaign, the men slept outside. Each soldier had a shelter half in his knapsack or rolled together in a blanket and slung across the body. When encamping, the men could find some trees to serve as poles, button two shelter halves together, and erect a tent to protect them from some of the elements. On active campaign, men too exhausted to bother pitching a tent slept out in the open. Walter Lenoir (37th NC) told of sleeping in all kinds of weather. One morning, his "socks were so wet that I wrung water out [of] them. . . before starting to march," he wrote in 1863. If the men were going to be stationary for few days, they used tents or improvised shelters of some type. Following the Seven Days battles, James Bellamy (18th NC) described a camp composed of "rude shelters made by boughs, blankets, &c—some are using hammocks made of their carpet blankets which once decorated the habituations of Carolina's Patriotic Daughters." A member of the 28th NC also wrote of just a single tent and two "flies," large pieces of canvas forming a roof, but no sides, for his entire company.[4]

After Fredericksburg, portions of the brigade were quartered in Sibley tents, large, bell-shaped canvas structures resembling teepees. "We slept on the ground, two and two, our feet towards the middle of tent and our heads to the wall," recalled William Miller (37th NC). "Our tent was small . . . only room for ten or 12 men. . . . It was supported by a big pole in the middle to which the rigging and canvas were fastened."[5]

Once the generals believed active campaigning season had ended, a camp was selected for winter quarters. Regulations specified camp lay out, the location of kitchens, officer's quarters, stables, and latrines. Winter quarters seemed to follow these guidelines. Lehman recalled the right-angled streets, one

3   O. J. Lehman, "Reminiscences of the War Between the States: 1862 to 1865." *The Union Republican,* October 19, 1922; Jordan, *NC Troops,* 9:121-22. Oliver Lehman organized and led the band at Bethania Moravian Church from 1856 -1921. *Bicentennial of Bethania Moravian Church, 1759 - 1959* (Winston-Salem, NC, 1959), 77.

4   Hickerson, *Happy Valley,* 83; Bellamy, "Diary," 40; Conrad, *Kinfolk of Jacob Conrad,* 303.

5   *Heritage of Ashe County, North Carolina,* 2 vols. (Winston-Salem, NC, 1984,) 2:28; Doctor Schaffner (33rd Regiment) also made mention of seeing Sibley tents following the battle of Fredericksburg. John Shaffner to "My Dearest Friend," December 21, 1862, Shaffner Papers, NCDAH.

for officers' quarters and the other for enlisted men. "The houses, or quarters," he wrote,

> were of many different styles of architecture—the best were built of rough logs, daubed with mud, a stick chimney also heavily daubed, covered with split boards which were held in place by heavy poles, as no nails could be had. Others were built up of logs about 4 feet and covered with tent cloth. . . . If we were encamped on a hillside, quite a number lived in 'dug-outs,' or under ground.

Surrounding forests were soon denuded of trees, and fences and vacant houses quickly dismantled for building materials. Men often used sticks and mud, and bricks when available, to build fireplaces in their cabins. George Cochran painted this picture of the winter of 1862-63:

> It was a very severe winter. . . . and before Spring opened, there were no trees . . . and even the stumps had been chopped off and burned. Snow covered the ground nearly all the time and it was bitter cold. . . . Our tents were so old and rotten that we could not stake them to the ground, and the walls hung like curtains. The wind sailed through the tents without let or hindrance. . . . We built a mud-and-stick chimney for our tent and made a platform of small pine poles which we covered with a thick bed of leaves, and put a blanket over them for a bed. For top covering we had three blankets and used our coats for pillows. . . . For a kitchen we made a dugout in the side of a hill just at the rear of our "residence' and covered it with split timber and earth. . . . That a man can 'get used to anything except hanging' was abundantly proved by Lee's veterans along the heights of the Rappahannock that winter.[6]

Officers like Cochran were usually quartered in tents. General Lane wrote in December 1864 that he and his aide, Lt. Everard Meade, had two tents put together: a front tent with a brick chimney "sitting room," and a back tent "sleeping apartment," along with plank floors and a real door. The "chamber" furnishings included: "bedstead and blankets, two trunks and a clothes pole (suspended from the ridge pole), which serves as an excellent ventilating wardrobe," Lane wrote. "In the front tent may be seen an old camp-table, a few

---

6   Lehman, "Reminiscences," *The Union Republican*, October 19, 1922; Cochran, *A Brief Sketch*, 35.

chairs, an old bent tin candle-stick, an inkstand and pens, tobacco and pipes, and sometimes a great deal of smoke."[7]

Rousing the men every morning was the hardest working soldier in each company: the orderly sergeant. He was ordered to memorize his company roll, just in case he was without his books. After taking the roll and examining the sick, he turned in a morning report to his captain for a signature. The company reports went up to the regimental staff, which tabulated each one. He was also responsible for punishing offenders and keeping records of various details. The orderly sergeant minded all company property, working with quartermaster and commissary sergeants, the company clerk and officers to tend mountains of required paperwork. Sick lists, morning reports, and the details of men for guards, detachments, and fatigue duty were submitted daily. Once a month, a report was sent to the Adjutant-General's department outlining any action; the names of soldiers killed and wounded; and the dates officers and enlisted men were transferred, resigned, or discharged. Every two months, the staff labored over the muster rolls and the required report on damaged arms. Quarterly reports on returned clothing, ordnance and ordnance stores, quartermaster property, and deceased soldiers were required—not to mention: certificates of disability, final statements, discharges, descriptive rolls, furloughs, passes and sick furloughs, inventories of deceased soldiers, and requisitions for forage, fuel, stationery, straw, arms, accouterments, ammunition, clothing, camp and garrison equipage, and quartermaster's stores. Lieutenant John Conrad (28th NC) complained in November 1862 that he had no time to write because he had to "work on some muster rolls, monthly returns, etc., and have just got through, but I have my pay-rolls to make out now and no one to help me."[8]

Of all the papers that passed through the hands of an orderly sergeant or company clerk, the one most sought-after by enlisted men and officers alike was the furlough home. Samuel Harding (28th NC) believed he deserved a furlough home in January 1863, because "I have done a heap of hard marching and hard Fighting." Men who wanted leave from the army received furloughs, but of course the number had to be limited. "They have commenced giving furlows," wrote Robert Francis (37th NC) on January 18, 1863. "The old soldiers will get

7   Lane, "Glimpses of Army Life in 1864," *SHSP*, 18:419.

8   August Kautz, *Customs of Service for Non-Commissioned Officers* (Philadelphia, PA, 1864), 131-49; August Kautz, *The Company Clerk* (Philadelphia, PA, 1865); Conrad, *Kinfolk of Jacob Conrad*, 316.

furlows first. Some start home today out of our Regiment." Often, only two men per company were furloughed at a time. A soldier had to return for the next one to leave. Furloughs could be for a few days, two weeks, or 30 days, possibly longer for medical reasons. General Branch had a furlough for a few days following the Seven Days campaign and chose to spend it with his family in Richmond. Yet, when combat seemed imminent, furloughs ceased.[9]

Breakfast followed roll call. Soldiers in camp for a lengthy period organized regular kitchens. Enlisted and officers alike often banded together in messes. "I expect you would like to no how we manage a bout cooking," Bennett Smith (37th NC) wrote home in 1862. "[T]here is fifteen of us messes together & that number a lowes us a cook that keeps one man from drilling while he is cooking I dont cook any I fetch water sometimes & make a fire & the rest cooks[.]" Messes could be just a few men, or, as Smith noted, more than a dozen. A year later, Smith informed his wife he did his own cooking, baking pies. "I think they eat prime," he said. Officers frequently messed together as well. Major Morris noted in November 1862 that he, Lt. Col. John Ashcraft, Chaplain Albert Stough, and commissary sergeant Charles Stowe messed together. They had hired a "free boy," paying him 12 dollars a month, to cook and wash.[10]

Confederate regulations stipulated each soldier was to receive daily "three-fourths of a pound of pork or bacon, or one and a fourth pounds of fresh or salt beef; eighteen ounces of bread or flour, or twelve ounces of hard bread, or one and a fourth pounds of corn meal," along with peas or beans, rice, coffee, sugar, and vinegar. In 1863, these ratuibs were modified to a half-pound of pork or bacon, or a pound of beef, and a pound and a half of flour or meal. The rations soldiers actually received varied greatly from those stipulated by law. Each regiment had a commissary sergeant who was overseen by the brigade-level assistant commissary of subsistence. Two men occupied the brigade commissary position during the war. The first was Maj. Daniel Carraway, whom Lane considered "an excellent officer," serving the brigade from its inception until June 1863, when he transferred to division staff. Captain (later major) Thomas McKoy, was the assistant commissary of subsistence in the 7th North

9   Samuel Harding to "Dear Mother," January 24, 1863, in Casstevens, *The 28th North Carolina Infantry*, 194; Robert Francis to "Cousin," January 18, 1863, private collection; *Weekly State Journal*, October 1, 1862.

10 Bennett Smith to Dear Jane, March 30, 1862, March 24, 1863, private collection; William Morris to "Deare Companion," November 19, 1862, Morris Letters, SHC/UNC.

Carolina. General Lane recalled after the war that McKoy had risen steadily through the ranks and sympathized "with the soldiers at the front and on their long, weary marches. He would always take charge of our cooking details," continued Lane, "and often sit up all night to prevent delay in preparing the rations." F. L. Alexander of the 37th Regiment was McKoy's assistant commissary of subsistence in the 7th Regiment.[11]

Army rations were often delivered to the nearest railroad station, and wagons from the various brigades picked up each brigade's allotment. Oliver Lehman (33rd NC) wrote that the commissary department issued rations every evening, and then the companies followed a set ritual:

> One man drew rations for his company, reporting the number of men in his company—the company was divided into squads of from 5 to 10 men. The ration was cut up into as many pieces as the mess contained, as near equal as possible. Then one was blindfolded, or turned his back, when another would call out 'who gets this?' pointing to a ration. The answer came, 'John Smith,' and again, who gets this? By this means, no one could complain of partiality being shown.[12]

Confederates often skimped or simply did without. Active campaigning often meant a disruption in the supply wagons. Lieutenant Colonel Speer recalled that during the battle of Chancellorsville, the men in the 28th NC had nothing to eat for three days. And on the retreat from Gettysburg his men went without bread for two days, while the Federals cut off any attempt to forage in the countryside. On other occasions, captured Federal haversacks helped sustain the men. Captain James Weston recalled the men of the 33rd NC fixing "a good breakfast on May 6, 1864, cooked from Yankee rations captured the evening before." John Conrad (28th NC) informed the folks at home in November 1862, he was drinking coffee captured at Shepherdstown two months earlier.[13]

---

11 *Confederate Regulations*, 191; Krick, *Staff Officers in Gray*, 28-34, 91, 201-10. Lane penned in "History of Lane's North Carolina Brigade,"*SHSP*, 10:208, that F. L. Alexander was commissary sergeant of the 37th NC, but no one with those initials served in that regiment. Each regiment also had an assistant commissary of subsistence, but Congress abolished it in 1863.

12 Lehman, "Reminiscences," *The Union Republican*, October 19, 1922.

13 Speer, *Voices from Cemetery Hill*, 101, 109; Clark, *Histories*, 2:570; Conrad. *Kinfolk of Jacob Conrad*, 316.

Food varied not only in quantity, but in quality as well. While stationed along the Atlantic coast in early 1862, for example, John Alexander of the 37th Regiment recalled receiving plenty of fish and sweet potatoes, but complained that the issued corn meal needed to be sifted, and the "bran was so large the boys spoke of it as Jeff. Davis' tomb-stones." In early 1864, Andrew Proffitt wrote of receiving plentiful rations in the 18th NC, including "shugar, coffee, rice and molasses, beeaf and corn meal," although he confessed to being tired of the latter. Proffitt wrote home again that September about their poor bread rations. Junius Little (28th NC) complained in the days following Wade Hampton's celebrated Beefsteak Raid behind Federal lines during the Petersburg Campaign in September 1864 that all he got to eat was "Steak for breakfast, steak for dinner and steak for supper." During active campaigning, droves of cattle frequently moved with the army, supplying the men with fresh beef when possible.[14]

At least during the war's early months, men often ventured out into the countryside to secure additional food. Andrew Proffitt confessed to eating stolen corn, and his fellow soldiers in the 18th Regiment "flank anything they run up with. We take corn, pumpkins, shugar cane or anything we can eat, anywhare we find it." Nicholas Gibbon, assistant commissary of subsistence for the 28th NC, wrote about having to scour the county side around Gordonsville to find a wagonload of flour, only to repeat the process two days later. During the campaign to destroy the railroad after their return from Maryland, Gibbon had to scrounge supplies for the brigade from the surrounding countryside. William Barlow (18th NC) wrote in a letter home in December 1862 that he and his comrades had only half enough to eat. He walked "6 or 7 miles to a mill and purchased half a bushel of meal," he explained. When he returned to camp, continued Barlow, he baked corn bread, sold part of it and kept enough to last himself two or three days.

Soldiers occasionally fished, but seldom hunted. The way men spent their money on food amazed Francis Kennedy, chaplain of the 28th NC. In January 1863 he noted someone had paid almost $20 for a half gallon of honey. William McLaurin of the 18th recalled being on picket, with the Federal pickets not far away, and between the lines was a stand of pine trees in which "a flock of wild turkeys lit down." One turkey had been shot during the day "and lay in full view

14 Alexander, *Reminiscences*, 82; Hancock, *Four Brothers in Gray*, 253, 281; Hahn, *The Catawba Soldier*, 172.

The 18th North Carolina's adjutant, William McLaurin, wrote of the men bagging a turkey caught between the lines, a supplement to the meager rations they otherwise received.

Histories of the Several Regiments and Battalions from North Carolina

of both picket lines. Disregarding the danger, each side determined to capture that turkey, and several men were gobblerized during the day. After sun down, George W. Corbett, in charge of the 18th skirmishers, played tactics to bring him in. Picking a man to help him, they approached in different directions, and succeeded in bagging the game. . . . The pot boiled that night." At other times, at least early in the war, people came to the camps to sell food to the soldiers. Bennett Smith (37th NC) noted in February 1862 a "gang of old nigars" just on the other side of the picket line selling "sweet bread" to the soldiers.[15]

To supplement their meager rations, soldiers implored those at home to send boxes of foodstuffs. "I want you to fetch us some dryed fruit if you do come and some honey, and some butter and some sausage meat," Samuel Harding (28th NC) wrote his father. "[I] want you to fetch me onions and some dride fruit and Some buter and Some grene fruit and molase," Thorton Sexton (37th NC) pleaded when he learned his father might be visiting the camps in late 1863. Almost all of these precious boxes came via the railroad. Samuel Harding (28th NC) complained to his father in 1862 it cost him $4 to get his box from home. General Lane wrote in December 1864 that he sent his own headquarters wagon to the depot to retrieve the boxes for the soldiers. Family members or fellow soldiers returning from furloughs could bring them, too. In

15   Hancock, *Four Brothers in Gray*, 281; Gibbon, Diary, 11, 20; William Barlow to "Dearly Beloved Wife," December 9, 1862, *Company Front*, 24; Kennedy, Diary, January 31, 1863; Clark, *Histories*, 2:46; Bennett Smith to "Dear Jane," February 4, 1862, private collection.

January 1864, an advertisement appeared in the *Western Democrat*, announcing that Abraham Torrence (37th NC) was at home on furlough. Anyone with boxes for soldiers in Company C could deliver them to Torrence, or to the railroad, and he would see they got to camp.: "I recd the trunk you Sent Me," William Morris (37th NC) wrote in April 1863. "Every thing right there. Was Not One of the Eggs broken." Calvin Holcomb (28th NC) confided to his brother in 1862 that he had received a box of apples from home, and it took five minutes to sell them all. Holcomb wished he had five bushels instead of just one box.[16]

Soldiers had one overarching challenge with food while on campaign: cooking it. Usually issued two or three or days' rations at once, the men spent most of the night before a movement taking turns around the fire preparing food that was either stashed in the haversacks or eaten immediately. When orders came to send baggage to the rear, this often included large cooking vessels. At times the soldiers were issued hardtack, which they often called crackers. John Green (33rd NC) complained his crackers were so hard he couldn't eat them. More often, Confederate soldiers were issued flour. Walter Lenoir left a vivid description of cooking on campaign:

> We were often without cooking utensils to prepare our rations, and the men would make their flour into dough, on oil clothes, and bake it into cakes at the bivouac fires on pieces of staves, around sticks, etc. The beef and bacon they would roast on sticks, but generally preferred to eat the bacon raw. I learned to eat fat bacon raw, and to like it. The beef roasted on sticks and the hard and dry army crackers which I generally used for bread, were so delicious to my taste after the fierce appetite gained by hard marching that I never enjoyed eating so much."[17]

After breakfast, men detailed for the day marched off to their duties, which could be working in the company kitchens, gathering firewood, or cleaning the parade ground. Noah Collins (37th NC) was detailed to dig a well in January

---

16 Harding to "Dear Father," January 24, 1863, Casstevens, *The 28th North Carolina Infantry*, 194, 195; Thorton Sexton to "Dear Father," November 5, 1863, Sexton Letters, DU; Lane, "Glimpse of Army Life," *SHSP*, 18:420; *Western Democrat*, January 12, 1864; William Morris to "Dear Famely," April 19, 1863, Morris Letters, SHC/UNC; C. M. Holcomb to "Dear Brother," February 19, 1862, *The Heritage of Yadkin County*, 1:143.

17 John Green to "Dear Wife," no date, *Stanley County Heritage*, 313; Hickerson, *Happy Valley*, 83.

1862. Many men told of building corduroy roads, or pole roads, in early 1863, trying to upgrade the route for supply wagons to get from the depot to the camps. General Lane had the men of the brigade making shoes and candles in camp during the war. George Cochran (37th NC), after the war, wrote of having to dig regimental sinks. Ten men were ordered to:

> go across a branch and dig a large sink on the side of the hill opposite the flag, which was the center of the camp. I had the sink dug about 30 feet long, near three feet wide and three and a half feet deep. . . . In a few weeks it was full to the brim. So another was dug just above it and the dirt from the new one thrown down the hill covering the old one.

Some men were detailed to serve as nurses, and a few to serve in wartime industries in various cities across the South.[18]

Possibly the most loathsome detail was picket duty. Whether in camp or winter quarters, each brigade was assigned an area between the lines to picket. Pickets were a warning system, delaying the enemy long enough to give their comrades time to reach the main lines from camp. When the entire regiment performed picket duty, part of it stayed in a reserve location, while the rest occupied some forward point. Regulations dictated that pickets were to be relieved every two hours. However, in the war's latter years, advance pickets occupied small pits dug in the ground in front of a regular picket line. Men might be in these pits for 24 hours and were only relieved under the cover of darkness. Most soldiers despised picket duty. William Bellamy (18th NC) wrote of heading toward the Chickahominy River in June 1862 for picket duty. "[D]read it," he said, complaining of the mosquitoes, frogs, and "Katy dids" that, "to our great regret assemble invariably at our post to entertain us for our Term of 12 hours." Noah Collins (37th NC) described the winter of 1862-63 as intensely cold, with "rain and snow," and "much unnecessary camp guard duty." A year later, Greenberry Harding (28th NC) reported being on picket duty every five days.[19]

18 Collins, Reminisces, 13; Clark, Histories, 2:476; Lane, "Glimpses of Army Life," SHSP, 18:207; Cochran, A Brief Sketch, 36.

19 Bellamy, Diary, 41; Collins, Reminisces, 35; Harding to Father & Mother, November 25, 1863, Casstevens, The 28th North Carolina Infantry, 195.

Standing picket posed many dangers. Bellamy recalled in early June 1862 a skirmish broke out one afternoon while he was on duty. Joseph Saunders wrote in December 1862 of being so close to the Federals he could hear them talking and giving orders. Conditions worsened when the armies bogged down in the trenches in 1864 and early 1865. "[W]e ar still lying in our ditches close to the yanks" wrote Thomas Alexander (37th NC) in June 1864. "[W]e can shoote from one breast work to other but the yanks a keepe close down if ver one puts his head above the works some Rebel sends a ball after him so we keepe them anoyed all the time ans they us[.]" Both sides staged frequent raids on picket posts late in the war, with officers trying to discern troop movements by learning what troops were in front of them.[20]

Pickets sometimes declared informal truces. Soldiers on both sides conversed freely and even traded goods. "We was on Picket Duty a fiew Days ago," wrote Morris (37th NC). "[T]he enemy on one Bank of the river & we on the other about 200 yds. wide. they are very Friendley & want to talk a Great Deal. they curce the war & Say there time will bee out Next May & will Go Home Peace or No peace & if the Abolitionist want the Negroes Set free they will have to Doo there own Fighting." On another occasion, Morris wrote the Federals on the other side of the river called out, asking for "a sorry corporal," or a run-down horse, which could be swapped for General Burnside. T. James Linebarger (28th NC) told the folks back home about a comrade trading a small piece of cornbread to a Federal soldier for a pocketbook or wallet Linebarger estimated to be worth $10.[21]

Men not on detail, or companies and regiments not on picket duty, drilled as platoons and companies in the morning, followed by regimental and, at times, brigade drill in the afternoon. Writing early in the war, John Conrad told his family Col. Lane was drilling the 28th Regiment every evening. "I wish you could see us drill," he wrote, "it is one of the most imposing and grand scenes ever you beheld, the guns and bayonets glittering in the sun and the whole battalion marching off at the same step in one solid column; I think we are improving rapidly and in a short time will be able to compete with any regiment

20 Thomas Alexander to "Dear wife," July 6, 1864, Thomas Alexander Letter, Petersburg National Military Park; Joseph Saunders to "Dear Mother," December 19, 1862, Saunders Letters, SHC/UNC.

21 William Morris to "Dear Fameley," December 28, 1862, January 22, 1863, Morris Letters, SHC/UNC; James Linebarger to Ann Linebarger, June 7, 1864, Ann Linebarger Snuggs Papers, SHC/UNC.

on a drill." In March 1862, John B. Alexander wrote the 37th NC was drilling five times a day. Drilling never ceased. Greenberry Harding (28th NC) noted in November 1863 the men were drilling twice a day when not on picket. Major Jackson Bost, commanding the 37th NC, felt drill remained an integral part of military life in early 1864. He issued a general order in late January 1864, covering several aspects of daily drill: twice a day, for at least two hours, if circumstances permitted; new recruits to drill a half hour longer than veterans; "old soldiers" who did not "drill well" to be lumped with the new recruits for extra drill. Squad drill was deemed the "very basis of all proficiency in military exercise." If soldiers did not master squad drill, then, according to Bost, it was impossible to master company and battalion drill. Anyone, new or seasoned, who did not drill properly was to be reported to the regimental commander.[22]

"If I had time I coul(d) tell you a Great Deal . . . but I have Drill all day & study at Night," Morris of the 37th wrote home in November 1861. Save for a handful of men, like Charles Lee and James Lane, graduates of military schools, or a few cadets from the North Carolina Military Institute in Charlotte, everyone was learning the fundamentals of drill at the same time. Morris and the other company-grade officers studied their manuals at night, and then practiced what they learned on their respective commands the next day. Thomas Wood wrote in 1861 the 18th Regiment used *Hardee's Rifle and Infantry Tactics*, while others used Winfield Scott's three-volume *Infantry Tactics*. Since North Carolina printed its own copies of a revised Hardee's, it may have been the primary infantry manual for the brigade. Other manuals identified as belonging to members of the brigade are rare. There is an older version of Hardee's drill manual belonging to William Callais (33rd NC). Two copies of William Gilham's *Manual of Instruction for the Volunteers and Militia of the Confederate States* survive and are attributed to brigade members: John Cain of the 18th Regiment and Ives Smedes of the 7th.[23]

22 Conrad, *Kinfolk of Jacob Conrad*, 290-91; John Alexander to "Dear Wife," March 18, 1862, Alexander Letters, UNC-Charlotte; Harding to Father and Mother, November 25, 1863, Casstevens, *The 28th North Carolina Infantry*, 195; Jackson Bost, General Order No. 2, Bost Papers, DU.

23 William Morris to "Dear Companion," November 12, 1861, Morris Letters, HC; Koonce, *Doctor to the Front*, 24; "Among Most Widely Used Confederate Infantry Manuals." Raynor's Historical Collectible Auctions. August 3, 2004. August 4, 2015. Http://www.hcaauctions.com /lot-3463.aspx. Cain's copy of Gilham's is at the Tennessee State Library and Archives, while Smedes's is located at the Library of Virginia.

At the end of the day came dress parade. The music played as the companies formed and their officers inspected them. Then the companies marched to the parade ground and formed the regimental line. Music proceeded orders to open ranks and present arms. Orderly sergeants presented their reports regarding the number of men present, sick, or absent. The regimental adjutants then read the orders. Adjutant William McLaurin (18th NC) wrote about General Lee's order congratulating Branch and his role in the battle of Hanover Court House being read to each regiment at dress parade on June 3, 1862. Such congratulatory orders were infrequent; more mundane communications were normal. Following the reading of orders, orderly sergeants took charge of the companies and dismissed them, while the officers lingered for further instructions from the commanding officer.[24]

Often on Sundays, the regiments formed for inspection. William Bellamy (18th NC) recalled these events as a day "always looked for with the greatest of horror & disgust imaginable." Everything, from the uniforms they wore, to the gear they carried and the quarters where they slept, was open to inspection. Those found deficient were assigned to extra duty, or had their pay docked. Pay could be docked for many different reasons, including the loss of equipment. Thomas Cameron and Levi Bass (7th NC) were both docked 25 cents in the winter of 1862 for losing canteens.[25]

Sundays frequently offered the religiously inclined soldiers, many of whom brought their beliefs with them when they joined the army, opportunities to gather and worship. Others found Christianity while they were in camp. "During the first two years of the war, soldier attendance at often infrequent religious services remained shockingly low." While this sentiment might be true for some regiments, others held regular services from the formation of the organization. Even before the 37th NC was formed, services took place every night about a half mile from camp. "[V]ery often 3 Sermons Going on at the same time," William Morris told his family. Colonel Lee was not only "A Military Man" but "a Devoted Christian" as well, he observed a few months later. One Sunday, after a service by a local preacher, Lee addressed the men. After reading a chapter from the Bible and praying, he preached what Morris considered "the Best Sermon I ever heard":

24 Clark, *Histories*, 2:24; *Confederate Regulations*, 33-34.

25 Bellamy, Diary, 22; Thomas A. Cameron, Roll 171, M270, Roll 109, CMSR, NA; Levi Bass, Roll 0171, M270, RG109, CMSR, NA.

The chaplain for the 37th North Carolina was Baptist minister Albert L. Stough. A church in Mecklenburg County is named for him.

Histories of the Several Regiments and Battalions from North Carolina

While we was Conyending for Our Wrights and Libertyes that we Should be Careful that While We was Engaged in a ware against the yankees Who Desire to bring us under Subjection & in to bondage that we be Not Slaves to a worse foe than Man. that foe he represented to be Sin. he contended that we was Engaged in a Just war but Not To Lay Down our arms that God had given us to defend our selves against that foe that would hold us in Chains through Eternity. he caled on us to Come out from under the bondage of Sin that we Might be free people indeed. he told us that we could Not Expect Sucksess in our Struggle for freedom as a Nation if we Stooped So low as to become Slaves to Sin.[26]

This religious current ran strongly through the 37th. Bennett Smith also noted in a letter home he was going to "preaching" every few days. The regiment's chaplain wrote the *Biblical Recorder* of his "attentive" men and the strong "religious interest" amongst them. Chaplain Stough requested additional "religious reading matter" and praised efforts to get more Bibles into the hands of the soldiers. "The enterprise is glorious in its origins, [and] the interest of our country, the happiness of our families, the preservation of pure religion, requires alike our exertions in supplying the destitute with the Gospel of the Son of God." In April 1863, Stough wrote of a third revival, in the 37th's ranks

26 George Rable, *God's Almost Chosen Peoples: A Religious History of the American Civil War* (Chapel Hill, NC, 2010), 90; William Morris to "Deare Companion," November 6, 1861, February 26, 1862, Morris Letters, SHC/UNC.

since the war started. In just two weeks, Stough had 119 penitents with 41 converts.[27]

Undoubtedly, Col. Lee was the driving force behind the 37th NC's Christian fervor. Such was not always the case in the early phases of the other regiments. Early in the war, the 18th NC had preaching from time to time, but the men showed little interest. Likewise, while the men of the 33rd NC "were among the best men on earth," said James Weston, they were not noted for piety.[28]

When first organized, the Confederate army excluded chaplains. Many believed the communities and denominations that sent chaplains should support them, not the military or government. In 1862, the Confederate Congress directed President Davis to create the post and to pay chaplains $85 (reduced to $50 two weeks later). Eventually, the salary was raised to $80 a month, and chaplains were allowed to draw rations equivalent to a private's. It was difficult to entice clergy to give up their local churches to take on the hard work as well as the hardships of camp life and battle. Plus, clergy were exempt from regular military service, and some believed they were simply trying to avoid the army. Eleven men served as chaplains in the Branch-Lane brigade. Only the 28th and 33rd Regiments had chaplains through most of the war. The 7th NC had two men, E. A. Best and M. M. Marshall, who served perhaps three months combined. One of the 18th's chaplains, Colin Shaw—the minister with "little attraction" for Wood—transferred in January 1863. William Jordan replaced him and resigned after a month. The 18th had no chaplain after September 1863. Three different men served the 28th NC: Oscar Brent from October 1861 to July 1862, when "ill health" forced him to resign; Francis Kennedy, from December 1862 until he transferred to a hospital in Charlotte in April 1864; and D. L. Henkle, December 1864 to the regiment's surrender in April 1865. Two men served with the 33rd NC. Benjamin Guthrie, appointed in April 1862, died of disease in camp a couple of months later. His replacement, Thomas Eatman, transferred out of Company A to fill the position, which he did until the surrender. Baptist minister Albert Stough served the 37th NC from

27 Bennett Smith to Wife, March 6, 1862, private collection; *Biblical Recorder*, March 5, 1862, May 6, 1863.

28 Koonce, *Doctor to the Front*, 15; Clark, *Histories*, 2:579. William Morris in the spring of 1863 thought the officers in the 37th Regiment were "verry wicked, Moore so Since Coln Lee was Killed." William Morris to "Dear Companion," April 15, 1863, Morris Letters, SHC/UNC.

November 1861 until ill health forced his resignation more than two years later.[29]

Chaplains performed a variety of roles. Francis Kennedy, the son of a minister, was admitted to the South Carolina Conference, Methodist Episcopal Church in the 1850s. In 1862, he helped deliver tracts from Charlotte to Richmond and was appointed chaplain of the 28th NC on January 3, 1863. Kennedy preached several times a week and spent his time visiting the sick, distributing tracts, Bibles, and hymn books. Conditions for his services varied greatly. On his first Sunday in camp, he had his "Bible and Hymn Book lying on an old goods box and the men gathered in a semi-circle" around his outdoor church on a "very raw and unpleasant," day on "very wet and cold," ground. Kennedy did not keep them for long. On other days, a great battle, or the elements, kept him from performing all of his tasks. Although a Methodist, Kennedy had to serve men of different denominations. In September 1863, he wrote of baptizing men by immersion in the Rapidan River for the first time. Two months later, after spending a day finding wine, he administered the sacrament to two Lutheran members of the 18th NC who had been condemned to be executed. Kennedy frequently had to pray with men who in a matter of hours were to be executed for crimes, most often desertion. "I don't think I shall ever forget the scene," he wrote after the execution of seven men from the brigade. He had baptized two of them just moments before they faced the firing squad.[30]

Kennedy was assigned to the 28th NC not long after fervent revivals began sweeping through the army. These meetings started after the Maryland Campaign in fall, 1862. Supplied with literature and missionaries from the churches back home, by the spring of 1863, the revival was well underway. "We have a revival going on in our Regt," Lt. Col. Speer wrote home in April 1863. "I hope it will go on till all of the men & officers become Christians." Chaplain Kennedy echoed Speer, reporting almost 300 church members in his regiment (28th NC) of 800 men, with 20 or 30 penitents. "We have Preaching Nearly Every day in camp," Morris (37th NC) wrote home in April. "I think the

---

29 Gardiner Shatturck, Jr., *A Shield and Hiding Place: The Religious Life of Civil War Armies* (Macon, GA, 1987), 63-65; Koonce, *Doctor to the Front*, 15; Jordan, *NC Regiments*, 4:407, 6:307, 8:111, 9:120, 470. The Confederate government stopped the practice of replacing chaplains with men from the ranks in 1863.

30 Kennedy, Diary, January 14, September 18, 26, 1863.

Soldiers are becoming More Interested in the Salvation of there Souls." The Gettysburg campaign slowed the revival to some extent, although Kennedy reported preaching to the men in both Pennsylvania and Maryland. Once back in Virginia, near Orange Court House, the regimental services resumed. Thomas Pritchard, chaplain for a Georgia brigade, reported preaching in Lane's brigade in September. Almost 30 came forward for prayer, and several were baptized. These meetings continued almost unabated through the spring of 1864. "I can say to you that there has been a big meeting going on in sight of our camps all day and is still going on," William Barlow wrote in February 1864. "There is a good many joining the Church. I have been 8 nights and one day and to baptizing one day."

In many instances, those joining the church were not only professing their faith in camp before their fellow soldiers, but were also desiring to connect with churches back at home. Chaplains often conveyed to the home churches the requests of new converts to join their fellowships. Elizabeth Robeson of Bladen County joyfully recalled in May 1864 that her son Evander had joined the church, according to a letter from the 18th NC's chaplain. Only the active campaigning, starting in May 1864, brought an end to the revivals in Lee's army.[31]

While some soldiers might attend a religious service, others found solace in many other diversions. Following evening parades, soldiers had a degree of free time. "There is awl sorts of amusements going on hear fidling dancing plaing bast bool pen jumping rasling and a heap of other things & some of the wikeds men you evry saw and the uglyes that you evr heard tel," Bennett Smith (37th NC) wrote home in early 1862. "I caint find out how it come I was fetch here," he confessed. Early in the war, camp life resembled a big holiday. Most of the men had never been away from home, and in some regiments, lax discipline prevailed. "Sometimes we would fall in at reveille with fishing lines in hand," recalled Thomas Wood (18th NC) "half dressed, and as soon as we broke ranks would dash across the sand dunes for the sea beach and fish for drums and whiting until breakfast time." The men always seemed to be close enough to a

31 Speer, *Voices from Cemetery Hill*, 97; J. William Jones, *Christ in the Camp or Religion in the Confederate Army* (Atlanta, GA, 1904), 332, 520; Morris to Dear Companion, April 15, 1863; Kennedy, Diary, June 26, July 15-23, 1863; William Barlow to William Barlow, February 22, 1864, *Company Front*, 41; *The Diary of Elizabeth Ellis Robeson, Bladen County, North Carolina, 1847-1866* (n.p., n.d.), 136.

body of water to fish. Yet their new roles in military life soon imposed tighter discipline.[32]

Some had trouble adjusting. John Alexander told of a fellow member of the 37th, Robert Sharpe, a "fine looking, active" soldier who "talked well and was a great ladiesman." Like many early in the war, Sharpe was:

> opposed to doing camp duty, for which the colonel had him put in the guard house for a week at a time. He was not in the least abashed; but drew the sign, "Sharp's Picture Gallery," and pinned it to his tent; and all day long he had applicants for pictures, which brought him considerable revenue. He did not object to going into all of the battles, but he would not stay in camp.

Any visitor was a welcomed distraction. "Pen cannot paint fully the air of cheerful content, irresponsible laughings, independent action, and practical spirit of jesting that 'obtains' ready to seize on any odd circumstance in its licenced levity," Dr. John Shaffner (33rd NC) wrote in December 1862:

> [A] cavalry-man comes rejoicing in immence top boots, for which in fond pride he has invested full fifty dollars of pay; at once cry from an hundred voices follows him along the line, "Come up out'er them boots!. Too soon to go into Winter Quarters! I know you're in thar—see your arms sticking out!" A green 'un rides by in an incommonly big hat, and is frightened at the shout, "Come down out'er that hat! Come down! 'Taint no use to say you ain't up that—I see your legs hanging out!" A fancy staff Officer was recently horrified at the irreverent reception of his nicely twisted mustache, as he heard from behind innumerable trees, "Take them mice out of your mouth! Take 'em out: no use to say they aint thar—see their tails hanging out!" Another sporting immense whiskers, was urged to "Come out of that bunch of har! I know you are in thar—I see your ears a-working!"[33]

Writing letters occupied many a soldier's free time in camp. These letters were "products of men struggling to depict a situation that was radically different than anything they had endured before. . . . in writing letters home they

---

32 Bennett Smith to Dear Jane, February 24, 1862, private collection; Koonce, *Doctor to the Front*, 13.

33 Alexander, *Reminiscences*, 81; John Shaffner to "My Dearest Friends," December 21, 1862, Shaffner Papers, NCDAH.

Joseph H. Saunders complained in January 1863 that they could not even get any good rumors in winter camp. Saunders would be wounded and captured during Pickett's Charge at Gettysburg, promoted to lieutenant colonel while still in captivity, and not be exchanged until the final weeks of the war.

Histories of the Several Regiments and Battalions from North Carolina

restored a degree of stability to their lives, even though they admitted to readers that they were navigating the unknown." Early in the war, the men passed on every rumor floating through the camps: the war would be over soon, or, they would be able to come home during the summer months when the heat and bugs made living in the coastal areas almost impossible. Once in Virginia, the Carolinians frequently relayed the rumors about being sent back home. "There is sum talk that we are going to be swapt for a regiment in N. C. & go to Wilmington," Andrew Proffitt (18th NC) reported in March 1864. Their letters became more realistic as the war progressed. Even in the middle of it, soldiers often had little news about the war. "It is so terrible dull here that it is almost impossible to write a letter home not even had any camp rumors for several days," Joseph Saunders (33rd NC) lamented in January 1863. Those who could not write themselves enlisted help. In 1862, William Barlow, for example, wrote letters for other members of his regiment. John Tally's 26 surviving letters demonstrate no fewer than 12 different scribes. Some soldiers used the postal service for letters back and forth between North Carolina, but ofttimes a soldier heading home on furlough transported letters, and more frequently, money, for comrades.[34]

34 Peter Carmichael, "Letters Home: Correspondence from Men at War," *The Civil War Monitor* (Summer 2014), 67; Hancock, *Four Brothers in Gray*, 255; William Barlow to unknown,

An abundance of downtime during the winter quickened soldiers' whimsy. For example, the *Fayetteville Observer* ran an ad in February 1864 announcing "A YOUNG MAN of good character and education, is desirous of opening a correspondence with some young Lady upon the subject of matrimony. . . . P.S. A lady in her 'teens' is preferred." Any interested young lady was asked to respond to Major Barney Barton, Lane's brigade."— Barney Barton was a wholly fictitious character.[35]

Soldiers rapidly consumed books and newspapers. Bennett Smith noted that one of his lieutenants, Harvey Bingham, received the *North Carolina Standard*, and his fellow members in the 37th "git to read hit hen we want hit." Chaplain Kennedy wrote in October 1863 he was starting to read Edward Bulwer-Lytton's *My Novel, or Varieties in English Life*.[36]

The men played cards seemingly non-stop. Men were "playing cards[,] ball[,] marbles . . . and almost everything that is wicked in the eyes of God," complained Marion Holland (37th NC). Gambling was against regulations. It cost Capt. Oliver Parks, (33rd NC) his commission, and he was forced to resign in the fall of 1863. He was charged with "conduct highly unbecoming an officer & gentleman" and with "play[ing] at a game of chance [chuck-a-luck] with sundry privates . . . betting & losing money." Even with Parks as a reminder, Brig. Gen. Lane had to publish an order in November 1864 re-emphasizing that: "Gambling in this Brigade is prohibited and those caught at it will be severely punished."[37]

Huge snowfalls made boys of battle-hardened men. The 37th's Octavius Wiggins recalled a "regular blizzard" during the winter of 1863-64. "The only event of interest was an exciting snow ball battle," he wrote, in which, "the 33rd regiment captured the 7th and 18th Regiments 'without a battle'." These three regiments then marched toward the camps of the 28th and 37th Regiments and

---

Company Front, 19; Joseph Saunders to "My Dear Mary," January 26, 1863, Shaffner Papers, NCDAH; Matthew Gianneschi, "A Man from Mecklenburg: 1st Sergeant John Tally and the 'Hornet's Nest Riflemen', North Carolina 37th Regiment, Company I." University of Denver (Master's Thesis) 1998, 118.

35 *Fayetteville Observer*, February 22, 1864.

36 Bennett Smith to "Dear Brother," April 13, 1862, private collection; Kennedy, Diary, October 23, 1863.

37 Marion Holland to unknown, n.d., Gaston County Museum; Jordan, *NC Troops*, 9:159; Special Order, No. 3, HQ, Lane's Brigade, November 18, 1863, General Order Book, 37th NC Infantry, CSA Collection, DU.

challenged them to battle. Skirmishers were thrown out "on the edge of a hill" and the

> enemy soon appeared across an open field with a strong line of skirmishers in front, and the battle opened by their driving our skirmish line in, the three assaulting regiments came to the attack beautifully, but one volley from the 28th and 37th drove them back down the hill; again they returned and again were driven back. Rallying in the valley, they re-formed and made a vigorous assault, breaking our center driving us into our camps, where we retreated to our shanties and surrendered to a pot of rice, bacon and corn bread.[38]

As night fell, many soldiers gathered around the campfires, where "The amateur talent of the regiment relieved the monotony of camp life with entertainments—drama, charade, burlesque." William McLauren of the 18th NC especially enjoyed "a 'Review of the Army,' in which our Irish wit, Ned Stanton, 'riding on an ass' colt,' easily took rank as the burlesque reviewer of the war." Many soldiers also sang songs, songs brought with them from home or learned during the war. Barlow told his wife the men loved to hear him sing, and he was writing songs for others in the 18th. Captain Edward Hale, Jr., Lane's assistant Adjutant General, wrote in early 1864 of the "humdrum notes of a country darkey who 'picks' his camp-made banjo, near our headquarters, each night." Daniel Robinson (37th NC) "played dances" on his fiddle, "including 'Philadelphia girls won't you come out tonight & dance by the light of the moon.' At the all-soldier dances, soldiers who played the girls would tie a rag around one arm."[39]

Lieutenant George Johnson, while the 28th NC was stationed in Wilmington, penned his own version of "Dixie's Land," showing quite a hand at rhyming in the process:

> Away down south in the land of cotton/Times of peace are not forgotten/Look away, look away, look away, Dixie Land.

---

38 Clark, *Histories*, 2:664.

39 Ibid., 18; William Barlow to Wife, December 26, 1862, *Company Front*, 36; *Fayetteville Observer*, February 15, 1864; Daniel Robinson, "Reminiscences," private collection.

For though the cloud of war hangs o'er/We soon shall see its form no more/Look away, look away, look away, Dixie Land.

Chorus:

Then shout "Hurrah for Dixie!" Hurrah! Hurrah!/In Dixie Land we'll take our stand/To live and die for Dixie/Hurrah! Hurrah! We'll live and die for Dixie! 'Tis true their ships our ports blockade/and cruel feet our soil invade; But when the 28th gets there,/The scamps will run in wild despair. When "Norman" brings his boys from "Surry."/The Yankees better move in a hurry The "Invincibles," if well equipped/and led by "Edwards," can't be whipped.

The Yankee rogues would better pack,/When the "Stanley Hunters" find their track! When "Lowe" shall bid his "Farmers" fire/His foes will reap destruction dire.

As "Barringer" leads on his "Grays,"/Full many a Yankee'll end his days. When "Kinyoun" comes with his "Yadkin Boys,"/He'll put an end to the Yankee joys.

And "Martin's Guards of Independence,"/Have fame in store for their destruction. And "Wright" with his "Cleveland Regulators,"/Will send dismay to the Yankee traitors.

And "Speer" with his brilliant "Yadkin Stars"/Will die in defense of the Stars and Bars; While the "Stanley Guards," by "Moody" led/Will be the Yankees' special dread.

The 28th is organized/With "Reeves" and "Lowe" both highly prized; If "Lane" will only be their colonel,/The Yankees' fate will be eternal.[40]

Camp was not always a musical setting: it could be quite dangerous. Chaplain Kennedy wrote in May 1863 that lightning struck a tree in the middle of camp, stunning one soldier. A year later, Capt. T. James Linebarger (28th NC) told of a wind storm that downed several trees while the different regiments were returning from drill. No one in Linebarger's unit was killed, but a falling tree hit a member of the 37th NC, and wounded several others. William McLaurin of the 18th wrote of a musket falling from a stack and discharging

40 Typescript copy in author's possession.

(because of the intense heat, he thought) a round that struck a sleeping George Huggins in the foot. The wound forced Huggins out of the army in 1864. "[T]he accidental discharge of a gun in the hands of a carless comrade" killed Abner Smith of the 37th in March 1862; Francis Groff (33rd NC) "drowned in the Neuse River" in April 1862; James Murphy (7th NC) in October 1862 simply dropped dead one morning during roll call.[41]

Some soldiers pined to see their loved ones. Others were more honest. "So long as I stay in camp, I never want to see you hear," Dr. Alexander wrote. "But if you value your modesty I beg you not to come into camp." However, there were some women in camp who came to nurse wounded family members. Frank Foxhall, a lieutenant in the 33rd NC, died in late June 1862 in the home of a Mr. Warwick, near Richmond. The *Tarborough Southerner* reported that Foxhall's last days were "blest with the presence of his wife" who "administered to his every want." The Warwick house was between the lines, so possibly the Foxhalls came under fire. Joseph Lipe (7th NC) wrote in December 1861 the wives of a couple of soldiers were in camp, and one was expected to stay "to attend to the cooking and make soups for the sick." Marion Holland (37th NC) reported in mid-1862 that Sidney Milholland, his wife, son, and daughter, had all been in camp. Not all women in or near camp were relations. John Conrad reported in October 1861 several washerwomen living just 10 steps behind his tent.[42]

Keeping personally clean, either in camp or on campaign, presented a constant challenge. Soldiers did almost all their bathing in local rivers and creeks. There are a few instances, like immediately after the Maryland campaign, in which entire companies were ordered to bathe in some local body of water. Soldiers frequently complained of a lack of soap and wrote home requesting more. When afforded the opportunity, the men also made lye soap in camp and sold the excess. Vermin, such as body lice, were a serious threat. "I have ordered a barrel of hot water to be brought in as I want to have myself scoulded and scraped," related Joseph Saunders (33rd NC) during winter 1862, "as I have for the first time been infested with the Maryland Rangers or in other words, I

41 Kennedy, Diary, May 14, 1863; Clark, *Histories*, 2:28; James Linebarger to Wife, May 3, 1864, Snuggs Papers, SHC/UNC; *Watauga Democrat*, September 6, 1917; Jordan, *NC Troops*, 4: 509, 9:152.

42 Alexander to Wife, April 7, 1862; *The Tarborough Southerner*, July 19, 1862; Conrad, *Kinfolk of Jacob Conrad*, 288; Lipes to Margaret, December 6, 1861, *Mooresville Tribune*, April 15, 1992; Holland to family, August 18, 1862, Gaston County Museum.

caught two lous on me the other day." Just a few months earlier, John Alexander wrote of seeing 500 men, "from privates to general officers," all with their shirts off, hunting "for those pesky little fellows." The battle with these vermin was one the soldier could never win.[43]

Men also played more comical sports. Several men in the brigade noted when the opportunity afforded itself in the winter months, they went skating. "Tommie," of the 37th NC—probably Thomas L. Norwood— told of this encounter one winter during the war:

> No doubt you had a very pleasant time during Christmas. I should like to have been with you. And I wish I was there now to have some fun skating, Providing my gallante would not lead me into such luck as happened a few days ago on the Rapid Ann river while I was skating. One or two of Virginia['s] fair sex were present and it happened that one of the hats of the crowd blew off and went across the river. I of course immediately darted after it. after having obtained this hat on my return my skate came off and I went through the ice in about twenty feet of water. Of course I fell in I let loose the hat. but soon I got out and found that the damsel had her hat. She (of course) said she was sorry—and (of course) I said it did not matter. (but it did make a considerable matter for I thought I would Freeze.) She insisted that I should take her shawl. I declined for I knew what the consequences would [be]. she might never get her shawl again. but she kept insisting I should take it so to my great pleasure she folded it around me. I immediately got on my horse and started for camp. But the best part now . . . when she put the shawl around me [I forgot] to inquire her name and her place of residence. so there I was—had some lady's large double shawl and I perfectly ignorant of anything about her.[44]

Regulations stipulated that soldiers were to be paid every two months. That responsibility fell upon the quartermaster's department. Every two months, the company officers labored over the muster and pay rolls,

---

43 Lane, "History of Lane's North Carolina Brigade," *SHSP*, 10:208; Saunders to "Dear Ann," December 27, 1862; Alexander, *Reminiscences*, 73. Schroeder-Lein writes the "initial discovery of lice on one's person embarrassed many soldiers, who sought to rid themselves of the pest in private." As time went on, it was realized everyone had lice, and the creative soldiers even caught the "greybacks" and held races with them. *The Encyclopedia of Civil War Medicine*, 186.

44 "Tommie" to "Mamie," January 20 [1864?], Giles Family Papers, SHC/UNC. It is unclear who wrote this letter, but the writer stated he was writing from the headquarters of the 37th Regiment.

documenting who was present, absent, on furlough, sick, captured, missing, or killed. These forms were forwarded up the chain of command. A private received $11 a month, a sergeant, $17, a captain, $130, and the colonel, $195. However, the system was disrupted frequently. Morris of the 37th reported in February 1862 that the quartermaster had been to Raleigh, but he could draw funds only in $100 bills—"[T]hat Sort of Money would Not be of any use in Camp," Morris lamented. The enlisted men often lined up in front of a table, and, after signing some type of receipt, received their pay. Officers were paid privately, often in their quarters. Letters home rarely failed to mention pay disruptions.

In October 1862, Morris reported that the men had not been paid in three months because the regimental quartermaster, Robert Oats, had been absent sick. Morris thought the men would be paid soon, but confessed he didn't wish to draw his pay until he had a way of sending a portion home. Joseph Joyner, the 7th's Regiment's ordnance sergeant, wrote in June 1864 that he had not been paid in eight months. The following month, he penned that the enlisted men were getting paid, but he still had no money because acting quartermaster Thomas Williamson had forgotten to get the muster rolls for the field and staff. The men's money—what was not spent on supplementing rations or squandered gambling—was sent home by the most secure means. It was still a risky venture. Chaplain Kennedy reported in mid-1863 that, while in Charlotte, he had the "misfortune" to lose his pocketbook that contained "6 or 7 hundred dollars . . . most the property of others." He was probably taking this money to families back home. If a soldier died in camp, a fellow soldier or family member often retrieved whatever money he had on him and held it for the family. Lieutenant Dan Boger (7th NC) wrote to his sister on the death of her husband, Nelson Bost, in August 1864. Bost had $100 on him when he died. Boger also sold Bost's canteen for $5.00, gave his tin cup to another soldier, and the soap he had to the entire company. If a soldier died while in service, his family could file a claim to receive any remaining salary due him. This process took time, however, and often involved the services of a lawyer. James Baxter (7th NC) died in a hospital in Richmond on August 5, 1862, after Frayser's Farm. A month later, his widow Margaret filed for the money owed to Baxter. Confederate authorities finally determined Baxter had been due $45.10 back pay, plus a $50.00 bounty. However, the funds were not released until April 1864.[45]

From time to time, the soldiers also received new clothing. A few companies arrived in camp already wearing uniforms. Company H, 18th NC, wore two buff-colored slings across their bodies, supporting a cartridge box on one side and a bayonet scabbard on the other. A breastplate adorned with an eagle, much like those worn by Federal soldiers, occupied the center. The kepis were of a lighter color gray, or sky-blue, with a darker band of material. The waist belts featured a common roller buckle. Another company of the 18th NC, Company E, arrived wearing dark-blue nine-button frock coats with red cuffs. Many of the other companies in the brigade arrived wearing their common, everyday clothing.

On May 27, 1861, a general order was issued to North Carolina regiments, creating a uniform for new troops: a gray sack coat of North Carolina manufacture, extending half-way down the thigh, with falling collar, six buttons, and, for infantry, epaulets of black cloth sewn onto the jacket; trousers were made of the same material, with a black stripe down the outside of each leg. Hats to be made of gray felt, and pinned on one side, with the company letter and regimental designation on the front. Per regulations, officers were prescribed to wear dark blue frock coats. Enlisted men were issued uniforms. Officers were not. Judging from photographs, it appears all of the regiments, save the 37th, received these early North Carolina Depot uniforms. Since scholars believe the supply of these early uniforms ran out in September 1861, it is possible most of the 33rd did not receive them either. New uniforms, with a shorter jacket sans the black trim, began appearing in spring, 1862. In October that year, the Confederate government assumed the responsibility of supplying uniforms to troops in its army. However, North Carolina continued to supply her soldiers with uniforms of her own manufacture. In 1863, the state began importing cloth from England through the blockade to supplement local production.[46]

---

45 *Confederate Regulations*, 109, 176; William Morris to "Deare Companion," February 8, 1862, October 5, 1862, Morris Letters, SHC/UNC; Joseph Joyner to "My Dear Mother," June 19, 1864, July 17, 1864, Joyner Papers SHC/UNC; Kennedy, Diary, August 6, 1863; Dan Boger to "Dear Sister," August 27, 1864, private collection; James Baxter, Roll 171, M270, RG109, CMSR, NA.

46 Mast, *State Troops*, 87, 88. Robin Smith and Ron Field, *Uniforms of the Civil War* (McLean, VA, 2001), 244.

Of course, actually getting state-supplied uniforms to the troops in the field was an entirely different challenge. Regiments lost everything except what they had on their backs when New Bern was abandoned in March 1862. The 37th NC moved personal effects to a nearby farmhouse right before the battle, and when it went against them, they were forced to burn the house and its contents. William Morris lost everything, including his uniform, and wrote home he was wearing his "Brown soote." Officers usually had a dress uniform, and something less formal for everyday wear or battle. An officer wearing his best, with braid, sash, and sword, made a conspicuous target. The weeks after New Bern were hard on the men. During active campaigning, clothes and shoes often wore out quickly. In battles like Chancellorsville and the Wilderness, the underbrush often tore their clothes, not to mention the effects of shot and shell filling the air.[47]

Soldiers in the Branch-Lane brigade were able to supplement their clothing with items gleaned from the fields following Federal defeats. Morris of the 37th noted after the Seven Days campaign, the enemy had left tons of equipment, including knapsacks, haversacks, weapons, and clothing. Not knowing how much he could carry, he contented himself with an oilcloth and pin case with a "very Nice Kneedle." Months later, after the capture of Harpers Ferry, he had acquired "Clothes plenty to Doo Ma all winter." Likewise, Leonard Alman (7th NC, wrote that the field at Chancellorsville was strewn with "Guns, knapsacks, blankets, overcoats, Haver Sacks, and everything you could think of. . . . this paper I am writing I took from a yankee knapsack also a nice portfolio for carrying pens ink & papers." John Conrad (28th NC) wrote home in November 1862 that the men in his company were purchasing blankets for $10 from the Confederate cavalry, who had captured them just a few days earlier. Once the men settled into trench warfare in mid-1864, these opportunities to supplement their clothing from the enemy virtually ceased.[48]

A visitor to a camp, or accompanying the army on campaign, would have observed many persons of color. A few of these were freemen who voluntarily

---

47 William Morris to "Deare Companion," March 16, 1862, Morris Letters, SHC/UNC.

48 Ibid., July 6, 1862, September 24, 1862; "Civil War Letters. . . Conrad," 317; Leonard Alman to "My Dear Wife," May 13, 1863, Leonard Alman Papers, DU. Overall, North Carolina did a good job supplying her soldiers with uniforms throughout the war. Photographs of brigade members show most men wearing what appears to be North Carolina depot clothing, with a couple of Richmond Depot-issued jackets. See, for example, Mast, *State Troops and Volunteers*, 41, 175, 252, 260, 300, 336, 349.

Aaron Perry was just one of an undocumented number of slaves who accompanied their masters to war.

North Carolina Museum of History

joined the Confederate army, such as William Henry Cousins and his brother Franklin of the 37th NC. They both lived in Watauga County and were kidnapped to serve as camp servants by a cavalry company commander headed to war. State representative Mark Holtsclaw secured their release, and the pair voluntarily joined the army in September 1861. Franklin was killed fighting at Manassas, and William Henry served as a teamster for much of the war. Another set of the Cuzzens family incuded Bloom and Lemuel Cuzzens (28th NC), free persons of color from Yadkin County. Bloom deserted on June 30, 1862, and Lemuel died of disease or "typhoid fever" the following month. John Polk, apparently a freeman from Gaston County, volunteered as a bodyguard for Col. Samuel Lowe, 28th NC.[49]

Some officers brought slaves from home to serve them in camp. Whether officially members of the brigade, or simply there as servants, they performed valuable service to the Confederate cause. William McLaurin (18th NC) wrote that often his "negro boy, Jack," brought him haversacks of food while he was on the front lines. John Ashcraft, originally a captain and later lieutenant colonel of the 37th NC, owned Aaron Perry, who likely went to work on the fortifications at Fort Fisher after Ashcraft left the army in May 1863. John Alexander (37th NC) struggled with his servant Bob, who had disappeared and

---

49 Mark Holesclaw to John Ellis, June 17, 1861, Noble J. Tolbert, ed., *The Papers of John Willis Ellis* 2 vols. (Raleigh, NC, 1964), 2:844; Jordan, *NC Troops,* 8:177, 9:488. The brothers' names are listed as Cozzens, Cossens, and Cousins. Jordan, *NC Troops,* 8:148. A John Polk appears in the 1860 US census, living in the King's Mountain area of Gaston County. Polk was a 35-year-old freeman.

was caught and jailed in Richmond. In July 1862, Alexander thought it best to sell Bob. In February 1863, he was still writing to his wife about Bob and what he thought he could get for him. Whether he ever parted with Bob is unclear. The number of people of color working in the camps, driving wagons, and serving in the ranks will never be known.[50]

Day-to-day life of the Tar Heel soldiers in the Branch-Lane brigade was a struggle. During the spring, summer, and fall, and even at times in the winter, they had to be ready to move at a moment's notice. At the same time, they spent days penned up inside their winter quarters, only moving about to go stand picket. Despite numerous diversions and times of gaiety and fun, they were still under the army's control, an experience many of them resented. For these, the long drum roll summoned them from the doldrums of camp life, and off they marched toward the enemy once again.

---

50 Clark, *Histories*, 2:55-56; Pension Application for Aaron Perry, Union County, NC, February 4, 1929, NCDAH; Jordan. *NC Troops*, 8:148; Alexander to "Dear Wife," July 26, 1862, February 21, 1863, Alexander Papers, UNC. Richard J. Rodrigues lists 12 black men who filed for pensions after the war, claiming service in the Branch-Lane brigade. *Black Confederates in the U.S. Civil War: A Compiled List of Africans who served the Confederacy* (Charleston, SC, 2010), 99-111.

Chapter 10

"I reckon the Devil himself would have run with Jackson in his rear."

Chancellorsville

Although not the coldest winter of the war, that of 1862-63 brought abject misery for Lee's army. Soldiers struggled to stay warm while fighting off the doldrums of winter quarters. On January 15, 1863, the brigade went into winter camp at Camp Gregg. Poor roads and heavy rains led the brigade to build a "pole" road in February, connecting the camp with the closest railroad depot. Many furloughs were granted, although never enough to suit the men, a few of whom slipped off home without permission. Some eventually returned, following an order encouraging men to rejoin their commands by March 10. If they did so, they were reprieved from disciplinary action for being absent without leave. Some deserters' cases were handled during a week of brigade-level courts-martial in mid-February. While these actions engaged many of the officers, common soldiers had little excitement.

March 27 was an official day of fasting and prayer, one of several during the war. "I preached this morning from Psalms 8th Cp., 3-4 verses, the largest audience I have ever addressed in camp—nearly the entire regiment was out and quite a number from neighboring Regiment [37th]," Chaplain Kennedy

(28th NC) wrote. "The men seem to appreciate the importance of a proper observance of the day. . . . Pretty nearly all the men too fasted. . . . I feel hopeful of the influence of the day's work in the Confederacy."[1]

Three days later, with the entire brigade formed into a hollow square, Kennedy witnessed the presentation of a sword, belt, sash, saddle, and bridle to General Lane by the brigade officers. Colonel Barber stood in the center as commanders of the other regiments escorted Lane. Speaking on the history of the brigade, Barber lamented the dead, particularly the "chivalric and high-souled Col. Campbell" of the 18th Regiment, the "pure and noble Lee" of the 37th, and the "gallant and patriotic" General Branch, who had "sealed his devotion to his country with his heart's blood, on the hard fought field of Sharpsburg." Barber then presented the sword to Lane promising him that "his brigade would never fail him." "Many of you," Lane declared in response to the men, "bear upon your persons *honored scars, silent witnesses* of the dangers you have encountered and bravely faced in defence of all that a freeman holds dear." At the conclusion of the brief ceremony, the men of the 28th Regiment wanted to give Lane three cheers, but Col. Lowe thought it "would appear rather out of taste."[2]

Little military action transpired during the winter months of 1863. Hill held a grand review of the Light Division on January 6. On January 19, Burnside launched a second attempt to cross the Rappahannock River. A winter storm that started during the evening of the next day quickly brought an end to the campaign, dubbed the "Mud March." On January 25, Maj. Gen. Joseph Hooker replaced Burnside as commander of the Army of the Potomac. In mid-February, General Lee dispatched two divisions of Longstreet's corps to southeastern Virginia in response to a build-up of Federal troops there. Otherwise all was quiet.

In late March orders sent surplus baggage to Richmond, suspended furloughs and reduced transportation— unmistakable signs to Lane's brigade and the rest of the army that campaigning season was upon them. Many soldiers observed Federal intelligence-gathering balloons floating off in the distance "[T]here is to be Seen two yankey Balloons in the air Every cleare day on the opposite Side of the river," one officer in the brigade wrote on April 15. "I recon they are afraid that old 'Stonewall' will pounce down on them unawares if

1   Kennedy, Diary, March 27-30, 1863, SHC/UNC.

2   *Western Democrat*, April 28, 1863.

they don't keep their eyes open," another member of the 37th wrote. Each day of warmer weather and drier roads shortened the time until the long roll beat and sent the men out of winter camps and toward the front; and everyone knew it. Many of the soldiers stood ready "to meet old Joe Hooker and his horde of vandals," wrote a member of the 28th NC, anxious to "give them such a thrashing that they will never more return."[3]

By April 29, an active campaign was clearly underway. Hooker's plan was three-fold: Federal cavalry would strike for the Confederate rear and break its lines of communication to Richmond; a portion of the Federal infantry would cross the Rappahannock River at Fredericksburg and threaten attack over the same ground Burnside had failed so miserably to carry that past December; finally, the bulk of the Army of the Potomac would march up the Rappahannock, crossing it and then the Rapidan River, and come up on Lee's flank and rear. The Army of Northern Virginia would thereby be forced to retreat, or to give battle on ground of Hooker's choosing. With Lee's army out of the way, Richmond would be vulnerable to capture. "My plans are perfect, and when I start to carry them out, may God have mercy on General Lee, for I will have none," Hooker wrote.[4]

Federal soldiers began marching on April 27, crossing Kelly's Ford on the Rappahannock River on April 28. Jackson quickly ordered his divisions to be on the road by 3:00 a.m. on April 29. Apparently those orders reached various commands slowly. Many in Lane's brigade remembered receiving orders to move at a moment's notice on April 29. A member of the 37th NC wrote that just 15 minutes elapsed between the preemptory order and the actual order to march, after which the men "left behind . . . a car load or two of used up articles." George Cochran recalled years later that the 37th NC marched out of camp and lined up while a fellow soldier was buried. "The thunder of artillery up the river reminded every one of us now attending the burial of a comrade would soon join the departed soldier from a field to be immortalized by another bloody battle between the soldiers of the North and South." Foggy, rainy weather helped conceal the movements of Jackson's corps. The Light Division arrived near Hamilton's Crossing that evening. Chaplain Kennedy had a prayer

---

3   OR 25,2:681; William Morris to "Dear Companion," April 15, 1863, Morris Papers, & Lewis Battle to Mother, April 17, 1863, Battle Family Papers, both in SHC/UNC; *North Carolina Standard*, April 8, 1863.

4   Stephen Sears, *Chancellorsville* (New York, 1996), 120.

with the soldiers of the 28th NC before bedding down shelterless in their rain-drenched trenches.[5]

April 30 dawned cool and misty. Scattered morning clouds gave way to a rainy afternoon. Later, the men worked on strengthening their breastworks. Yet tools were sparse, only one axe and one spade per company. A member of the 37th remembered they "used bayonets and anything with which we could gouge up dirt." Throughout the day, Federal artillery shelled the men as they reinforced their position. "At first the whizzing messengers came at long intervals," remembered one, "and the famous expression 'nobody hurt' would move pleasantly along the line, but as they came nearer and rapidly, the boys adopted the better part of valor, and lay close in their entrenchments."[6]

Although it took time for Lee to discern Hooker's plans, by May 1, he had concluded that the Federals in his front at Fredericksburg were but a ploy. The real threat was coming from the west. Yet the Federals at Fredericksburg were more than a mere line of skirmishers; some 60,000 of them confronted Lee there. His own army, with Longstreet's two divisions still absent to the east, numbered but 61,000 men. Contemporary military theory dictated that a general should never divide his army in the presence of a numerically superior foe. Audaciously, Lee did exactly that. Early's division, augmented by William Barksdale's Mississippi brigade, with artillery, remained at Fredericksburg to hold the Federals. Hooker had another estimated 70,000 Federal soldiers moving toward Lee from the west. Lee had already dispatched the divisions of Richard Anderson and Lafayette McLaws westward, building breastworks and blocking the roads, and Jackson's entire corps soon followed them.

Jackson had his men on the march around 4:00 a.m. on May 1. The 10-mile march took all day. The column marched two or three miles then halted and waited, probably at Salem Church, frequently stopping thereafter. Octavius Wiggins (37th NC) witnessed General Lee pass the marching column, greeted by "deafening" cheers. Around 11:00 a.m., Jackson sent Anderson and McLaws toward the Federals. Once contact was made, Hooker lost his resolve and pulled his forces back toward the village of Chancellorsville, into a heavily wooded area known as the Wilderness. Late in the day, Lane's brigade was ordered to load weapons, and Wiggins recalled seeing Lee and Jackson "seated

---

5   *North Carolina Standard*, June 2, 1863; Cochran, *A Brief Sketch*, 38; *Weekly State Journal*, May 20, 1863; Kennedy, Diary, April 29, 1863, SHC/UNC.

6   *North Carolina Standard*, June 2, 1863; Cochran, *A Brief Sketch*, 39.

under a tree where we filed out of the road . . . to form a line of battle." Hill ordered Heth's, McGowan's, and Lane's brigades to push on toward Chancellorsville. Heth encountered stiff resistance, though, and with daylight fading, the advance halted about a mile and a half from the hamlet. Enemy shelling wounded several men as Lane formed his brigade into a line of battle. At some point that evening, the 18th NC, in support of an artillery battery, sustained a few casualties when a nearby caisson exploded. Sporadic skirmishing continued throughout the night.[7]

Meanwhile Lee and Jackson were meeting nearby, devising a plan to defeat the Federal army. Confederate cavalry reconnaissance indicated that the Federal right flank was "hanging," unfortified and unanchored. In light of this intelligence, Lee again chose to divide his command, sending Jackson with 28,000 men, his entire corps, across the front of the Federal army, to attack their exposed flank and rear. The movement left Lee with just 13,000 men, supported by artillery, to distract Hooker and his army while Jackson executed his flanking maneuver.

While Jackson wanted the march to begin at sunrise, it was 7:00 a.m. before the lead elements stepped off. The Light Division, bringing up the rear of the column, did not move until 10:00 a.m. Adjutant McLaurin was sent to recall the 18th NC skirmishers while other orders to the regiments mandated that officers, accompanied by a strong guard with bayonets fixed, be sent to the rear of their commands to prevent straggling. Jackson was spotted riding to the right. When he returned a short time later, Lane's brigade moved off, under orders not to cheer Stonewall if he passed. "The march was quite slow," remembered Octavius Wiggins, "until we passed the 'Furnace.'" An opening in the woods provided the Federals with a glimpse of the flanking force as it passed, allowing Federal artillery to fire on the moving column. From that point on, all the regiments moved at the double quick through the opening. "Then we let out in earnest," Wiggins continued. Despite previous hard marches, "this differed from all others in severity. There was no particular road part of the time, and it would seem as if we were marching in a foot-path just broad enough for one man. When we would pass that, of course, a double quick was in order." In another account, Wiggins wrote: "On we rushed jumping bushes, branches up and down hills." Several Federals reported the presence of Jackson's

---

7 Harris, *Historical Sketches*, 29; Octavius Wiggins, "Address to the United Daughters of the Confederacy." NCDAH; *The Weekly Standard*, June 3, 1863; OR 25/1:919.

command, but Hooker believed the Confederate army was retreating toward Gordonsville.[8]

The head of Jackson's column turned right on the Orange Turnpike about 2:30 that afternoon. They had covered 12 miles, but were only 5-6 miles from where they had started a few hours earlier. It took time to deploy two infantry divisions: Rodes in the front, followed by Colston, in the thick woods on either side of the turnpike. For many years the trees had been harvested to make charcoal, and the returning vegetation was thick, almost impassable in places. Confederate troops lined both sides of the turnpike. Pender's and Heth's brigades of the Light Division were posted behind Colston's command to the north of the road. Lane's brigade, just coming up, remained in column on the turnpike. Federal infantry waited just one-half mile to the east. Although not all of his infantry was up, Jackson checked with Rodes and gave the order to launch the assault. I was about 5:30 p.m. Bugles sounded, followed soon by a scattering of shots from pickets and the blood-curdling screech of the Rebel yell. The Confederates had caught the Federal line on the flank and quickly routed an entire corps. Federal soldiers "did run and no mistake about it—but I never blamed them," Wiggins wrote. "I would have done the same thing and so would you and I reckon the Devil himself would have run with Jackson in his rear."[9]

Jackson's advance caught the Federals in the midst of fixing supper. "Fires were burning in every direction over which were pots filled with fresh beef. The Yankees were cooking supper for Jackson's men." Apparently, Confederate commissaries issued no rations the morning before the advance, so many of Jackson's troops quickly grabbed something as they charged. "It was an easy thing to slip out of ranks and charge some of these pots and many an old 'reb'. . . brought his supper from the bottom of them on the point of his bayonet " There was more than just food for the taking. In their haste, the Federals abandoned or threw away anything impeding their flight, such as "napsacks an

---

8   Clark, *Histories*, 1:191, 2:36; *The Daily Review*, April 10, 1884; Wiggins, "Address to UDC," NCDAH. An anonymous member of the 37th, writing about the same time as Archer, states Lane's brigade stepped off "near eight o'clock." *The Weekly Standard*, June 3, 1863. The 10:00 a.m. start time is based upon a letter written on May 8, 1863, most likely by a member of the 33rd. *Weekly State Journal*, May 20, 1863.

9   Wiggins, "Address to UDC," NCDAH.

blankets an overcoats an a heep of ther coking utensels," according to William Howard (18th NC).[10]

Lane's troops struggled to keep up with the advancing lines of battle. As the main Confederate lines crashed through the woods, Lane's men ran double quick down the road. Dead and dying Federal soldiers "lay thick in every direction." Lewis Battle (37th NC) said, "Our spirits were so high we could scarcely hold ourselves to the ground, for we could see as we passed along the road at least ten dead Yankees to our one," including the wreckage of an ill-conceived Federal cavalry charge.[11]

By 7:30 p.m., the Confederate advance began to falter. Rodes's and Colston's divisions became intermixed, tangled in the terrain and spent by their march and pursuit of the foe. General Rodes called a halt to try reorganizing his command. The sun had set about an hour before, and the moon, just one night shy of being full, began to rise, casting eerie shadows throughout the twisted, snarled woods. Not only did the two lead divisions stop, but so did Lane, who was following artillery, still standing in the road. Near the brigade stood some earthworks the Federals had built the previous day. Jackson was nearby, attempting to help other officers rally and untangle the Confederate infantry. As Jackson rode by the 18th NC, one of its captains remembered making "that wilderness ring with their cheers" as he passed. Jackson "took off his hat in recognition of their salutation." During this lull in the fighting, Jackson ordered Hill to bring up his men. He meant to continue the advance and cut off the Federal line of retreat at U.S. Ford over the Rappahannock. Hill picked Lane's brigade to spearhead a rare night-time attack. He ordered Lane to throw out a regiment as skirmishers and form the rest of the brigade behind them. Once in position, Hill wanted Lane "to push vigorously forward."[12]

Confederate artillery just ahead of Lane on the road opened fire, drawing a response from a nearby enemy battery. Shell fragments covered the road, and Lane ordered his men to lie down where they were, while he and the rest of his staff dismounted and sought shelter in the woods on the left side of the road. "[W]e. . . buried our faces as close to the ground as possible," wrote one

10 Ibid.; Howard, Diary, May 2, 1863, NCDAH.

11 *Raleigh Weekly Standard*, June 3, 1863; Lewis Battle to Mother, May 22, 1863, Battle Papers, SHC/UNC.

12 Krick, *Civil War Weather*, 94; JL to August Hamlin, 1892, Lane Papers, AU;, Early, *Autobiographical Sketch*, 213; *Fayetteville Observer*, February 20, 1884; OR 25/1:916.

Carolinian, "and I expect some of us rubbed the skins off our noses trying to get under it . . . one of my men resorted to prayer—I expect we all did the same thing. . . . He went down low and loud—long and strong." Another wrote that "Burning shells, shriek and scream through the heavens in all directions." Morris of the 37th NC recalled an artillery round going off feet in front of him, wounding him in the foot and killing several members of the 18th Regiment. Morris rolled into a cut on the side of the road to shield himself from further shrapnel.[13]

Hill sent one of his staff officers to inquire why Lane's brigade was not deploying as ordered. Lane told the officer he didn't want to lose his brigade and was "unwilling to attempt to form my line in the dark, under such a fire and in such a woods." In a post-war letter, Lane wrote, "All old soldiers know how difficult it is to maneuver the bravest troops in the dark under a murderous fire, through scrubby oaks & pine thickets, & over the abatis of the enemy's abandoned works." Lane suggested that Hill order the artillery to stop firing, which would perhaps silence the Federal artillery. The staff officer traversed the fragment-strewn road again, delivering Lane's response, and Hill ordered the Confederate artillery to desist. Soon thereafter, the enemy counter-battery fire indeed halted as well. The artillery duel had lasted some 15 minutes.[14]

Lane ordered Col. Avery to deploy the 33rd as skirmishers. Avery took his regiment and advanced 250 yard to the crest of a hill on their front, fanning out on either side of the Orange Plank Road to cover the brigade. Lane cautioned Avery not to fire into Rodes's men, whom Hill's division had come to relieve. Avery soon reported no other Confederates to their front. The brigade advanced about 100 yards after the bombardment before deploying to either side of the road, according to one Carolinian. The 7th and the 37th NC filed off to the right, with the 37th's left anchored on the Plank Road. The 28th and 18th NC filed off to the left, with the right of the 18th likewise still on the road. Portions of Stuart's Horse Artillery maintained a position on the Plank Road in front of the brigade's center. "The woods in front of our right was of large oaks with but little undergrowth," wrote Lane, "in rear of our right there was a pine

13 JL to August Hamlin, 1892; Wiggins, "Address to UDC," NCDAH; *North Carolina Standard*, June 2, 1863; `William Morris to JL, January 3, 1895, SHC/UNC.

14   JL to Marcellus Moorman, "Narrative of Events and Observations Connected with the Wounding of General T. J. (Stonewall) Jackson," *SHSP*, 30:111-13; JL to Augustus Hamlin, 1892, AU.

Lt. Gen. Thomas J. "Stonewall" Jackson, commander of the Second Corps, was mortally wounded at the height of his fame after leading a crushing attack against the exposed right flank of the Army of the Potomac.

Library of Congress

thicket . . . to the left of the road there was a dense growth of 'scrubby oaks' through which it was almost impossible for troops to move."[15]

Once Lane formed the brigade, he rode back to the Plank Road, seeking further orders from Hill. Stonewall Jackson recognized Lane's voice in the darkness engulfing the Wilderness. "Lane, whom are you looking for?" he called out. "Gen. Hill," came the reply, "who ordered me to form my line for a night attack, which I have done, and I now wish to know whether I must advance or await further orders . . . but General, I do not know where Gen. Hill is." To save time, Lane asked for orders. "[W]ith a gesture with his right hand in the direction of the enemy," Jackson responded. "Push right ahead Lane." After this, Jackson rode forward, and it "was the last time I ever saw him." Lane rode toward his line's right to get his command moving.[16]

Jackson, with several members of his staff and escort following behind him, rode down the Orange Plank Road. They passed the left flank of the 37th Regiment first. Thomas Lowery, according to his family, saw the general ride by, and warned him. "I wouldn't go in there now. It's too dark, and your men may take you for the enemy and shoot you." Jackson and his staff rode on,

15 Harris, *Historical Sketches*, 28; JL to Henry McClellan, May 14, 1885, *The Life and Campaigns of Major General J. E. B. Stuart* (Boston, MA, 1885), 242; James Lane, "The Death of Stonewall Jackson," *Fayetteville Observer*, January 23, 1884; 494; Wiggins, "Address to UDC," NCDAH; Moorman, "Narrative of Events," SHSP, 30:115; JL to Augustus Hamlin, 1892, AU.

16 *Fayetteville Observer*, January 23, 1884; JL to Augustus Hamlin, 1892, AU.

though, past the 18th's right flank. A member of the regiment, Richard Reeves, recalled many years later "standing under a large oak tree," when "Jackson came riding up. He told us the enemy was very near us and we must watch and listen and at the least noise, Fire, as it would be the foe. He rode away looking the gallant soldier he was." A moment later, Hill rode up with his staff, stopping on the Orange Plank Road to converse with Jackson. After urging Hill to push the attack forward, Jackson rode toward the 33rd and the Federal lines, leaving Hill there on the road between the 18th and 37th Regiments.[17]

Lane rode back along his line to his brigade's far right. Near 9:00 p.m., he instructed his colonels to "keep a bright lookout, as we were in front of everything & would soon be ordered forward to make a night attack." However, as he approached, Lane encountered a dilemma. Nearby Federals were calling out to their enemies, wanting to know whose brigade they were. "General Lane's," was the reply. "Tell General Lane to come in," retorted a Federal. Unsatisfied with their inquiry, Lt. Col. Levi Smith of the 128th PA, stumbled into the 7th NC, bearing a white flag. Smith stated he was simply trying to learn whether the troops in front of him were friends or foes. Much to Smith's chagrin, Lane refused let him return to the Federal lines. Instead he sent his brother and aide, Oscar Lane, back to Hill for instructions about what to do with Smith. Meanwhile, Lt. Col. Junius Hill approached Lane, imploring him not to advance. Hill had heard "noises which satisfied them that troops of some kind were on" the brigade's right. Lane agreed, and Hill sent Lt. James Emack with four men to investigate.[18]

Out in front of the brigade's line of battle, the 33rd was spread out in a line large enough to cover the brigade's front. Colonel Cowan and Lt. Col. Saunders, once the line was posted, returned toward the main line and found General Hill, probably on the Orange Plank Road. The General told the pair their objective was Chancellorsville, "to push on, drive the enemy out of that, then we would have them on the hip." On the far right of the skirmish line, a Federal officer rode into the lines, shouting for General Williamson. First Sergeant Thomas Cowan called out to the officer, Brig. Gen. Joseph Knipe,

---

17 Note, Ray Lowery to author, June 12, 2001, in my possession; Richard Reeves, "Our Confederate Veterans," Richmond NBP; Robertson, *Stonewall Jackson*, 726. Hamlin's account says some officers in the 18th NC claimed Jackson turned off the road and passed to their rear. Hamlin, *The Battle of Chancellorsville*, 108.

18 *OR* 25/1:916, 918; JL to Augustus Hamlin, 1892, AU.

who identified himself as a friend. "[F]riend to which side?" was Cowan's inquiry, to which Knipe answered "to the Union." "All right," Cowan responded, stepping back to his company and ordering his men to fire into the area of the voice in the darkness. This brought a quick response from Federal infantry and artillery.[19]

Emack and his squad, probing for information about the troops ahead of them, had stumbled off into the woods toward the brigade's front and right. Out in the darkness, the Federals were demanding the return of their colonel. Not far from the brigade's front, Emack ran into the 128th Pennsylvania, and, raising his sword, yelled "Men, Jackson has surrounded you; down with your guns, else we will shoot the last one of you." Almost 200 Pennsylvania troops surrendered. The Union lieutenant colonel, Smith, standing by Lane, protested as his men were marched into Confederate lines. Lane, he said, "had no right to capture them under the circumstances," Smith's protest was cut short when fire from Federal small arms and artillery raked Lane's lines, in response to the incident between Knipe and the 33rd. The Union prisoners took shelter behind the abandoned works to Lane's rear, ironically, the same works they had been sent to occupy.[20]

Colonel Purdie positioned the 18th Regiment to the left of the Orange Plank Road, with the 28th to his left. His adjutant, William McLaurin, claimed later he did not know the 33rd had been deployed on the brigade's front as skirmishers. Upon hearing noises on his unit's front, Purdie called for McLaurin, and the two of them walked out into the darkness along the Plank Road. Soon they encountered Col. Avery and Capt. George Sanderlin of the 33rd NC, whereupon a scattering of shots somewhere "two or three hundred yards in our front, to the right side of the road," led Purdie and McLaurin to hasten back toward the 18th.[21]

19 *Fayetteville Weekly Observer*, February 6, 1884. Ernest Furguson gives a slightly different account of the exchange between Cowan and Knipe. see *Chancellorsville 1863: The Souls of the Brave* (New York, 1992), 198. Lane, in his account to Hamlin in 1892, writes Emack was detached with four other men. In a widely reprinted 1873 article, Lane writes Emack was sent out with five men. See *The Wilmington Morning Star*, January 4, 1873.

20 Moorman, "Narrative of events"; JL to Augustus Hamlin, 1892, AU; Captain John Young (18th NC) and his company escorted the prisoners to the rear. When Young returned later that evening, he distributed several captured swords among the officers of his regiment. Harris, *Historical Sketches*, 29.

21 Clark, *Histories*, 2:37.

The 7th NC had joined the 33rd in blazing away at the Federals, raising a racket that "gave it every semblance of a battle." Having just captured almost 200 Federal soldiers not far from their front, they assumed other enemy troops could be nearby. Lane cautioned his men to keep a "bright lookout" ahead. The 37th NC, to the left of the 7th Regiment, joined them in emptying their muskets toward an unknown foe in the darkness, toward the Orange Plank Road. There Moorman's artillery had just limbered up, waiting to be relieved by a fresh battery. Moorman rushed toward the 37th, crying out, "What are you firing at? Are you trying to kill all my men in front of you? There are no Yankees here." Noah Collins (37th NC) wrote he had fired one round and had loaded to fire again when the officers regained control of the men.[22]

The firing rolled on down Lane's line. In front of the 18th Regiment came the sound of horses in the woods, moving in their direction from the Orange Plank Road. Colonel Purdie, still out in front of the regiment, ordered the men to "Fix bayonets; load; prepare for action!" Someone in the regiment yelled "Cavalry," and the men poured a volley into the woods. "Cease firing! You are firing into our own men," came a desperate shout through the smoke and darkness. "Who gave that order!" retorted Major Barry (18th NC). "It's a lie! Pour it into them, boys!" With that, sheets of flame from the rifles and muskets leapt out once again into the darkness. John Frink (18th NC) recalled a stricken horse falling just three feet in front of him. The 28th Regiment likewise fired a volley into the night.[23]

Nevertheless, the voices crying out in the Wilderness had been correct. Unbeknownst to the brigade's officers and all but a few in the ranks, Stonewall Jackson and A. P. Hill, with their staffs, had ridden through the lines and toward the enemy. Some accounts have Jackson taking the Mountain Road and stopping behind the 33rd's skirmish line, listening to the Federals bringing up reinforcements and strengthening their lines. Other accounts have the group advancing on the Orange Plank Road. Adjutant Spier Whitaker later wrote that

---

22 Wiggins, "Address to UDC," NCDAH; Moorman, "Narrative of Events," SHSP, 30:115; Collins, "Reminisces," 36.

23 *Fayetteville Observer*, January 2, 1884; Clark, *Histories*, 2:73, 5:99; *Land We Love* (July 1866), 181. Alfred Tolar (18th NC) wrote after the war the "night was calm and the tramp of thirty horsemen advancing through a heavy forest at a rapid gait, seemed to the average infantryman like a brigade of cavalry." Clark, *Histories*, 5:99. According to ordnance returns, the 18th, 28th, and 37th Regiments all carried some smoothbore muskets. Jackson was struck by the buck-and-ball rounds these muskets fired. Ordnance Returns, Bryant Papers, SHC/UNC; *The San Angelo Daily*, April 20, 1926.

Major John D. Barry of the 18th North Carolina believed Federal cavalry was attacking the brigade's position that night. He would later command the brigade for a short time.

Library of Congress

Jackson and his staff passed through the lines of the 33rd NC, reconnoitering the Federal position. With the firing on the Confederate right, Jackson's entourage "came galloping back and across our line to the right of the road to escape the artillery fire." In all probability, the muskets of the 37th Regiment drove Jackson and his party from the Orange Plank Road into the woods in front of the 18th NC, who mistook the mounted officers for Federal cavalry. Hill's staff, closer to the 18th, was decimated by the fire. More of Jackson's staff members survived, but Stonewall himself was struck three times.[24]

Escaping the withering small arms fire, A.P. Hill quickly ran toward the 18th NC, crying, "You have shot my friends! You have destroyed my staff!" Jackson lay wounded in the darkness. Hill soon found him, personally tending his wounds while sending orders for an ambulance and surgeon. Jackson was

24 Clark, *Histories*, 5:98. David Kyle, an area resident who served as a guide for Jackson, has the party taking the Mountain Road. *Confederate Veteran* (September 1893), 4:308-309. An anonymous account published in 1866 keeps the party on "the pike." *Land We Love* (July 1866), 181. It is possible this account was written by aide-de-camp and Jackson's brother-in-law William Morrison; see Robert Krick, *The Smoothbore Volley that Doomed the Confederacy* (Baton Rouge, LA, 2002), 9n12. Captain Richard Wilbourn, who was riding alongside Jackson, corroborates the idea the 37th Regiment fired on Jackson first: "our little party was fired upon by about a battalion . . . a little to our right and to the right of the pike—the balls passing diagonally across the pike. . . . At this firing our horses wheeled suddenly to the left. " Richard Wilbourn to Jubal Early, February 19, 1873, *SHSP*, 6:267.

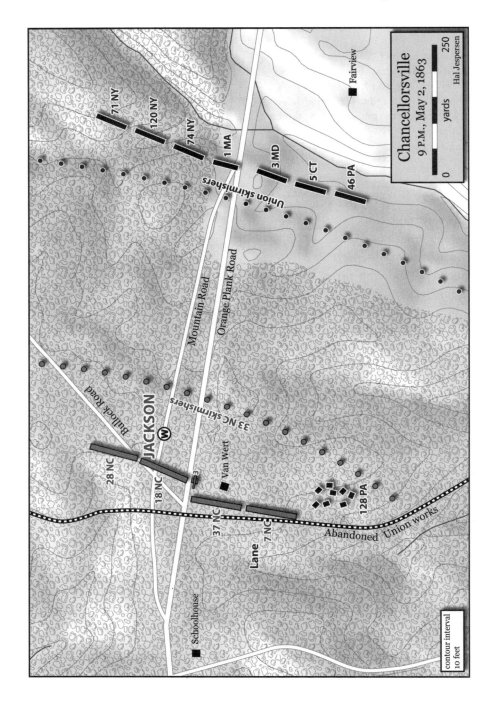

Chancellorsville
9 P.M., May 2, 1863
Hal Jespersen

0   yards   250

contour interval
10 feet

moved behind the lines. The wounded Major Morris may have caught a glimpse of Jackson being carried down the road. "A party of men carrying a wounded man on a litter [which] halted within ten or fifteen feet of me," he later wrote, "and someone said: 'Gen. are you suffering much?'" Jackson was transported to an ambulance behind the lines, and then taken to the rear, where his left arm was amputated early the next morning.[25]

Shortly thereafter, General Hill was also wounded, this time by artillery shrapnel across the back of both legs. According to two different officers, Hill stumbled into the lines of the 18th, demanding the regiment's identity. Upon learning it, Hill asked, "Who commands it?" "Col. Purdie," answered Capt. Van Richardson. "Almost at the same moment he was met by that gallant officer." Hill chastised Purdie "for firing at a noise." McLaurin later recorded a member of the regiment taunting Hill: "A body knows the Yankee army can't run the 'Light Division,' and one little general needn't try." Sometime in next few hours, Hill sought out Purdie and publically apologized.[26]

"Our regiment was fully aware of the terrible mistake that they had made, within ten minutes after it happened," Capt. Alfred Tolar (18th NC) wrote after the war. "Imagine, if you can for no tongue or pen will ever be able to describe the anguish of sorrow that rankled in the bosom of his devoted soldiers as it was whispered from one to another, 'Gen. Jackson is wounded,'" chronicled a member of the 37th. Lane, still on the right of his brigade dealing with the captured Federals, heard his name being called. He found fellow brigade commander William Dorsey Pender, who advised him of Jackson's wounding and of the likelihood that it had been caused by Lane's command. Upon reaching the 18th, Lane encountered Maj. Barry, who confessing knowing nothing of Jackson and Hill's riding to the front. Furthermore, "he could not tell friend from foe in the dark & in such a woods, that when the skirmish line fired there was heard the clattering of approaching horseman & the cry of

25 Hill quoted in Robertson, *Hill*, 187; William Morris to JL, January 3, 1895, Lane Papers, AU. In December 1883, a T. J. Capps, claiming to be a member of the 18th NC wrote he saw the ambulance bearing Jackson off the field, and that Jackson was wounded before sunset on May 2. Capps's identity remains a mystery. A James Thomas Capps was in the 18th Regiment; however, he died of wounds received during the battle of Hanover Court House in 1862. Several former brigade members wrote, countering Capps's claims, including General Lane. For the original letter, see *The Daily Review*, December 1, 1883. For rebuttals, see *The Fayetteville Observer*, January 2, 1883, January 23, February 6, 1884.

26 Clark, *Histories*, 2:38; *Fayetteville Weekly Observer*, February 20, 1884.

cavalry & that he not only ordered his men to fire, but that he pronounced the cry of friends to be a lie" and kept his men firing. McLaurin added that neither Jackson nor Hill was in the habit of riding to the front.[27]

Some blamed Lane and his Tar Heel brigade for the tragedy played out in the darkness of the Wilderness. "General Lane got scared," wrote one staff officer in his official report, "fired into our men, and achieved the unenviable reputation of wounding severely Lieutenant-General Jackson and wounding slightly Maj. Gen. A. P. Hill." After the war, Lane told an early Chancellorsville historian: "In all my intercourse with Genl. A. P. Hill I never heard him, nor have I ever heard any one else censure the 18th regiment for firing under the circumstances." The debate still continues.[28]

Regardless of who was to blame, Lane's brigade confronted a tense situation on the front lines in the murky woods. The wounded A. P. Hill passed command to Maj. Gen. J. E. B. Stuart. However, Stuart was not at hand, and it took time to contact the famed cavalry general, give him the news, and wait for his arrival. Maj. Gen. Rodes assumed temporary command of Jackson's corps, while Heth assumed command of the Light Division and countermanded the order for a night attack. Around 11:00 p.m., when Pender's brigade came on line, Lane shifted the 18th and 28th regiments across the Orange Plank Road, extending his line, while at the same time, withdrawing half of the 33rd Regiment; the other half still covered the front of the brigade, which was now entirely south and below the Orange Plank Road. The 37th's left still rested on the road, with the 7th on their right, followed by half of the 33rd, the 18th, and the 28th.

Around midnight, a Federal corps launched its own night attack to regain some of their lost ground, and possibly the baggage wagons of the III Corps. The Federal soldiers soon lost their way in the thick woods. The 18th Regiment poured a volley into part of the Union line, and for a short time, bayonets were crossed. A portion of the 28th actually refused its flank, an attempt to keep the Federals from gaining the Confederate rear. In the confusion, though, Federal forces started attacking one another in the darkness, while their artillery raked

---

27 *Fayetteville Weekly Observer*, January 2, 1884; Wiggins, "Address to UDC," NCDAH; JL to Augustus Hamlin, 1892, AU; Clark, *Histories*, 2:38.

28 OR 25/1:1010; JL to Augustus Hamlin, 1892. For other accounts and assessments, see Hamlin, *Battle of Chancellorsville* (Bangor, ME: n.p.), 103-17; John Bigelow, Jr., *Chancellorsville* (New Haven, CT, 1910), 315-21; Krick, *Smoothbore Volley*, 1-41.

friend and foe alike. In the end, the enemy retreated from Lane's front, leaving behind several prisoners, along with the 3rd Maine's blue regimental flag.[29]

Lane's Tar Heels settled down for an uneasy night. Additional Confederate brigades arrived, extending the line to the right. One soldier in the 18th recalled, "the least noise brought on a volley. With empty stomachs we slept on our arms, as best we could, between the firings." Romulus Linney (18th NC) recollected that during the night a Union soldier came into Confederate lines and sat down by the flag. A few moments later, he popped up and said "Why, this isn't my flag!" No, it wasn't, and one company captain directed the man to the rear as a prisoner. "I guess not," he replied as he leveled his rifle and pulled the trigger. "The whole brigade turned loose . . . and he was torn to pieces," Linney reported.[30]

Orders went out before dawn for the advance. The three brigades south of the Orange Plank Road planned to start the movement, swinging to the left to align on the road before a general advance of the whole Light Division. About sunrise, the attack began, just as Federal artillery fire blanketed Confederate lines. Archer's brigade, on the far right, quickly pushed the Federals out of the clearing at Hazel Grove. However, Archer's men ran into a second line of works, which, despite repeated attacks, held. McGowan's brigade was next, but it lost contact with Archer's brigade as the advance continued. They quickly took the first line of works they encountered, but bogged down 70 yards from the second line. While Archer fell back to regroup, McGowan was driven back by a counterattack.[31]

Lane's brigade came next. The general wheeled his men through the woods to the left, aligning on the Orange Plank Road, and then set off toward the Federal works, some 500-700 yards away. "Keep cool, men and do your duty," Capt. William Nicholson (37th NC) told his company. "Yes, men do as Captain Nicholson tells you," Col. Barber echoed, "and let us die on this battle field or gain the victory." The brigade advanced through woods swept with artillery and

29 JL to Augustus Hamlin, 1892, AU; OR 25/1:917. Company E, 28th NC captured the flag, according to Lane. Clark, *Histories*, 2:467. Lane told Hamlin he gave the fragments of the flag to his future wife, who burned it the night Richmond was evacuated.

30 Clark, *Histories*, 2:39; *The Atchison Daily Globe*, July 2, 1898.

31 One historian of the battle concludes Archer and McGowan misunderstood their orders. Charged with simply bringing their brigades on line with those on the left of the Orange Plank Road, they attacked instead. Further, he believed Stuart gave Lane his orders in person. Bigelow, *Chancellorsville*, 346.

small arms fire. Robert McAulay (18th NC) crumpled to the ground wounded, got back up, yelling "Forward" to his men, and was struck twice more. Intermixed with the unearthly "Rebel Yell" was the cry, "Stonewall Jackson!" The brigade surmounted the first line of works and pressed onward. On the right, a portion of McGowan's brigade passed in front of the 28th NC, which Lane ordered (except for Companies B and G which were still clear) to support the troops in front. This effectively removed the 28th from the actions of the rest of the brigade. For some reason, Lane's brigade drifted to the left, possibly due to the crowding of McGowan on the right. The 37th actually crossed the Orange Plank Road during the charge. Firing and reloading in the process, the brigade surged ahead. Once it hit the main Federal breastworks, the 37th found "many. . . miserable Yankees. . . still crouched trembling for their lives" behind it "as we bounded over, out they bounced and took to the rear."[32]

Likewise, the 18th NC, to the right of the 37th, pressed ahead. Unable to advance past the second line of captured works, the regiment was ordered to lie down and continued to fire. Trying to hold the captured works was a "desperate struggle." The 33rd Regiment was next, followed by the 28th. One brigade member, possibly from the 18th, recalled five days after the battle, what he witnessed: "Many are falling on the right hand and on the left, still we falter not. The brave and intrepid Col. Purdie, while in the act of discharging a rifle at the foe, and when in about forty yards of the intrenchments, falls, killed, with his face towards the enemy, by a rifle ball in the head." Several members of the regiment, including Heartford Love, bore Purdie's body off the field. Lane's brigade reached the main Federal lines first during the primary charge, driving off the defenders. "[B]ut the shot and shell are playing havoc in our ranks and the men are falling on either side. Within a space of about forty yards the bodies of seventy-six men were found dead."[33]

For almost an hour, Lane's brigade tenaciously held the captured works. They were able to converge small arms fire on a Federal artillery section out in front and drive it from the field. Causalities mounted quickly. Wiggins recalled one of his men showing him his wounded arm when the poor man was struck twice more in the thigh. In another instance, Wiggins tapped a soldier with his

---

32 Wiggins, "Address to UDC," NCDAH; OR 25/1:921; "Sketch of the Life of Lt. Robert McAulay"; *North Carolina Standard*, June 2, 1863.

33 Harris, *Historical Sketches*, 29; OR 25/1:919; *Weekly State Journal*, May 20, 1863; Heartford Love to "beloved companion," May 9, 1863, Fredericksburg and the Wilderness NMP files.

Lieutenant Colonel Junius L. Hill of the 7th North Carolina was killed "while gallantly leading a charge against the enemy breastworks" at Chancellorsville.

Histories of the Several Regiments and Battalions from North Carolina

sword to get his attention. As the soldier started to rise, a bullet slammed into his head and he fell dead into Wiggins's arms. George Cochran, also of the 37th, was struck in the shin by a lead ball from an artillery shell he saw burst right in front of him. He managed to make it to the first set of works but could not drag himself over them. Though he considered the wound but a scratch at the time, it would cost him his leg. Cochran's twin brother, Marion, was killed during the attack.

The 33rd Regiment suffered heavily losses. Both field officers were wounded, Col. Avery slightly, Maj. Thomas Mayhew, mortally. At least half of the regiment's company grade officers were killed, wounded, or captured that morning. The general's own brother, J. Rooker Lane, was killed. George Barringer, a member of the 28th NC, serving as a brigade courier, recalled lying behind a stump with the younger Lane. Lane asked Barringer to shift a little, "as the shells were coming on his side." Barringer moved about four inches when "grape shot struck him [Lane] between the shoulders and went entirely through his body" throwing him back about ten feet. When Barringer got to him, Lane told him: "You can do me no good," and soon died. The intense engagement exhausted ammunition: "Cartridge boxes are cut from both friend and foe and strewn on the ground by the men," one soldier wrote.[34]

---

34 Sears identifies the section as belonging to Battery H, 1st US Artillery. Sears, *Chancellorsville*, 321; Wiggins, "Address to UDC," NCDAH; Mannie Yeary, *Reminiscences of the Boys in Gray, 1861-1865.* (Dallas, 1912), 41. Cochran, *A Brief Sketch*, 43-44.

Lieutenant Colonel John B. Ashcraft was wounded during the fighting at Chancellorsville. The injury, coupled with his declining health, led to his resignation from the 37th North Carolina.

Mark A. Ashcraft

With no support forthcoming and low ammunition, Lane's only option was to order his men to fall back toward the first line of works. About the same time, Federal infantry counterattacked. Harris (7th NC) remembered the Federal infantry being concealed in a "deep ravine" between the lines. When McGowan's brigade fell back, Lane's right flank was exposed, and the retreat ordered. Not everyone escaped. After the 18th's color sergeant fell the evening before, Andrew Proffitt dropped his rifle and bore the flag. He was lying down like the rest of the brigade, and the Federals were up and over the works before he could get away. A Federal soldier from a New Jersey "grabed the flag out of my hand & said to me, 'Fall in John. . .' John fell in but did not like to do it." This was the first flag lost during the war since the creation of the brigade.[35]

Noah Collins (37th NC), was wounded in his right thigh and captured that morning. Collins was able to drag himself to the Orange Plank Road, which lay lower than the surrounding area, to shield himself from the battle. Once the Confederates retreated, Union soldiers found him and told him to go to the

---

35 Harris, *Historical Sketches*, 29; Hanock, *Four Brothers in Gray*, 196-64. John Barry (18th NC) gives another version of the events: Proffitt was killed and the flag picked up by Cpl. Owen Eakins, he writes. Eakins did not hear the order to retreat, and Lt. Alfred Rowland ordered him to the rear. The soldiers did not see when Eakins was killed, and the flag fell into the hands of the Federals. OR 25/1:893. The North Carolina Museum of History acquired the flag of the 18th, captured on May 3, 1863, in 2009; see *The Washington Times*, January 21, 2009.

Corporal Owen Eakins may have been carrying this flag during the battle of Chancellorsville when he was killed. The flag was captured by a member of the 5th New Jersey. *North Carolina Museum of History*

rear, but upon discovering his wound, they carried him back to Union lines. Collins recalled what happened next:

[W]hen coming into the Union lines, I became so weak sick and faint that I commenced lying down to rest; when a Union Captain seeing me, commanded me to go on . . . that was no place for me to stop at; when I replied that I could not possibly go any further, still lowering myself down to the ground; upon which he drew back his sword, advancing two or three paces towards me at the same time, and angrily told me I must and should go on. . . . I replied to him . . . I must have assistance; when the same two soldiers that bore me into Union lines, carried me to the hotel at Chancellorsville,

Colonel Samuel Lowe of the 28th North Carolina escaped the Battle of Chancellorsville unwounded. He was not as lucky at Gettysburg, where he was wounded in the left thigh. He never returned to his regiment.

Histories of the Several Regiments and Battalions from North Carolina

amidst a very severe and destructive shower of Rebel cannon shot and shells, and set me down behind the hotel, to shelter me from the same.

Collins claimed that not long after he was brought into the Chancellor House, General Hooker, the Army of the Potomac's commander was wounded on the porch. Collins stayed there for some time, until some Union soldiers carried him for a third time further behind Union lines. He was eventually recaptured.[36]

Separated from the balance of the brigade, Col. Lowe led eight companies of the 28th Regiment into the fray. For a time, Lowe held the regiment behind McGowan's brigade, exposed to a "murderous fire." Eventually he fell back to the first line of works and reformed his men. When J.E.B. Stuart soon rode up and ordered the regiment to charge, the 28th surged ahead, fighting "with the most determined courage." Federal forces caught them on the flank, however, and forced the Tar Heels to fall back. Lowe headed off to find Lane for further orders, turning command of the regiment over to Capt. Edward F. Lovill. Whereupon Stuart rode up again, singing "Old Joe Hooker, Get Out of the Wilderness," and ordered the 28th to support fresh Confederate batteries.[37]

Brig. Gen. Robert Ramsuer's brigade advanced toward Lane and the Federals. Lane pleaded with Ramsuer to shift to the right, not to attack over the

---

36 Collins, "Reminisces," 37-38.

37 OR 25/1:921; Clark, *Histories*, 2:477.

J. Rooker Lane, one of General Lane's brothers, started out the war in the 5th Virginia Cavalry. In early January 1863, he was detailed as an acting volunteer aide-de-camp on Lane's brigade staff. The younger Lane was killed in the bloody fighting at Chancellorsville.

College of William and Mary

same ground his men had just trod. Yet Ramsuer had his orders, and his brave Tar Heels likewise charged, and were soon forced to fall back.[38]

Lane led his men farther back behind the lines to re-form their ranks and refill their cartridge boxes. In the process he encountered the wounded Maj. Morris, who had ridden to the front but was unable to join the men in battle with his damaged foot. Lane, Morris recalled years later, had tears in his eyes. His brigade had suffered staggering losses. One-third of the 2,700 men Lane led into battle had been killed, wounded, or captured. Colonel Purdie was dead, and colonels Avery, Barber, and Haywood were all wounded. Even more wrenching to Lane was the death of his younger brother Rooker. Lane turned over command of the brigade to Morris and headed farther toward the rear. In a few moments, he returned, telling Morris he had found a cup of coffee, the only nourishment he had taken for 24 hours.[39]

Once his men replenished their cartridge boxes, Lane was ordered to take his brigade to the far Confederate left, across the Orange Plank Road, to serve as a reserve for Brig. Gen. Alfred Colquitt's men. Federal artillery blanketed the area, setting the woods on fire. The "heat was excessive," Lane wrote in his official report, "the smoke arising from burning blankets, oilclothes, &c., very offensive. The dead and dying of the enemy could be seen on all sides enveloped in flames, and the ground on which we formed was so hot as to be

38 JL to Augustus Hamlin, 1892, AU.

39 William Morris to JL, January 3, 1895, Lane Papers, AU.

disagreeable to our feet." Lane later recalled that the "dropped rifles of the dead and wounded and the enemy's shells with imperfect fuses exploded in every direction as the flames swept over them; the dead of both armies were being burnt to a crisp and the helpless Federal wounded begged to be taken out of line of the rapidly approaching and devouring fires." Eventually, Lane's brigade was ordered forward, and once the woods burned over, he sent out skirmishers. The skirmishing was heavy during the evening, and the men spent the night in a line of battle in the smoldering wilderness, covered in ash.[40]

Led by the flamboyant Stuart, Jackson's men, succeeded, after repeated assaults, in driving Federal soldiers from Fair View and the Chancellor House area. This enabled the wings of the Confederate army under Lee and Stuart to reunite. Federals in Fredericksburg had managed to overwhelm the greatly outnumbered Confederate defenders, but with Hooker's army now forced back into a defensive position on the Rapidan, Lee was able to divert Confederate forces from there back toward Fredericksburg.

After some skirmishing on May 4, Lane formed his brigade and proceeded behind the lines. His men spent the night asleep "in ashes under those charred scrub oaks." Lane wrote years later: "it was hard to tell whether we [were] white or black, Federal or Confederate so far as the color of our clothes were concerned." Other Confederate soldiers greeted them with "boisterous laughter & cheer," due to their appearance. Yet many of Lane's gallant band were as heartbroken by the grim losses as their commander was. Lane placed those losses at more than 927 men, men who included favorite commanders, childhood friends, neighbors, and even family. "There are periods in every man's life when all the concentrated sorrow and bitterness of years seem gathered into one short day or night of agony," Lane wrote after the war. "Though victory was assured," he continued,

> imagine my feelings as I lay all black with soot and smoke under an oak reckoning the fearful cost; and reflecting, that in less than forty-eight hours one-third of my command had been swept away, one field officer, only, left fit for duty out of thirteen carried into action—the rest all killed or wounded—most of them being my warmest friends; my boy brother who had been on my staff lying dead on the field; and Stonewall Jackson, my old professor, whom as a boy I had not fully appreciated and

whom, as my commanding officer, I dearly loved, lying mortally wounded and probably dying, shot by my own gallant command.[41]

The brigade spent May 5 skirmishing and shifting their lines to conform with those the Federals established near the river. The rain falling on the battlefield that day helped mask the Federal army's retreat, for Confederate skirmishers discovered the bulk of the Federal army gone on the morning of May 6. They left nothing but the debris of war, including thousands of wounded now in the Confederates' charge.

Lane's brigade returned to its winter camp on May 7. Obviously it was easier to return to their former camp with its established supply route since several of the men complained about lacking rations for three days. Not long after returning to camp, the brigade's soldiers gathered to vote on their nominations for the medals of distinction. At the first dress parade after a battle, as stipulated by presidential act, non-commissioned officers and enlisted men were to select a soldier from each company who had demonstrated "courage and good conduct" during battle. The nominations were then forwarded to the president, and medals were authorized to be struck and awarded to the soldier, or his widow or family. At least two regiments in the brigade, the 18th and 37th, submitted lists. Later, when it became impossible to find the material for the medals, the act was altered, and instead of medals or badges, the names were published on a "Roll of Honor," which was read to the regiment and published in state newspapers. If a regiment in the Branch-Lane Brigade contributed to the Roll of Honor at any other point, it has been lost to history.[42]

The five regiments of Lane's brigade marched to the parade ground on May 10 where a missive from General Lee was read to the men, announcing the dreadful news that Stonewall Jackson had died of complications attending his wounds. "Language is inadequate to portray the picture of sorrow stamped upon the faces of his faithful devoted soldiers," Wiggins wrote after the war. "In their old ragged gray jackets with no handkerchief to brush away the scalding tears pouring down their bronzed and battle scared faces, seeking some

41 JL to Augustus Hamlin, 1892, AU; Lane, "Chancellorsville," *SHSP*, 8:496; Lane, "Reminiscences of Stonewall Jackson", AU. The losses in Lane's brigade had been the greatest in the Confederate army. Sears places them at 910 men, including 165 killed and 633 wounded. Sears, *Chancellorsville*, 497.

42 Speer, *Voices from Cemetery Hill*, 101.

secluded spot upon the banks of the river there to shed tears that come truly from the aching heart." The past two years had brought many triumphant victories, but also many a tear shed over the loss of friends, families, and commanders like Colonels Lee, Purdie, and Campbell, and now, the mighty Stonewall Jackson. Many tears were yet to come.[43]

43 Wiggins, "Address to UDC," NCDAH.

Chapter 11

". . . with waving banners pressing into the very jaws of death."

The Gettysburg Campaign

Following

the much-lamented loss of Jackson, Lee decided to reorganize his army from two infantry corps to three in order to make it easier to maneuver and control. His decision required the elevation of two more commanders to the rank of lieutenant general.

Richard Ewell, a career army officer who commanded a division under Jackson until being wounding at the battle of Second Manassas, was selected to lead Jackson's former Second Corps command. Lee promoted the Light Division's own Ambrose Powell Hill to lead his new Third Corps. The elevation of Hill left the Light Division in need of a new commander.

Hill wrote to Lee about two possible candidates to lead his former division. The first was Maj. Gen. Henry Heth, whom Hill considered "a most excellent officer, and gallant soldier . . . there is no man I had rather see promoted than he." Then Hill wrote of William Pender, the Light Division's senior brigade commander. Pender had been wounded four times and "never left the field," recorded Hill, and he led the "best drilled and disciplined Brigade in the Division." Lee recommended Pender's promotion to command the Light Division, and it was accepted. Pender, a Tar Heel himself, was a 29-year-old

Brigade commander William Dorsey Pender was elevated to replace A. P. Hill as commander of the Light Division.

Library of Congress

West Point graduate. The new Third Corps of the army comprised Maj. Gen. Richard Anderson's Division (transferred from Longstreet's Corps), the Light Division (from Jackson's former corps), and a third division commanded by Henry Heth made up of two brigades from the Light Division, plus two additional brigades. Lane's brigade remained part of Pender's Division, Hill's Corps, Army of Northern Virginia.[1]

Leadership in Lane's brigade changed as well. With Purdie's death and the resignation of the wounded Lt. Col. Forney George, command of the 18th NC passed to Maj. John Barry, just 24 years old, and before the war, a Wilmington banker. Both Col. Clark and Lt. Col. Cowan of the 33rd were out wounded, and Maj. Thomas Mayhew died of his Chancellorsville wounds on May 12. Joseph Saunders was promoted from company commander to major, and led the regiment during the upcoming campaign. Colonel Barber of the 37th, although wounded at Chancellorsville, appears to have returned to the regiment before the campaign commenced. Lane's staff shifted as well. Assistant commissary of subsistence Daniel Carraway joined the brigade staff on April 11 but transferred to division staff at the end of June. Edward Nicholson, a lieutenant in the 37th NC, transferred in May to brigade staff as acting assistant adjutant and inspector general.[2]

1   Douglas Freeman, ed., *Lee's Dispatches* (New York, 1915), 91-92; Brian Wills, *Confederate General William Dorsey Pender: The Hope of Glory* (Baton Rouge, LA), 2013.

2   Jordan, *NC Troops*, 6:306, 400, 9:118-19, 468; Krick, *Staff Officers in Gray*, 91, 231.

There was some discord in the brigade following Chancellorsville. On May 19, at least 25 members of Company A, 37th Regiment, deserted, taking their arms with them. Thomas Norwood, a member of that company who had risen through the ranks to lieutenant, claimed they left over a disagreement concerning company promotions. The men had just been paid, noted General Lee, who complained that deserters often left in squads, with extra ammunition, passing themselves off as "guards or patrols in search of deserters. . . . I need not enlarge upon the extent to which this evil will grow if not at once stopped." Three men also left the 18th's Company D on June 12 while others simply trickled away as opportunity afforded. Enlisted men were not the only disgruntled ones. Colonel Barber (37th NC) asked for the resignation of Lt. Thomas Kerns, because of unsatisfactory conduct "on the battlefield." In endorsing Kerns's resignation letter, Barber added that this course was quicker than preferring charges. When the resignation was accepted on June 1, Kerns enlisted in his former company as a private.[3]

The brigade was still unevenly armed. As of June 30, 1863, Lane's soldiers had some 1,000 Richmond rifles on hand, plus an additional assortment of 598 rifles and muskets. Some of the regiments also received new battle flags. Unlike the original pattern flags, with battle honors painted in white, these new flags conformed to the standard issued to other regiments in the army: battle honors in blue, with the regimental designation in yellow above and below the center star.[4]

For nearly a month, the brigade occupied its former camp, being called out for 24-hour picket duty only every few days. That all changed on June 3, when Lee's army was put in motion. Lee had decided to march north, into Maryland and Pennsylvania, hoping that an invasion there would lessen Union pressure on the key Confederate strong point on the Mississippi at Vicksburg. Plus, Lee's army in Virginia needed supplies. Both men and horses had been on reduced rations through the winter. Lee had even sent a portion of Longstreet's corps to

---

3 Thomas Norwood to Uncle, June 16, 1863, Lenoir Papers, SHC; Thomas Nixon to Uncle, May 20, 1863, Nixon Papers, DU; OR 25/2:814-15; Jordan, NC Troops, 3:346-49, 9:472-83, 498; Thomas Kerns, Roll 0403, M270, RG109, CMSR, NA. Lee noted there were 32 deserters from the 37th.

4 James Bryan, Roll 0033, M331, RG109, CMSR, NA. It is unclear if all the regiments in the brigade received this issue. The 28th Regiment continued to carry the older flag. All of the brigade flags of this issue survive, except the 37th Regiment's. Additional brigade weapons included: 506 .58-caliber rifles, probably Springfields; 84 smoothbore .69-caliber muskets; and 8 .72-caliber Belgian muskets.

Suffolk, VA, to gather supplies, reducing the pressure in the main Confederate camps around Fredericksburg. James Longstreet's men returned after Chancellorsville, but the supply shortages remained acute. A Confederate army on Northern soil could forage liberally, addressing the supply problem while diverting the Federal army and allowing the farmers in Virginia to tend to their crops. Moreover, a victory on Northern soil might pressure the Lincoln administration to negotiate an end to the war, or lead to foreign recognition and alliances.

Lee began moving his army toward Culpepper Court House on June 3. To mask the movement of the other two corps, Hill's corps was left behind to man the Fredericksburg trenches and observe the Federals across the Rappahannock. If the Federals evacuated their position, Hill could cross the river and pursue, "inflicting all the damage you can upon his rear." Orders went out June 4 for Lane's brigade to be ready to move at a moment's notice, and the orders came as church services were concluding on Friday, June 5. The men marched throughout the night, reaching Hamilton's Crossroads just after daylight on June 6. A hospital was established while skirmishers drove Federal pickets beyond the Port Royal Road. William Barlow (18th NC) expected "a powerful fight here," probably a common sentiment.[5]

Although they skirmished every day, a general battle did not commence. Once Hooker learned two enemy corps were moving through Culpepper and Sperryville, orders were issued for the withdrawal of the Federals before Fredericksburg. Confederates knew they were gone by the evening of June 14. Andrew Proffitt (18th NC) noted capturing a "wagon load of spades picks and shovels." The next morning the men were ordered to cook two days' rations, and, at noon began moving toward the upper fords of the Rappahannock. One company of the 7th Regiment was sent to patrol Fredericksburg.[6]

As Hill's corps stepped off, Pender's men of the Light Division were left behind to make sure the Federals didn't double back. Finally, at 4:00 a.m. on June 16, Lane's brigade moved out, crossing the Rapidan River at Ely's Ford. Many men fell out of the ranks during the sweltering two days following. Proffitt (18th Regiment) dropped out, and from Winchester wrote describing hundreds of men doing the same and being placed in crowded, rickety

---

5   OR 27/3:859; Kennedy, Diary, June 5-6, 1863, SHC/UNC; Harris, *Historical Sketches*, 32; William Barlow to Elizabeth Barlow, June 8, 1863, *Company Front*, 32.

6   Hancock, *Four Brothers in Gray*, 206; Harris, *Historical Sketches*, 32.

ambulances. His feet were "worn out," Proffitt wrote, and he was given a "pass to shift for" himself, before winding up in a private home. His brother Alfred also gave out on the march and was eventually shipped to Chimborazo Hospital in Richmond. It is unclear how many fell victim to the heat. Doubtless most of them suffered from the army's six-month reprieve from significant long-distance marching.[7]

By June 20, the brigade had reached Chester Gap in the Blue Ridge Mountains. The 7th and 37th Regiments were ordered to wait until the wagon trains had passed, bringing up the rear. The brigade moved through Berryville on June 23, and Shepherdstown on June 25. In Shepherdstown, a member of the brigade pioneer corps took an axe to a flagpole flying the Stars and Stripes. "We will move at 2 o'clock to cross the Potomac," Hill proclaimed to his corps, "and conquer a glorious peace on their own soil!" About noon, the men forded the Potomac River, then marched through Sharpsburg, through Hagerstown the next day, and on June 27, crossed into Pennsylvania, camping about a mile and a half from Fayetteville. A British military observer appraised the division's troops as "a remarkably fine body of men, and looked quite seasoned and ready for any work. Their clothing is serviceable . . . but there is the usual utter absence of uniformity as to color and shape of their garments and hats; grey of all shades, and brown clothing, with felt hats predominate."[8]

Lee issued two orders while on campaign. The first on June 21 set forth proper foraging procedures. Goods were to be bought at fair market value, and the property of private citizens had to be respected. Lane recalled after the war that his brother had found him a trunk in a shop and returned to camp for his money when Lee's order arrived preventing Confederate money being forced upon the Pennsylvania citizens. In a second order on June 27, Lee reminded his men that they were not waging war upon unarmed and defenseless people. Any soldier caught abusing private property would be arrested and punished. Iowa Michigan Royster, recently transferred to the 37th NC, wrote home on June 29 about the "most beautiful country you ever saw, the neatest farms, large white barns, fine houses, and good fences. The whole country side is covered with the finest crops of wheat, such wheat as is not seen in our country." However, on the two previous days, Royster noted how "our soldiers plundered far and

---

7   Hancock, *Four Brothers in Gray*, 211.

8   Kennedy, Diary, June 26 - June 29, 1863, SHC/UNC; Hill quoted in Robertson, *Hill*, 201; Arthur Fremantle, *Three Months in the Southern States* (London, 1863), 229-30.

wide—taking butter, milk, apple-butter, fruit, chickens, pigs and horses and everything they could lay their hands on. . . . I never saw people so submissive and badly scared. . . . It must be conscience. They know how their soldiers have desolated Virginia and they fear that ours will retaliate." In light of Lee's order, Royster believed the plundering would stop. Chaplain Kennedy used the occasion to preach to the 28th upon the subject of taking items from unarmed civilians.[9]

June 28 found Lane's brigade stationary. The men were ordered to wash clothes and clean rifles. "There was many a chicken eat today," William Mauney (28th NC) chronicled in his diary. Kennedy preached to "a pretty good congregation," and many soldiers got mail. Up early on June 29, the men were eating breakfast at 4:00 a.m., with orders to march at five. While awaiting those orders, they were inspected. In a classic illustration of the paradox of military life, orders did not come until early afternoon, when the men were told to return their extra rations and cooking utensils to the wagons, and be ready to move at once. About the time they had completed their packing, orders arrived instructing the men to cook three days' rations. On the next day, June 30, orders came from Lee to Hill: move his corps from the vicinity of Fayetteville to Cashtown. Lane's brigade stepped off at 5:00 a.m., passing through Fayetteville and re-crossing the Blue Ridge Mountains, arriving in Cashtown 12 miles away.[10]

While Lane's brigade trudged down South Mountain, Pettigrew's brigade of Heth's division encountered Federal cavalry at Gettysburg. Pettigrew's Carolinians fell back, and the general explained first to Heth, then to Hill, that what he observed riding into Gettysburg had been veteran Federal cavalry, not militia. His superiors doubted Pettigrew's assessment. Heth gained permission to take his entire division to Gettysburg the next morning, and he set out early July 1. An hour later, Hill ordered the Light Division to head the same direction. A Federal cavalry officer fired the first shot at the advancing Confederates at 7:30 a.m. The enemy cavalry slowed Heth's advance, forcing him to deploy two of his four brigades. Dismounted Union cavalry soon gave way to Federal infantry. Eventually, Heth's entire division came on line.

---

9   OR 27/3:912-22; *The Wilmington Messenger*, November 2, 1892; Iowa Royster to Dear Ma, June 29, 1863, Royster Papers, & Kennedy, Diary, June 28, 1863, both SHC/UNC.

10 Mauney, Diary, May 28, 1863; Kennedy, Diary, June 29, 1863; Harris, *Historical Sketches*, 35.

As the Light Division marched within three miles of Gettysburg, Pender positioned his brigades across the Chambersburg Pike. Perrin's and Scales's brigades moved to the right, while Lane's and Thomas's brigades moved to the left of the road. From the turnpike to the left were the 7th, 37th, 28th, 18th, and 33rd Regiments. "We have advanced . . . [and] the ball is opened 10-o'clock," a member of the 37th wrote in his diary. The Division advanced for about a half-mile then halted along a creek for the men to refill their canteens. Another half-mile advance brought them up behind Confederate artillery on Herr's Ridge, dueling with the Federals. The soldiers stopped there and dropped to the ground. Pender, concerned about the appearance of Federal cavalry on his right, pulled Lane's brigade out of line and sent them in that direction. Lane extended Pender's line, while deploying the entire 7th Regiment "as a strong line of skirmishers . . . and at right angles to" Pender's line of battle. In effect, the 7th guarded the right flank of the entire Confederate army.[11]

Pender called for an advance at 4:00 p.m. Lane's brigade followed the remnants of Archer's brigade forward into the woods near Springs Hotel on Herr's Ridge. On the right flank, the 7th, moving by their left flank, struggled to keep up. Eventually, they became separated from the rest of the brigade. As Lane emerged from the woods, he discovered that Archer's men were no longer to his front, and that the 7th had failed to keep up on his right. Apparently, Lane's men had shifted somewhat farther to the right. Federal cavalry was still "annoying" Lane's line "with an enfilade fire." Colonel Barber sent a company, 40 men, from the 37th NC, under Capt. Daniel Hudson's command to the right to keep them at bay. Lane then ordered his brigade to charge, and his Tar Heels "rushed forward at a double-quick, the whole of the enemy's force beating a hasty retreat to Seminary Hill." Lane pushed on a little farther, into the peach orchard near the McMillan farm. Orders from Pender told Lane to advance farther only in a general advance. With Federal artillery raining death, Lane ordered his men back a few yards, behind a stone fence. The 7th eventually rejoined the brigade, their fight for the day done. The brigade's losses for the day were light.[12]

11 William Alexander, Diary, July 1, 1863, William Alexander Papers, SHC/UNC; OR 27/2:665.

12 OR 27/2:665. Pender's division medical officers established field hospitals in various farms along the Chambersburg Pike and Willoughby's Run. The Light Division and possibly wounded from Heth's Division as well used hospital sites at the Samuel Lohr farm and the Andrew Heintzelman Tavern and adjoining farm. Gregory Coco, *A Vast Sea of Misery: A History*

Fellow brigade commander Col. Albert Perrin, commanding McGowan's South Carolina brigade, criticized Lane's actions on July 1. "I found myself without support either on the right or left," he wrote. "General Lane's brigade did not move upon my right at all," and at the time of Perrin's attack, wasn't even in sight. One South Carolinian said Lane's Tar Heels "saw Yankee cavalry on their right. No doubt looked at it through the stone fence in front." Lane had been in this same position, as the right flank of the army, just two months earlier in the woods at Chancellorsville where his men had captured a Federal regiment in the darkness, massed for attack just beyond his flank. Now, Lane, with his flank being harassed, could see a brigade of Federal cavalry posted to his front, Federal infantry and artillery stood to his left, and he did not know the identity of the body of troops lying just over the hill. Many historians over the decades claim Lane formed his men—or at least part of his command—into a square, which is a defensive maneuver to protect against attacking Federal cavalry. In fact, the credit for forming a square on Gettysburg's first day goes to the 52nd NC of J. Johnston Pettigrew's brigade. That North Carolina regiment was posted on the right to protect the Confederate flank, and its adjutant confirmed that his regiment formed a square early on the afternoon of July 1. Neither Lane nor any of his men mentions utilizing such a maneuver.[13]

July 2 found Lane's brigade near the McMillan farm, enduring an early morning shower, but the afternoon temperatures grew to be oppressively hot as the day wore on. Lee's battle plan for this day was to attack both flanks of the entrenched Federal position south of the town. Longstreet's corps would attack on the Confederate right, and Ewell's corps, the left. Hill's corps would menace the Federal center, applying enough pressure to keep it from reinforcing the flanks. Lane's brigade spent more of the day fighting the heat than the enemy. At some point, Lane sent the 18th and 33rd Regiments to his left, beyond

---

and Guide to the Union and Confederate Field Hospitals at Gettysburg, July 1-November 20, 1863 (Gettysburg, PA, 1988), 135-36; Kent Brown, *Retreat from Gettysburg: Lee, Logistics, and the Pennsylvania Campaign* (Chapel Hill, NC, 2005), 109.

13 OR 27/2:662; Washington Shooter, July 20, 1863, quoted in J. Michael Miller, "Perrin's Brigade on July 1, 1863," *Gettysburg Magazine* (July 1995), 13:25-27; John Robinson, "Fifty-Second Regiment," Clark, *Histories*, 3:236. For two modern claims that Lane formed a square, see Bradley Gottfried, *Brigades of Gettysburg: The Union and Confederate Brigades at the Battle of Gettysburg* (New York, NY, 2012), 313, and Allen Guelzo, *Gettysburg: The Last Invasion* (New York, NY, 2013), 202. Historian Harry Pfanz correctly attributes the square formation to the 52nd. See Harry Pfanz, *Gettysburg: The First Day* (Chapel Hill, NC, 2001), 289.

Garnett's battalion of artillery, "that they might be better sheltered and at the same time be out of the enemy's line of fire."[14]

As Longstreet battled the Federals on Little Round Top, Lane and Perrin were ordered to drive skirmishers out of a farm lane to their front, back toward the Emmitsburg Road. According to Lt. Wilson Lucas (33rd NC), Pender rode to Col. Avery, looking for 75 men to take the farm lane. Those picked men were placed under the command of Lucas and Lt. John Caldwell and presented to Pender. "Can you take that road in front?" he asked Lucas. The lieutenant wasn't sure. "If you can't take it say so," Pender retorted, "and I will get some one who can." Rankled, Lucas told Pender, "We can take it if any other 75 men in the army of Northern Virginia can." This satisfied the general. "That is the way I like to hear you talk." Instructed to hold his fire as long as possible, Lucas related:

> We formed the men in line, I commanded the right and Lieut. Caldwell the left. We had to charge through an open field, with no protection whatever. . . . When we got within two hundred yards of the Federals, we charged with a yell, and they stood their ground until we were within ten steps of the road, then a part of them ran, but 26 surrendered. And the very last time they fired upon us, which was not more than twelve or fourteen feet from them, they shot Lieut. Caldwell in the left breast. I did not see him fall. As soon as we were in the road one of the men told me Lieut. Caldwell was killed. I went at once to the left and found him, lying partly on his back and side . . . I called two men, and we placed him on his back and spread his oil cloth over him. He was warm and bleeding very freely when I got to him. I could not send him out to the regiment, for it was such an exposed placed the Federal skirmishers would have killed a man before he could get a hundred yards, as we were lying close to each other.[15]

Lane sent other troops under the command of Maj. Owen Brown (37th Regiment) toward the sunken lane, and drove the Federals back toward Cemetery Ridge. When the Carolinians began firing on the Federal gunners, the

---

14 OR 27/2:655.

15 *The Morganton Herald*, November 21, 1895. John Caldwell was the son of Tod R. Caldwell, a state senator and later governor of North Carolina. Discussion of the death of John Caldwell took considerable column space in postwar newspapers. Many believed Caldwell was killed on July 3, during the charge. See *News and Observer*, September 10, & *The Charlotte Observer*, October 9, 1887. Lucas, however, goes on to write he had Caldwell buried on Seminary Ridge the night of July 2, near "two honey-pod trees . . . not far from an old two-story house."

enemy infantry counterattacked, driving the Confederates back. Once they reformed, the Confederates drove back the enemy once more. This time, they maintained control of the area. "It was the hottest place for a while I was ever in during the war," Lucas wrote many years later. About 10:00 p.m, Lane sent two companies of the 7th NC, under Capt. James Harris, to reinforce Brown. Upon arrival, Harris learned that Rodes's division was out in front of the skirmish line. These troops had been ordered to attack the Union position at night, but the attack was soon cancelled. Some of Rodes's men fell into Long Lane with Lane's skirmishers, crowding out the two companies of the 7th, which Maj. Brown sent back to the brigade after midnight. Losses for the day are unknown.[16]

Late in the day, Lane observed Gen. Pender riding from the left of his brigade, toward the division's right. At some point, Pender dismounted and climbed a nearby boulder to better observe the terrain. Given intensifying federal artillery fire, Pender expected a coming attack. Suddenly, a shell burst, and a jagged piece of hot iron tore into Pender's thigh; the general was carried behind the lines while a staff officer from Thomas's brigade found Lane, and informed him of Pender's wound. Lane, the senior brigade commander in the Light Division, assumed command, handing over his own brigade to Col. Clark Avery of the 33rd NC.[17]

Skirmishing and artillery duels flared up in the darkness. When those sounds faded, the groans of the wounded, crying for water or mercy, intermingled with the martial music of bands from both sides. Meanwhile the warm night temperatures—in the seventies throughout—simply amplified the suffering. The rising sun burned off an early morning patchy fog and some dark clouds. Heavy skirmishing continued through the morning, and Lane was forced to use large segments of Thomas's and Perrin's brigades to reinforce the skirmish line.[18]

Not long after the war, Lane wrote that early on the morning of July 3, General Lee "appeared in front of my line, reconnoitered the enemy's position and when he was about to leave, he remarked that 'he needed more troops on the right, but that he did not know where they were to come from.'" The

---

16 OR 27/2:655; *The Morganton Herald*, November 21, 1895; Harris, *Historical Sketches*, 35; Pfanz, *Gettysburg: Culp's Hill and Cemetery Hill* (Chapel Hill, NC, 1993), 148, 280.

17 Willis, *Pender*, 234.

18 OR 27/2:666.

previous evening, Lee had ordered Ewell and Longstreet to renew their flank attacks. The Confederates still held a portion of Culp's Hill, taken the night before. Both sides renewed the attack early Friday morning, and while the Confederates had more infantry, the Federals had better artillery. Portions of Ewell's corps captured part of the Federal position on Culp's Hill, but they couldn't hold it due to a lack of reinforcements. Longstreet, on the Confederate right, never fulfilled his orders of launching an attack, and Lee was forced to concoct a new battle plan. Since the flanks had been attacked, the Federals must have pulled reinforcements from the center. Lee concluded the Federal center must be weak: he would launch his attack there.[19]

About noon, Hill's units received their orders. Lane was to take the two brigades that formed his second line, his own under Avery and Scales's brigade, and move right and report to Gen. Longstreet. Lane's orders were to form his two brigades behind those of Henry Heth's division, which was now under Gen. Pettigrew since Heth's wound to the head on the first day of the battle. The woods screened Lane's view of the division to his front. Not long after they took position, Maj. Gen. Isaac Trimble arrived and assumed command of Pender's division; Lane returned to the command of his brigade and Avery to the 33rd. A West Point graduate and civil engineer, the 60-year old Trimble had commanded a brigade under Ewell until being wounded at Manassas in August 1862. His stint as commander in the Light Division was short.

Trimble and Lee rode over to inspect the two brigades. When he spotted a number of men sporting bandages, Lee is said to have remarked, "Many of these poor boys should go to the rear; they are not fit for duty." Trimble only had about 1,533 men present in in total for both brigades. "On taking command of these troops, entire strangers to me," he explained, "and wishing . . . to inspire them with confidence, I addressed them briefly, ordered that no gun should be fired until the enemy's line was broken, and that I should advance with them to the farthest point." Octavius Wiggins (37th NC) recalled seeing Trimble riding down the lines and stopping at various regiments to speak with the men. As he later noted, "[H]e was a stranger to us and had been sent to command us in the absence of our wounded general, and would lead us upon Cemetery Hill at 3 o'clock."[20]

19 *Richmond Times*, April 11, 1867.

20 20OR27/2:666; *Richmond Times*, April 11, 1867; Clark, *Histories*, 2:661. Trimble's comments are found in a letter from Lane to the *Raleigh Observer*, November 30, 1877.

The brigade was positioned, from left to right: the 33rd, 18th, 28th, 37th, and 7th Regiments. Scales's brigade was to the right, and Pettigrew's of Heth's division was to their front. At 1:00 p.m., more than 150 Confederate cannon opened upon the Federal defenses along Cemetery Ridge. Around 80 Federal artillery pieces responded. Thomas Sutton (18th NC) thought it "the heaviest fire of the enemy's field artillery that our brigade ever experienced during the war." Confederate artillery had little effect, and Union guns, to save ammunition, went silent. Confederate artillery chief, Col. E. P. Alexander, thought the Federal artillery had been driven off, and about 3:00 p.m., Longstreet ordered the Confederate infantry to advance. Pickett's Virginia division on the right, and Heth's division, under Pettigrew, stepped off toward the Federal line. About 150 yards behind Pettigrew came Lane's and Scales's brigades. After passing through the Confederate artillery, the men emerged onto a mile-long open field, but one crisscrossed with numerous fences. "It was a grand site," a member of the 37th wrote, "as far as the eye could see to the right and left two lines of Confederate soldiers with waving banners pressing into the very jaws of death."[21]

Not long after clearing the line of woods, wounded and straggling men from Pettigrew's command began filtering back into Lane's troops. To keep cohesion in his own ranks, Maj. Turner ordered the 7th to charge bayonets, forcing the stragglers to move around his flanks. Lane, moving his Tar Heels at the double-quick, pressed onwards past the smoldering ruins of the Bliss farm and Steven's Run. "My command never moved forward more handsomely," he reported later. Colonel Lowe (28th NC) was struck in the left thigh by a minie ball and carried to the rear. Lieutenant Colonel William Henry Asbury Speer took command of the regiment, leading his men through "all sorts of missiles" Federal artillery threw "into our ranks." As the regiment moved across the field, a shell exploded amid the 28th's ranks, knocking down Speer, killing two men, and wounding three others. Shortly before reaching the Emmitsburg Road, conflicting orders ripped Lane's brigade asunder. Brockenbrough's brigade, on Pettigrew's far left, crumbled under Federal fire and streamed to the rear. Ohio and New York troops, behind a covering stone wall, began pouring an enfilading fire into the rest of Pettigrew's command. Lane guided his brigade in that direction. At the same time, Trimble ordered his two brigades forward. The

---

21 Clark, *Histories*, 2:74, 661; see Alexander, *Fighting for the Confederacy*, 258-59, and *Military Memoirs*, 423.

conflicting orders split the 37th Regiment in two: half moved forward, along with the 7th Regiment, while the rest of the 37th, 18th, 33rd, and 28th veered left. The right of Lane's brigade crowded the left of Scales's brigade as both charged toward the Emmitsburg Road.[22]

Pettigrew's attack stalled along the Emmitsburg Road. Small squads of men struggled over the fence and on toward the enemy line along upper Cemetery Ridge. One Carolinian recalled seeing Lane "on horseback . . . riding just behind and up to his men, in the attitude of urging them forward with his hand; a moment later a large spurt of blood leaped from the horse as he rode up, and rider and horse went down in the smoke and uproar." A courier from General Longstreet braved the fire by finding Lane and ordering him to move his command toward the left. As soon as the general could free himself from his "wounded, plunging horse," he passed the assignment to Col. Avery, ordering the 33rd NC to change direction to the threat. "My God General," Avery retorted, "do you intend rushing your men into such a place unsupported and when the troops on the right are falling back?" Enemy fire began decimating Lane's three and a half regiments on the left side of the command. Major Joseph Saunders, Avery's second in command, was struck in the mouth, the round knocking out several of his teeth. Although Saunders was reported dead in North Carolina newspapers, he in fact had survived and was captured. "[A] bomb shell exploded near [Mathias O'Neal's] face shocking & otherwise injuring him." Company F of the 28th NC took in 24 men, and finished the day with only four unwounded. Every member of Company A was killed, wounded, or captured. Family tradition records Greenberry Harding being struck five times, and David Hefner four times. Surprisingly, both survived the war.[23]

"My left was here very much exposed," Lane wrote, "and a column of the enemy's infantry was thrown forward in that direction, which enfiladed my whole line." To his right Lane saw troops streaming to the rear. So he ordered his men to withdraw: "We fell back as well as could be expected." He left hundreds of killed and wounded soldiers as he moved back over the Bliss farm

22 OR 27/2:666; Speer, *Voices from Cemetery Hill*, 109; *Raleigh Observer*, November 30, 1877. According to Lowe, the brigade in front of his dressed to the right, while Lane's brigade dressed to left: "[I]n less than half the distance [these movements] uncovered us and left us [in the] front line."

23 Clark, *Histories*, 3:91; Clement Evans, *Confederate Military History.* 12 vols. (Atlanta, GA, 1899), 4:191; *Richmond Times*, April 11, 1867; Raleigh *Observer,* November 30, 1877; Jordan, *NC Troops*, 8:144; 9, 193; Speer, *Voices from Cemetery Hill*, 109.

Private Sidney Choplin of the 28th North Carolina was one of six brothers serving in the Confederate army. Sidney was killed during Pickett's Charge at Gettysburg on July 3, 1863. Two of his younger brothers, Joseph and Robert, had been killed the previous year during the Seven Days' Battles in Virginia outside Richmond, and another brother would fall in 1864.

Cheryl T. Martin

and toward the Confederate artillery. The 28th Regiment left its flag behind in the Emmitsburg Road. A short time later, the banner was scooped up by a member of the 126th New York Infantry.[24]

Lane's other commands, the 7th and half of the 37th, fared no better. After the brigade spilt, these men rushed ahead into the Emmitsburg Road. The 7th crowded Scales's brigade for some time, but officers were able to get the lines straightened. As they advanced, the men were "cheering for the 'Old North State' with such volume . . . as to be heard above the din of battle." With momentum on their side, the men threw down one section of the fence bordering Emmitsburg Road and dropped into the road. However, the fence on the other side proved too difficult to remove while under fire. Major Turner, leading the 7th, climbed over the fence, with the majority of his men following him. Turner advanced about 10 yards closer to the stone wall that provided some cover for the Federals and was shot in the foot. Turner ordered his men to return to the road, and he himself crawled in that direction. Just as he was passing command to Capt. James Harris, a ball passed through Turner's waist,

24 OR 27/2:666-67. The 28th's flag was captured by Capt. Morris Brown, who was later awarded a Medal of Honor by the US Congress. Sent to the War Department, the flag had #66 stenciled on it. It was sent to the Museum of the Confederacy in 1905. Richard Rollins, *"The Damned Red Flags of the Rebellion": The Confederate Battle Flag at Gettysburg* (Redondo Beach, CA, 1997), 227.

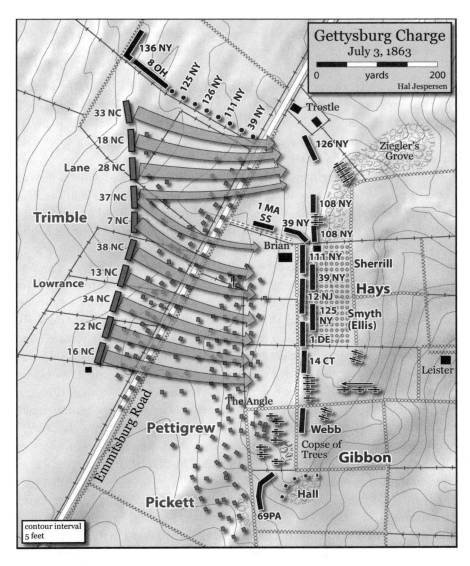

striking his spine and paralyzing his lower body. For a short time, the 7th maintained its position in the road. But with mounting pressure from their left, and a threat of attack on the right, action was required. Many years later Harris wrote:

> To remain and be captured or run the gauntlet of the enemy's batteries and escape was our only alternative and the latter (the bravest act of the day), was resorted to, every

man going to the rear as fast as his well nigh exhausted nature would admit, spurred onward by dangers which the heroic courage of the day failed to surmount.

Turner, who thought his wounds mortal, was left in the road. He actually survived, and was even able to help another Confederate apply a tourniquet to a leg of a wounded soldier. The 7th NC also lost its newly issued flag. A member of the 1st Delaware Infantry picked it up after each member of the entire color guard was struck down and the flag left on the field.[25]

Of Lane's five regiments, the 37th probably advanced closest to the Federals posted behind the stone wall. Like the 7th, the Tar Heels in the 37th found the eastern side of the fence along the Emmitsburg Road impervious to their attempts to tear it down. Instead, under fire, they leapt over the fence and continued up the hill toward the enemy. With some of the Federals abandoning their positions, Lt. Thomas Norwood "rushed forward thinking the day was ours." Norwood was only twenty paces from the Federal works when Lt. William Mickle shouted that the Confederates were retreating. At that moment, Norwood was shot in the left shoulder, the ball passing completely through. Mickle, too, was hit "at the same moment," Norwood wrote. "He uttered one shriek, was afterwards motionless and quiet." Iowa Royster was singing "Dixie" and "waving his sword" when he was struck for a second time, possibly by canister, in the chest. "I can see him now," Octavius Wiggins wrote in 1901, "in his new uniform with flashing sword, he cheered his men on apparently totally oblivious of the fact that a shrapnel bullet had already passed through his leg." Major Owen Brown sustained a leg wound, and Lt. Col. William Morris was captured. The remainders of his men streamed back to their starting place, as Lane attempted to reorganize them.[26]

During the fight, Trimble had also been hit in the leg. As he passed by Lane, he remarked, "If the troops I had the honor to command today couldn't take that position, all hell can't take it!" Command of the Light Division once again rested with Lane. Colonel Avery assumed command of the brigade. Meanwhile, a cheer went up from the Federal lines: their bands were playing, and many

---

25 Harris, *Historical Sketches*, 36-37; Raleigh *Observer*, November 30, 1877. The 7th's flag was captured by Pvt. John Mayberry. It was sent to the War Department and #44 was stenciled on it. Mayberry was awarded the Medal of Honor by the U.S. Congress. Rollins, *Damned Red Flags*, 221.

26 Raleigh *Observer*, November 30, 1877; Raleigh *Daily Progress*, August 11, 1863; Clark, *Histories*, 2:674.

Iowa Michigan Royster of the 37th North Carolina Troops was mortally wounded during Pickett's Charge while charging up the grassy slope east of the Emmitsburg Road on July 3, 1863.

Histories of the Several Regiments and Battalions from North Carolina

---

Confederates thought their enemies were launching a counter attack. Members of Lane's brigade, those wounded on the field and in the road, saw mounted Union officers ride by trailing captured Confederate battle flags in the dust. Most likely, one of the flags belonged to the 28th North Carolina. A Federal private recalled:

> General Hays took a Rebel flag captured by a captain of the 126th New York, on which was inscribed "Harper's Ferry," and the names of ten battles, and two of his staff, each with a captured flag, rode down in front of his command, and in the rear, trailing the Rebel colors in the dust, and amid the deafening shouts and cheers of the men who for a moment forgot the terrible battle scenes and thought only of the glory of their victories.[27]

Confederate wounded poured toward the rear. At some point on July 3, the hospital for Lane's brigade, and possibly Pender's Division, shifted locations, perhaps to be nearer the battlefield. Chaplain Kennedy had trouble finding it: "the Medical Department was badly managed today causing a good deal of unnecessary pain and trouble to the wounded." Lane placed his losses at 660

---

27 Leslie Tucker, *Major General Isaac Ridgeway Trimble: Biography of a Baltimore Confederate* (Jefferson, NC, 2005), 179. Robertson has a slightly different quotation from Trimble, this one made to Lee, not Lane. *Hill*, 224. Federal quotation found in Rollins, *Damned Red Flags,* 191-93.

Wesley L. Battle, 37th North Carolina, was charging beside Iowa Royster on July 3 when he, too, was killed.

Histories of the Several Regiments and Battalions from North Carolina

men, out of 1,355 men present. Lane's brigade held its position behind the Confederate artillery for the rest of the day. One brigade member thought the evening rain "reduced the temperature, and made it more pleasant." The rain did not stop for days.[28]

That night Lee chose to retreat. Avery shifted the brigade back toward the McMillan farm on July 4, and the soldiers labored on breastworks. The wounded were moved three miles behind the lines, and the slightly wounded were sent on toward Cashtown. Light skirmishing took place between the armies throughout the day, but both sides were exhausted. The constant rain did not help the army preparing to retreat with its wounded, numerous wagon trains, impressed supplies, and thousands of livestock. Kennedy recorded in his diary that the division commissary and quartermaster trains were already on the road before orders came for the medical trains to embark. The wounded who could not be transported were left behind. "I had my feelings sorely tried when telling officers and other men goodbye who were so seriously wounded as to disqualify them for traveling," Kennedy wrote. Assistant Surgeon John McLean (33rd NC) and hospital steward Edwin McAulay (7th NC), along with at least

28 Kennedy, Diary, July 3, 1863, SHC/UNC; *OR* 27/2:667; Harris, *Historical Sketches*, 37. Gregory Coco writes Scales's brigade of Pender's division might have had a temporary field hospital at the Michael Crist farm near McPherson's Ridge. Furthermore, he identifies the 1881 farm of W. H. Gelbach as a possible burial place for the dead from Lane's brigade. This probably would have only been the dead from the fighting on July 3. *Gettysburg: The Aftermath of a Battle* (Gettysburg, PA, 1995), 143, 224.

three enlisted men, were left behind with the brigade's wounded. They were all captured. Lack of transportation forced the mobile wounded to walk.[29]

Chaplain Kennedy accompanied the divisional supply train that left late on July 4 and moved on through the night. "I was in the saddle . . . in a pouring rain, thoroughly wet all night," he wrote. "Our progress was impeded by the multitudes of troops, artillery and wagons along roads, so that when we stopped about 8 o'clock this morning, on this side of a little village called Fairfield, we had travelled about 8 miles." After resting until 1 o'clock, the wagons embarked in the rain once again. Augustus Floyd (18th NC) struck in the leg, apparently by a piece of grape shot, on July 3 was a part of the caravan of wounded. Floyd made his way to a field hospital two miles behind the lines. A surgeon probing the wound discovered Floyd's pants did not have an entry hole, "but [were] driven with the ball to the bone." Floyd was loaded into a wagon and sent toward the Potomac. During the trip, one of his brogans fell through a hole in the wagon's floor, so he "threw the other away." His wagon eventually made it to Williamsport, but like so many others, he had to wait to be floated over the rain-swollen river. In his post-war autobiography, he mentioned the attack of Federal cavalry and how they "were driven back," but he failed to mention if he was among the many wounded Confederates armed to prevent the capture of the trains.[30]

Lane led out the Light Division once darkness fell, with the 37th NC in the van. Hill's corps, occupying the center of Lee's shortened line, left first, also on the road to Fairfield. "The extreme darkness, heavy rains, and muddy roads rendered our progress necessarily slow," James Harris (7th NC) wrote. Longstreet's corps followed Hill; Ewell came next, with the cavalry bringing up the rear. The men crossed over South Mountain on the night of July 5. The next day, they waited for other troops to pass to the front before setting out at 3:00 p.m. That night, they stopped near Hagerstown, MD. July 7 found the brigade about a mile and a half beyond Hagerstown. The incessant rain raised the Potomac River. That, coupled with the loss of the pontoon bridge to Federal cavalry, effectively trapped the Army of Northern Virginia near the community of Williamsport.[31]

---

29 Kennedy, Diary, July 3-4, 1863, SHC/UNC; Jordan, *NC Troops*, 4:407, 9:120.

30 Kennedy, Diary, July 4, 1863; Floyd, Autobiography, 9.

31 Alexander, Diary, July 5-7, 1863, William Alexander Papers, SHC/UNC; Harris, *Historical Sketches*, 38. Brown writes one company from each brigade was detailed out of line and into the

James Harris reported that the 7th NC was on picket duty along the Cumberland Pike much of July 8, but it rested on July 9. Confederate generals were working on a defensive line between Hagerstown to the north and Downsville to the south. Lee needed to buy time for his engineers to construct a pontoon bridge at Falling Waters to aid crossing his army over the Potomac River. When the waters receded sufficiently, Ewell's corps forded at Williamsport, while Longstreet's and Hill's corps crossed over the new bridge.

On July 10, one of the 37th's missing men arrived in camp. Thomas Norwood had been wounded on July 3 close to the Federal lines during Pickett's Charge. He attempted to retreat, but collapsed from the loss of blood. Federal soldiers eventually collected him and sent the wounded soldier to a hospital about three miles behind the front lines. "For my part, I lost everything," lamented Norwood, "and lay two days and nights on the ground with nothing on me but a pair of pants and half a shirt, and it raining all the time." After Lee's retreat, most of the Confederate wounded (including Norwood) were transferred to the Gettysburg College or the Lutheran Seminary buildings. Loosely guarded, Norwood planned his escape. When he found a "student's blouse," he put the garment on and slipped out about two hours before sunset. After walking for several hours, he found a Southern sympathizer and spent the night with his family. The next day Norwood swapped his clothes for those of a common laborer, although his host was a smaller man. "[S]o you can imagine the figure I cut in his clothes," Norwood chronicled. Eventually, the injured soldier stumbled into the rear of the Federal army, which was moving southward in pursuit of the Army of Northern Virginia. However, his luck held when a local farmer hired him to work beyond the Confederate lines toward Hagerstown. Once he secured a pass, Norwood made his way through the Federal pickets and eventually reached friendly lines. "Our guards sent me to General Johnson . . . who sent me to General Ewell, and he again to General Lee." Norwood arrived at Lee's headquarters near midnight. The next morning, he wrote, "Lee received me very politely, got from me the information I had discovered about the Yankee Army. . . . He complimented me upon my adventure and then insisted on my taking breakfast with him, which I accordingly did, sitting by the General in my uncouth garb

---

countryside to forage, but did not clarify which company came from Lane's brigade. *Retreat from Gettysburg*, 300.

and feeling at ease." After reporting to his regiment, Norwood was sent to a hospital in Richmond.[32]

Confederate soldiers began entrenching new lines on July 11: Ewell on the left, behind Hagerstown, Hill in the center, and Longstreet on the right. Harris (7th NC) reported the Federals "came in sight" during the afternoon hours and there was some skirmishing, but no general engagement. Confederates continued to entrench the following day. A publicized general order from Lee praised the men for their previous actions and urged them to continue the struggle. Possibly, Lee's order had the desired effect. William Alexander (37th NC) recorded that "we have made good earthworks, the men are anxious to fight." Lieutenant Colonel Speer (28th NC), echoed these thoughts, writing home that if the Federals attacked, "they will get what no army has got before." That same day, the Heth and Pender divisions were consolidated, while Lane returned to the command of the brigade and Avery to the 33rd Regiment.[33]

Lane reported on July 13 an attack on his skirmish line about 2:00 p.m. by a strong line of Federal skirmishers. Twenty-nine of Lane's men were captured, and another soldier was killed "in the works." At the same time, several Federal sharpshooters took up position in a barn not far from the Confederate lines, annoying Lane's Tar Heels. "A few shots from a battery drove them out," one Carolinian wrote. As evening set, the incessant rains intensified. Lee, perceiving time was limited, ordered his army across the river under the cover of darkness. His perception had been right: the Army of the Potomac had orders to attack the next morning.[34]

Lane took his brigade out of line to cross the Potomac via the improvised bridge at Falling Waters. On through the night they trudged. Thomas Sutton (18th NC) found the road "miserable." General Lane remembered the march "through mud and rain, was worse than that from Gettysburg which was 'awful.'" Around 10:00 a.m. and about a mile and a half from the bridge, Lane's brigade filed off in a field and stacked their arms while awaiting their turn to cross. Heth was ordered to deploy his division as a rear guard for the rest of the

---

32 Harris, *Historical Sketches*, 38; Thomas Norwood to father, July 16, 1863. Federal Maj. Gen. Darius Couch, in his official report, complained of an unknown number of Confederates who escaped with the help of local citizens. OR 27/2:214.

33 Harris, *Historical Sketches*, 38; Alexander, Diary, July 12, 1863; Speer, *Voices from Cemetery Hill*, 109; OR 27/2:667.

34 OR 27/2:667; Harris writes the skirmishers were captured on July 12, not July 13. Harris, *Historical Sketches*, 39.

army. Lane was in the process of taking arms and proceeding to the pontoons when Federal cavalry attacked Heth's lines. In the melee, Brig. Gen. Pettigrew was mortally wounded. Lane ordered his men to fix bayonets, "as our guns were generally unloaded," and continued on toward the bridge, when a staff officer rode up with orders for Lane and Scales to deploy. Lane posted his brigade and dispatched skirmishers under Lt. James Crowell (28th NC) with orders not to fire until the Federals were close, and to fall back toward the river as the main line did. Lane soon added the entire 18th NC to the skirmish line, under Col. Barry, while Col. Avery had command of the right. The men of Heth's division filed to the rear toward the bridge while Lane's brigade assumed the rear guard of the Army. Slowly the Tar Heels fell back, covering Heth's withdrawal. Finally, Lane's men scampered across the bridge, with the 28th bringing up the rear. "Lieutenant Crowell's command," Lane wrote in his report, "was the last organized body to cross the bridge." As the Federals gained the Maryland shoreline, the pontoon bridge was cut and swung back to the Virginia side. The brigade kept marching until near Martinsburg, where they camped for the evening. For the first time in three days, the men received rations.[35]

On July 15, the brigade went into camp near Berryville and rested for six days. The men were able to bathe, and stragglers unable to make the march slowly rejoined the ranks. Save in the annals of history, the Gettysburg campaign came to a close for members of Lane's brigade. Confederate losses had been severe, and while many hard-fought victories awaited, the Army of Northern Virginia would never be itself again.

---

35 Clark, *Histories*, 2:74, 476; OR 27/2:667; Harris, *Historical Sketches*, 40; Alexander, Diary, July 13, 1863.

Chapter 12

"Perhaps we are to be shot or hung."

The Plight of the Prisoner

William G. Morris was just one of thousands of Confederate soldiers captured at Gettysburg. After being hauled over the stone wall, the disgruntled lieutenant colonel of the 37th NC found a nearby barn, stuck his sword blade in it, and snapped it in two, to keep it from the enemy, he later claimed. Kept in a pen for a few days while the railroad was repaired, Confederate prisoners were then shipped off to various prison camps. Morris was briefly detained at Fort Delaware before being transferred to Johnson's Island, Ohio, where he remained for almost two years.[1]

The plight of prisoners of war during the conflict might best be described as a catastrophe. Of the 410,000 men held as prisoners, 52,000 died while incarcerated. "[N]o wartime experience . . . ," historian David Blight writes, "caused deeper emotions, recriminations, and lasting invective than that of prisons." At the outset of the war, neither side prepared for prisoners. Most

---

1   Minnie Puett, *History of Gaston County* (Charlotte, NC, 1939), 204; Jordan, *NC Troops*, 9:469.

probably believed prisoner processes would follow the historic European model of paroling the men and allowing them to go home until properly exchanged. However, the U.S. government, believing the official paroling and exchange of prisoners constituted recognition of the Confederate States of America, refused to do anything. While local or individual commanders could parole prisoners, the Federal government, as a policy, did nothing.[2]

Before the brigade was officially formed, more than 400 Confederate soldiers attached to Branch's command had been captured at the battle of New Bern in March 1862. Columbus Turner, at the time a corporal in the 33rd NC, was one of the unlucky soldiers. Turner and some of the other prisoners were kept for a month on board the *Albany* in the Neuse River. During the day, they were permitted on deck, but at night, were shoved below decks to "sleep on broad shelves . . . the air close, and the whole place . . . rather damp and offensive." While on board, Turner discovered he had body lice, "that pestiferous tribe of insects" which "seized [him] with a feeling of loathing and disgust." The only food issued was soup, but there was a dearth of spoons. Turner was finally able to purchase a cup. The *Albany* eventually made her way up to New York City, an open-sea journey leading many to "become very sick . . . [they] crawled about on deck and to the sides of vessels like lizards." Turner was sent to Castle Williams on Governor's Island first, and then transferred to Fort Columbus. Prisoners were kept within the fort itself, sleeping on the floor at first, and later on straw pallets. The men again ate soup, which was brought from outside. Once the detail reached the grounds, "a general rush was made . . . the prisoners would crowd and press around, heave and set—some would rush between the legs of others—some would mount the pile of human beings crowding around like a herd of hogs about a slop trough and over the[i]r heads walk down into the cans to fill cups." Turner's stay in prison was short, especially compared to those of other prisoners later in the war. He was paroled and transferred to Aiken's Landing, on the James River in Virginia, on July 12, 1862, and declared exchanged.[3]

Typically, officers were sent to Johnson's Island. While the Federal authorities repurposed some structures as prisons—like the Old Capital

---

2 David Blight, *Race and Reunion: The Civil War in American Memory* (Cambridge, MA, 2011), 152.

3 Kenrick Simpson, ed., *Worthy of Record: The Civil War and Reconstruction Diaries of Columbus Lafayette Turner* (Raleigh, NC, 2008), 1-4; Jordan, *NC Troops*, 9:123.

Captain William Farthing was captured at Hanover and imprisoned at Johnson's Island. He was released on November 10, 1862, submitted his resignation on November 12, 1862, and died in a hospital in Winchester on November 28, 1862.

Cliff Farthing

building in Washington, D. C.—the prison on Johnson's Island , Ohio, on the edge of Lake Erie near Sandusky, was built for that singular purpose. The compound, which included a block- house, a cannon, and barracks for the prisoners, was enclosed by a 14-foot fence with a guard parapet. A ship, with its guns pointed toward the compound, was anchored off shore. Colonel Clark Avery of the 33rd NC, along with four other company-grade officers, was sent to Fort Columbus first, and then on to Johnson's Island, where they arrived on June 21.[4]

In late May, 609 members of Branch's brigade were captured following the battle of Hanover Court House. Cut off from the rest of the brigade, the majority came from the 28th NC. After spending a night on the battlefield, the prisoners were marched eight miles before being herded onto a train and transported to White House Landing. There, they boarded a steamer for Fortress Monroe, where they were transferred to another vessel. As they made the five-day voyage to New York, the men pondered their fate. "[H]ow we would be treated, if we would be exchanged or paroled, or perhaps we are to be shot or hung," crossed many a mind. At Governors Island, the officers were separated from the enlisted men and transferred to Fort Columbus, while the enlisted men made their way to Castle Williams. The officers were given some

4 Lonnie Speer, *Portals to Hell: Military Prisons of the Civil War* (Mechanicsburg, VA, 1997), 77-79; Jordan, *NC Troops*, 9:118.

Colonel William Lee Davidson was wounded in May 1863 at Chancellorsville, captured a year later at the Wilderness, and became a part of the Immortal 600.

John Anderson

freedom of the grounds and were allowed to play ball, read local newspapers, visit with the enlisted men, and even watch a yacht race.[5]

About three weeks after their capture, the majority of the officers were transferred to Johnson's Island. Ferried across the channel and loaded onto railroad cars, the officers were marched into the stockade on the island a day and a half later. Instructed to hand over any money they had, William Speer (28th NC) noted that "This was quite humiliating." Prisoners were told they could draw upon their accounts for needed purchases. Troubled by loss of the freedom he enjoyed at Fort Columbus and distressed over the conduct of the guards, Speer lamented: "This is dreadful," putting Confederates "in prison & then shoot them like they were savages." News soon arrived of the battles for Richmond. A newspaper account made its way into camp and a colonel read it to "over 1,000 men, every now & then shouting & waving hats & slapping hands in wild enthusiasm." The following day, Speer and the other prisoners were warned another such display would bring swift retaliation from the guards. "We are now duly notified that we are liable to be shot at any time. Think of this condition to be in, liable to be shot down at any time without any self defence." This problem was not unique to Johnson's Island, but also occurred at other prisons. Prisoners lived under the constant threat of the guards, who could fire at the least perceived infraction.[6]

---

5   Speer, *Voices from Cemetery Hill*, 63, 68; Johnston, Diary, June 8, 1862.

6   Speer, *Voices from Cemetery Hill*, 75, 76, 78.

While Avery was incarcerated at Johnson's Island, a fellow prisoner was "brutally murdered by a sentinel." The ensuing uproar found prisoners plotting to overpower the garrison. Avery approached another officer: "Colonel," he said, "with blazing eyes, 'we can't stop this thing-we must lead it.'" After meeting with other field officers on the island, they planned to "attack . . . the sentinels, burst down the plank fence & take the guard's guns & try to secure the block house & take the cannon." They eventually gave up on the idea. The senior officers were able to convince their fellow officers of the folly of the movement. "If we had got out, how then would our case have been any better, for we then still would have been entirely surrounded by water," Speer wrote, also noting two others were wounded, plus random shots had come into their quarters.[7]

His industrious fellow captives made "rings, breastpins, shirt buttons, bracelets & watch fobs" out of the shells men found while bathing in the lake, Speer noted. John Croom (18th NC), was captured in 1864 and incarcerated at Elmira, NY. In November 1864, he got a letter asking him to make a ring for a friend. Though confessing he did not see how he could get the ring to her, he did ask for the young lady's initials, to carve on the ring. Other diversions for prisoners at Johnson's Island were swimming and bathing in Lake Erie when the weather permitted it, cards, books, and, when available, newspapers.[8]

Prison life brought a new level of melancholy and loneliness. Captain George Johnston (28th NC) had been captured along with many others following the battle of Hanover Court House. "I almost went mad in the intense longing, the almost utter despair which overwhelmed me," he wrote, thinking about his wife. Speer reported many "long faces" in August 1862 among men who believed they would not be exchanged, but hanged. The senior officers at Johnson's Island even agreed to draw straws to see who would go first.[9]

On July 22, 1862, the two sides reached an agreement, known as the Dix-Hill Cartel, that established a scale to manage the exchange of soldiers. An army colonel was worth 15 privates. A captain, six privates. The majority of enlisted men were taken to Aiken's Landing on the James River, below Richmond.

7   *The News Herald*, October 5, 1922; Speer, *Voices from Cemetery Hill*, 83.

8   Speer, *Voices from Cemetery Hill*, 77; John Croom to friend, November 12, 1864, private collection, copy in author's possession.

9   Johnston, Diary, June 8, 1862, NCDAH; Speer, *Voices from Cemetery Hill*, 83.

Captain Simon Bohannon of the 28th North Carolina was captured at Spotsylvania Court House in May of 1864 and sent to Charleston, South Carolina, as part of the Immortal 600. He survived his ordeals and was paroled on June 16, 1865.

Histories of the Several Regiments
and Battalions from North Carolina

Officers captured at New Bern and Hanover Court House were sent to Vicksburg. "On our way home at last," wrote George Johnston, "Thank God Thank God." The prisoners were taken to Sandusky and then by rail to Cairo, Illinois, where the group was transferred to steamboats for the journey down the Mississippi River. It took Avery 20 days to reach Vicksburg: he arrived on September 20, 1862. He, along with Speer and Johnston, was not officially declared exchanged until November 10. Early in the war, most of the officers and enlisted men were allowed a short period of time at home before rejoining their commands.[10]

At times, parole came quickly. Brigade soldiers at Fredericksburg and Chancellorsville were paroled within a few days. Andrew Proffitt (18th NC), captured at Chancellorsville, spent just 13 days as a prisoner, part of that time in Washington, D.C. A few escaped captivity. Thomas Norwood (37th NC) donned civilian clothes and walked out of a Federal hospital at Gettysburg and made his way to Confederate lines. Lt. Octavius Wiggins (37th NC) was captured on April 2, 1865. At City Point, he was placed aboard a steamer bound for Washington, D.C., and then on railcars rolling toward Johnson's Island. Somewhere near Harrisburg, Pennsylvania, Wiggins jumped from the moving train, survived the fall, and, cutting the military buttons from his clothing,

10 Speer, *Portals to Hell*, 97-102; Johnston, Diary, June 8, 1862; Jordan, *NC Troops*, 9:118.

disguised himself as a common laborer. Working his way south, Wiggins arrived in Richmond only to discover the war was over.[11]

In December 1862, the prisoner exchange system began to break down after William Mumford was hanged in New Orleans for tearing down a United States flag. Disagreements between the two governments led to a suspension in the exchange of officers, and after the publication of the Federal General Order 100, also known as the Lieber Code, in April 1863, of enlisted men as well. Later problems stemmed from the Confederate government's refusal to acknowledge black Union troops as soldiers–instead of escaped slaves and, therefore, criminals—and from the fact that the Lieber Code essentially rewrote the laws of war. Thus tens of thousands of prisoners, North and South, languished in prisons for almost two years.[12]

Early in the war, Federal recruiting officers routinely swept through prison camps, looking for recruits for their regiments. The first such sweep of Branch-Lane brigade members was August 1, 1863. William Harris and Joseph Sewers of the 33rd NC and James Clarke of the 7th NC all joined the Delaware Heavy Artillery. By the end of August, Patrick Brannon (7th NC) had become the first of 11 brigade members to join the 3rd Maryland Cavalry (US). Apparently, not only were the men released from prison, but they also received a $25.00 bounty, plus a $2.00 signing fee. The number of Confederate prisoners willing to take the Oath of Allegiance and swear loyalty as Federal soldiers increased in 1864. Recruiting moved from Fort Delaware to Point Lookout. At least 36 brigade members joined the 1st US Volunteers, while eight men enlisted in the 4th US Volunteers. All told, six US Volunteer regiments were made up of Confederate prisoners of war. These regiments went out West, to guard the frontier and battle Native Americans. Two members of the brigade joined the 1st CT Cavalry; 18 went into unknown Federal regiments.[13]

While conditions at all prisons were bad, for a chosen few prisoners, 1864 brought new horrors. Confederate authorities constantly moved prisoners because of overcrowding. June 1864 found 50 Union officers being held in a

---

11 Hancock, *Four Brothers in Gray*, 199; Clark, *Histories*, 2:671.

12 Signed by the president and promulgated as a general order in April 1863, the Lieber Code dictated the conduct of soldiers in wartime. Among other subjects, it dealt with treatment of prisoners of war. It is in OR/3, 3:148-64.

13 Clark, *Histories*, 4:444; 9, 152, 230; Henry Brinkley, M384, Roll 0032, RG109, CMSR, NA; Speer, *Portals to Hell*, 220.

residential section of Charleston, SC. Enemy shore and naval batteries frequently shelled the civilian sections of the city, and Federal authorities claimed that the placement of prisoners was intentional, making them human shields. Union prison authorities quickly selected 50 Confederate officers to also be deliberately used as human shields, and placed them on a ship bound for Charleston. Among the 50 were Lt. Cols. William Barber (37th NC) and William Davidson (7th NC), both captured in May 1864 during the overland fighting in Virginia. The 50 left Fort Delaware around July 26 and spent three anxious weeks aboard a ship in Charleston harbor before an agreement was reached to exchange the officers. Hostilities were suspended for the day in Charleston, and the prisoners treated to a banquet before returning to their respective sides.[14]

Not long after these 50 Federals left Charleston, the Confederates moved 600 more into the city from Macon, GA. While these officers were ultimately destined for other prisons, U.S. officials believed the prisoners were being detained there to deter the Federal forces from shelling civilian centers of the city. Hence they selected 600 Confederate officers to send to the area, including 13 members of Lane's brigade. All but two, Capt. William Alexander (37th NC) and Lt. John Cowper, both incarcerated since Gettysburg, had been captured in the spring of 1864.[15]

Captain Walter MacRae (7th NC) was one of the prisoners selected on August 13, 1864. Word had filtered back to the captives that the 50 who had gone before had been exchanged. "We were so certain that this last move was a bluff that every one was anxious to go," MacRae later wrote. On August 20, they boarded a steamer and set out. Only one hatch was left open to provide fresh air for the men. "Imagine then the situation in this foul hold," wrote MacRae, "near the steaming boilers, and glowing furnaces, with 600 sea-sick men, already enfeebled by close confinement, sweltering and gasping for water, which was doled out hot from the condensers." As the vessel neared Hilton Head, 40 detainees were sent to the base hospital. Critcher was among them,

14 Mauriel Joslyn, *Captives Immortal: The Story of the Six Hundred Confederate Officers and the United States Prisoner of War Policy* (Shippensburg, PA, 1996), 17-22.

15 Besides Alexander and Cowper, the members of the brigade selected were 7th NC: Capts. John Knox, Walter MacRae; 18th Regiment: Lts. David Bullard, George Corbet, John Elkins, John Frink, Franklin McIntosh, and Capt. Thomas Lewis; 28th NC: Lt. Henry Andrews, Capt. Simons Bohannon; 37th Regiment: Capt. Ander Critcher. Joslyn, ibid., 294-306.

suffering with chronic diarrhea. He was paroled on December 14 and made his way home to Watauga County.[16]

Dubbed the "Immortal 600," the prisoners arrived on September 7 at Morris Island, a long sand spit partially facing Charleston. Their pen, one and one-half acres of sand surrounded by logs, included 160 A-frame tents, four men per tent. According to one description, the stockade was:

> built immediately in front of what was formerly Battery Wagner. Our position was such that every shot or shell from the guns on Sumter and Moultrie and other Confederate batteries, must either pass close over our heads, or right through the pen. Any which fell short, or exploded a tenth of a second too soon, must strike death and destruction into our crowded ranks.

The Federals commenced firing soon after the prisoners arrived, but the Confederate artillery was slow to return the fire. MacRae believed they seemed unwilling to endanger their own men. One morning, after the Federal batteries opened fire, "we saw a puff of smoke blow out from Fort Moultrie, and almost immediately, heard the rush of a fine, large shell. It passed howling over our heads and smashed into the nearest embrasure, where it exploded within with much havoc." After seeing Federal ambulances removing the wounded, the prisoners "fervently shook hands with each other, and not one lifted up a voice of lamentation. It was a good shot!" At night, "the burning fuse [of Confederate shells] was plainly visible" to the prisoners and one could mark the flight of the shells from the moment they left."[17]

MacRae had much to say about the food. Their rations, he wrote:

> consisted of sour corn meal, meal which would stand alone when the barrel was knocked from it—stuff, as we were informed, which had been condemned by the Union Commissaries as wholly unfit for their troops. Occasionally we received a piece of hog meat, about one inch square, and, say half inch thick, with as many pickles, put up in something near akin to vitriol, as we wanted. Of the rotten meal we received daily six or eight ounces.[18]

16 Clark, *Histories*, 4:714; Mauriel Joslyn, *The Biographical Roster of the Immortal 600* (Shippensburg, PA, 1992), 81.

17 Clark, *Histories*, 4:716.

18 Ibid., 716-17.

No prisoner was wounded by Confederate fire. Yet exposure killed several of the men, including Cowper, who died of pneumonia on October 7. He was buried on Morris Island. Federal prisoners in Charleston were transferred to Columbia, SC, by the first of October. Three weeks later, the Confederate prisoners were told to pack their few belongings, and they were transferred farther south, to Fort Pulaski near Savannah. Many had believed they were going to be paroled. However, they were transferred farther south, to Fort Pulaski near Savannah, Georgia. While they were not subjected to the roar of cannon and the whistling of shells, clothing and blankets were scarce during the winter, and the rations were poor, mostly corn meal and pickles, supplemented by cats and rats. A few were so ill they were ultimately released. Henry C. Andrews (28th NC) was paroled on December 15, in Charleston. He spent time in a Richmond hospital before being transferred to the Invalid Corps. On March 4, 1865, the remaining prisoners were transferred back to Fort Delaware. Most of the Immortal 600 weren't paroled until May and June 1865.[19]

Despite the tragic experiences of the Immortal 600, their fellow captives in prison camps fared just as badly, even if their suffering was less public. As the war dragged on, conditions at various camps deteriorated. In mid-1864, as the prisoner of war exchange system ground to a complete halt, prison populations swelled. Confined to inadequate facilities, they begin suffering a host of deadly maladies exacerbated by malnutrition, limited medical care, and exposure. While most of those who perished in 1862 died of typhoid, caused by unsanitary drinking water, those in 1863-64 primarily succumbed to chronic diarrhea, and, during the winter of 1864-65, pneumonia. A small number of soldiers died from scurvy, heart disease, and small pox. William Montgomery (33rd NC), was the first documented brigade member to die as a prisoner of war—of unknown causes at Fort Columbus on March 14, 1862. The last brigade member to die a prisoner was Miles Ballard (28th NC), who expired from "ch[ronic] diarrhoea & scurvy" on July 28, 1865, in a Washington, D. C. hospital. Overall, September 1864 was the deadliest month for the brigade's POWs in terms of the number of men who died. Twenty-five brigade members succumbed that month.[20]

---

19 Joslyn, *Captives Immortal*, 176-78.

20 A survey of Jordan, *NC Troops*, showed 294 brigade members who died as prisoners. Thirty died of typhoid, 115 of dysentery or chronic diarrhea, and 54 of pneumonia. Many had no cause of death listed, and many more had incomplete records.

Those who didn't perish also suffered and sought constantly to distract themselves from the miseries of their condition. In October 1863, from one of the barracks on Johnson's Island, William Morris began writing home to his wife in Gaston County. Many of the letters, which were limited to one page, made it through the lines in what was called the "Dixie Mails." Prisoners could receive packages from home, or "close relatives." Though censored, Morris's letters provide a unique glimpse into an officer's life as a prisoner of war. Confederate currency was worthless except to exchange with another prisoner. A fellow officer loaned Morris some Federal currency when he first arrived at Johnson's Island, while another friend supplied clothing. At first, Morris could supplement his rations, buying anything he wished from the prison sutler. Over time, prison officials clamped down, only allowing sick prisoners to purchase additional foodstuffs. In several letters, Morris pleaded for a box of tobacco. "It would answer Me the Same purpose as Money," he wrote in July 1864, but his letters do not specify if he ever received the tobacco.[21]

At first, Morris was content with the food he received or was able to purchase. "I am in fine health & weigh 170," he wrote in December 1863. In July the next year, Morris told of several boxes "of eatables" that had come through the lines. His wife would be surprised to "see us figuring around a stove preparing our Meals," Morris thought, and wished he could invite her to join their dinner mess. In September 1864, he noted that prison officials began restricting their access to food and cutting their rations. "We are Not living so well." A month later, he confessed, "I am Not so fleshy as I was." He said the same in January 1865. While he never mentioned it, many of the prisoners at Johnson's Island (and elsewhere) supplemented their meager daily rations with rats.[22]

Joseph H. Saunders, lieutenant colonel of the 33rd Regiment, wounded and captured at Gettysburg, was like Morris, incarcerated at Johnson's Island. He likewise mentioned the "Dixie Mails," and complained when they were suspended or late. On February 11, 1865, about six weeks before his release, Saunders provided an intimate look at the life of a late-war prisoner:

---

21 Roger Pickenpaugh, *Captives in Gray: The Civil War Prisons of the Union* (Tuscaloosa, AL, 2009), 99; Morris to "Dear Companion," October 21, 1863, Morris Letters, SHC/UNC; July 29, 1864.

22 Morris Letters, SHC/UNC , December 21, 1863; July 7, September 14, October 20, 1864; Speer, *Portals to Hell*, 185.

James Summers rose from sergeant to command a company in the 33rd North Carolina. He was captured twice, once at Chancellorsville and again on April 2, 1865, during the Petersburg breakthrough.

Histories of the Several Regiments
and Battalions from North Carolina

I have changed so much that I scarcely know my self[.] one of the unaccountable to me is that beyond my pipe stem (have the same old pipe and bag that Florida gave me) have not made attempt to make a single thing[.] have [no] taste for those little things that use to amuse me[.] My Mind has almost entirely employed in thinking of the past—present and future none very pleasant.[23]

In September 1864, the opposing sides agreed to exchange dangerously sick prisoners. The next January talks opened on exchanging prisoners man for man, and an agreement was reached on February 4, 1865. Prisoners, in groups of 500, were scheduled for release over the next few weeks. Morris and seven other officers from Lane's brigade were paroled on March 14,. They, with many others from Johnson's Island, arrived at Cox's Wharf on the James River, VA, where they were received on March 22, for exchange.[24]

Lane's brigade lost its final lot of men as Confederate defenses fell in April 1865. Scores of soldiers from the depleted regiments were nabbed as the Federals stormed the works. Scores more were captured in hospitals across Richmond. These men swelled prison populations, and for a brief time after Lincoln's assassination, the release of Confederate prisoners ceased. George Benson (33rd NC), one of the many captured in the last days, had served since

23 Joseph Saunders to "My Dear Sister," February 11, 1865, Saunders Letters, SHC/UNC.

24 Jordan, *NC Troops,* 9:467.

October 1861, although at times he had been sick, and between December 1863 and May 1864, was absent without leave. After the war, he related that following his capture on April 2, he was placed on a steamer and transported to Point Lookout. "O what an auful place for poor Soldiers to be confined at," he wrote of his new surroundings. He wasn't released until June 23, 1865.[25]

Timothy Pridgen, a sergeant in the 18th Regiment, was the last brigade member released from prison. He had been wounded in the left thigh and captured on July 28, 1864. He was taken to City Point, and then transferred to a hospital in Alexandria. In February 1865, he was moved to a hospital in Washington, D.C. He wasn't released until November 9, 1865, when his broken femur had finally knit. The infection and damage necessitated a lengthy treatment, and Pridgen endured lifelong suffering. He wrote to Alexander Graham in 1867, trying to learn more about educational opportunities for disabled veterans like himself. He eventually married and settled in Sampson County, dying in 1907. Though the prison camp experience did not kill Pridgen and the other brigade members who survived the ordeal, it profoundly affected the rest of their lives, no matter how long they were.[26]

25 Ibid., 210; George Benson, "My Last Fighting and Prison Life," Private Collection.

26 Jordan, NC Troops, 6:421; Max Williams, ed., The Papers of William Alexander Graham, 8 vols. (Raleigh, NC, 1984), 7:313-14.

Chapter 13

"[B]ullets whistling all about them."

The Bristoe and Mine Run Campaigns

The bloodletting of Chancellorsville and Gettysburg left Lane's brigade in shambles. Colonels commanded the 18th, 33rd, and 37th, yet the 7th was led by a captain and the 28th by a wounded lieutenant colonel. Battlefield losses, sickness, and desertion had all thinned the ranks. "Oh! how my heart bleeds for our loved comrades who went down in the fierce onslaught at Gettysburg," lamented a member of the 28th. "Only a few more such bloody battles and North Carolina's host, the flower of the South, will be no more." The campaigns of May-July had cost the brigade 1,640 men.[1]

Soldiers absent without leave were a serious concern following the Gettysburg campaign. Men typically stole away by themselves, or with a trusted friend. Yet near the end of July, seven members of Company E, 33rd NC, left en masse, bound for their Carolina homes. Another six members of this company were declared deserters sometime during the same month. Of the 13,

---

1 North Carolina *Standard*, July 20, 1863; Lane, "History of Lane's North Carolina Brigade," *SHSP*, 10:73.

Maj. Gen. Cadmus Wilcox

Library of Congress

only five returned. Historian Mark Weitz contends the massive losses from Chancellorsville and Gettysburg, coupled with low morale following the retreat, drove men from the army and back toward their homes. Painfully aware of the depletion, Lee went so far as stationing pickets along the Staunton and Dan River crossings in the foothill areas in an attempt to catch the deserters. It "would be a great benefit . . . to catch them, in order to make some examples as speedily as possible," he told Secretary of War James Seddon.[2]

Besides trying to catch deserters and rebuild the ranks of his army, Lee needed to recommend a replacement for Pender. Following his wounding on July 2, Pender was transported by wagon to Staunton, VA, where his leg was amputated on July 18, but Pender succumbed to his wounds. Lane was the senior commander of the division, and permanent command should have devolved upon him. Yet when it came time to recommend someone for the position, Lee passed over Lane, writing "Lane the senior brigadier of the division is not recommended for promotion," before laying out his reasons for recommending fellow brigadier general Cadmus M. Wilcox instead. Wilcox, Lee continued, "one of the oldest brigadiers in the service, a highly capable officer, has served from the commencement of the war and deserves promotion. Being an officer of the regular army he is properly assignable

---

2 Jordan, *NC Troops*, 9:174-83; Mark Weitz, *More Damning than Slaughter: Desertion in the Confederate Army* (Lincoln, NE, 2005), 87; OR 27/3:1052. Six of the 13 deserters were transferred on July 14, 1862, from Company B, Cohoon's Battalion of Infantry.

anywhere." Wilcox had other advantages besides seniority. He was born in North Carolina, and many at home clamored to see fellow Tar Heels in higher commands; Wilcox was also a West Point graduate and decorated veteran of the war with Mexico, had served in the pre-war regular army, taught military tactics at West Point, toured Europe, and had written a book on the infantry evolution of the Austrian Army. He was serving as a regular army captain in the Fourth Infantry in the New Mexico Territory when the war began. Furthermore, his brother, John Wilcox, represented the state of Texas in the Confederate Congress, and might easily have championed Cadmus's approval as a major general. Wilcox's promotion to command of the Light Division was dated August 9, 1863. There does not seem to have been any dissent among the various brigades regarding his assignment.[3]

Federal forces crossed the Potomac River at Harper's Ferry on July 17, 1863, and advanced up the Loudoun Valley. Eventually cavalry, followed by infantry, arrived at Manassas Gap protecting Washington, D.C., pressuring Lee's supply line. Lee reacted by taking two corps through Front Royal and toward the vicinity of Culpepper. Lane's brigade moved around July 21. The Tar Heels found the road dusty, the weather hot, and their progress impeded by wagon trains. James Harris (7th NC) said the march had been hampered for two hours on July 25 by elements of Federal cavalry. According to Kennedy, the skirmish killed two members of the 28th and wounded nine others. The brigade went into camp on July 27, two miles past Culpepper Court House.[4]

A second Federal foray brought another change of scenery for Lane's brigade. On August 1, the second battle of Brandy Station began. For the next week, there was light skirmishing, and Lane's brigade was called up to support Confederate cavalry on August 2, but was never engaged. The following day, the brigade changed camps, passing through the Cedar Mountain battlefield,

---

3 Wills, *Pender*, 237-38; Freeman, *Lee's Dispatches*, 115-16; Freeman, *Lee's Lieutenants*, 3:202; Gerard A. Patterson, *From Blue to Gray: The Life of Confederate General Cadmus Wilcox* (Mechanicsburg, PA, 2001). Patterson writes Wilcox first met Lee in Mexico and served as second in command at West Point while Lee was superintendent. Some contend Jackson's wounding by Lane's men kept Lane from higher promotion. However, Wilcox's resume was far more impressive than Lane's, and his promotion clearly warranted. See Paul Bradley, "Was General Lane a Scapegoat?" *America's Civil War* (May 2013) 26/1:51. McDaid in "Four Years," 228, argues Lane and Wilcox were close friends for the remainder of their lives.

4 Harris, *Historical Sketches*, 40; Kennedy, Diary, July 23-25, 1863, SHC/UNC. The Kennedy and Harris dates are off by one day. Kennedy has the skirmish on July 24, and Harris writes they encountered Federal cavalry on July 25.

fording the Rapidan River, and eventually going into camp near Orange Court House. Picket posts were established at Morton's Ford, but active campaigning came to a standstill for the next six weeks.[5]

While the brigade was not actively fighting, conflict and struggle were still a part of everyday life. In early 1863, back in North Carolina, a peace movement began to gain traction. The leader of the movement was the editor of one the state's largest newspapers, the *Raleigh Standard*, William Woods Holden. Conscription laws, the impressments of agriculture and livestock, and the heavy-handedness of Confederate officers and officials all contributed to some citizens' strong dislike of an overreaching Confederate government. Holden threatened in June of 1863 to initiate a movement to remove North Carolina from the Southern Confederacy. More than 100 peace meetings were held in various North Carolina counties during July and August, with many adopting resolutions opposing the war effort to one degree or another. These resolutions, coupled with Holden's editorials, and the suffering of families back in North Carolina, all contributed to the demoralization of Tar Heel soldiers in the armies. One soldier in the 7th Regiment wrote there was "a good deal of dissatisfaction among the N. C. Troops," mostly on account of "Old Holden's press."[6]

Something had to be done. Officials called for a convention of North Carolina troops to meet at Orange Court House on August 12. More than 30 Tar Heel regiments sent representatives who proceeded to approve resolutions supporting the continuation of the war, many of which were published in state newspapers. At these meetings, a member of each company was appointed to a committee to write resolutions. As the committees toiled, calls were made for speeches. Most of the resolutions that passed passionately denounced the peace movement. We "have witnessed with profound indignation the course pursued by the *Raleigh Standard*," read the resolution of the 37th Regiment, "in reference to our existing affairs, and that the sentiments enunciated by these journals, are in the highest degree treasonable, meriting as they receive, an almost unanimous repudiation by our soldiers in the field." The wording from the 28th Regiment was just as strong:

---

5 Harris, *Historical Sketches*, 41; Lane, "History of Lane's North Carolina Brigade," *SHSP*, 9:71.

6 Robert Yates, "Governor Vance and the Peace Movement," *North Carolina Historical Review* (1940), 27/1:2-3; C. F. Mills to Harrison Mills, September 6, 1863, C. F. Mills Papers, DU.

> Resolved, That those who seek thus to bring the Commonwealth of North Carolina in
> conflict with the Government of the Confederate States, who thus create discord and
> disturbances at home and furnish our defeated foe with further encouragement
> towards our further subjugation, and prevent our depleted ranks from being filled, as
> the law directs, are not only guilty of giving aid and comfort to our enemies, but are
> treating North Carolina soldiers in the field with neither consideration nor justice.[7]

Resolutions adopted in camp rejecting the peace movement back home did little to improve morale. "There is much excitement among the N. C Troops about the peace talk at home," William Speer wrote, adding prophetically that he believed the meetings and resolutions "will amount to but little." The Confederate government did attempt to entice deserters and those absent without leave to return to the army via the issue of amnesty proclamations, including one by Jefferson Davis on August 1, 1863, giving men 20 days to return to their regiments. Instead of luring men back to the ranks, it gave many without furloughs the impetus to visit home. The problem of absent soldiers only worsened as 1863 dragged on.[8]

Active campaigning started again in September. Longstreet's corps was transferred to Tennessee, beginning on September 8. Lee staged a review of his two remaining corps, Ewell's on September 10 and Hill's on September 11. Federal cavalry, supported by an infantry corps, crossed over the Rappahannock River on September 13. Finding no Confederate infantry, the Army of the Potomac's commander, Maj. Gen. George G. Meade, gained permission to move the rest of his army across the river on September 15. The Federals established headquarters at Culpepper Court House. Once again the opposing forces cautiously watched each across a river, this time, the Rapidan.

A Confederate victory at Chickamauga goaded Lee from his defensive mindset. Even without Longstreet, Lee's numbers were increasing. Speer reported the ranks of the 28th NC had grown from 118 men after Gettysburg to 453 men. Word also filtered back to Lee that the Federals had moved two corps, probably to the West. While Meade's army still outnumbered Lee's, the odds were better for the Confederates. Lee could not attack the Federals from where he was. Instead, he chose a flanking maneuver, one that was often successful.

---

7   Yates, "Governor Vance and the Peace Movement," *North Carolina Historical Review*, 2-3; *The Evening Bulletin*, August 20, 1863; *Weekly Raleigh Register*, August 26, 1863.

8   Speer, *Voices from Cemetery Hill*, 110.

He divided his army into two columns, with Hill's corps having the longer distance to cover. Lane's brigade moved on October 9, appearing to have served as the rear guard of the column, protecting the wagon train and reserve artillery. While Confederate cavalry fought repeatedly with their Federal counterparts, infantry contact was limited. They advanced at times through rain, and at times on roads through forests cut by the Confederate pioneer corps. Most days they were up early to march. On October 12, however, cattle for the day's rations arrived just before dawn, so the men did not move out until 8:00 a.m., once the butchering process was complete and the meat prepared. Hill's column traveled through Warrenton, Chestnut Hill, New Baltimore, and toward Buckland on the Broad Run. On October 15, elements of Heth's division, in front of Wilcox's men, engaged the Federals near Bristoe Station. Two Confederate brigades were chewed up in the fighting, and a battery of artillery was lost. Lee criticized Hill for attacking instead of waiting for other portions of his corps to come up. Lane's brigade was deployed, but save for the "bullets whistling all about them," not engaged.[9]

Lee's campaign to flank the Federals out of their position came to naught, and the general had to make a choice. Confederate forces were close to Washington, D.C., and any further pursuit would simply push the Federal army into the extensive works lining the city. Such a move would also leave Richmond uncovered. Moreover, Lee's army had no rail link for supplies. The Federals had wrecked the bridge over the Rappahannock River, and rations would have to come via wagon until the span was rebuilt. Therefore, Lee chose to move back to where he started. To deny the Federals the use of the railroad, he ordered the tracks dismantled. Lane's brigade commenced demolishing the tracks of the Orange and Alexander Railroad, three to four miles from Bristoe. His men "had become expert" at tearing up tracks, Lane wrote after the war. "Perhaps it may be of interest to know how this was done," Octavius Wiggins (37th NC) added. "The rails were ripped up and pens made of the cross-ties, the rails then laid on the pens which were set on fire, the irons soon become red hot in centre, when half a dozen soldiers would seize each end and run to a telegraph post, or tree, and play circus by running rapidly around it—bending the rail three or four times around the post." Their work done, Confederates

9 Speer, *Voices from Cemetery Hill*, 115; Harris, *Historical Sketches*, 43; Clark, *Histories*, 2:569; William Henderson, *The Road to Bristoe Station: Campaigning with Lee and Meade, August 1 - October 20, 1863* (Lynchburg, VA, 1987), 78-163.

headed back toward their former camps. "The Federal forces immediately followed, rebuilding the railroad as they advanced," complained a member of the 7th Regiment.[10]

Lane's brigade went into camp at Brandy Station, remaining inactive until November 7. Federal infantry attacked a Confederate position at Rappahannock Bridge that day, capturing large portions of two brigades from Ewell's Corps. Lee placed Hill's corps on alert, and the men were ordered to prepare one day's rations. Before dawn on November 8, Lane's brigade marched toward Culpepper Court House, eventually catching the rest of the Light Division and going into a line of battle, with the 18th NC on the far left protecting the Confederate flank. A couple hours later, Lane's brigade was also ordered to the left, along the Warrenton Road, to subdue Federal cavalry and reinforce the 18th. Lane placed the 7th and 37th NC under Col. Barber's command. The Federal horsemen were close enough to fire into these two regiments as they deployed. Once into position, the Tar Heels gave the "familiar 'Rebel Yell'" and a volley that emptied "a number of saddles and sent the cavalrymen flying to the rear in confusion." The 7th and 37th chased the Federals for about half a mile, when they were ordered to halt, and the two regiments returned to the "reserve picket post." An anonymous brigade member wrote that had not Lane's brigade arrived, the Federal cavalry most likely would have turned the Confederate flank "and in fact, [put] our entire rear at his mercy." The action cost the brigade two killed and 11 wounded. Skirmishing continued throughout the remainder of the day.

Under the cover of darkness, the Carolinians headed toward their former camp. Chaplain Kennedy complained of weather, bitterly cold and "disagreeable . . . The fences for miles along the line of march were all ablaze and such straggling I have never witnessed. Thousands were gathered around the fires." Despite the cold, the soldiers forded the Rapidan, and Kennedy made several trips, ferrying soldiers over on his horse.[11]

---

10 Clark, *Histories*, 2:479, 663; Harris, *Historical Sketches*, 42.

11 Harris, *Historical Sketches*, 42.; *The Charlotte Democrat*, November 24, 1863; Kennedy, Diary, November 9, 1863, SHC/UNC. William McLaurin in his history of the 18th Regiment says the whole attack was an ambush. Confederate cavalry fell back, while the 18th, positioned in some woods, cut off the line of retreat. The Federals discovered the trap but still lost several troopers. Clark, *Histories,* 2:45. General Lane never mentions the ambush. See "History of Lane's North Carolina Brigade." *SHSP,* 9:72.

Lane's brigade returned to winter quarters at Liberty Mills, spending the next couple of weeks picketing a bridge over the Rapidan and along the Stanardsville Road. With tents in short supply, the men built improvised shelters. Blankets and overcoats were also sparse, and mornings were frosty. Besides picket duty, camp routine was punctuated by lively religious revivals and the execution of several members of the brigade for desertion and misbehaving before the enemy. That fall, Lane had to quell some discontent in his brigade. Colonel Clark Avery, the third senior colonel in the whole army, sought a promotion to brigadier general. One idea Governor Vance passed along to Secretary of War Seddon was formation of a new military district in western North Carolina, with Avery in command, but when the district was created, command went instead to the governor's brother. A month later, Vance again wrote Seddon, recommending a new brigade composed of the 1st, 3rd, 33rd, and 55th NC Regiments, with Avery in command. Avery told Vance he "never had the slightest difficulty with Gen Lane," but believed "the universal opinion of the Brigade is that he has never done my regiment justice in his official reports." Seddon referred the matter to General Lee. Catching wind of the possible breakup of his brigade, Lane wrote to one of Lee's staff officers that he was "opposed to having my command reduced to gratify the aspirations of any subordinate officers." Wilcox endorsed Lane's letter, adding, "if there should be such a scheme in contemplation, I beg that the brigade of General Lane may not be mutilated." Lee, who had final say in the matter, squelched the idea, writing after the first of the year that he believed the "men. . . would be satisfied if let alone." On November 17, the troops were ordered to prepare two days' rations and be ready to move. This was in reaction to a reported Federal cavalry raid at Morton's Ford. The order was later countermanded.[12]

Spurred by leaders in Washington, D. C., Federal forces launched another offensive on November 23, 1863, aiming to slip between Lee and Richmond and force the Confederates out of their works and out into the open. Lee did leave his entrenchments, planning to attack the Federals while they were shifting to the southeast. Federals were near the Confederate right flank. Late on November 26, the Federals crossed the Rapidan River. Hill's corps occupied

12 Lane, "History of Lane's North Carolina Brigade." *SHSP*, 9:72; Joe Mobley, ed., *The Papers of Zebulon Baird Vance*, 2 vols. (Raleigh, NC, 1995), 2:283; OR 29/2:867-69; Harris, *Historical Sketches*, 43.

the left flank. Lane's brigade set out about 2:30 the following morning. They trudged 23 miles before going into camp in a pine thicket.[13]

On arriving, Confederate troops began building breastworks. For the remainder of the war, any time they stopped, the men started digging in. Wilcox's division occupied the center of Hill's line, across the Orange Plank Road, with Anderson's division to his right and Heth's division to his left. Federal probes discovered weakness on Hill's left, so on November 29, Federal Maj. Gen. Gouverneur K. Warren moved into the area. Hill quickly responded, shifting his entire corps to the left of the Plank Road. Skirmishing took place between the opposing sides, but no general battle commenced. Instead of fighting the foe, the soldier fought the elements. Since no fires were permitted, Lane wrote the pickets out in front of the lines were rotated off every half hour.[14]

The clothing and shoes of the men during this march and deployment were in deplorable condition because of persistent problems in the Confederate quartermaster's department and the state of North Carolina. "The scenes of suffering at Valley Forge in the old Revolution which are so historically famous, are surpassed in the present war," lamented one member of the brigade. Lane recalled these conditions in his postwar history of the brigade. He reported seeing a young soldier of the 7th Regiment,

> barefooted, without drawers, and his pants in front split up to the knee, take off his knapsack, take out an dirty counterpane—the only thing, by the way, it contained—and when he was in the act of replacing his knapsack upon his shoulders, some three or four merry-hearted fellows ran up, crying out, "Hold on, Jake, hold on, and let us help you!" Yelling and laughing, they helped him on with it, and when he folded his counterpane and wrapped it around his shoulder, another glorious old rebel, almost as "seedy" looking, who had been sitting with his back against the works, watching the whole performance in silence, yelled out, "Now Jake, you have fortified one end, what are you gwine to do with t'other?" Jack's only reply was a back-step and a double-shuffle, the wind all the while making streamers of his torn pants. This performance was greeted with shouts and uproarious laughter from every looker on.[15]

13 *Charlotte Democrat*, November 24, 1863; Kennedy, Diary, November 27, 1863, SHC/UNC.

14 Lane, "History of Lane's North Carolina Brigade," *SHSP*, 9:72.

15 Ibid.; Kennedy, Diary, November 27, 1863, SHC/UNC.

When the Federals did not attack, Lee took the initiative. Wilcox and Anderson's divisions were moved out of the trenches and around the Federal flank. When day broke on December 2, the enemy was gone. The army quickly returned to winter quarters. Serious campaigning ended until the spring.

Following the Bristoe Station and Mine Run campaigns, life for the soldiers settled down into the tedious routine of winter quarters, with clothing poor and rations slim. William Campbell (37th NC) wrote home in late December: "we are suffering without a doubt[.] we are drawing flower [rations] but mute [meat] not regular a tall[;] we hante drawn but one rashing of meat in five days until today. . . one pint of flower and nothing with it aint a nuff you know for a man a day. Wife if you have anything you can spare and has a chance please send it me." A general order read to the men in mid-January apologized for the reduction in rations, but admonished the men to remember the sacrifices their forefathers had endured during the Revolution. Rations had not improved by March 12, when Augustus Shore (33rd NC) complained they: "keep getting a little shorter[.] we dont get but two oz of meat some times for one day[.] but we grin and endure it and keep in good spirits[.]" Lee allowed a greater number of men to obtain furloughs over the winter months, up to eight men per one hundred present. Others were detailed home to retrieve boxes of provisions and clothing for the men in camp.[16]

One officer in the 37th reported in late January half his company was without shoes. The cobblers in the brigade, using camp-crafted tools, labored to construct shoes when leather could be found. Boots in need of repair were brought to the brigade cobblers as well. Captain Edward Nicholson, the brigade Assistant Adjutant General, was charged with the management of the shoe shop. Revivals continued to sweep through the camps, when the weather permitted. However, in April 1864, Chaplain Kennedy was reassigned to a post in Charlotte. Lane lamented his loss, adding the brigade was left with one chaplain following Kennedy's departure. Fortunately, the number of executions, which had reached a war-time high in the fall of 1863, dwindled.[17]

---

16 William Campbell to Parents, December 29, 1864, private collection; J. F. J. Caldwell, *The History of a Brigade of South Carolinians* (Philadelphia, PA, 1866), 168; Jordan Council to wife, January 17, 1864, Mary Council Papers, DU; Thomas Norwood to Uncle, January 30, 1864, Lenoir Papers, SHC; 37th Letter Book, 2:22, Confederate Military Collection, DU; Augustus Shore to Mother, March 12, 1864, Shore letters, EU.

17 Lane, "Glimpses of Army Life in 1864," *SHSP*, 18:407-11; *Fayetteville Observer*, February 15, 1864.

Dreadful weather sometimes plagued the camps. In mid-February, Noah Collins wrote it was so cold that if a soldier dipped his hands in water to wash his face, the water would have "a skim of ice" on it before the hands returned. As during the winter before, the soldiers engaged in great snowball battles. The one in late March 1864 pitted the 7th, 18th, and 33rd Regiments against the 28th and 37th. Other men skated on frozen ponds. Some soldiers used their time to make trinkets for those at home. "I have a ring to send you the first chance [I get]," wrote John Tally (37th NC), "a nice bone ring." General Lane related a story that in April 1864, there was a "tournament" attended by several ladies and generals. Thirteen "knights" competed at saber, pistol, jumping, taking a ring, and other feats. There was a master of ceremonies, the brigade band playing between rounds, and a dance following the festivities. "Everything passed off very pleasantly, both at the tournament and dance," Lane recorded.[18]

There were several memorable events in the winter of 1863-64. Three regiments in the brigade, the 18th, 28th, and 37th, had to re-enlist. Each of these had re-enlisted for two years in the spring of 1862, and their enlistment was set to expire. Every veteran within the ranks knew he really had no say in the matter. Those who did not re-enlist would be conscripted right back into the army. Officers were instrumental in the process. A captain in the 28th Regiment "was wild with enthusiasm, and jumping in front of it, he yelled out 'Good for all Company A! Men, I love the very ground you stand on,'" when his company re-enlisted. Captain Gold Holland exhorted his company to "Be firm." When his company all re-enlisted, he asked his colonel if the men could raise three cheers. Permission was granted, "and the biggest sort of an old Rebel yell was raised at once," Lane wrote. Men who declined re-enlistment in the 28th and 37th Regiments were pulled out of the ranks, lined up, and threatened with being labeled "revolters, deserters and base cowards" in local newspapers. Later, Col. Barber gave them another chance by circulating adopted resolutions, promising to have the names of re-enlistees removed from the forthcoming article. Twenty men still held out, objecting to several aspects of the resolution: its call for the execution of deserters, for example, its declaration of satisfaction with the regiment's officers, and its pledge to continue the fight until war's end. Noah Collins, one of the dissenters, wrote he "could not see how any person possessed of reasonable sense, or regard for man, justice, or obligation, to say

18 Collins, "Reminisces," 47; John W. Tally to Wife, December 15, 1863, private collection; Lane, "Glimpses of Army Life in 1864," *SHSP,* 18:411.

nothing about the future, could vote for such resolutions." In the end, all of the men in the 18th and 28th Regiments re-enlisted unanimously. When the resolutions of the 37th Regiment were published in state newspapers, the names of the 20 objectors were not reported.[19]

In an effort to boost morale among North Carolina troops in Lee's army, and to influence voters in the upcoming gubernatorial campaign, Governor Vance visited various brigades' camps in late March and early April 1864. Vance was originally scheduled to speak to Lane's brigade on April 1, but rain and a sore throat postponed the speech. Many of the men cried "April Fools" as they slogged back to camp. Vance was rescheduled to visit Lane's brigade on April 6. On the day before, Lane, and Captains Nicholson and Hale rode over to Scales's brigade to get a preview of Vance. Hale reported the events for his father's newspaper, the *Fayetteville Weekly Observer*. An estimated crowd of 3-4,000 men from four different brigades attended. For an hour and 40 minutes, the governor spoke on the folly of the peace movement, North Carolina's support for the Southern Confederacy, and the prowess of the Confederate soldier. "The yankee fights for pay. . . . The yankee will cease to fight when fighting ceases to pay," Hale recorded him saying. The number of speeches, along with the bad weather, Hale wrote, had made the governor hoarse. Yet the soldiers "were at one moment convulsed with laughter: at the next, in some instances, moved to tears at his touching eloquence, or excited with fierce determination." Lane and Kennedy both believed Vance did a good job. Colonel Barber introduced Vance when it came time to speak in front of Lane's brigade, and when he finished, numerous cheers rose up. He didn't satisfy everybody, however. George Williams (7th NC) was offended by Vance's belief the fighting "should be carried on until hell froze over and then waged on the ice." The soldiers were "not willing to fight as long as that," Williams believed, "and think Mr. Holden is not fighting that long and he is our choice By [sic] a large majority." Despite Williams's predictions, Vance handily defeated Holden in the election.[20]

19 Lane, "Glimpses of Army Life in 1864," *SHSP*, 18:407; Collins, "Reminisces," 47; *The Daily Confederate*, February 19, 1864. Lee mentioned the re-enlistment of Lane's brigade in a letter to Samuel Cooper on February 15, 1864. *OR* 33:1173.

20 Kennedy, Diary, April 1, 1864, SHC/UNC; *Fayetteville Semi-Weekly Observer*, April 14, 1864; Lane, "Glimpses of Army Life in 1864," *SHSP*, 18:408; George Williams to Father, April 5, 1864, Williams-Wobble Papers, NCDAH. Alfred Profit writes Vance was due to speak to Lane's brigade on April 2 or 3, but the weather was bad. Hancock, *Four Brothers in Gray*, 256.

Along with other brigade commanders, Lane started organizing a sharp-shooter battalion for his brigade in the fall of 1863. The best marksmen from the various regiments were organized in a battalion, with Capt. John Knox (7th NC) in command. These sharp-shooters performed no camp or picket duties. Once they mastered the basic drill, they learned to judge distances. According to Lane, the men were "drawn up in a line, and one of their number having been sent forward, it was their duty to guess how far distant he was. When the first guesses were read aloud and the correct distances known, loud laughter and amusing remarks soon convinced many that their untrained eyes were anything but accurate." As the men became proficient in judging distance, they were issued 22 rounds of ammunition and required to fire at 100, 300, 600, and 900 yards. The names of the five best shots were forwarded to division headquarters. During the next couple of weeks, marksmanship improved. Lane had the targets brought back to camp and the names of the best shots written on them and displayed for all to see.[21]

Besides rotating on and off picket duty, the brigade was called out on several occasions. On January 29, they were ordered to have three days' rations on hand, one cooked, and be prepared to move in an instant. Half of the 28th NC was on picket on February 6, when the Federals probed the lines. The rest of the regiment and all of the 33rd were sent to reinforce the picket line. On February 7, the entire brigade was on line. With rifle and cannon fire sounding in the distance, Lane's brigade, along with those of Scales and McGowan, embarked with Stuart's cavalry on a three-mile march in an attempt to flank the Federals. Wilcox was absent, and Lane was in charge of the Light Division. Much to the Confederates' chagrin, the Federals were gone by the time they arrived. The regiments were called out again on March 1, when a large force of enemy cavalry was spotted moving toward Richmond. Amidst abysmal

---

William Speer writes the speech took place on April 4, 1864. Speer, *Voices from Cemetery Hill*, 122-24. Hale, in his letter dated April 5, says Vance was to speak to Lane's brigade next, possibly on April 6.

21 Lane, "History of Lane's North Carolina Brigade," *SHSP*, 10:206; *Charlotte Observer*, August 20, 1893; Fred Ray, *Shock Troops of the Confederacy: The Sharpshooter Battalions of the Army of Northern Virginia* (Asheville, NC, 2006), 94-95. It is unclear just how many men served in this battalion. In Thomas's brigade, two to four men from each company were selected. However, a post-war account from a member of the 33rd Regiment states the battalion was composed of three men from each regiment. *The Morganton Herald*, August 30, 1894. Caldwell writes in his history of the Gregg-McGowan brigade that their sharpshooter battalion was composed of six officers, ten non-commissioned officers, and 160 privates. *The History of a Brigade of South Carolinians*, 172.

weather—rain, sleet, and snow—Hill's corps was ordered to Madison Court House. After a couple of miserable days in the bitter cold, the brigade returned to their camps, disappointed they were unable to trap Federal cavalry.[22]

As the doldrums of winter gave way to the rebirth of spring, everyone knew time for active campaigning was nigh. Furloughs were suspended in March, and on April 18, Lee ordered all surplus baggage to be sent to the rear. "The sunshine and the winds were fast hardening the roads, and hourly hastening the impending struggle which, it was conceded by all, would decide the fate of the Confederacy," a member of the 7th NC wrote in hindsight. Indeed, there was still a year of hard war left, and indeed it would "decide the fate of the Confederacy."[23]

22 Collins, "Reminisces," 46-50; Kennedy, Diary, January 7-April 5, 1864, SHC/UNC; *Fayetteville Observer*, February 18, 1864. It is unclear who led the brigade during the February encounter.

23 Freeman, *R. E. Lee*, 3:266; Harris, *Historical Sketches*, 44.

Chapter 14

"Mahone took his cussing."

The Overland Campaign

Over the winter months of 1863-64, Lane's brigade grew. Men wounded during the Chancellorsville and Gettysburg campaigns returned to the ranks, while more conscripts arrived from North Carolina. The spring of 1864 found 2,350 men in the ranks, making it the largest brigade in the Army of Northern Virginia. Colonels commanded at least three of Lane's regiments. The 28th was under Lt. Col. William Speer, while the 7th NC was commanded by Lt. Col. William Davidson. The men were issued clothing in late April and were well armed, but undoubtedly could have used improved rations. Overall, Lee's army mustered around 65,000 men.[1]

While George Meade still commanded the Army of the Potomac, Ulysses S. Grant, recently named commander of all Federal armies, made his camp with Meade's army, exercising tactical control. On May 3, the Federal army of some 120,000 men crossed the Rapidan River, intent on flanking Lee out of the Mine

---

1   Alfred Young, III, *Lee's Army During the Overland Campaign: A Numerical Study* (Baton Rouge, LA, 2013), 139.

Run defenses and moving quickly through the Wilderness to draw out the Army of Northern Virginia into the open. The movement of the Potomac army was in conjunction with planned offensives east of Richmond, in the Shenandoah Valley, in north Georgia, and around Mobile, Alabama. By applying simultaneous pressure on multiple points, Gen. Grant hoped to keep the Confederates from using interior lines to reinforce threatened sectors.

About 1:00 p.m. on May 4, several members of the brigade observed a courier hastily riding into Lane's camp. Within a few moments, officers were barking orders, with men scurrying about, packing tents and wagons, and falling into ranks. Shortly thereafter, Heth's division, followed by Wilcox's, was on the march toward the same ground where they had fought a year earlier. About 11:00 that night, Wilcox's division camped at the village of Verdiersville.[2]

Up before daylight on May 5, the men passed through the old Mine Run defenses and moved along the Orange Plank Road. Just before noon, the report of skirmishers' rifles sounded ahead. Lee planned to secure the intersection of the Orange Plank Road and the Brock Road, and deployed Heth's division. To the north, Ewell's corps, moving along the Orange Turnpike, engaged the Federals as well. To seal the gap between Heth's division and Ewell's corps, Hill was ordered to send Wilcox's division into the slot. With Lane's brigade in the lead, Wilcox moved the division off to the left. Two brigades from the division were sent to the right as they passed through the Chewing farm, while Lane and Thomas continued ahead. Lane deployed his brigade as they neared Wilderness Run, while Captain Knox fanned out the sharpshooter battalion in front of the brigade. At least part of the brigade advanced toward the Federals as the sharpshooters became seriously engaged. In a matter of moments, they had captured 147 Federal soldiers, while incurring no losses. On Heth's front, massed enemy infantry attacked, and Hill sent word to Wilcox to hurry his division back toward the Orange Plank Road to support Heth.[3]

Quickly, Wilcox's men shifted toward Heth's position. As Lane transferred his brigade to the south side of the road, Federals were reported "approach[ing] from the left of the road," the same direction they had just come. To protect their rear, the 37th NC wheeled out of line and into position along the road. Lane ordered his Tar Heels to drop knapsacks and deployed the rest of his

2   Harris, *Historical Sketches*, 44; J. H. Harris to "Captain," July 19, 1864, Lane Papers, AU.

3   Harris, *Historical Sketches*, 45; James Lane, "History of Lane's North Carolina Brigade," *SHSP*, 9:124-29.

Lieutenant Frank Craige, 33rd North Carolina, was saved from serious injury at the battle of the Wilderness when a bullet struck his belt buckle.

Histories of the Several Regiments and Battalions from North Carolina

brigade from the left: the 7th, 33rd, 28th, and 18th NC Regiments, with the brigade sharpshooters to the right of the 18th. Soldiers described "dense," woods with plenty of "mire and mud."[4]

There was as much confusion now in the Wilderness as there had been a year earlier, when Jackson rode out in front of his men, and they accidentally shot and killed him. Hill informed Lane that part of Scales's brigade had been driven from the front, and Lane needed to restore the line. Once he positioned his brigade, Lane called for an advance, cautioning the 7th not to fire, as there were Confederates somewhere in their front. Almost 2,000 Tar Heels raised the "Rebel Yell" as they crashed through the woods. Lane described the advance as "necessarily slow, as we had to move through a swamp filled with dense undergrowth and dead fallen trees." Heavy fire from enemy rifles slowed the brigade's advance as much as the terrain did, yet the Confederates pushed the Federals back. In the evening twilight, the men in the 7th could see shadowy forms to their left. Heeding Lane's warning, they withheld fire as they moved closer. Suddenly, there was a cry for the 7th to surrender, followed by "a destructive volley" of musketry, and the left of the regiment collapsed. Those not killed, wounded, or captured streamed to the rear. Unable to find Lt. Col. Davidson in the confusion, Capt. Harris took command of the right wing and what he could find of the left, and pulled the

---

4   Clark, *Histories,* 2:570, 665; Harris, *Historical Sketches,* 44; Samuel Cowan to "Captain," July 9, 1864, Lane Papers, AU.

7th Regiment back into line with the 33rd Regiment. Harris later gave the losses in the 7th Regiment as 5 killed, 39 wounded, and 31 captured.[5]

Lane's right endured an equally difficult struggle. As he advanced, the 38th NC of Scales's Brigade came up behind Lane's line. The 18th NC and the brigade sharpshooters shifted to the right, while the 38th went on line between the 28th and 18th. Lane reported the pressure on the right so great that Col. Barry had to refuse the two right companies of his command. Further heated attacks forced Barry to turn the entire 18th to the south, at right angles to the rest of the brigade. An enemy bullet struck one soldier in the 18th, Richard Reeves, as he loaded his rifle. The round hit his bent arm, passing through four times. The 18th held its position a short time but was eventually forced to give way.[6]

In the center of Lane's line, the 28th and 33rd NC still held against an enemy so close that "We could almost hear [them] breathing," one officer in the 33rd wrote. The 28th NC continued advancing and, according to Col. Speer, drove the Federals from a third line of defenses. Speer soon discovered he had outpaced the troops to his right by some 200 yards. Furthermore, the 28th was running low on ammunition. His men had to raid the cartridge boxes of friend and foe alike near their position. At some point, Wilcox ordered McGowan's brigade, on Lane's left, to withdraw, which exposed Lane's flank. Confronted by the partial collapse of the 7th, Federals working their way around the refused 18th NC, and men running low on ammunition, Lane ordered his brigade to withdraw and reform on a rise above the swamp. Polycarp Lail recalled that he and Adley Holler, serving as the color guard for the 28th NC, failed, along with Ensign Junius Little, to see the retreat of their regiment in the intense fighting. Lail attributed their escape to "Providence," which saved them "from being mangled with bullets."[7]

5 JL to "Major," September 8, 1864; James Harris to "Captain," July 19, 1864, both in Lane Papers, AU.

6 JL to "Major," September 8, 1864; Richard Reeves, "Reminiscences." RNBP. The position of the 18th Regiment on the evening of May 5 isn't clear. Regimental Adjutant William McLaurin wrote many years later that his regiment was sent "near a mile" beyond the Orange Plank Road, where he found the 38th NC fighting. It is unlikely the 18th traveled "near a mile" past the brigade's position in the dark, in the Wilderness, to fight. Clark, *Histories*, 2:47.

7 Clark, *Histories*, 2:570; William Speer to "Captain," July 19, 1864, JL Papers, AU; Hahn, *The Catawba Soldier*, 187. Lail contends Little was wounded, but Little's wounding is not reported in his compiled service record.

Junius Little escaped with the flag of the 28th North Carolina during the battle of the Wilderness, but was captured at Spotsylvania Court House.

Histories of the Several Regiments and Battalions from North Carolina

On his way to the rear, Lane encountered Barry Benson, a sharpshooter in McGowan's brigade. "Are you bringing in cartridges?" Asked Lane, thinking Benson was coming up to re-supply his brigade. "Yes, in our cartridge boxes," was Benson's reply, as he and his pards held up their cartridge boxes. "That's right," was Lane's reply, according to Benson.[8]

Many men became confused in the darkness. Lieutenant Colonel Davidson, for example, "stumbled on the Federals," while wandering in the woods. They "quietly put out their hands and drew him in. Not a word was spoken." William McLaurin, the 18th's adjutant, was also wandering in the woods, having "lost my bearings," in the constant movement. He stumbled "in the darkness [and] got into Hancock's corps and had to tack variously to get out." For two hours he blundered his way toward Confederate lines, eventually finding the plank road.[9]

It took most of the night for members of Lane's brigade to find their comrades. The core of the brigade had been moved behind Scales's command. As McLaurin hustled down the Orange Plank Road, he spied "General Wilcox's white horse" and approached the general. "Out of wind, and gasping between words, I told him that I was just out of Hancock's corps, and that there was not a man between him and Hancock's skirmishers." Wilcox did not believe the story, "and was not over polite in letting me know it." McLaurin eventually

---

8   Berry Benson, "Reminiscences," Berry Benson Papers, SHC/UNC.

9   Clark, *Histories*, 2:47, 570.

found his brigade and told Lane and Colonels Barry and Avery the same thing. When Lane went to Wilcox, the general rejected it again: Heth's division was in front, he said, and his tired soldiers were not to be disturbed.[10]

McLaurin was correct. Save for the dead and wounded, no Confederate troops were in front of Wilcox. Eventually Wilcox realized it. Several times throughout the night, he and Heth went to General Hill, pleading for permission to reorganize their lines. Each time they were told Longstreet's corps would be up before dawn to establish a line in front of Hill's spent divisions. Wilcox even went to Lee's headquarters at the Widow Tapp's Farm and fruitlessly pled his case there.[11]

Benjamin F. White (18th NC) recalled once the day's battle ended, the soldiers "slept on their arms in a stone's throw of each other . . . the plaintive voice of the whippoorwill added to the dreariness and suspense . . . of the great tragedy." The two sides were so close they could hear each other talking, according to White. "About midnight a big owl sitting in a tree broke the stillness with his hoot— 'who, who, who-are-you?' A soldier of the 18th answered back, 'The 18th North Carolina Regiment, A damn fool!' The thing was so ludicrous the Confederates and Federals roared with laughter."[12]

Unfortunately for White and the other Confederates on the right of Lee's line, Wilcox waited too long to take the initiative. About 4:00 a.m., he ordered the division's pioneers to "come to the front with axes, spades, etc., to fell trees and construct works." Yet the pioneers found the Federal lines too close to their own. Before Longstreet could arrive on the field, two Federal corps crashed into Confederate lines. Scales's brigade quickly gave way, its survivors streaming back into Lane's bivouac. Lane was struggling to position his brigade. Although he had not received orders, he had moved the 33rd, 18th, and 37th NC into a position fronting the enemy, with a portion of the 33rd bent back toward the Orange Plank Road. The 28th and 7th Regiments had not yet re-deployed and were probably near the road. James Weston recalled that the 33rd had just settled down to "a good breakfast cooked from Yankee rations captured the evening before, when, suddenly, sharp and rapid firing was heard in our front." The 18th and 37th NC quickly crumpled under the weight of the

---

10 Ibid., 47.

11 Gordon Rhea, *The Battle of the Wilderness, May 5-6, 1864* (Baton Rouge, LA, 1994), 279.

12 *Wilmington Messenger*, January 30, 1898.

Colonel Cark M. Avery was mortally wounded trying to stem the Federal breakthrough at the Wilderness during the second day of fighting. He lingered for more than a month before dying on June 18, 1864.

North Carolina Museum of History

Confederate soldiers pouring through their ranks from in front of them. "[T]he men were willing to fight," Octavius Wiggins wrote, "but had no chance. . . . The 37th was borne gradually back . . . *without firing a gun.*" The 7th and 28th also collapsed. Ensign Junius Little had the colors of the 28th Regiment. Captain Edward Lovell attempted to grab the flag to rally the men, but Little resisted. He reached "for his pistol," Little remembered later, [giving] "the Captain to understand that he was man enough to carry that flag and for him to let it alone."[13]

Only the 33rd Regiment held. The men moved quickly to some improvised breastworks and opened fire upon the Federals. Colonel Avery was walking behind the men, encouraging them to stand fast. "Colonel, shelter yourself behind these breastworks," Maj. James Weston warned. "If you walk about in that way, you will certainly be killed." "No, no. . . It will make the men fight better," was Avery's reply. A member of the 16th NC overheard Avery saying, "we will give them one volley before we go" shortly before a bullet ripped into the colonel's left arm. Although a stretcher came forward, Avery refused to be taken to the rear. Instead, he was carried along the lines, continuing to encourage his men. Despite its valor, one regiment could not thwart the enemy's advance, and the 33rd was forced to retreat. Two lieutenants—John

13 Cadmus Wilcox, "Lee and Grant in the Wilderness," *The Annals of the War Written by Leading Participants North and South* (Philadelphia, 1879), 495; Clark, *Histories*, 2:570, 665; Hahn, *The Catawba Soldier*, 174-75.

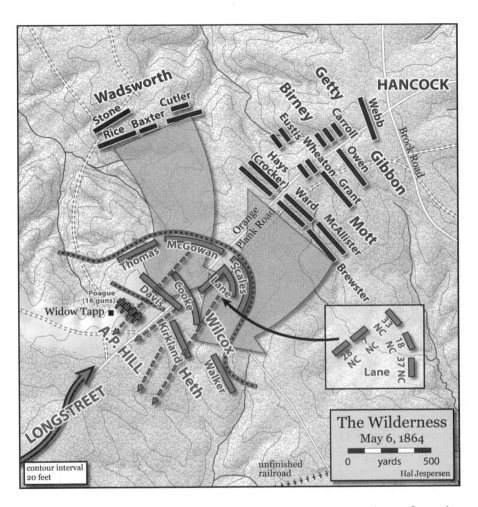

The Wilderness
May 6, 1864

0   yards   500

unfinished
railroad

contour interval
20 feet

Hal Jespersen

Fain and John Rencher—were wounded attempting to carry Avery from the field. The colonel himself was struck four times, in the leg, neck, and through the body. Eventually, Avery was transported to field hospitals located at Parker's Store and then Orange Court House, where he succumbed on June 18, 1864.[14]

14 Clark, *Histories*, 2:570; George H. Mills, *History of the 16th North Carolina Regiment (Originally 6th North Carolina Regiment)* (Rutherfordton, NC, 1901), 47; *The News and Observer*, March 28, 1895; Robert Cowan to "Captain," July 9, 1864, Lane Papers, AU; James Lane, "History of Lane's North Carolina Brigade, *SHSP*, 10:126.

Lost in the melee was the 33rd NC's flag. Several enemy soldiers rushed it, and while another soldier grappled with the color bearer, Sgt. Joseph Kemp of the 5th MI cut the flag from the pole and scampered rearwards with his trophy. Only the pole remained in Tar Heel hands.[15]

Many of Lane's men never had a chance to fire their rifles. They were simply pushed back in one confused mess. The 18th tried to stop, reform, and fight, but a renewed Federal charge drove them back again. At least once, according to McLaurin, they were fired upon by their own troops. His group contained "fifty or seventy-five . . . composed of men from all of Lane's soldiers." As the brigade members streamed to the rear, they ran into the lead elements of Longstreet's command, who were astonished at the sight of their erstwhile comrades. "Some wanted to know if we belonged to General Lee's army," Octavius Wiggins (37th NC) recalled of the chaffing they received. "We didn't look like the men they had left here—'we were worse than Bragg's men.'" Slowly Lane's men reassembled, coming by themselves, in small groups, and in half regiments. Meanwhile Lane saw to the replenishment of their ammunition and the cleaning of their fouled arms.[16]

Once the brigade reformed, Heth and Wilcox's divisions were ordered to fill the gap between Longstreet's and Ewell's Corps. Longstreet's men had been able to drive back the Federals who overran Hill's lines earlier that morning and had even managed to launch a flanking attack. Yet once again tragedy befell the Confederate army: Longstreet was mistakenly severely wounded by his own troops. He survived but would not return for months. Major General Richard Anderson was placed in temporary command of Longstreet's corps. The Confederates on the left under Ewell also attacked, but they lacked the numbers to drive off the Federals. Eventually, the four-day battle of the Wilderness was a Confederate victory, with Grant's forces stalled in the tangled undergrowth. Lane's brigade lost 415 men: 43 killed, 229 wounded, and 143 captured. Among brigade leadership, Col. Avery was mortally wounded; Lt. Col. William Lee (7th

15 *Detroit Free Press,* July 21, 1909; OR 36/1:1020. Alexander, "We Fought them Like Tigers," 220. The official records listed the flag as belonging to the 31st North Carolina Troops, but that regiment was not present at the Wilderness. Furthermore, the flag returned to North Carolina was marked 129 and is stenciled with "33" and "N.C.," plus the names of 16 battles. Kemp was awarded the Medal of Honor for the capture of this flag, an award not presented until 1909. The flag was returned to Richmond in 1914.

16 Clark, *Histories,* 2:48, 665. Longstreet's troops had been on extended duty with Bragg's Army of Tennessee since the battle of Chickamauga, the previous September.

NC) and Capt. John Knox, the sharpshooters' commander, were both captured on the evening of May 5.[17]

The men should have been able to rest after this ordeal. Yet Lane reported their moving frequently along the Plank Road and with "untiring energy," felling trees, constructing abattis, and digging entrenchments at every halt. Smoke from fires started by artillery and small arms hung in the dense underbrush. One Carolinian complained of drawing but one day's rations for four days. "I have to thank God that I have been allowed to live where so many have fallen," wrote Fain, undoubtedly a near-universal sentiment. "I have been two days of terrible fighting . . . we lost pretty heavily in killed and wounded. . . the enemy attacked us in tremendous force but affected nothing."[18]

A year earlier, when Lee stopped the Federal army in the same tangled woods, the enemy retreated back over the Rapidan River to rest and refit. Grant, however, determined to move off to the east in an attempt to get between Lee and Richmond and force Lee to give battle on ground of Grant's choosing. Grant's eastward movement set Lee's army into motion.

Confederate cavalry barely outpaced the Federals to the intersection of Brock Road and Old Court House Road near Spotsylvania Court House. Anderson's infantry soon arrived and handily repulsed a Federal attack. Lane's brigade and the rest of A. P. Hill's corps were on the road heading east by 2:00 p.m. on May 8. Unusual heat and a lack of water plagued the soldiers on the march. Halted about two in the morning May 9, the column was back on the road by 6:00 a.m. Lane's brigade reached Spotsylvania Court House around noon. Hill's corps, now under the command of Lt. Gen. Jubal Early because of Hill's poor health, took the Confederate right. The brigade moved a couple of times on May 10. Lee chose to shift two Confederate divisions to the Po River. First Lane's brigade filed in next to Brig. Gen. Robert Johnston's brigade of Ewell's corps. Lane's brigade slid into their position later when Johnston was moved. By the end of the day, only Wilcox's division manned the Confederate right. That evening, the Tar Heels could hear the battle taking place on the far Confederate left. Ordered to prepare for a counter attack, they hurried toward

17 McDaid, "Four Years," 265.

18 James Lane, "History of Lane's North Carolina Brigade," *SHSP*, 10:127; Collins, "Reminiscences," 50, NCDAH; John Fain to "My Own Dear Mother," May 8, 1864, Archibald Erskine Henderson Papers, DU.

the fighting at the "double-quick," but then were ordered to return to their original position.[19]

Every time the brigade arrived at a new position, the men constructed new works, or strengthened those started by their predecessors. Felled trees and the fence rails from nearby farms were encased in dirt. Many soldiers placed head logs atop their works, leaving an opening large enough to thrust their rifles through to shoot. The brigade even built traverses "to protect ourselves from shots" enfilading their lines, wrote one Carolinian.[20]

Save for the lightning and severe rain on the afternoon of May 11, Lane's men were not engaged. Instead, they worked on their position on the division's left flank. Brigadier General George H. Steuart's brigade of North Carolina and Virginia troops stood to their left, the far right brigade in a mile-long Confederate bulge known as the Mule Shoe. Lane's brigade was divided into two parts. A gap of 100 yards separated Lane's left from Steuart's right. The 28th, followed by the 18th Regiment formed Lane's left. A swampy area came next, and then the 37th, 7th, and 33rd Regiments.[21]

Massed columns of Federal infantry struck the Mule Shoe early on the morning of May 12. Masked by fog—so thick neither friend nor foe was distinguishable at 10 feet, according to one Tar Heel—the enemy drew close upon the works before being discovered. Copious amounts of rain had dampened many Confederate rifles. Since Lee believed the Federals headed toward Fredericksburg, he ordered most of the artillery out of the Mule Shoe the evening before. Confederate defenses were quickly overrun. Lane cautioned the 28th to hold its position and went to see what was happening farther to his left. Satisfied the Federals were working their way through the fog behind his position, Lane ordered Lt. Col. Speer to move his regiment by the right flank, toward a section of older works. Before this could happen, the Federals struck the 28th's ranks. With Federals swarming on both sides of his regiment "[M]y men left as best they could," Speer confessed. He had 113 men captured, Junius Little among them. A member of the 63rd PA captured him, along with the

19 James Lane, "History of Lane's North Carolina Brigade," *SHSP*, 10:127; Harris, *Historical Sketches*, 46. Grant's failure to attack Wilcox on May 10, wrote one historian, "was perhaps the most tragic" failure of Grant during the Spotsylvania campaign. Gorden Rhea, *The Battles for Spotsylvania Court House and the Road to Yellow Tavern, May 7-12, 1864* (Baton Rouge, LA, 1997), 181.

20 Clark, *Histories*, 2:49.

21 JL to "Major," September 16, 1864, Lane Papers, AU.

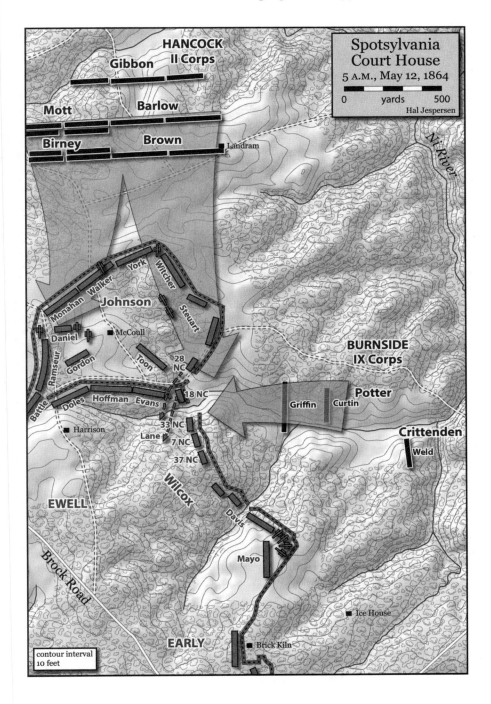

HANCOCK
II Corps

Gibbon

Mott   Barlow

Birney   Brown

Landram

Spotsylvania
Court House
5 A.M., May 12, 1864

0   yards   500

Hal Jespersen

York   Witcher

Walker   Steuart

Monahan

Johnson

Daniel   McCoull

Ramseur   Gordon   Toon   28 NC

Battle   Doles   Hoffman   Evans   18 NC

Harrison   33 NC

Lane   7 NC

37 NC

Wilcox

Davis

EWELL

BURNSIDE
IX Corps

Potter

Griffin   Curtin

Crittenden

Weld

Mayo

Brock Road

Ice House

EARLY   Brick Kiln

Ni River

contour interval
10 feet

As the Federals swarmed over the left of Lane's position on the morning of May 12, 1864, the 28th North Carolina lost its second flag of the war. *North Carolina Museum of History*

battle flag he brought safely through the entanglement at the Wilderness. The remaining portion of the regiment rallied on the 33rd, now commanded by Lt. Col. Robert Cowen.[22]

The 18th NC was also caught up in the melee. Colonel Barry ordered the regiment to fall back toward the nearby 33rd. Augustus Floyd recalled being "foolhearted," in following "our Colonel with others and got out with three or four bullet holes through my coat and pants." Pushed back even farther, it took

22 JL to "Major," September 16, 1864, John McGill to "Captain," September 9, 1864, William Speer to "Captain," July 19, 1864, all in Lane Papers, AU. The flag of the 28th Regiment was captured by Cpl. John M. Kindig. He was awarded the Medal of Honor for the flag's capture. The flag was sent to the War Department and assigned number 134. It was returned to North Carolina in 1905. Dedmondt, *The Flags of Civil War North Carolina*, 123.

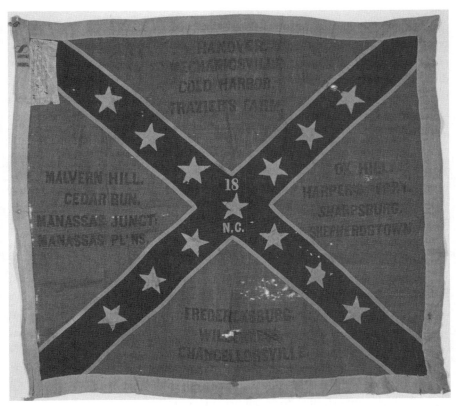

A lieutenant from a Pennsylvania regiment is credited with capturing the 18th North Carolina's flag at Spotsylvania Court House. *North Carolina Museum of History*

time to get the survivors of the 18th reformed. Ensign John Frink, bearing the 18th's flag, was taken by a Pennsylvania lieutenant. Frink recalled an enemy soldier coming up to him and demanding his flag. Unaware, because of the fog, that the Federals were encircling his line, Frink told the Federal "to get back to the rear—'you d— Yank.'" A blow from the man's rifle knocked him to the ground. If "it hadn't been for a large pair of blankets around my shoulders, he would have killed me," Frink said. He spent the rest of the war as a prisoner. Lieutenant Colonel McGill reported 113 members of the 18th captured on May 12.[23]

23 Floyd, "Autobiography," 11; John McGill to "Captain," September 9, 1864, Lane Papers, AU; *The San Angelo Daily*, April 20, 1926. Alexander Mitchell, 105th PA, was awarded the Medal of Honor for capturing the 18th's flag, which was sent to the War Department, with captured

Sensing the danger, or possibly under orders from Lane, Col. Barber refused the left company of the 37th. This gave the 33rd and 7th Regiments an anchor upon which to reform. The Tar Heels filed into a traverse—a shallow ditch—and waited. Portions of the 28th rallied and joined the brigade line on the left. "In the best of spirits the Brigade welcomed the furious assault which soon followed," Lane wrote after the battle, "with prolonged cheers and death dealing volleys—the unerring rifles of the 37th and part of the 7th thinning the ranks of the enemy in front while the rest did good execution in rear." Wave after of wave of Federal soldiers attempted to drive Lane from his improvised position. James Harris (7th NC) recalled several columns of Federals advancing to a hill formerly occupied by Lane's men, "some 40 or 50 yards" to their front, "only to be repulsed with great slaughter." Harris described the unbelievable bravery of the 7th and 33rd NC troops: Lt. Col. Cowan atop the works, "encouraging the men to still greater efforts in rolling back" the enemy force; 1st Sgt. Isaac McCurdy (7th NC) also on the works firing until "instantly killed"; Richard White of the ambulance corps, "wounded . . . himself pierced by an enemy's bullet, and his lifeless form sank to the earth." Barber wrote of an assault along his front as well, enfeebled by "the nature of the ground." "Men could not fight better nor officers behave more gallantly," Lane wrote proudly in his report of this repulse of the enemy. "We justly claim for this Brigade alone the honor of not only successfully stemming but rolling back the tide of Federal victory which came surging furiously to our right."[24]

Not long after the attack began, Lane sent his brother Oscar, an aide-de-camp, back to Wilcox, asking for reinforcements. Wilcox ordered Thomas's and Scales's brigades to Lane's assistance. Scales's brigade moved to the left of Lane's men. Doles's brigade of Georgians also arrived, and, according to Lane, Doles suggested a counter-attack. After informing Wilcox of his plans, Lane swung his line to the right and rode up behind the 33rd. James Weston recalled Lane's "lips quivering with the glow and ardor of battle. 'You must hold your ground,' he said. '[T]he honor and safety of the army demand it.'" Cowan

number 118 stenciled on it. The banner was returned to North Carolina in 1905. Dedmondt, *The Flags of Civil War North Carolina*, 104.

24 William Barber to "Captain," September 8, 1864, Lane Papers, AU; Harris, *Historical Sketches*, 46, 48; JL to "Major," September 16, 1864, Lane Papers, AU. Edward Hale wrote after the war the brigade front was composed of two regiments, with the remnants of the other three behind them. Loaded rifles were passed to those in front in rapid order. *Fayetteville Observer*, May 12, 1897.

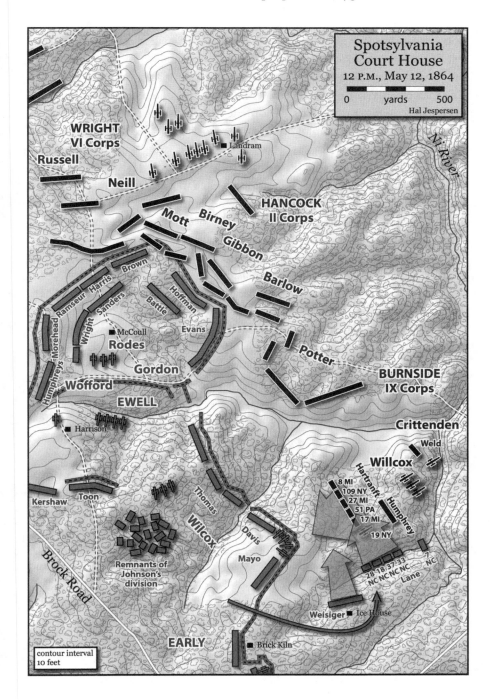

Spotsylvania
Court House
12 P.M., May 12, 1864

0   yards   500

Hal Jespersen

WRIGHT
VI Corps

Russell

Neill

Landram

HANCOCK
II Corps

Mott

Birney

Gibbon

Barlow

Brown

Harris

Ramseur

Morehead

Sanders

Hoffman

Wright

Battle

McCoull

Evans

Rodes

Humphreys

Gordon

Potter

BURNSIDE
IX Corps

Wofford

EWELL

Harrison

Crittenden

Weld

Willcox

8 MI
109 NY
27 MI
51 PA
17 MI

Hartranft

Humphrey

Kershaw

Toon

Thomas

Wilcox

19 NY

Davis

Mayo

Remnants of
Johnson's
division

28 18 37 33
NC NC NC NC

7
NC

Lane

Brock Road

Weisiger

Ice House

EARLY

Brick Kiln

Ni River

contour interval
10 feet

grabbed the flag of the 33rd, and "with a loud shout rushed upon the foe." The rest of the brigade followed and advanced some three or four hundred yards, and "swept everything before them." After the men had proceeded through a pine thicket, an aide from Wilcox found Lane and ordered him to return to the works. Lane sent word back to the Confederates manning the trench to his rear, warning that they were coming. Finding the works occupied, Lane formed in a secondary position.[25]

Lane's brigade played a role in thwarting the attack. Had he faltered, the Federal attack might have succeeded and resulted in a decisive Union victory at Spotsylvania. Lane did not act alone, however. Confederates to the left and rear of the Mule Shoe, notably Brig. Gen. John Gordon's three brigades, also rallied and pitched into the foe, driving them back across the works. In some areas along the salient Federal soldiers clung to one side with Confederate soldiers on the other, grappling in some of the hardest bloodletting of the war. William McLaurin (18th NC) saw the "Bloody Angle" portion of the Mule Shoe. "There was an oak woods to their rear, and an oak tree twenty inches in diameter was so riddled with minie balls, several feet from the ground, that its top-weight wrung it down. I saw the tree . . . and the many dead, on each side of the breastworks were silent witnesses of the fighting qualities of both armies."[26]

Despite Lane's brigade's heroism in the early morning of May 12, the battle was far from over. At noon, Lane was ordered to move his Tar Heels back into the main works, to a new position right of where he took his stand earlier, just below a spot known as Heth's Salient. Federal artillery, massed upon a rise of ground a quarter of a mile to the east of this salient, poured a destructive fire into Confederate lines. A piece of shell mortally wounded Lane's brother Oscar while he stood talking to the general and Capt. Hale.[27]

Though vicious, the fighting along the Mule Shoe had been indecisive: The two sides fought to a stalemate. Grant now chose to attack Heth's Salient, while Lee tried to capture the artillery enfilading his lines, and more importantly, relieve pressure on other Confederate troops. Lee came to Lane's position and

---

25 Clark, *Histories*, 2:571; JL to "Major," September 16, 1864.

26 Rhea, *The Battles for Spotsylvania Court House*, 255; Clark, *Histories*, 2:51.

27 Lane, "History of Lane's North Carolina Brigade," *SHSP*, 9:150; Harris, *Historical Sketches*, 47; *The Monroe Journal*, October 29, 1912. A June 7, 1864, article in the *Semi-Weekly Standard* reported Oscar Lane "had his leg shot off below the knee and a part of his right foot shot away."

Prior to the war, Oscar Lane, General Lane's brother, served in the 61st Virginia Militia. Like brother J. Rooker Lane, Oscar also served with the 5th Virginia Cavalry before transferring to Lane's staff. Oscar was mortally wounded at Spotsylvania Court House on May 12, 1864.

College of William and Mary

sent his sharpshooter battalion on a mission. Lee wanted to know if infantry was supporting the Federal artillery. After Capt. Knox's capture, Capt. William Nicholson (37th NC) had assumed command of the Sharpshooter Battalion. Nicholson selected five men, and with a stretcher, they set out beyond the picket line. An officer there cautioned Nicholson that simply raising his head would produce a hail of bullets. The mission, Nicholson assured him, was authorized by General Lee. According to one postwar account, Nicholson took one soldier with him and walked unmolested to a rise. Once there he raised his field glasses and "sharpshooters for six hundred yards each side of him" opened fire, fortunately to no effect. At some point, Nicholson's party spied a Federal peeping from

William T. Nicholson served as adjutant and a company commander, and then as commander of the brigade sharpshooters.

Histories of the Several Regiments and Battalions from North Carolina

behind a tree. They agreed one of them should fire upon the Federal, and when he took aim, the other should "plug" him, "and another soldier was added to the list of the dead in Grant's great army."[28]

Nicholson soon had the information Lee sought, but his companion had sustained a leg wound in the process. Nicholson carried him over his shoulder back to the picket post. Moving across the field under fire, Nicholson came across a dead enemy officer with a "very fine water proof coat rolled around his neck and shoulders." Without setting down the wounded man, Nicholson "reached down and pulled the coat off the dead officer's head." As he made his way to the rear, other Confederates placed the wounded soldier upon a litter and started him toward the lines. Unfortunately enemy artillery spotted the litter party, opened fire, and killed the wounded soldier.[29]

With Nicholson's information in hand, Lee decided to capture the Federal batteries. He selected Lane's brigade to lead, supported by Mahone's former brigade of Virginians under the command of Col. David Weisiger. Lane, his staff, and regimental officers dismounted. Under Lee's watchful eye, Lane sent the 7th and 33rd NC over the works, under Lt. Col. Cowan's command. Two companies from both regiments were thrown out as skirmishers, with Capt. Thomas Williamson (7th NC) commanding. Cowan began pushing the Federal skirmishers back, through some woods to their front, while Lane brought up the rest of the brigade. Lane's orders were to advance into the "oak woods near the ice house" and "to face to the front after the left of my line had gotten well into the woods." Once "well into the woods," Lane caught up with Cowan and positioned his brigade, left to right: 28th, 18th, 37th, 33rd, and 7th Regiments. The first four faced the battery's flank, while the 7th Regiment, at a 90-degree angle to the rest of the brigade with Lane's skirmishers in front, protected Lane's right flank. Weisiger's brigade was 100 yards behind Lane.[30]

---

28 JL to "Major," September 17, 1864, Lane Papers, AU; *Charlotte Observer*, August 20, 1893

29 William Alexander, undated reminiscence, Alexander Papers, SHC/UNC. Alexander identified the dead officer as Maj. John Piper, 1st Michigan Sharpshooters.

30 *The Monroe Journal,* October 29, 1912; JL to "Major," September 16, 1864, James Lane Papers, AU. Lane writes in 1867 and again in 1893 that Lee was present when he launched his attack on the afternoon of May 12. See JL to Peter Parker, in *Monroe Journal* and *The Weekly Sentinel,* September 24, 1867. As the brigade crossed over the works, "Lee was riding very close to us," Wiggins wrote. Clark, *Histories,* 2:666. Ross Gaston (28th NC) writes Lee dismounted and attempted to "lead the charge and our boys made him go back." It is unclear if Gaston refers to an earlier event, or when the charge on the afternoon of May 12 was made. Civil War

Lieutenant Charles T. Haigh had just left the Virginia Military Institute and joined the 37th North Carolina, only to be killed at Spotsylvania on May 12, 1864.

Virginia Military Institute

Lane advised Weisiger to follow the Tar Heels at a supporting distance. Within moments, with every soldier in place, Lane ordered the advance. As soon as the Tar Heels cleared the woods, their "Rebel Yell" filled the air. Lieutenant Charles Haigh, a recent VMI graduate, rushed ahead of the 37th. It was an unusual move, as officers typically stayed behind their companies. Federal gunners now turned some of their pieces toward Lane's men, belching forth iron that ripped into the brigade. "One shell exploded in" the 37th, killing a "Captain and eight men." Out in front, Haigh "with hat in one hand and sword in the other, shouted to his men to come on." "Charge, boys! charge! the battery is ours!" As they neared the battery, the 37th stopped and delivered a volley. In that instant, "poor Charley Haigh fell dead" at Wiggins's side, shot in the head. Wiggins considered Haigh "the bravest of the brave."[31]

Federal artillery plaguing the Confederate lines was quickly silenced. James Wheeler, an 18th NC private, claimed the 19th NY Light Artillery's flag. Nevertheless, Lane's men did not stop at the battery. They surged into the woods on the other side. At that instant, a division of the IX Corps, dispatched by General Grant to attack the Confederate line, passed the front of the brigade. Lane's triumphant charge plowed into the Federals' flank, hitting the 17th MI

Collection, Box 70, Folder 52, NCDAH. One of Lee's staff officers remembers Lee galloping under a hail of artillery fire down the line to stop Confederate batteries as Lane charged. William Chamberlaine, *Memoirs of the Civil War* (Washington, D.C., 1912), 100-101.

31 JL to "Major," September 16, 1864; Clark, *Histories*, 2:667; *Fayetteville Observer*, May 26, 1864.

Ensign Robert M. Staley rose through the ranks of the 37th North Carolina, bearing the flag until wounded at Spotsylvania Court House.

Histories of the Several Regiments and Battalions from North Carolina

and 51st PA. The struggle quickly devolved into what one eyewitness described as "a scene with clubbed musket and bayonet," with the Federal regiments collapsing into one another.

James Grimsley (37th NC), with 25 to 30 men, rushed up to a dozen members of the 17th MI, including the color sergeant. Upon Grimsley's demand for surrender of the flag, the sergeant agreed, asking only, that he be allowed to carry it to the Confederate rear. At the same time, he untied the flag's oil-cloth case from around his waist and gave it to the Carolinians. They granted his request, and heading back toward Confederate lines, they encountered a lieutenant colonel and an additional 15-20 soldiers. "Grimsley went up to him and remarked that he (the colonel) was completely surrounded, and in order to save his own life and the lives of his men they had better throw down their arms and be conducted to the rear. The colonel agreed, telling his men, 'Boys, we are surrounded and had better surrender.' They did" and were escorted to the rear. Likewise the Pennsylvanians also collapsed. Lane believed he could accomplish more with reinforcements. (The 18th Regiment had taken only 39 men and officers into the fight.) As two batteries of Federal artillery opened up on Lane from the right, he sent Hale to bring up Weisiger's brigade. Artillery to the brigade's right also opened fire. With such a small force, Lane chose to pull back his men.[32]

Unexpectedly, rifle fire ripped into the brigade's rear. Instead of coming up to support Lane, Weisiger's brigade sent a volley into its ranks. A frantic rush to

32 Harris, *Historical Sketches*, 51.

the rear by Lt. Cols. McGill and Cowan succeeded in stopping the Virginians' fire. Extraction proved difficult for Lane, with enemy soldiers pouring into the fight. A member of the 17th MI captured Col. Barber, and Maj. Jackson Bost assumed command of the 37th. Lane himself came close to capture more than once. A small group of enemy soldiers, for example, demanded his surrender in a pine thicket on his way back. Lane boldly commanded them to throw down their arms. They were hardly inclined to obey an unarmed man until Lane added, "Very well, wait a moment, till my line comes up." The Federals dropped their weapons, and the general made his escape. Soon thereafter, Lane, walking "cap in hand . . . found myself face to face with two Yankees going to the front. As one of these fellows leveled his gun to fire on me, I heard some one cry out 'What are you about?' Then followed quickly the sharp crack of an unerring rifle, and as that Yankee fell dead, almost at my feet, I dashed by the other one." As Lane passed by his savior, whom he later learned was Peter Parker (37th NC), he remarked "This is no place for us and the sooner we get out the better."[33]

Lane then spied Wiggins (37th NC), backed up against a tree "and daring two burly Yankees to fire on him." Rushing into a field between the lines, Lane skirted back along the edge of the woods and soon encountered Wiggins again. Lane's presence in the field apparently distracted the two Federals long enough for Wiggins to escape. Soon they stumbled upon the color bearer of the 51st PA. "Hello, Yank! That won't do, bring us that flag," Wiggins called out. Since they were Confederates, the Federal soldier, not noticing both Lane and Wiggins were unarmed, surrendered. Wiggins, Lane, and their captive quickly parted company. Lane worked his way back to the lines and collapsed on a pile of rails. Two young members of his brigade, their "faces . . . almost black . . . from biting so many cartridges," found the general and wanted to carry him back farther away from danger. Lane refused. "[I]t would never do for them to lug me out of the woods, in the presence of my Brigade when I was not wounded, only physically exhausted." The pair remained with Lane until he could go on. As they found the brigade, Lane "could not keep back the tears as I listened to their prolonged cheers of delight."[34]

33 John McGill to "Captain," September 9, 1864, Lane Papers, AU; Clark, *Histories*, 2:667; JL to "Major," September 16, 1864; *OR* 36/3:806-807.

34 JL to "Major," September 16, 1864; *The Charlotte Democrat*, May 24, 1864; *The Monroe Journal*, October 29, 1912.

Some of his men ran into additional trouble making their way back to Confederate lines. Riding amongst the brigade survivors and their prisoners, Brig. Gen. Mahone demanded to know if there was an officer present. Lieutenant Colonel McGill (18th NC) came forward, and the general demanded to know where he was going. After hearing the answer—to the rear to reform—Mahone angrily ordered McGill back into the fight. The "d__d North Carolinians were deserting his brave Virginians," he said. McGill and Mahone argued about what was happening in the woods. Not satisfied, Mahone "commenced abusing the Brigade generally." As the heated exchange continued, McGill told Mahone he could "'go to Hell' or any where else but as for me, I would form with my command and accordingly move forward." More than 30 members of the brigade had gathered around McGill by this point.[35]

Mahone rode on, finding a group of Lane's men, with captured flags and prisoners in tow. The Virginian began to claim "everything," wrote William McLaurin after the war, and

> began to gather our flags, which was stopped instanter. Col. Cowan, of the 33rd, and myself were close together near two flags and in easy pistol-shot of Mahone. Being foiled in his flag-gathering, he turned toward us and those with us and began upbraiding all for retreating in "cowardly disorder." Cowan's red head literally got on fire. He poured forth a volume of cuss words that Jude Early or Major Hampton might have honored as their own without injury to their reputation. Advancing toward Mahone with his hat in one hand and his pistol cocked in the other, he told him how he had run from instead of going with us into the charge; that his brigade also acted badly, and neither had anything to do with the captured flags. Among other severe epithets, he called Mahone a cowardly son of b—h, and told him he would have to apologize for his language toward us or he would kill him on the spot. I advanced with Cowan, with my pistol ready for business if Cowan's failed. Mahone took his cussing without a word back, made a profound apology, and rode inside of the breastworks.[36]

Still not finished, Mahone unsuccessfully tried to snatch the flag of the 51st PA as Wiggins crossed into the works. A little more than a week later, Mahone petitioned Lee, arguing that the flag Grimsley captured had in fact been captured by a member of the 41st VA. The controversy raged, at least on paper,

35 Ibid.

36 John McGill to "Captain," September 9, 1864.

for several weeks. In the end, Lane's brigade was credited with capturing three flags on May 12 (the 19th NY Battery, and the 17th MI and 51st PA Infantry).[37]

Lane's men reformed near the courthouse, while Capt. Hale of Lane's staff led Weisiger's brigade out of the woods. One act remained to play out before day's end. Lee again called on Lane and his sharpshooter battalion to gather some information down the Fredericksburg Road. Lee said he had "witnessed the gallantry of his sharp-shooters as well as the alacrity with which they had borne the hardships of the day." However he did not have the "heart to order them forward again." Lane was certain the men would do whatever Lee ordered "cheerfully." "I will not send them unless they are willing to go," Lee responded. Captain Nicholson was called, and Lee explained what he needed, but "enjoined him to let his men know that he did not order them, but *requested* them to make the reconnaissance for him." Everyone was "elated," Lane wrote. As the battalion marched by, "Every cap went off and was twirled in air. Yell followed upon yell. General Lee . . . gracefully doffed his hat, but said not a word." Nicholson and his sharpshooter battalion soon returned with the needed information.[38]

In addition to the three flags captured by Lane's brigade, the regiments also claimed almost 400 captured Federal soldiers. Burnside's attack was blunted, and the Confederate position saved. But it had come at a cost. Lane counted some 470 losses within the brigade: 47 killed, 116 wounded, and at least 307 missing and presumed captured. The only colonel he had left was the 18th's John D. Barry. A lack of horses and roads forced the captured Federal battery to be left on the field, quickly to be reclaimed by the enemy. Lane's men reformed in front of Spotsylvania Court House, and the 7th NC rejoined them. The men were moved in a vacant section of the Confederate works, and rations issued. "[A]fter so. . . hard a days work we had done," Speer wrote, the men "rested for the night."[39]

---

37 *Landmark*, September 14, 1893.

38 *The Charlotte Observer*, August 20, 1893. Lane wrote a slightly different version of this story in 1907. "Soon after those brave men were twirling their caps over their heads and yelling, as they passed General Lee, and gracefully sitting on his horse, watched them as they quickly crossed the works, deployed and disappeared to the front, the troops in the works wildly cheering. It was grand." James Lane, "Personal Reminiscences of General Lee." *The Wake Forest Student* (January 1907), 26/5:310-11.

39 JL to "Major," September 16, 1864; Harris, *Historical Sketches*, 47; William Speer to "Captain," July 19, 1864, Lane Papers, AU.

Everyone from rank private to the army commander realized exactly what James Lane's brigade had accomplished on May 12. "The stubborn fight made here by Lane's Brigade certainly saved the day," Lt. Col. Speer (28th NC) scrawled in his diary about the morning struggle. James Weston (33rd NC) later observed, "there can be little doubt that Lane's Brigade saved Lee's army from a terrible defeat [at Spotsylvania]. I never saw such heroism as was then displayed, both by officers and men," he continued. "It was impossible to surpass it." Lane was justifiably proud as well, writing four months later that it was "impossible for me to speak too high terms of my command in repulsing this terrible attack of the enemy—men could not fight better, nor officers behave more gallantly."[40]

A member of Lee's staff, Col. Charles Venable, wrote the Federal breakthrough that morning had been "checked by Lane's brigade," by throwing his left flank back from the trenches, confronting their advance." Lieutenant General Early, commanding the corps, believed the Federal attack "was checked by the prompt movement on the part of General Lane." Even an English newspaper correspondent, according to Weston, commended the brigade, writing: "Lane's North Carolina veterans stopped the tide of Federal victory as it came surging to the right."[41]

The high tribute paid to Lane's brigade did nothing to arrest the ongoing war. Save for posting skirmishers in rifle pits 10 paces apart in front of the lines, the brigade remained stationary from May 13-18. The men spent their time strengthening the works and bracing for the next attack. One-third of each brigade manned the trenches every night. At three every morning, the rest of the men arose and took their positions in the works, ready to receive an attack. Instructed to keep their gear on them at all times, the troops were not allowed to leave the encampment. Despite the abject hardships of trench life, morale remained remarkably high. "Half such a whipping would have sent McClellan, Hooker, Burnside or Meade to the other side of the Rappahannock," believed T. James Linebarger (28th NC). "It seems Grant is determined to sacrifice his army or destroy Lee's." The captain also thought that a few more attacks against

---

40 Speer, *Voices from Cemetery Hill*, 132; Clark, *Histories*, 2:571; JL to "Major," September 18, 1864, Lane Papers, AU.

41 Ibid.; Jubal A. Early, *Autobiographical Sketch and Narrative of the War Between the States* (Philadelphia, PA, 1912), 355; Clark, *Histories*, 2:571.

Captain T. James Linebarger was wounded at Fredericksburg, Chancellorsville, and again at Gettysburg. He surrendered with the 28th North Carolina at Appomattox.

Histories of the Several Regiments and Battalions from North Carolina

the sprawling and well-placed Confederate entrenchments and the enemy "will have expended his strength."[42]

Federal infantry charged a portion of the line on May 18, and Lane's brigade was pulled into a supporting position to the rear of Pegram's brigade. However, the crisis passed. Suspecting that the Federals were on the move, Lee ordered a reconnaissance on May 19. He sent all of Ewell's Corps except the artillery on a flanking march around the Federal right. Lane's brigade's left moved into a supporting position for some of Ewell's guns and returned to their section of the lines later that evening.[43]

May 20 passed relatively quietly, with just some skirmishing somewhere to the brigade's right. Federal soldiers began abandoning their works that evening, bound for the North Anna River. All through the next day, small skirmishes broke out as both sides probed to see if their enemy was either underway or screening troops on the move. Determined to settle the matter, Lee ordered two brigades from Wilcox's division toward the Federal lines late in the day. After passing a church and turning left, Lane formed his brigade. He deployed the 33rd, 28th, and 37th NC in front, with the 18th and 7th held in reserve. The Carolinians pushed through the dense undergrowth ("an almost impenetrable abattis," Lane said) and struck the Federal skirmish line. Confederate artillery weighed in, and the brigade rushed forward, seizing the main enemy line. Lane

---

42 Harris, *Historical Sketches*, 49; Caldwell, *The History of a Brigade of South Carolinians*, 202; Linebarger to family, May 15, 1864, SHC/UNC.

43 Harris, *Historical Sketches*, 48.

posted one company from each regiment as skirmishers out in front of his position. The two brigades were ordered back to the main Confederate lines at nightfall. Lane reported his losses as two killed, 13 wounded, and three missing. The ease with which his troops had overrun a portion of the main Federal line confirmed to Lee the enemy was abandoning his front.[44]

Orders came for a night march. The men in Lane's brigade were kept on the move until 2:00 a.m. and allowed a short rest before resuming the march on May 22. They crossed the North Anna River at Island Ford, and marched until they reached the tracks of the Virginia Central Railroad, where they encamped. His soldiers "much needed and greatly appreciated" the rest, Wilcox wrote. It was the first such break not in the presence of the enemy in more than two weeks. On May 23, Hill's corps moved from Hewlett's Station east to Anderson's Tavern, camping in an oak woods. Captain Hale marveled at the word "camp." For "the first time since leaving Orange [Court House] our wagon came up, we had some rice and ate out of plates." He was looking forward to clean clothes and a bath.[45]

William McLaurin (18th NC) described hearing shots nearby. "Pop! pop! pop! bang! bang! bang!" Just moments before, one of the soldiers sent out with a load of canteens came running back, asking McLaurin for his "army colt." McLaurin pointed to an oak tree where his belt was hanging. Not long after the shots, an elderly farmer came into the brigade's camp and was directed to Gen. Lane. The farmer was complaining of missing sheep. Lane had each regiment searched. If the guilty party were found, orders were to send him to Lane under guard. The adjutant of the 37th had almost completed his search when a private "stepped up the slope right near headquarters with a leg of mutton in his hand." Lane ordered the guilty soldier to walk in a "circle with a billet of wood, and the leg of mutton on his shoulder." Once the consequences for the soldier became apparent, the farmer asked Lane to release the man and let him have the mutton. Then the farmer let the other Tar Heels have the rest of his sheep, probably concluding that the nearby enemy troops would take them anyway.[46]

Hill's corps was on the left of the Army of Northern Virginia, with the Light Division on the left of Hill's line. Wilcox was concerned about Jericho

44 JL to "Major," September 16, 1864, Lane Papers, AU; Harris, *Historical Sketches*, 49.

45 Clipping Scrapbook, 172-73, Cadmus Wilcox Papers, LC; Clark, *Histories*, 2:54; *Fayetteville Observer*, June 2, 1864.

46 Clark, *Histories*, 2:54-55.

Mill, on the North Anna River, about three miles from the division's position. He therefore sent McGowan's brigade there to guard the army's left flank. A brush between Confederate and Union cavalry did nothing to alert Lee of his flank's vulnerability. Thinking the main Union army headed elsewhere, Lee chose not to reinforce the river crossing. Word arrived about 2:00 p.m.: the Federals were crossing the North Anna at the mill. Hill, now back in command and less convinced than Lee, ordered Wilcox to move the Light Division toward McGowan's position. Writing a letter home, Capt. Hale was just penning the words "at last we have some rest," when word came for the men to fall in. Lane marched his brigade up the railroad until he reached McGowan, where he took position on his right. The brigade's sharpshooters were sent to the front, and, not long thereafter, the 7th NC was detached and sent to one of the river's fords. Lane positioned his four remaining regiments, left to right, 18th, 37th, 33rd, and 28th. Thomas's brigade stood to McGowan's left, with Scales's brigade behind him.[47]

Wilcox thought he faced only a couple of Federal cavalry brigades. So four infantry brigades supported by artillery should easily be able to chase two cavalry brigades back across the river. Yet it was not cavalry he faced, but, rather the better part of an entire Federal corps. Wilcox launched his attack. The Light Division crossed the railroad, descended a slope, and plunged into the woods. Federal skirmishers scampered back to their works. Somewhere in the woods, Lane and McGowan became separated. Lane sent word back to Wilcox through Capt. Hale that the troops on his left had given way. Wilcox ordered Lane to "push on," because he had just out-paced them. The brigade was half way across an open field when Federal infantry rose from behind some improvised works and delivered a stunning volley into the Tar Heels. They stopped to return fire, and after a few minutes, the 37th began to waver and eventually broke for the rear. Witnessing this, the other members of the brigade, recalling what had happened just a few hours earlier, "began bleating like sheep. . . . It was ludicrous in the extreme—fighting for all we were worth and bleating like sheep," recalled McLaurin.[48]

Lane withdrew the entire brigade into cover of the woods and rallied the 37th. Again the brigade advanced. Combined small arms and artillery fire stalled the attack, and the 37th broke for the rear again. The 18th, 28th, and 33rd stood

47 JL to "Major," September 20, 1864, Lane Papers, AU; *Fayetteville Observer*, June 2, 1864.

48 JL to "Major," September 20, 1864, Lane Papers, AU; Clark, *Histories*, 2:55.

fast, until ordered to pull back. Part of Wilcox's command achieved some success, flanking the enemy position and almost cutting off its line of retreat. Massed Federal artillery and fresh troops drove back Thomas's and Scales's brigades. Not long after nightfall, Lane pulled back his men. Company B of the 33rd shouldered their rifles, "as though on drill," and led the brigade off the field. Lane then deployed a strong protective line of skirmishers, and buried the brigade's dead, and gathered the wounded. Years later, Edward Lovell recalled Nathaniel Nixon, a member of the 28th NC, who lay desperately wounded between the lines. His friend, Mark Freeman, called to him, and Nixon answered, saying the Federals had "been to him and given him water." Freeman dropped his rifle and stripped off his accoutrements, calling loudly "Natt, I'm coming after you. I am coming unarmed, and any man who shoots me is a damned coward." Freeman found Nixon and, unscathed, brought him back. Nixon later died in a field hospital. Overall, Lane gave his losses as 11 killed, 79 wounded, and 10 missing.

Later, Lane criticized the 37th's performance during the battle of Jericho Mills. The regiment "broke in a disgraceful manner and ran back," he reported. After rallying and advancing again with the brigade, the regiment "again broke and ran in a still more shameful and disgraceful manner." Yet a couple of years after the war ended, Lane came to the regiment's defense. The *Richmond Index* wrote Lane's and Scales's brigades "behaved most disgracefully, and were replaced by Davis' and Cook's troops of Heth's Division." Responding, Lane said only the 37th faltered that day, which he attributed to their loss of leadership. The loss of so many officers during the battle of Spotsylvania had left a void in command.[49]

With the fighting well over, Davis's brigade of Heth's division replaced Lane's troops around 11:00 p.m. Lane's men took up positions on the railroad and began fortifying it, but before daylight, orders sent them to their camp near Anderson's Station where they remained for the next couple of days. Baiting the Federals, Lee was daring them to once more attack the entrenched Confederate lines. James Harris (7th NC) recorded heavy skirmishing with artillery on the afternoon of May 25. Confederate forces discovered at dawn two days later that the Federals had evacuated the south bank of the North Anna River and were again maneuvering to turn Lee's flank. Lee had his army on the move soon

---

49 JL to "Major," September 20, 1864, AU; John Arthur, *Western North Carolina: A History from 1730 to 1913* (Johnson City, TN, 1914, 1996), 624; *Wilmington Journal*, September 27, 1867.

thereafter. Lane's brigade marched to Ashland, and on May 28, shifted to Atlee's Station, then to the Totopotomy Creek on the 30th. The men had to build breastworks "under a very severe Artillery fire," Col. McGill complained, wounding eight members of his 18th Regiment.[50]

Lee began consolidating his men near the previous Gaines Mill battlefield on May 31. Most of Hill's corps held their former positions until June 2, when Lee ordered them to the new front. Wilcox's division arrived about 3:00 p.m. and took a position to the right and rear of Hoke's Division. Before arriving on scene, Lee had ordered Confederate forces to occupy Turkey Hill, a key artillery position. Lee personally ordered Breckinridge's division to take the hill when he arrived and it had not been done. About 5:00 p.m., two brigades of Wilcox's division, Lane's and McGowan's, were ordered to support Breckinridge. Lane's brigade formed in an open field behind Wharton's brigade during the successful attack, which drove off the Federal defenders.[51]

While the brigade's losses for the day were light, everyone was deeply concerned when a sharpshooter's round slammed into Lane's groin. "I feared from the profuse bleeding that the artery was cut," Capt. Hale wrote. The general was quickly borne to the rear. Hale learned "the artery was not cut nor was the bone struck." However, "the wound is a very severe one indeed. . . . It is very sad to lose him even for a time." A post-war biographer wrote, Lane "was so dangerously wounded that he was not expected to live." Lane was transported to Richmond to convalesce.[52]

John Barry, the senior colonel present with the brigade, took command in Lane's absence. A year earlier and not far away, Barry was denying the presence of friends riding in the tangled thickets in front of him when he ordered his men to fire that fatal volley into the darkness at Chancellorsville. Barry moved the brigade back into line, strengthening the entrenchments as a torrential rain fell. The Federals attacked early on the morning of June 3. By noon, when enemy officers refused to lead any further attacks against the heavily entrenched position, approximately 6,000 Federal soldiers lay dead or wounded on the field. Wilcox's division, on the far Confederate right, played little part in the

---

50 John McGill to "Captain," September 9, 1864, Lane Papers, AU; Harris, *Historical Sketches*, 48.

51 Ibid., 50; Freeman, *R. E. Lee*, 3:383.

52 *Fayetteville Observer*, June 9, 1864; William Cox, "A Sketch of General James H. Lane, C. V.," [1908], Lane Papers, AU.

slaughter. "We watched the fight with intense interest," Hale wrote. Confederate artillery posted near the brigade opened an enfilade fire, and in turn, "a battery or two . . . enfilade[d] our Brigade, and the balls come very close when they open on us." Sharpshooters, too, continued to ply their trade. They were blamed for Lane's wounding on June 2 and the fatal wounding of Capt. James Hunt (33rd NC), who was struck in the chest on June 3 and died in a Richmond hospital three days later.[53]

The next 10 days were spent in the trenches. "They have got to fighting of a night," Lt. Col. Speer (28th NC) wrote home on June 5. "We can't sleep any. . . . We have fought behind breastworks. It is raining on us and quite disagreeable. The Men are getting sick very fast." Speer estimated only four days not spent under fire out of the past 32. . "I have never seen anything like this in my life." Michael Talley (37th NC) echoed Speer: "I am well enough in health but am about Broke down a marching & throwing up breast-works to gether every day . . . we have pretty hard times in the hot sun & raining every 2 or 3 days untill we are all completely broken down."[54]

Hale provided a valuable glimpse of the life of a brigade member while on the lines after the battle of Cold Harbor:

> We have a hole in the top of our quarters made by a shell, through which we see nearly all the skirmishing, and watch the flight of the shell, or rather their bursting, for you can't see them in the day except when they are coming at you. But at night you cannot imagine what a grand sight it is, to see the lightning flash along the horizon, then the flames belched forth, amid the screaming of the shells, the sharp report and brilliant flash and scintillations of light as the missiles explode; while the woods and open fields are lighted up, as if by fire-flies, with the smaller jets of flame jutting out from thousands of small arms, and high in air the shells from their mortars (for they have a mortar battery just over here) describe their graceful curves—a strange noise it all makes in the night with the ringing cheers of combatants, as one line or the other line of skirmishers gains an advantage.[55]

53 *Fayetteville Observer,* June 9, 1864; Jordan, *NC Troops,* 9:159.

54 Speer, *Voices from Cemetery Hill,* 136, 138; Michael Tally to "Dear Aunt Susan," June 7, 1864, private collection.

55 *Fayetteville Observer,* June 13, 1864.

On June 5, orders came down from headquarters. Officers were instructed to carefully inspect their lines, replenish ammunition as needed, and issue rations, while keeping at least one-third of the men on duty at all times. A second missive ordered all detailed men to return to the ranks, while a third criticized officers allowing able-bodied men to go the rear for little or no reason. Lee occasionally shifted troops in his lines, and every evening, about 9:00 p.m., bombarded the enemy, hoping to reduce Grant's chances to make an orderly withdrawal.[56]

Ten days after the early June battle of Cold Harbor, Confederate scouts reported the Federal army once more on the move. The 33rd and the 7th regiments inched toward Federal lines to verify the intelligence. All the Tar Heels found were 10 Federal stragglers. The brigade moved out at 5:00 a.m. on June 13, crossing the Chickahominy River at McClellan's Bridge, across the York River Railroad bridge, and through White Oak swamp before encountering Federal cavalry near Riddle's Shop. Gen. Wilcox posted McGowan's and Scales's brigades in the front, with Lane and Thomas taking up positions in support. John McGill (18th NC) later complained the brigade was formed under a "severe artillery fire," losing three enlisted men wounded. Various sharpshooter battalions from the division advanced to chase off the Federal troopers before Wilcox's main lines became engaged. Lane's brigade took several losses during the brief fight. Later that evening, He moved his command to the main line on the right and advanced with the other brigades, but eventually fell back and entrenched.[57]

The brigade stayed at Riddle's Shop the next couple of days. Moving ever so slightly, it then commenced building new or strengthening existing works. Lee was trying to discern Grant's movements: was the enemy army preparing to storm the Richmond defenses once again, or were they moving south, to attack Petersburg? Slowly Lee realized the latter was true. On June 17, Wilcox was ordered to move his division from Chaffin's Bluff toward the works at Bermuda Hundred. The following day, they were ordered to the works outside Petersburg. Setting out at 3:00 a.m., Col. Barry led the brigade across pontoon

---

56 Circular, ANV, June 3, 1864, Dowdey and Manarin, *Wartime Papers*, 762-63; Freeman, *R. E. Lee*, 3:400.

57 Harris, *Historical Sketches*, 51; James Harris to "Captain," September 9, 1864; John McGill to "Captain," July 18, 1864; William Speer to "Captain," July 19, 1864, Lane Papers, AU; *Fayetteville Observer*, June 27, 1864.

bridges near Drewry's Bluff, and after marching all day, finally halted near Battery No. 37.

For Lane's brigade, trudging through the heat and dust east of Richmond, the Overland Campaign came to an end with the crossing of the James River.[58]

58 Harris, *Historical Sketches*, 51.

Chapter 15

"I have to be shot to death."

Crime and Punishment

"**My** Dear Wife," Joseph Honeycutt wrote home on March 3, 1865. "I have to state to you the sad news that tomorrow at 12 o'clock that I have to die. I have to be shot to death for starting home to see my wife and dear children."

Honeycutt was a 44-year-old farmer and shoemaker in Stanley County with at least five children living at home in 1860. A post-war account claimed he was a Union man, forced into the Confederate army during the final months of the war. On the last day of February 1865, Honeycutt, with his comrades Daniel Furr and Winchester Palmer of the 7th NC, along with "three hundred others," chose to desert. Honeycurr, Furr, and Palmer left out early and were missed at roll call. Lane had the guard doubled, preventing the others from leaving. After waiting for two hours beyond the camp, the three made their way back though the lines and were within "fifty yards of their tents" when they were arrested and sent to the guard house. A quickly assembled court martial acquitted Palmer because "he was a son of a bloody war man." The other two were sentenced to execution on March 4, 1865. "I drempt last night of seeing you but I shall never," Honeycutt wrote home on March 3. "I don't mind death like I do to leave my family for I have to suffer so much here that I don't fear. I don't want you to grieve for me for I feel like I am going home to die no more." Other members of the regiment interceded, but Honeycutt and Furr became just two more soldiers lost to the cause.[1]

Once a citizen was mustered into the Confederate army, or received pay as a soldier, he was bound under the 101 Articles of War. Confederate regulation required the articles be read to the soldiers "every month, after the inspection," and in certain cases, when related to specific duties, "every week." The articles encouraged soldiers to "attend divine services," and forbade dueling, profane language, or criticizing elected Confederate leaders. Enlisted men and officers were required to pay proper respect to their superiors and fight against mutiny. Guidelines were established for military courts to try those deemed guilty of infractions. The articles also mandated punishments. Officers could be cashiered for falsifying muster rolls or returns, while enlisted men could suffer the death penalty for desertion or corporal punishment for fighting.[2]

Given the large numbers of men who suddenly found themselves together and removed from the moral restraints normally imposed by family and community, coupled with the boredom of camp life, there were numerous infractions of military regulations. Some of these could be minor, like losing issued equipment. Pay was often docked in such cases. In other instances, regimental commanders took action quickly. George Cochran recalled a fellow member of the 37th NC, Anthony Keller, who stated he enlisted to escape a murder charge. Upon returning from being sick, Keller discovered his favorite rifle missing. He refused thereafter to do any duty or obey orders, and many were afraid of him. Once he learned of it, Col. Lee "ordered Keller arrested and made to walk before the sentinel six hours with hands tied behind him with a gun hung on his back." It was Cochran's job to keep Keller in line as the brigade moved to a new camp. When Keller verbally abused him, Cochran "wrote out a charge against him" and sent it to Col. Lee. Keller was again arrested, and Lee ordered the same punishment as before. Keller swore that once free, he was going to kill Cochran. Having borrowed a pistol, Cochran was prepared, but another officer intervened with Lee, who kept Keller confined. Cochran was

---

1 *Stanly County Heritage* (Waynesville, NC: Walsworth Publishing Co., 2001), 313. The service records of Honeycutt (also spelled Huneycutt), Furr, and Palmer, end in October 1864. The story is unsubstantiated.

2 *Confederate Regulations*, 394, 407-20.

wounded not long thereafter, and while he was away from the army, Keller was released. On July 31, 1862, Keller deserted and was dead by the end of year. For more serious offenses, regimental commanders called for regimental courts-martial. When officers were tried or charges could result in the death penalty, a general court-martial was called. These courts consisted of 3 to 13 officers. A majority of the court had to agree with the verdict, and at least two-thirds had to vote in favor of a death sentence.[3]

Confederate courts-martial records were among the papers destroyed when Richmond was abandoned in April 1865. Piecing together a complete account of the role of military justice in the Confederate army is thus impossible. According to Jack Bunch, at least 325 courts-martial within the regiments of the Branch-Lane brigade occurred during the war. Twenty-three of those took place before formation of Branch's brigade, leaving 302. The first brigade courts-martial took place in mid-April 1862, near Kinston. In a two-week span, 12 members of the 33rd and 37th Regiments were tried. Only two have their offenses listed. Henry Harmon (37th NC) was tried and acquitted for desertion on April 25, 1862. Kinsion Wall (33rd NC) deserted on February 7 and was apprehended two days later. On April 17, he was convicted and sentenced to be flogged. The two officers tried, Lt. Henry Fite and Capt. James Potts, were both acquitted. The remaining eight were all convicted of unknown infractions and sentenced to confinement on bread or water, or hard labor. Active campaigning brought an end to courts-martial, and the brigade reported only 13 trials between September-November 1862.[4]

A soldier charged with a crime, once apprehended, was placed in the guard house. Sometimes this was a tent, and in more permanent quarters, possibly a cabin. George Cochran (37th NC) was detailed as a guard at the guard tent early in the war. No one was allowed to communicate with the prisoners. One morning, a member of the regiment tried to get past Cochran, who would not permit it. Soon, someone reported Cochran to Col. Lee, stating he had allowed prisoners to buy pies from a local lady. Lee instructed the officer of the guard to pass by Cochran at the changing of the guard, forcing him to stand guard two additional hours. Cochran complained to his captain, who went to Lee and got

---

3   Cochran, *A Brief Sketch*, 22; Jordan, *NC Troops*, 9:558. Cochran says Keller was killed while hiding out in the Brushy Mountains in Alexander County.

4   Jordan, *NC Troops*, 9:233; Jack Bunch, *Roster of the Courts-Martial in the Confederate States Armies* (Shippensburg, PA, 2001).

the decision over-turned. Cochran tried fruitlessly to learn the identity of the informant. Had he been successful, Cochran was prepared to "instantly knock [him] on the head with" his musket. Later, he confessed it was probably best his accuser remained anonymous. John Alexander (37th NC) recalled a grossly intoxicated fellow soldier making so much racket "the citizens thought the yankees had taken the town." A detail sent to arrest the soldier returned empty handed, confessing to their captain they would have to kill the soldier to capture him. He was "backed up against a house with a big Bowie knife in his hand, threatening to kill any one who offered to take him. Without saying a word," the officer "sprang up and ran to the house and seized him by the collar and led him off to the guard house."[5]

When it came time for a trial, a panel of officers was chosen and the accused brought in and seated at a table beside the judge advocate facing the "jury," often officers from the unit. Orders convening the court were read, and if the soldier had no objections to the officers present, they were administered the oath. A field-grade officer normally presided, while the judge advocate served not only as counsel for the accused, but the government's prosecutor. Once the charged man was identified, the judge advocate read the charges against him. A plea of guilty or not guilty was then entered for each count. Witnesses for the government testified, and the prosecution closed. The accused could then present witnesses, all of whom could be cross-examined. Once testimony ended, the court deliberated in closed session. When court members reached a decision, the president and judge advocate signed the official document which was then sent for approval to the officer authorizing the court. After review, a three-part general order was issued. Part I identified the court, time and place of its meeting, and under what authority it was called. Part II included information on the soldier, specifications against him, and the court's decision on each charge. Information was also included on specific punishments for the guilty. Approval or disapproval of the court's findings by the convening officers comprised Part III, along with orders implementing the approved punishment. In death sentence cases, the reviewing officer could suspend execution until the President reviewed the verdict.[6]

---

5 Cochran, *A Brief Sketch,* 8-9; Alexander, *Reminiscences of the Past Sixty Years,* 82.

6 Jack Bunch, *Military Justice in the Confederate States Armies* (Shippensburg, PA, 2000), 17-18; Aldo Perry, *Civil War Courts-Martial of North Carolina Troops* (Jefferson, NC, 2012), 7.

Francis M. Cochran was mustered in as a corporal, but reduced back to the rank of private in March or April of 1862. He rose to first sergeant before being killed at the battle of Chancellorsville in May 1863.

Catawba Soldiers in the Civil War

Fifty-eight of the 326 recorded courts-martial in the brigade resulted in acquittal. Six others had their sentences remitted, while four were simply reprimanded. Another 16 paid fines or had their pay suspended. The majority of soldiers convicted of some infractions were ordered back to their companies for punishment. Brigade band member Oliver Lehman recalled seeing soldiers "with a board strapped on their backs with large letters 'I am a thief' or 'I stole my comrade's rations' and other offences marching through the camp, up one street and down the other with a drum corps in front of them making all possible noise to attract attention." Lehman also recalled soldiers "sentenced to walk in a circle about 50 feet in diameter, carrying on his shoulders a billet of wood weighing from 60 to 90 lbs for an hour each day, for a day or a week according to the offence. A guard, with a musket stood by and kept him moving until his time expired." [7]

Non-commissioned officers could be punished by reduction back to the ranks. Corporal William Rogers had served in the 18th Regiment for almost two years before being busted back to private for "cowardly conduct" in August 1864. Officers could be cashiered from the service. A few were forced to resign. Not long after Lt. Allen Croom's appointment in the 33rd, he submitted his resignation and was granted leave. Croom went on to organize a new company to which he was appointed captain before his resignation was approved. This

7   Lehman, "Camp Life."

Captain Oliver Parks was forced to resign from the 33rd North Carolina for conduct unbecoming of an officer and a gentleman.

Histories of the Several Regiments
and Battalions from North Carolina

action infuriated Col. Avery, who considered Croom incompetent and of "no account whatever," and in July, demanded his resignation. Colonel Haywood demanded Lt. William Green's (7th NC) resignation following the battle of Gaines Mill in June 1862. If he did not resign, then Haywood intended to prefer charges. Captain Thomas Brown, Jr. (18th NC), twice ran away during battle. The first was during Hanover Court House, and he was captured soon thereafter. At the battle of Fredericksburg, he likewise "shamefully runaway and desert his Command." Colonel Purdie recommended that Brown be "dropped from the rolls of the army in disgrace and published for one week in" various North Carolina newspapers.[8]

While there is no record of either Branch or Lane ever being brought up on charges, Col. Edward Haywood (7th NC) could not say the same. In December 1863, he was charged with being intoxicated on duty. A court-martial found Haywood guilty and sentenced him to be cashiered from the service. However, because of his prior "gallant service," the court-martial board, field officers in the brigade, and even Robert E. Lee, all recommended the charge be remitted. Davis agreed, and on April 23, 1864, ordered Haywood released from arrest and restored to duty. Yet in the meantime, Haywood had disappeared. In September 1864, Lane laid out the facts as he understood them to Gen. Samuel

---

8   Jordan, *NC Troops* 6:416; Clark Avery to Samuel Cooper, July 15, 1862, Roll 0379, M270, RG109, CMSR, NA; William Green, Roll 0173, M270, RG109, CMSR, NA; Thomas Purdie to "Dear Sir," December 30, 1862, Roll 0260, M270, RG109, CMSR, NA.

Cooper. On February 27, 1864, Haywood had obtained a 21-day leave of absence to take his sick wife back to North Carolina. A month later, Haywood obtained an extension of his leave, due to illness. Extensions continued to be granted through the spring and summer.[9]

When Lane returned to the army following his wounding, Haywood was still missing. Lane wrote in April, trying to get information, complaining that the officer had been long absent from command, and even when present, he did "very little duty rarely even going on picket." Lane wrote again in September, asking that Haywood be ordered to report to his command at once. His absence was unfair to the officers and men in the 7th Regiment. Haywood had been with the 7th since being appointed lieutenant colonel on May 16, 1861. Promoted to colonel following the death of Reuben Campbell at Gaines Mill in 1862, Haywood was wounded at both Second Manassas and Chancellorsville. In late 1862, a swell of support for Haywood's promotion to brigadier general came to naught. While on sick furlough in Raleigh, he was writing to Army headquarters, seeking permission to go before a board of medical examiners and be declared incapacitated for further field duty. Haywood eventually got his examination, was found to be suffering from chronic cystitis, and was retired to the Invalid Corps on November 28, 1864. On a couple of different occasions, he requested an appointment as commander of the post in Raleigh, and then Salisbury, but apparently spent the rest of the war on leave, waiting to be assigned.[10]

Soldiers did just about everything they could to keep from being caught breaking the rules in camp. John Alexander (37th NC) told of a soldier who had a barrel of brandy shipped to him. The soldier buried the container in his tent and sold small drinks for 10 cents. This went on for a few days, until a customer complained 10 cents should buy two drinks. When told he could go buy his drink some other place, the disgruntled soldier reported the "blockader." His barrel was confiscated and turned over to the surgeons. In another instance, Albert Johnson and two companions from the 7th Regiment slipped out of camp late one afternoon to purchase food from a local farmer. On their return,

9   Jordan, *NC Troops,* 4:405; JL to Samuel Cooper, April 27, 1864; Special Order #95; Edward Haywood, Roll 0173, M270, RG109, CMSR, NA.

10 JL to Samuel Cooper, September 23, 1864; Edward Taylor to Samuel Cooper, October 10, 1864; Edward Haywood to Walter Taylor, October 12, 1864; Edward Haywood, Roll 0173, M270, RG109, CMSR, NA.

a guard arrested them. Johnson "earnestly besought the sentinel to turn him loose." The guard refused and began escorting the men back to camp. They were crossing a "deep washout" when Johnson "caused the sentinel to fall into the pit." The trio made their way quickly to their command. The next day, company commanders ordered their men to fall in, and the guard walked through the ranks looking for his escapees. He was able to pick out one man, a Mr. Robison, but the others eluded capture and subsequent punishment. Johnson confessed that while being inspected, it took a great deal of "effort . . . to maintain his equilibrium."[11]

Whiskey, fisticuffs, insubordination, and thievery were all problems officers had to face. Yet desertion, leaving camp without official permission, was the worst. All soldiers knew that Article of War #20 made desertion a crime punishable by death, but leniency was possible, for the next article granted the officers of the courts-martial discretion.[12]

Explaining the motivations of more than 300 deserters in the Branch-Lane brigade is a challenge. Soldiers seldom gave the reasons that led them to abandon their comrades. Historian Mark Weitz concludes most Confederate soldiers viewed their service as "contractual, not indefinite." Soldiers left for two primary reasons: either dissatisfaction with the army, or concern for the family back home.[13]

Throwing together men from different classes and backgrounds caused consternation among the volunteer citizen soldiers. "We are under very strict discipline, some of our boys take it very hard," John Kinyoun (28th NC) wrote early in the war. An officer in command, giving orders and expecting obedience, had been a friend back home.. After spending 19 months in service, Bennett Smith, a private in the 37th NC, voiced his displeasure at army life to his wife. He spoke for many:

> I am tird of so many masters & Sutch tite rules. I want to get So I can go when I pleas & wher I pleas with out a pas. it is pore living the way we hav to liv hear no liberty a tal & hav to do jest as others Say. I long to Sea the time when the officers has no longer any

---

11 Alexander, *Reminiscences*, 81; "In Memoriam," *Kinfolk and Connections* (September 1990) 8/2:1-11.

12 *Confederate Regulations*, 410.

13 Weitz, *More Damning than Slaughter*, 11.

cawl for their offis So they can quit exercizen authority over men that is as good as they
are if not better than a heap of them. [14]

Dissatisfaction was rampant in the 37th NC in 1863; at least 25 members
left following the battle of Chancellorsville. Disagreement over promotion
policies led to the mass exodus. While there were other cases of men absenting
themselves from their commands, usually in the battle, the men who walked out
of Company A, 37th NC, inspired others. Three from Company D, 18th NC
left on June 12, 1863; 10 from Company E, 33rd NC deserted around July 24,
1863. As the war ground on, more men voluntarily vanished. Three members of
the 33rd, Company F, deserted as the brigade relocated from Petersburg to east
of Richmond in September 1864. Another 11 members of Company F joined
them while the brigade moved on December 9. Three members of Company C
and five of Company H, 18th NC, slipped off into the woods in early February
1865.[15]

As the war dragged on, deteriorating conditions back in North Carolina
drove many out of the ranks and back toward home. "[W]hat really motivated
Southern soldiers was home, community, and to a much greater extent, family,"
Weitz writes. "It was the defense of home, fireside, wife, and children that had
real meaning for these men." Many a soldier marched away, expecting to return
home before a year ended. That never happened. Beginning in April 1862 and
never ceasing, conscription continuously pulled more men from communities.
The absence of these men on farms, coupled with poor weather conditions,
meant many families started to go hungry. In many cases, the threat of
conscription drove men avoiding service from their cabins and into the woods
and organized bands. Yadkin County attorney R. G. Armfield wrote to
Governor Vance in February 1863:

When the time came for them to go perhaps nearly one hundred in this county took to
the woods, lying out day and night to avoid arrest, and although the militia officers
have exerted themselves with great zeal, yet these skulkers have always had many more

14 Kinyoun to "Dear Wife," October 13, 1862, Kinyoun Papers, DU; Bennett Smith to "Dear
Wife," April 16, 1862, private collection.

15 Thomas Norwood to "Uncle," June 16, 1863, Lenoir Papers, SHC/UNC; Jordan, *NC
Troops*, 3:345,349, 6:335-37, 391-99, 9:174-79, 185-94, 472-82.

active friends than they need, and could always get timely information of enemy movements to arrest them and avoided it.[16]

About the time Armfield wrote, 20-30 conscripts and deserters gathered at the Bond Schoolhouse in Yadkin County, planning to cross over the mountains into Union lines. Alerted, the local militia surrounded the school. A pitched battle soon followed, with several wounded or killed on each side. "O what a sad affair. . . poor men killed," wrote William Speer (28th NC). The conscripts, he thought, would be better off in the ranks where they "might have lived &, if killed, they would have died like men and not Torries." The surrounding counties witnessed several pitched battles in the months to come, and word filtered back to camp of the depredations happening, especially in the state's western communities. Wilkes County was once reported as having 1,500 deserters in a single camp. Robert E. Lee actually ordered former brigade officer Robert Hoke, with part of a brigade, into the area in the summer of 1863 to round up the deserters.[17]

Former as well as current brigade members were sometimes involved directly in the inner civil war taking place within the state. Isaac Wilson, for a brief while in 1861 a lieutenant in the 37th Regiment, later on served as a recruiting officer. While at home in Ashe County on furlough, he was shot and killed while out plowing a cornfield. His murder was believed to be in retaliation for the murder of a local dissident earlier that year. One county south, another former member of the 37th, Harvey Bingham, worked to corral deserters, conscription evaders, and dissidents in Watauga County. Wounded in the head at Second Manassas, Bingham resigned a short time later, because of "disease of the lung." To quell the growing unrest in the western part of the state, Governor Vance created the home guard in mid-1863. Bingham was placed in command of the 11th battalion, which eventually comprised two companies, one of which was commanded by another former 37th officer, Jordon Cook. Bingham, Cook, and the others were constantly fighting both deserter bands and Union soldiers from East Tennessee. Any soldier they caught without a

16 Weitz, *More Damning than Slaughter*, 26; R. G. Armfield to Zebulon Vance, Feb. 19, 1863, Vance Papers, NCDAH.

17 Casstevens,*The Civil War and Yadkin County*, 85-96; Speer, *Voices from Cemetery Hill*, 90. One of those involved in the Bond Schoolhouse affair was Anderson Douglas, who joined the 28th Regiment on October 27, 1863. He lost an arm at Reams Station on August 25, 1864. Jordan, *NC Troops*, 8:177.

proper furlough was escorted under guard to Salisbury and forwarded back to his regiment.[18]

Naturally worried about their families at home, and unable to procure furloughs or to stay home long enough to help, soldiers simply left their regiments, often under the cover of darkness. Many struggled with the decision to stay or go. Bennett Smith described the group in 1863 that "runaway" out of the 37th Regiment. "I dont think that I will go yet," he wrote. "I want to wait fore the bigest crowd & then I will go[.]" Circumstances were hardly better in February 1865 when Alfred Proffitt (18th NC) noted many fellow soldiers deserting into Union lines. "I hardly think I shod go, but if I ever run away . . . thare is whar I shall go. I would not pretend to come home. Thare are things that would make me go but it is not worth while to say what those things are at present." Obviously, desertion was a viable option for hundreds in the brigade.[19]

Officers did everything they could to coax back those overstaying their furloughs and declared absent. Newspaper advertisements began appearing in mid-1862. At first, officers tried to shame deserters back into the ranks. An ad from the 7th Regiment informed the people back home of more than 200 men absent at that time, and threatened "their names will be published as deserters" if they did not report back immediately. The same type of advertisement ran once again that December.

A few weeks later, the threat became reality. Officers in Company I, 28th NC, published the names of 24 soldiers absent. If they remained so, not only would they be treated as deserters, but their pay would be stopped. In mid-1863, officers of Company D of the 33rd published a list of 28 names, and offered a $50 reward for the arrest and delivery of each man. One member of the 7th NC wrote a state newspaper in July 1863, recommending that a deserter's property be confiscated and given to those in need. "If such a course was pursued, my honest conviction is that ere long the *woods, mountains,* and *caves*

18 Jordan, *NC Troops*, 9:524. For more information on Wilson, see Sandra Ballard and Leila Weinstein, eds., *Neighbor to Neighbor: A Memoir of Family, Community, and Civil War in Appalachian North Carolina* (Boone, NC, 2007); for more information on Bingham and the war in Watauga County, see Michael Hardy, *Watauga County, North Carolina, in the Civil War* (Charleston, SC, 2013).

19 Bennett Smith to "Dear Wife," May 17, 1863, private collection; Hancock, *Four Brothers in Gray*, 287.

would be a desolate habitation." Shortly after the letter appeared, all notices for the apprehension and reward for deserters ceased.[20]

Officers were sometimes detailed to return to their home counties to round up the absentees. Whether William Morris was granted a leave of indulgence or detailed for the purpose isn't clear, but he started back to the army from Gaston County in March 1863 with three deserters from the 37th Regiment. Once they boarded the cars in Charlotte, one of his charges, Eli Rudisill, gave him the slip. Morris arrived back in camp with the other two, Jacob Rudisill and Oilver Byrd, who were not punished because they had returned willingly. A few months later, Lt. Thomas Norwood was sent to Ashe County "to persuade my lost sheep to return to duty" in his company in the 37th NC. Norwood discovered several of them had been abducted and enrolled into the 21st VA Cavalry. The Virginia regiment's colonel refused to release the men without an order from the Secretary of War. Though it took a little time, Norwood got his letter, and 15 members of his company rejoined the 37th.[21]

Confederate or state officials made several attempts to encourage absent soldiers to return. The orders came from three different sources: the War Department, Robert E. Lee, or Governor Zebulon Vance. On August 1, 1863, Jefferson Davis issued one of those proclamations, encouraging soldiers to return to the army and promising no disciplinary action if they did so within 20 days. While some did come back, many others decided to either leave or stay gone, believing they could be pardoned once they returned. General Lee issued the last amnesty on February 9, 1865, again pardoning all who returned within 20 days. Those who had already received a pardon, or who deserted after February 9 were not included.[22]

Soldiers often included instructions and advice for absent comrades in their letters home.. "i want you to tell Jo Sexton that he had better come back as quick as he can for he is reported as absent with out leave," Thorton Sexton (37th

20 *Weekly State Journal*, June 18, 1862; *The Daily Journal*, December 19, 1862; *Semi-Weekly Standard*, January 2, 1863; *Raleigh Register*, June 17, 1863; *Charlotte Daily Bulletin*, July 25, 1863. The militia, and later home guard battalions, did catch a few. Phillip Griffin (37th NC) deserted on December 15, 1862, and was caught by A. L Meeks three weeks later. Upon delivery to Richmond, Meeks was paid $30 for his efforts. Phillip Griffin, Roll 402, M270, RG109, CMSR, NA.

21 William Morris to "Deare Companion," March 4, 1863, Morris Letters, SHC/UNC; Norwood to "Dear Uncle," September 25, 1863, Lenoir Papers, SHC/UNC.

22 Weitz, *More Damning than Slaughter*, 84, 135, 155, 281.

NC) wrote home in November 1863. Based upon a statement by William Barlow (18th NC) in June 1863, the regiments kept separate lists of absentees. Those who were expected to return were listed as absent without leave, while those not expected to come back were deserters.[23]

Soldiers who voluntarily returned to their regiments, or were caught and brought back under guard, had to face the consequences of their actions. Greenberry Harding (28th NC) wrote in late 1863 of several members of his regiment in the guardhouse for desertion and forced "to wear a ball & chain for two months." Alfred Proffitt told his parents of a returned deserter in the 18th who had the letter "D" branded on the left hip, while a member of the 37th was drummed through camp wearing a board painted with the word "deserter." In another case, a soldier had

> one side of his head shaived and he had to toat a stick of wood waying 50 lbs. round a ring 30 feet in diameter evry other hower in the day and then ware a barrell shirt throu the streets with two drums after him beating Yankee Doodle. Allso a man after him with a bayonet for desearting. On his barrell shirt thare are big letters, "Deserter."

Allen Absher (33rd NC), found guilty of deserting in the fall of 1862 and ordered to forfeit three months' pay, had no prospect of leave for six months, and had to clean the camp two hours daily for three months. A few deserters found guilty had their death sentences reduced to hard labor. Green Morris (28th NC) was sent to Castle Thunder in Richmond for seven months, and he transferred to a different regiment upon his release.[24]

In some cases, there were attempts at appeals for the condemned. Jesse Luther deserted from the 28th NC some time before September 1863. He was caught, tried, found guilty, and sentenced to death. The sentence was suspended until reviewed by the president. In the meantime, his regiment exerted a strenuous effort on Luther's behalf to spare his life. The 28th's officers signed a petition asking for clemency, and Chaplain Kennedy delivered

---

23 Thorton Sexton to "Dear Father," November 13, 1862. Thorton Seton Letters, DU. William Barlow wrote, "Tell Thomas M Barlow that James Gilbery said that they took his name off the list and they did not expect him to come back." Barlow to Dear Wife, June 8, 1863, *Company Front*, 33.

24 Greenberry Harding to "Dear Father," November 25, 1863, Casstevens, *The 28th North Carolina Infantry*, 195; Hancock, *Four Brothers in Gray*, 190, 204; Perry, *Civil War Courts-Martial of North Carolina Troops*, 27.

Chaplain Francis Milton Kennedy, 28th North Carolina, frequently had to pray with men right before they faced execution.

Histories of the Several Regiments and Battalions from North Carolina

it to the president's office in Richmond. A few months later, Kennedy noted Luther's sister was in camp. He lent her his horse, and she went to see Lee on her brother's behalf. Finally, on March 3, 1864, the War Department announced: "The sentence of death against Private Jesse M. Luther, Company E, 28th. . . is commuted, by order of the President to four months hard labor at such place as the commanding general may appoint."[25]

For a few, desertion warranted the ultimate payment: death. "On the 19th of September," James Harris (7th NC) wrote in 1863,

we were called to witness for the first time, a military execution for the crime of desertion. The unhappy victims (two in number) were members of . . . 33rd Regiment. . . . They were tried by a court martial, found guilty, and the death penalty imposed. The brigade was drawn up in three sides of a square, and the condemned men, accompanied by their spiritual advisers marched in front of each regiment with arms tied behind their backs, and the band meanwhile playing the "dead march." after which they were tied to stakes a few feet apart and blind folded. The guard—24 in number, were about fifteen feet distant, and, at the command, Fire, the unfortunate men were instantly killed. The different regiments were then marched by the dead men so that each one might see for himself, the terrible consequences of desertion.[26]

25 Perry, *Civil War Courts-Martial of North Carolina Troops*, 29. Kennedy, Diary, September 23 - November 9, 1863.

26 Harris, *Historical* Sketches, 41.

A couple of weeks later, the men were drawn up once again to witness the execution of seven brigade members—three each from the 18th and 37th, and one from the 28th. The order had been read to the brigade announcing their deaths, and then the men were given one week to prepare. The brigade formed a hollow square, and the "unfortunate" soldiers were marched along the lines before being secured to stakes. Chaplain Kennedy spent time with the men: he had baptized two of them earlier that day. "All professed to have obtained peace with God save one poor fellow who did not seem satisfied with his condition." Twenty-four soldiers were lined up in front of the condemned, half of them with muskets loaded with blanks in an effort to ease the psychological impact of execution. Once the prisoners were blindfolded, the officer gave the command to aim and fire. As the smoke cleared, six of the seven were killed outright. Yet the seventh "received five balls in his bowels, but they were aimed too low to cause instant death. He was again bound to the stake, six men brought forward and immediately ended his suffering." The scribe believed the executions were having a positive effect on the brigade.[27]

In some instances men probably not guilty were executed. For example, two men executed in September 1863 were brothers Jacob and Elkana Lanier (18th NC). They had slipped out of camp on August 25 and were apprehended five days later. "We left camp to get some apples and green corn . . . we do not get more than half enough to eat," Jacob wrote home while awaiting trial. . He had no idea what fate awaited him but believed officials could not "hurt one much." Their trial began on September 9; on the 20th both brothers were found guilty and sentenced to death. Jacob wrote his parents again, informing them of his fate. "All the other consolation is after they have killed the body they can go no further." He had put his trust in his Savior and believed his officers were doing what they could. Elkana promptly wrote his wife, regretting he would never see her and his children again. Both brothers wrote again on September 24. Elkana wanted his wife to rear their children "right and try to give them an education so that they can read the Word of the Lord." While he knew it would be hard on his family, he cast his impending death in a positive light, writing more than once, "Glory be to God I am going home." "I hear them making the coffins for our bodies," he wrote, adding verses to hymns such as "Come Ye Sinners" and "Amazing Grace." Jacob was less buoyant. "It goes hard for me to write so solemn a doom," he wrote. "I have spent my time reading the Holy

---

27 Kennedy, Diary, September 26, 1863 SHC/UNC; *Fayetteville Observer*, October 5, 1863.

Bible and in prayer to God. . . . I am exceedingly sorrowful on your account. Read the 88th Psalm—the reason plainly to be seen." Yet were the Lanier brothers guilty? Of being absent without leave, certainly. Of desertion, probably not.[28]

At least 22 North Carolina soldiers in the Branch-Lane brigade were executed during the war. An unknown number of others were caught at home and executed by the local militia or home guard. Hundreds of others ran afoul of the military justice system for infractions great and small. Many harbored bitter feelings for the punishments their officers doled out. Jordan Council (37th NC) was found guilty of desertion and thought he had received justice until Col. Barber imposed his punishment: forfeit of pay, police duty, and wearing a ball and chain. The last chaffed Council, who swore if he survived the war, the colonel "will fare but midlen." For many in the brigade, surviving the war was still long odds.[29]

28 Shayle Edwards, *The Lanier Brothers: "Apples and Green Corn"* (n.p., 2000), 13-16. Perry, *Courts-Martial of North Carolina Troops*, 29-30.

29 The number of 22 came from a survey of Jordan, *NC Troops*. This number differs by one. Perry, *Civil War Courts-Martial of North Carolina*. The difference is Dulin Starnes (37th Regiment), who was "shot to death" on an unknown date. Jordan, *NC Troops*, 9:589. Jordon Horton to "Dear Wife," January 17, 1864, Council Papers, DU.

Chapter 16

"The canons are all rouring like if they were going to tair up evry thing."

The Petersburg Campaign

Federal troops came close to capturing Petersburg in mid-June 1864. Confederates east of the city were pushed out of two sets of works, retaking only one on the night of June 17. Lee, unsure of the disposition of the Army of the Potomac, kept the bulk of his army east of Richmond, facing Federal forces near Bermuda Hundred. Not until late in the day on June 17 did he realize that the main Federal army had given him the slip. He moved Hill's corps from Four Mile Creek to Chaffin's Bluff. Early on June 18, Lee ordered Hill to cross the James River and march rapidly towards Petersburg. Confederate forces already east of Petersburg abandoned the second line of works overnight, moving into a new third line. This new line held against repeated attacks as the main body of Lee's army arrived and went into position.

Late on June 18, Col. John D. Barry led Lane's brigade below Petersburg, going into position near Battery 37. Regiments were shuffled around the following morning. The 7th NC was posted between Batteries 36 and 37, while the 18th was near Battery 34. The other regiments doubtless filled in the gaps, strengthening the position. Lane's brigade occupied the far left of Hill's corps,

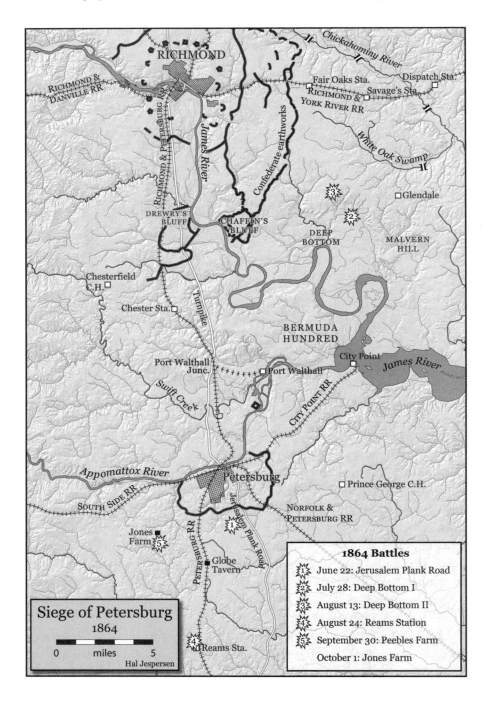

RICHMOND & DANVILLE RR

RICHMOND

Chickahominy River

Fair Oaks Sta.

Dispatch Sta.

Savage's Sta.

RICHMOND & YORK RIVER RR

White Oak Swamp

RICHMOND & PETERSBURG RR

James River

Confederate earthworks

Glendale

DREWRY'S BLUFF

CHAFFIN'S BLUFF

DEEP BOTTOM

MALVERN HILL

Chesterfield C.H.

Chester Sta.

Turnpike

BERMUDA HUNDRED

City Point

James River

Port Walthall Junc.

Port Walthall

Swift Creek

CITY POINT RR

Appomattox River

Petersburg

Prince George C.H.

SOUTH SIDE RR

PETERSBURG RR

Jerusalem Plank Road

NORFOLK & PETERSBURG RR

Jones Farm

Globe Tavern

Reams Sta.

Siege of Petersburg
1864

0   miles   5

Hal Jespersen

1864 Battles

1. June 22: Jerusalem Plank Road
2. July 28: Deep Bottom I
3. August 13: Deep Bottom II
4. August 24: Reams Station
5. September 30: Peebles Farm

October 1: Jones Farm

connecting to the right of Mahone's division. As the Union forces moved toward the Weldon Railroad on June 21, Mahone's and Wilcox's divisions were ordered out to confront them. About 2:00 p.m., Barry moved the brigade down the Halifax Road, halting near Globe Tavern where they wheeled off into the woods and began digging in. At one point, Wilcox ordered an advance, but contact was sparse. They captured 20-30 prisoners and passed a few dead infantry and cavalry. By 10:00 p.m., the Confederates were on their way back to the Petersburg entrenchments.[1]

Wilcox again unleashed the Light Division the next day with Federals reported moving in the same area. They were on the move by 11:00 a.m. After marching down the railroad tracks, Wilcox turned the division off to the left, or east, and advanced more than a mile down a "country road." McGowan's and Thomas's brigades were deployed south of the road, with Lane's and Scales's north of it. Barry posted the brigade from the left: 37th, 7th, 18th, 28th, and 33rd Regiments, with the 33rd's right on the left of Scales's brigade. "The woods and undergrowth was so thick," Wilcox wrote, "that it was not possible for a Colonel to see his regiment in line." Barry deployed the sharpshooter battalion under Maj. Wooten, and the two brigades advanced uncontested more than a mile, stopping at the edge of some woods. Wooten ordered his battalion to lie down and sent word back to Barry. No enemy was seen in the Union works 50 to 100 yards to his front, but several flags flew over the breastworks. Possibly Wooten's sharpshooters did not cover the brigade's entire front.

When A. P. Hill arrived at 2:00 p.m., he ordered Lane's and Scale's brigades to advance through dense woodlands. The 18th NC drove the Federal skirmishers back toward their works, capturing several while suffering three casualties. Lieutenant Colonel Speer reported that the 28th NC, likewise encountered "the enemy's skirmishers, fought them, drove them in and took some 40 prisoners . . . [all] under a heavy fire in which I lost some good men." James Harris (7th NC) recalled a protective rise to their front with "men lying flat to deliver their fire over the crest of the hill."[2]

1   James Harris to "Captain," July 19, 1864 Lane Papers, AU; John McGill to "Captain," July 18, 1864, Lane Papers, AU; Caldwell, *History of a Brigade of South Carolinians*, 163-64; Cadmus Wilcox, "Petersburg Campaign Report," Lee Headquarters Papers, Virginia Historical Society.

2   Wilcox, "Petersburg Campaign Report," VHS; Thomas Wooten to Hale, September 24, 1864; John McGill to "Captain," September 9, 1864; William Speer to "Captain," July 31, 1864, Lane Papers, AU; Harris, *Historical Sketches*, 51. Wilcox wrote he had orders from Hill to avoid bringing on a general engagement. see Freeman, *Lee*, 3:453-54.

After the almost hour-long fight, the division was directed to redeploy in support of Mahone's division. The brigade lost seven killed, 50 wounded, and five captured, more than any other brigade in the Light Division for June 22. Leaving his skirmishers with orders to fall back first to the railroad, and then to Petersburg, if the Federals advanced, Wilcox pulled the Light Division back and to the left. For a while, the men endured a severe shelling from Federal artillery. Eventually they moved in support of Wright's Georgia brigade, but at darkness, they were ordered back to the main Confederate works. Though he had checked a Federal corps well short of its objective, Wilcox had shown little enthusiasm in that or in supporting Mahone's division. On June 23, Lane's brigade shifted left under small arms and cannon fire, replacing the Florida brigade. Losses were reported as six killed and 12 wounded.[3]

For two days, Mahone's attacks south of Petersburg netted success, wrecking several Federal divisions. A third attack launched on June 23 met with similar success, but an attack on the enemy left, along the Appomattox River the following day, was defeated. The Federal advantage in sheer numbers doomed any lasting result for Lee. He had to send a portion of his army away to contend with a Federal advance in the Shenandoah Valley. While the remaining Confederate forces successfully checked a Federal advance west of the Weldon Railroad, the railroad itself was lost.

"I can tell you that I have not seen any pleasure for the last 45 days," wrote Noah Wagner (28th NC). "[I]t is aweful to think ever since the 4 of may I have not seen one day but the canons are all rouring like if they were going to tair up evry thing we have been in line of battle or marching all the time if onley for Gods sakes this awful war would end so that we could live in pease." The war was taking its toll on the brigade. Almost every day brought a casualty. William Edwards (28th NC) was killed on June 23; Thomas Trivett (37th NC) was wounded by a "stray shot" on June 24. In that same 45-day stretch Wagner mentioned, Lane's brigade lost 1,153 irreplaceable men killed, wounded, and missing.[4]

---

3 Lane, "History of Lane's North Carolina Brigade," *SHSP*, 9:357; William Speer to "Captain," July 31, 1864. The fallout over the captured flags at Spotsylvania might have led to Wilcox choosing "to carry on his own movement rather than rushing to the aid of Mahone"; see McDaid, "Four Years," 295.

4 John Hatley and Linda Huffman, *Letters of William Wagner, Confederate Soldier* (Weldon, NC, 1983), 91; Jordan, *NC Troops*, 9:189, 483; Lane, "History of Lane's North Carolina brigade," *SHSP*, 9:357.

On June 25 Lt. Col. Speer noted being so close to the Federal works his men could not "stick up our heads without getting shot at. . . . As soon as a man shows his head he is plugged at & often killed or wounded." There was no shade, no rain, and "the hottest weather I ever did see. . . . I tell you, dear Father, it is horrible to be in this place." The next day, the brigade rotated out of the trenches to a spot behind the lines relatively unexposed to Federal fire where they stayed until July 2.[5]

After the war, Jubal Early claimed General Lee had stated that if the Federals reached the James River, the campaign would "become a siege, and then it will be a mere question of time." Grant not only reached the James, but crossed it, and now Lee's army was committed to holding a 19-mile-long system of defenses stretching from the White Oak Swamp above the James River, all the way south to the Weldon Railroad. Lee had to protect the vital railroads leading from the west into Petersburg—part of the key supply line to Richmond—while preventing Grant from making a sudden dart toward the capital, all with a numerically inferior army. For the next 10 months, Grant's strategy was to feign attack on Richmond, while massing to strike Confederate lines below Petersburg, or extending his own line farther west, further stretching the already-thin Confederate defenders. Lee was thus compelled to shuttle his insufficient forces across the James and Appomattox Rivers to blunt Grant's breakthrough attempts. Hill's corps became the de facto mobile strike force of Lee's army.[6]

Grant pursued the idea of a two-front war even as the initial attempts to capture Petersburg disintegrated on June 18. Grant selected Deep Bottom, on the James River, as a crossing point to "divide the attention of the enemy's troops, and to confuse them as to whether to expect an attack upon Richmond or Petersburg." Federal soldiers were sent to the area, and a pontoon bridge constructed over the river. Lee learned of the Union entrenchments at Deep Bottom by June 21 and sent Henry Heth's division to the area on June 22. Confederate artillery harassed Federal infantry and gunboats. To bolster the Confederate presence in the area, Lane's brigade set out July 2 for Deep Bottom. They marched throughout the night and arrived on July 3. Grant knew Lane's brigade was near Deep Bottom by the evening of July 4. Area

5   Speer, *Voices from Cemetery Hill*, 140, 142; Harris, *Historical Sketches*, 52.

6   J. William Jones, *Personal Reminiscences, Anecdotes, and Letters of Gen. Robert E. Lee* (New York, NY, 1875), 40.

Henry A. Conrad was just 16 years old when he enlisted in the 28th North Carolina in August 1861. He was killed on July 28, 1864, at the first battle of Deep Bottom.

Catawba Soldiers in the Civil War

commander Maj. Gen. Benjamin Butler wrote Grant, reporting a deserter had given the disposition of Confederate brigades in the area. Rumor of attack had one-third of the brigade under arms at all times. On July 15, the 33rd Regiment was ordered to the support of a battery of 20-pounder Parrotts bombarding both transports in the river and Federal infantry entrenchments. A Federal buildup compelled Lee to transfer additional troops to the area. A member of the 7th reported that on July 24, Lane's brigade rotated out of the works, replaced by men from Maj, Gen. Joseph B. Kershaw's division.[7]

On July 24, the process began to have John D. Barry appointed as a temporary brigadier general and assigned to permanent command of Lane's brigade. Hill didn't consider the brigade's senior colonel, Edward Haywood, suitable, and the next senior, William Barber, had been captured. Lee signed off on Barry's promotion, as did Jefferson Davis. Barry led the brigade in a skirmish on July 27, and lost two fingers when he was struck in the right hand. Colonel Robert Cowan (33rd NC) replaced Barry as brigade commander, while Capt. William Callais took command of the 33rd. It is possible Lane returned to the army the day Barry was wounded. Several newspapers reported the carriage bringing Lane back to the brigade was the same that took Barry to Richmond. Lane later wrote that Lee would not allow him to return to active duty, "as he

---

7 Horace Porter, *Campaigning with Grant* (New York, NY, 1906), 216; Harrison, *Historical Sketches*, 52; OR 40/2:633.

was afraid my leg was not strong enough." He was allowed, however, to look after the well-being of his men, and when he felt like he could withstand the rigors of the campaign, to report back to Lee.[8]

Both sides decided to attack on July 28. Two brigades from Kershaw's and Wilcox's divisions were chosen to lead the assault, while Heth's division held the New Market line. Brigadier General James Conner led the attacking column aiming at turning the Federal right and driving them back to Curle's Neck where they could be beaten in detail. Conner placed Lane's brigade on the right, with McGowan's brigade in the center and Kershaw's brigade on the left. Cowan positioned the brigade, from the left: 7th, 18th, 37th, 28th, and 33rd Regiments. Troublesome terrain bedeviled the advancing lines of battle. Two hundred yards of dense woods opened onto a road, beyond which lay a marsh along a branch of the White Oak Swamp. Then came a cornfield split by a finger of woods. Cowan sent the brigade's sharpshooters to the front. About the time the advance was called, Cowan reinforced his sharpshooters with three companies from the 7th.[9]

Sometime between 11 a.m. and noon, Confederate forces stepped off and encountered Federal skirmishers in the swamp; the morass tore the regiments and brigades apart. Daniel Moore, carrying the flag of the 33rd NC, and Capt. David Corzine broke into the cornfield and discovered they had outpaced their regiment. Corzine was killed and Moore struck twice. McGowan's brigade, to the left of Lane's, split in two, with part of it crowding and possibly overlapping Lane's brigade. The regiments attempted to reorganize as they moved into the cornfield, but the advance continued relentlessly. A portion of McGowan's brigade out in front of the advance prompted Cowan to order Lane's brigade to double-quick in an attempt to catch up. As the brigade moved across the cornfield, the regiments just became further entangled. The 18th overlapped the 37th, which overlapped the 28th. On the brigade's right, the 33rd drove the Federals all the way to a small ridge, only to discover the enemy overlapped their right. To straighten out his lines and bolster his right, Cowan ordered Maj. Bost, who had just gotten his regiment moving forward, to move the 37th by

8   John Barry, Roll 0017, M331, RG109, CMSR, NA; Harris, *Historical Sketches*, 53. Barry was absent until early 1865. His temporary promotion was cancelled September 18, 1864. Lane, "Personal Reminiscences of General Lee," 311; *Fayetteville Observer*, August 4, 1864; *Richmond Dispatch*, July 29, 1864.

9   Harris, *Historical Sketches*, 52.

The 28th North Carolina carried this flag through the Overland Campaign, only to lose it to a member of the 9th New York Cavalry in a small fight near Malvern Hill in July 1864.
North Carolina Museum of History

---

the right flank in that direction. "What I could make understand to move to the right of the brigade I marched by the flank to the right," Bost reported.[10]

Bost and Captain Callais simultaneously discovered that the enemy troops had worked their way around the brigade's right and were enfilading the Confederate line. To escape being cut off and captured, Callais called for a retreat. As his men plowed into the 37th moving behind them, both regiments

---

10 *Confederate Veteran*, (May 1902), 10:216; Jackson Bost to "Captain," August 3, 1864, Lane Papers, AU.

broke to the rear. Cowan, in view of his crumbling right, ordered the 7th to form at an angle to the remnants of the brigade, but a Union charge collapsed the rest of the Confederate right. Tar Heel soldiers attempted to re-form on a fence bordering the cornfield. Once again the Federals advanced on Lane's brigade and pushed the Tar Heels back through the swamp, back toward where the attack commenced.[11]

General Conner witnessed his line collapsing. With his staff all away, he quickly appointed Lt. Spier Whitaker, the 33rd's adjutant, his temporary aide. He and Whitaker rapidly set about reforming the brigade, and his new aide "discharged the duty so well and efficiently as to merit my highest approval," Conner wrote.[12]

Lost in the confusion was the newly issued flag of the 28th NC. Pvt. Samuel Malleck, 9th NY Cavalry, picked it up. Details about its capture are unknown. Early on, the color bearer of the 18th NC was wounded and passed the regimental colors to Cpl. David M. Barefoot. Barefoot "bore them at the front until I ordered the Regiment to retreat," Lt. Col. Speer reported. Yet Barefoot was one of the missing. Timothy O'Conner, a member of the 1st U.S. Cavalry, captured this flag. The 9th NY Cavalry historian recalled many years later the two captured flags. One was "old and nearly worn out: while the other was new and had the names of 17 battlefields." The 18th's flag was issued in early 1864, while the 28th's flag replaced a banner captured at Spotsylvania.[13]

The left of the Confederate attack pushed the Federals back, but with the collapse of their right, the attackers retreated toward their earthworks. All along, North Carolina had been fighting cavalry. Federal infantry arrived later in the day, but the attack was not renewed. After the war, Lane placed the brigade losses at the battle of Deep Bottom, or Gravel Hill, at 138: 11 killed, 50 wounded, and 77 captured. On the evening of July 29, Federal forces re-crossed

11 James Harris to "Captain," & John McGill to "Capt.," both July 29, 1864; William Speer to Capt. E. J. Hale, Jr. & W. G. Callis to "Capt.," July 29, 1864; Jackson Bost to "Captain," August 3, 1864, all in Lane Papers, AU.

12 *News and Observer*, July 11, 1901.

13 Newel Cheney, *History of the Ninth Regiment, New York Volunteer Cavalry* (Jamestown, NY, 1901), 200. The 28th's flag was sent to the War Department and the number 149 stenciled on it. Malleck was awarded the Medal of Honor. The 18th's flag was sent to the War Department and assigned number 150. O'Conner was awarded the Medal of Honor for its capture. Both flags were returned to North Carolina in 1905 and are currently at the NCMH. Dedmondt, *The Flags of Civil War North Carolina*, 105, 124.

the James River, as more Confederate troops arrived for a planned advance. Early the next morning, Confederate forces discovered the Federals gone. Word undoubtedly spread through the ranks about the explosion of the mine under Confederate lines outside Petersburg, and the ensuing battle of the Crater.[14]

Voting for the new state governor took place on July 29. The 7th Regiment cast 94 votes for Vance, while W. W. Holden, de facto leader of the Peace Party in North Carolina, received 23 votes. William Speer took time to write Vance, informing him the 28th Regiment cast 179 for him, and 31 for Holden. Vance won the election by a landslide. Occasional shells thrown into the works contributed the only other real events of note for the next couple of weeks. The brigade shifted positions a few times. William Mauney (28th NC) reported it moved two miles on August 1, occupying a line of works between Chaffin's farm and Malvern Hill. Normal picket duty ensued, but the front stayed quiet until August 13 when Federal gun boats shelled the area. That same day, Col. Barber (37th NC), recently exchanged after his capture at Spotsylvania, returned and took command of the brigade.[15]

Lee sent even more of his troops into Northern Virginia in early August, hoping to weaken the Federal stranglehold on the Petersburg front. Grant returned to the strategy of applying pressure on both Confederate flanks. Two Federal corps, with cavalry support, started across the James River on August 14. Several in the brigade reported "Considerable musketry and artillery firing" to their left. That evening, the brigade's skirmishers were forced back, and the men slept on their arms. Lane's brigade moved from Chaffin's Bluff to Gravel Hill the next day, spending much of their time strengthening their works. With General Lee personally directing troop movements, two additional brigades from Mahone's division arrived. One of those, Wright's Georgia brigade, was positioned to the right of Lane's. About noon, the Federals began their advance using ravines to close on the Confederate works. With a dash, they struck the Confederate line, quickly pushing back Wright's brigade, and as they poured over the works to the right, Lane's brigade also began to falter.[16]

14 Lane, "A History of Lane's North Carolina brigade," *SHSP*, 9:357; Harris, *Historical Sketches*, 54.

15 Ibid., 53, 54; Speer, *Voices from Cemetery Hill*, 145; Mauney, Diary, August 1, 1864, KMHS.

16 Harris, *Historical Sketches*, 54; Mauney, Diary, August 2, 1864, KMHS.

Barber rallied the brigade under the eyes of Lee near the Darbytown Road. They "must not fail," Lee told the Tar Heels. As they surged ahead toward the Federals, Barber took a wound in the left leg. (The 28th's William Speer, just recently promoted to colonel, took command of the brigade after Barber fell.) The Tar Heels were wavering once more when brigade adjutant Edward Hale rallied the men and "charged at the double-quick." Some 60 yards from the works, the brigade stalled again and, for 15 minutes, "kept up a terrible fusillade" with the enemy. Then "raising a wild yell, the brigade rushed upon the breastworks," recapturing the whole line. Inside the works, an enemy soldier "wantonly killed" Lt. Camden Lewis (7th NC). Climbing on top of the works, the Carolinians "poured volley after volley into the flying masses of the enemy." Farther down the line, the enemy was firing into the brigade's flank. A force of 150 men from Lane's brigade used one of the ravines fronting their works to sneak up on to the Federals' flank and rear. A determined volley or two put them to flight.[17]

Hale noted the brigade captured 600 prisoners, a flag, arms, and "plenty of rich booty," while itself losing eight killed, 59 wounded, and 27 captured. Some of the wounded, like Noah Cline (28th NC), who was struck in the knee, lingered for weeks until they died of their wounds. "All the army are complimenting us," Hale wrote. Our "noble brigade again saved the day, as they did twice on the 12th May at Spotsylvania . . . . The whole thing was done by our Brigade and a few Georgians who straggled in. It was glorious." Even Wilcox complimented the brigade as "distinguish[ing] themselves highly."[18]

The battle of Fussel's Mill, or Second Deep Bottom, was the first time Lane's Tar Heels had encountered the United States Colored Troops, black Union soldiers. They were dressed in new uniforms, James Harris (7th NC) noted, with "shoes neatly blacked, presenting somewhat the appearance of holiday soldiers." Many of the black soldiers, Harris thought, "rather than take the chances of escape, surrendered and were sent to the rear." William McLaurin (18th NC) described the dead and wounded Federal soldiers sprawled around as "blue-black birds lying on that battle field."[19]

17 Harris, *Historical Sketches*, 55; *Fayetteville Observer*, August 25, 1864.

18 *Fayetteville Observer*, August 29, 1864; Jordan, *NC Troops*, 8:198-99; Wilcox, "Petersburg Campaign Report"; Clark, *Histories*, 2:57.

19 Harris, *Historical Sketches*, 54; Clark, *Histories*, 2:57.

Everything was relatively quiet the next four days. A truce was called to bury the dead on the evening of August 17. A member of the 7th NC recalled a "frightened negro soldier" shot while running through the Confederate picket line. Various brigade detachments rotated pulling picket duty. Then, on the morning of August 21, Confederates discovered the Federals gone. On August 17, Grant had launched a second attack to solidify his control of the Weldon Railroad. A. P. Hill, with Heth's division and some of Mahone's men, once again blunted the advance, capturing some 1,800 prisoners. Other attacks followed over the next three days. In the end, the Federals continued to hold the area. Supplies for Lee's army, brought in on the Weldon RR tracks, had to be unloaded 20 miles south of Petersburg and brought into the city in wagons. Detecting Federal troops moving south and crossing the James, Lee ordered the two brigades under Conner, Lane's and McGowan's, to the Petersburg trenches.[20]

As these two brigades crossed the river and reported to Wilcox, James Conner was relieved of his demi-division command, and on August 18, placed in command of Lane's brigade. The 35-year-old lawyer had already served with distinction: in Hampton's Legion, as a Confederate district attorney, and as colonel of the 22nd NC. Now, on June 1, 1864, he was appointed a brigadier general and assigned command of McGowan's brigade. When McGowan returned to the army after convalescence, Conner was assigned to command Lane's men.

Lane's brigade crossed the James on August 21 and boarded a train at Rice's Turnout. By 9:00 p.m. that evening, the men were encamped near Battery 37, below Petersburg. The next morning they moved another quarter of a mile and began building breastworks. One soldier described the works: "33 feet broad on the top and 90 feet thick at the base." The Tar Heels continued to wield "pick and spade" until orders arrived on August 24. They then marched from 2:00 p.m. to 9:00 p.m. when they stopped and encamped on the Vaughn Road, near Holly Church.[21]

Confederate cavalry had found an isolated Federal corps near Reams Station, engaged in destroying more of the railroad. Lee selected and moved what forces he could spare to intercept them. The Confederate attack force

---

20 Harris, *Historical Sketches*, 55.

21 Mauney, Diary, August 21, 1864, KMHS; Harris, *Historical Sketches*, 55; Wilcox, "Petersburg Campaign Report," VHS.

comprised seven brigades from Hill's corps. Lee's marching orders sent these troops on a circuitous route that avoided the Federals at Globe Tavern. Wilcox's men moved out at 8:00 a.m. Harris recalled marching "somewhat leisurely in the direction of the Weldon Railroad." About two miles from Reams Station, Wilcox halted the division, and for two hours did nothing, thereby, according to historian John Horn, throwing off the timing of the Confederate attack. Federal infantry eventually pulled back into their defensive position just south of Reams Station. Wilcox likewise redeployed his division, posting McGowan's and Scales's brigades in a pine thicket, with Lane's brigade in reserve behind McGowan. At some point, Wilcox ordered two regiments from Lane's brigade up to the left of Scales's brigade, extending the line. However, Wilcox soon ordered them back. Anderson's brigade was sent forward, while McGowan's men demonstrated on their section of the line. According to Edward Hale, some of Anderson's force reached the Federal breastworks but could not carry them. The "Georgians broke and ran over our Brigade which was lying in the woods behind."[22]

Wilcox decided a second attack, with more men, might succeed. Heth's division was arriving. Instead of taking time to move McGowan, Heth threw his own men into the attack. The new line comprised three brigades: MacRae's on the right, Cooke's in the center, and Lane's on the left. Conner positioned the brigade, from the left: 7th, 28th, 37th, 33rd, and 18th Regiments. Confederate artillery opened upon the Union position at about 5:00 p.m., and the infantry stepped off shortly thereafter. After advancing 200 yards through the pines, Confederates entered a field covered with heavy "abattis [sic], sharpened stakes, trees felled crosswise, &c. Raising 'a ringing rebel yell'" the Tar Heels charged, each soldier making his way the best he could through the obstructions—all the while, under a storm of small arms and artillery fire. The left of Lane's brigade began faltering. The 7th NC moved about 100 yards, into the woods, where the officers worked on reforming the ranks. As the 28th charged, Colonel Speer fell mortally wounded, struck in the head. Speer died four days later in Petersburg. Major Samuel Stowe assumed command of the regiment, but confessed they were "terably Exposed," and many men faltered. "The sacrifice was truly fearful in my Regiment," Stowe recounted later. Both the 37th and 33rd NC likewise

---

22 Harris, *Historical Sketches*, 44; John Horn, *The Destruction of the Weldon Railroad* (Lynchburg, VA, 1991), 126; *Fayetteville Observer*, September 8, 1864; Wilcox, "Petersburg Campaign Report," VHS.

Captain Gold Holland rose through the ranks to command a company in the 28th North Carolina. One fellow soldier wrote that he could often be seen carrying a stool and frying pan into battle.

*Histories of the Several Regiments
and Battalions from North Carolina*

floundered, although some of the 37th penetrated the enemy works. Only the 18th Regiment, its right resting on Cooke's brigade, did not seem to waver during the charge. Cooke's and MacRae's brigades, with a portion of Lane's, swept into the works, flanking several Union regiments. Captain Gold Holland (28th NC), who wore a knapsack and could often be seen carrying a camp stool and frying pan, was the first into the Federal works, a postwar source claimed. "Yankees, if you know what is best for you, you had better make a blue streak towards sunset," he yelled on cresting the entrenchments. Some of Lane's men threw handfuls of dust into the eyes of the Federals as they topped the works.[23]

Thomas M. Hanna (37th NC) was slightly wounded in the charge. He wrote his wife about his ordeal few days later:

Dear wife: . . . God has spared my life through another bloody battle . . . . The day I commence it we were marched all night and fought the yankees at Ream Station . . . . we had to march 20 miles to get around them in the hottest weather I ever felt. We had a desperate fight, made the attack and drove them from their breast works . . . . We also lost pretty heavily . . . . I myself slightly wounded in the right breast. The ball struck my pocket Bible, and went half way through it [it] kill[ed] a man dead just in front of me

23 *Fayetteville Observation*, September 8, 1864, May 3, 1894; Clark, *Histories*, 2:575; James Harris, Samuel Stowe, Benjamin Rinaldi to "Captain," August 28, 1864, & William Callars, Jackson Bost to "Captain," August 29, 1864, all in Lane Papers, AU; James Lane, "A History of Lane's North Carolina Brigade," *SHSP*, 9:353-54.

and the doctor said it would have killed me if it had not struck my pocket Bible. I told them I was killed when I was hit, it hurt me desperately, and I thought I was shot in the heart. I went to the rear and stayed there two or three hours and went back again. But the Book saved my life . . . . I have the bullet. It stopped in the Book. It went through my coat . . . . I don't know what I will do for a Bible, mine is ruined, torn and bursted all to pieces.

After this scary moment, Hanna struggled back to the front through the storm to join his comrades.[24]

Disaster beset the Federals around Reams Station. Forced to flee and pushed back about a mile, the Federals had experienced a disaster. They lost at least 2,700 men, with more than 2,000 captured, in addition to 9 cannons, 3,100 stands of arms, and 12 flags. Quite possibly the 37th NC captured two flags belonging to the 111th PA. Major Bost's short report says only that the brigades were so intermingled he "lay no particular claim to any thing particularly." Lane's brigade lost 115: 12 killed, 97 wounded, and 6 missing. Confederate losses totaled 720. Many sang the praises of the North Carolina brigades for their success at Reams Station. Lee himself congratulated Lane. The North Carolina brigades "had by their gallantry not only placed North Carolina, but the whole Confederacy under a debt of gratitude which could never be repaid." The general even wrote to Governor Vance on August 29. While he had frequently commented on the bravery of Tar Heel soldiers in his army, "their gallantry and conduct were never more deserving of admiration than in the engagement at Reams Station."[25]

As darkness fell, one Tar Heel noted "a thunder storm gave a sublime and graphic ending to the bloody scene as the roar of battle died away, and was lost in the stillness that succeeded the storm." Confederate cavalry replaced the infantry, which began the tramp back toward Confederate lines. On the evening of August 26, Lane's brigade went into position near Battery 45. The following

24 Hanna to "Dear Wife," undated, private collection. Many years later a Gaston County pastor related that the bullet had made "a track through [the Bible] from Genesis to John." Ironically, the minie had come to rest on the "14th chapter of John . . . 'Peace I leave with you, my peace I give unto you.'"

25 Jackson Bost to "Captain," August 29, 1864; Lane, "History of Lane's North Carolina Brigade," *SHSP*, 9:357; *OR* 42/1:940; Clark, *Histories*, 2:480-81. Lee's letter was widely published across the state; see *The Daily North Carolinian*, September 5, 1864. The historian of the 111th NY, attributes the capture of at least one of the regiment's flags to the 37th NC. Martin Hust, *The 111th New York Infantry* (Jefferson, NC, 2009), 159.

day, the brigade moved to its former position on the Vaughn Road and resumed building breastworks.[26]

Lane returned to his brigade on August 27. As he left Lee's tent, the army commander called him back, pulled a box of peaches from under his cot and gave Lane several. "The ladies are always sending me nice things, and I want to share these with you." When Lane got back to camp, he shared the peaches with his staff: Assistant Adjutant General Edward Hall, Ordnance Officer James Bryan, Assistant Quartermaster Anthony Cazaux, Quartermaster Edward Herndon, Assistant Adjutant and Inspector General Edward Nicholson, Assistant Commissary of Subsistence Adam Nisbet, Assistant Quartermaster John Sudderth, and Everard Meade, his future brother-in-law, as aide-de-camp.[27]

The brigade spent much of the next month in the trenches. James Harris (7th NC) reported on September 2 that the command had moved to the right to fend off a cavalry raid, but saw no fighting. Wooten led the brigade sharpshooters in quick dashes on Federal picket posts at least three times, once on August 31 at the Davis house off Vaughn Road. This action earned Wooten letters of thanks from both Hill and Wilcox. Days later on September 8, Wooten captured several Federals, and eight days later he and his men captured 98 more. Lane termed the maneuvers of the sharpshooter battalion "Wooten's Seine Hauling." Wooten's technique included taking "the whole or part of his command," and moving

> by the flank, in double ranks, toward the enemy's line, taking advantage of all natural features; and sometime the command would crawl until within easy running distance. Then they would quietly rush forward. Wooten would halt on the line of pits, and when the rear of his command reached him he would order both ranks to face outward and wheel. Wheeling on Wooten as the pivot, they would return at a run in single rank, empty every pit before them, and never fire a gun.[28]

26 Harris, *Historical Sketches*, 56.

27 Lane, "Personal Reminiscences of General Lee," 311; Krick, *Staff Officers in Gray*, 388.

28 Harris, *Historical Sketches*, 56; Collins, Reminisces, 61; Mauney, Diary, September 1-17, 1864, KMHS; *Charlotte Observer,* August 20, 1893. The skirmish at the Davis house isn't entirely clear. Dunlap says it took place on August 23, with Charles Watson, in charge of the sharpshooters of McGowan's brigade. However, before he could charge, Wooten and Lane's sharpshooters "anticipated Watson's movement and captured the post just before Watson got there." W. S. Dunlap, *Lee's Sharpshooters* (Dayton, OH, 1899, 2000), 156-57.

There was some opportunity for communication between the opposing lines. Nicholas Gibbon, detached from the 28th Regiment and serving on Wilcox's staff, told his diary about a letter from his brother, John, on September 11. He had proposed securing a pass and meeting with Nicholas, their sister Catherine, and if possible, brother Robert. "I shall be very glad to see you," he wrote. John Gibbon, however, was a major general in the Union army, and told his brother he had permission to meet under a flag of truce at Aiken Landing. Nicholas wrote back on October 8: "It is not agreeable that I should meet you under the circumstance in your note, although I have no doubt that I could obtain permission from General Lee if I desired it." One final letter from John, dated October 30, said that he regretted Nicholas's decision. He assured him, however, "that under no circumstances could such a meeting with one of my brothers prove disagreeable to me." Rumor had it the brothers never spoke again.[29]

A new Federal offensive got underway at the end of September. Grant wanted to sever more ties between North Carolina and Virginia and prevent Confederate reinforcements to the Shenandoah Valley. With Richmond under threat, Union soldiers launched an attack to cut the Southside Railroad on the Petersburg front. Crossing to the north of the James on September 29, they captured a portion of the Confederate defenses at Chaffin's Bluff. Lane's brigade was withdrawn from the works and went into position near Battery 45. Lee planned to shift nine brigades and seven batteries north of the James to smash through the Federal lines. Early on the morning of September 30, Lane's brigade passed through Petersburg, crossed the Appomattox, and headed toward the James. Two to three miles north of Petersburg, a courier caught up with the troops, and Lane's and McGowan's brigades were ordered back to the Petersburg defenses. Federal forces were driving back Confederate cavalry. They had been "put on the Zig Zag," Noah Collins (37th NC) complained. The brigade went into a position near Battery 45, and then about 4:00 p.m., both brigades were ordered out.[30]

After moving down the Boydton Plank Road, the brigades of Lane, McGowan, and MacRae turned onto Church Road, occupying some light entrenchments near Old Town Creek. Lane was on the right of Church Road,

---

29 Gibbon, Diary, 24-25, UNC-Charlotte; C. Brian Kelly, *Best Little Stories: Voices of the Civil War* (Naperville, IL, 2006), 96-97.

30 Harris, *Historical Sketches*, 56; Collins, "Reminisces," 62.

William Barber, colonel of the 37th North Carolina Troops, was wounded six times during the war.

Courtesy of Betsy Barber Hawkins

with McGowan on the left, MacRae in reserve. Wilcox ordered Lane's and McGowan's sharpshooters thrown forward. With the Federals almost upon them, Wooten deployed his men at the double-quick. Advancing through the boggy bottom around a creek and moving forward several hundred yards, they killed several and captured 12 Federal soldiers. Many of the enemy were fortified within the Jones House, and Wooten shifted his line to the right, "thus isolating the enemy who had taken possession of the house, from their line which had been driven across the field to the edge of a pine thicket." This maneuver allowed McGowan's sharpshooters to capture 40 Federals in and around the farm house. A quick Union counter-attack forced Wooten back some 150 yards. The sharpshooters met advancing Confederates as they fell back, and Wooten shuffled them to the right of the brigade. Lane deployed his regiments from the left: 18th, 7th, 28th, 37th, and 33rd. As the regiments were moving into position, a "chance shot" struck Col. Barber (37th NC) in the hip; Jackson Bost again assumed command of the regiment. Many believed the colonel's sixth wound of the war was slight.[31]

Sensing an opportunity with the enemy struggling to get into position, Wilcox ordered his brigades to advance. Colonel Cowan had already seen an opportunity and had the 33rd up, with the 37th following. A small stream separated these two regiments from the rest of the brigade, and they became

---

31 Thomas Wooten to "Captain," October 7, 1864, Lane Papers, AU; *Fayetteville Observer*, October 17, 1864; Clark, *Histories*, 2:669.

engaged first. "On reaching the top of the hill I halted," Cowan wrote, "and delivered Several volleys into their flank." The rest of Lane's brigade, along with McGowan's, joined in the attack, and the Federals fled. "To the delight of all this battlefield was rich in oil cloths, blankets, knapsacks and the like," Lane reported. "Some of the knapsacks, judging from the appearance of the straps, were cut from the shoulders of their owners in their hasty retreat under a murderous fire, accompanied with that well known 'rebel yell.'" In the chaos swirling around the Jones farm, one of Lane's soldiers captured 60 enemy men and officers in the cellar. A portion of the brigade succeeded in turning and coming up on a portion of the Federal line's rear. The Carolinians opened an "oblique reverse fire" upon them, and then watched as they "skedaddled." Gold Holland, then in temporary command of the 28th NC after Capt. Lovell's wounding, estimated the enemy fell back more than a mile, from the Jones farm to the Peeble House.[32]

During the advance, Lane passed one of his Tar Heels "kneeling over his dying brother, indifferent" to the the "whistling bullets." When the 7th regiment's soldier caught Lane's eye, he asked if he could stay behind, adding "I am no straggler." "I know what it is to lose a brother under similar circumstances," Lane said, continuing his move to the front, "and I haven't the heart to order you forward. But your brother is shot through the head and is insensible—you can do him no good." Soon, with rifle in hand, the soldier passed Lane. "Here I am, general, I have thought over what you said and I am going to the front." In another instance, Lane berated one of the troops for plundering in the midst of battle. He "only wanted a blanket to sleep on these cold nights," the man replied. Lane later saw him "running to the front with a fine Yankee blanket under his arm." Later, the general noted the number of "sugar-loaf hats, blue overcoats, oil-cloths, shelter-tents," he spotted in his camp.[33]

While a resounding success, the attack had sown a great deal of confusion in Lane's ranks. The brigade pulled back about 200 yards to a fence bordering a cornfield. The 33rd, after having moved first to the right, and then deploying again on the brigade's left, ended up possibly fighting with McGowan's brigade. Holland complained the 28th NC was intermingled with other Lane regiments,

32 Samuel Cowan to "Captain," & Gold Holland to William Nicholson, October 3, 4, 1864, Lane Papers, AU; Clark, *Regiments*, 2:481; Lane, "Glimpses of Army Life in 1864," *SHSP*, 9:412.

33 Lane, "Glimpses of Army Life in 1864," *SHSP*, 18:413-15.

and with MacRae's brigade as well. Lane collected the brigade and spent the night in the rain near the Jones farm.[34]

Hill planned to renew the fight on October 1. While Wilcox feigned an attack on the front of IX Corps, Heth's division, reinforced overnight, would flank the V Corps. Wilcox had McGowan's and Lane's men up early, moving toward the Federals by 7:00 a.m. Thick woods masked their advance, and while awaiting the sound of Heth's guns, Wilcox had his men tear down a fence and build temporary works. Shortly after eight, Heth launched his attack. Wilcox ordered his artillery to open fire. Shortly, the sharpshooters of the two brigades moved forward, creeping along a ravine of Arthur's Swamp, beyond the enemy left flank. Their stealth eventually captured more than 200 Union infantry hiding in a depression seeking protection from the Confederate artillery. So many prisoners were hurried toward the rear that Confederate artillery sensed another attack and again opened fire. This forced Wooten's men to seek shelter, wounding three Confederates and killing several prisoners. Wooten sent four men back to the battery to try to halt the firing. After three of his sharpshooters were wounded, he himself set out towards the rear "to ascertain the reason why the firing still continued." When the guns finally quieted, Wilcox ordered Wooten to continue the advance. A quarter mile farther found the Federals heavily entrenched, and Wooten was ordered to hold this line. Lane's and McGowan's brigades occupied the Federal works near the Pegram House.[35]

Wilcox's two brigades successfully completed their assignment. Heth, however, failed to turn the Federal right. Thus both Heth and Wilcox withdrew. Fighting around the Jones Farm on September 30 cost the brigade 111 men: 9 killed, 97 wounded, and 5 missing. Peebles' Farm, on October 1, produced a dozen more: 4 killed, 8 wounded. The 18th Regiment had been reduced to a "mere skeleton," Thomas Sutton complained. Almost everyone mourned the loss of Colonel Barber. He had died in a Petersburg hospital on October 3. Just a few days before, he had tendered his resignation. Once again, there was high praise for the Tar Heel brigade. One general described Wooten's charge on

---

34 Gold Holland to William Nicholson, October 2, 1864. Exactly what role the 33rd played in the rest of the battle is unclear. Cowan wrote he moved left and linked up with McGowan. Historian Richard Sommers believes they joined MacRae's brigade, fighting alongside the 26th NC; see Samuel Cowan to "Captain," October 3, 1864, James Lane Papers, AU, and Richard Sommers *Richmond Redeemed: The Siege at Petersburg* (California, 1981, 2014), 275-77, 279-80.

35 *The Charlotte Observer*, August 20, 1893; Thomas Wooten to "Captain," October 7, 1864.

September 30 to Lee as " the handsomest thing of the kind he had seen during the war."[36]

Wilcox's men held their position until dark on October 1, when they retired back inside Confederate defenses near Battery 45. The following day, they were back at the Jones farm, building breastworks. Save for a couple of occasions, the brigade spent the rest of October working on entrenchments and building winter quarters. Twice it was ordered out, once around October 9, and again on the 27th. Both times the men went to the right to support other troops, but they never saw action. Noah Collins and a couple other members of the 37th decided on one of these forays to examine a Confederate mortar in a nearby fort. During their inspection, the Federals fired a mortar of their own. "I heard a mortar shell coming, making a curious noise through the air, perpendiculary or straight above us," Collins observed. "When upon looking up and discovering it, I dashed as close to the wall . . . as I could get and the other two ran out of the fort; about which time the mortar shell struck in the edge of the magazine and sank so deep in the ground that when it exploded . . . not a single piece of it flew out." As the trio returned to the ranks, Collins noticed a shell explode "about the height of a man's head, about six feet in the rear of Company B . . . which fortunately injured no person." That same month, Lane was amused to see artillerists "running out and picking up the fragments of shells." Large buckets of such iron and lead were sold to Richmond foundries to be melted down and recast as munitions.[37]

Lane's brigade had 1,732 men present for duty at the end of October. They were drilled frequently, both in the manual of arms and school of the company. Yet even with the drill, an inspector found the 28th Regiment "badly in need of discipline." Though their clothing was shabby, the overall health of the brigade was "never better." Few were reported sick, because, some thought, the camp was far from "hucksters, whose vending of miserably cooked pies . . . incapacitates so many for duty." Yet the local "houses of ill fame," plagued many. Despite frequent roll calls, some of the soldiers "will go to these places regardless of punishment . . . there is but one way of stopping it. Drive these

36 Clark, *Histories*, 2:76; William Barber, Roll 399, M270, RG109, CMSR, NA; *Charlotte Observer*, August 20, 1893. Noah Collins (37th Regiment), who had numerous run-ins with Colonel Barber, wrote in his diary: "I had the pleasure of seeing Colonel William B. Barber . . . fall mortally wounded, about fifteen paces to my right, to rise no more." Collins, "Reminisces," 63.

37 Collins, "Reminisces," 65; Lane, "Glimpses of Army Life," *SHSP*, 18:414.

lewd wretches from the community and keep on the watch detectives to prevent their return." November passed as quietly as October. On November 15, the men were ordered to build winter quarters at their camp near the Jones Farm. Had "my house up," Alfred Proffitt (18th NC) reported on November 20. They had also just been issued "Some of the prettiest kind" of clothing.[38]

Federal forces thrust again against the Weldon Railroad in early December, attempting to cut even more of the line to the south. Lee pulled most of Hill's corps out of the trenches to intercept the blue-clad soldiers. With Lane commanding the Light Division, the brigades marched out of camp on December 8. The following evening, "a ground-covering and timber-breaking sleet" commenced falling. Wilcox arrived, and Lane returned to the command of the brigade. By the time Hill's corps arrived at Jarratt's on December 10, other units had driven back the Federals who left piles of smoldering railroad ties and twisted rails.[39]

The brigades began the trip back the following morning. They made it across the Nottaway River, camping in Dinwiddie County. The next two nights were the "coldest and windiest nights that I was exposed to during the war." Noah Collins (37th NC) thought. On the eleventh, Collins witnessed "two small fly-tents burned over some soldiers, and some of the soldiers' wet blankets froze under and over them." The following night, the men had to "throw the snow and ice from around our camp-fires with spades, to get a position to sleep on." Collins wrote he and the others had suffered "indescribly much from cold" back at their winter quarters. At the camps near the Jones Farm, Lane discovered someone had stolen the chimney he and Lt. Meade constructed. Hence they were forced outside, "sitting around a real camp-fire."[40]

Active campaigning was finally finished for 1864. Yet with the two opposing armies so close, the war never quite disappeared. When the brigade inspector came around at the end of December, he noticed that the heavy details of men drawn from the ranks prevented drilling. Every day some 200 men from Lane's brigade stood picket duty, and an additional 363 constructed breastworks. Lane had his cobblers at work, and they made better quality shoes

38 Inspection Reports, Records of the Adjutant and Inspector General's Department, M935, NA; Hancock, *Four Brothers in Gray*, 284.

39 Collins, "Reminisces," 68.

40 Ibid.; Lane, "Glimpses of Army Life," *SHSP*, 18:416-17.

than those issued. Many soldiers complained that meat had not been issued in some time, but the inspector described "double rations of coffee and sugar, and the usual ration of flour or hard bread."[41]

Major Wooten and the brigade's sharpshooters engaged in the only real action. Lane received orders to send the sharpshooters out "to catch two or three Yankees," late on the evening of December 18. Lee was trying to ascertain the location of the XIX Corps. After Lane's explanation of the mission, for several moments, Wooten pondered and reportedly thought the assignment impossible since the moon would soon be up. Then he recalled a nearby ravine that could provide cover and set off. The sharpshooters advanced to within 100 yards of the Federal works, fired several volleys, and then rushed the rifle pits. They captured 11, according to Lane, while a different account mentions 12 "fat ones." Another raid took place on December 31, and the sharpshooters of Lane, McGowan, and Scales captured another 30 Federal soldiers.[42]

Winter was grueling for the soldiers. Collins (37th NC) complained of being assigned to fatigue duty on December 20 and serving for 26 days. He and his comrades "suffered a great deal" due to the weather while working on the fortifications. "[M]any days . . . it snowed, ice and water was full knee-deep in the moat or ditches in which we had to labor." Rations, as usual, were in short supply. Concerned citizens in Richmond had made a concerted effort to supply the soldiers with a good Christmas dinner, but there was little to go around. Proffitt of the 18th NC complained on January 1, 1865, that the soldiers had drawn rations of meat only two days out of the past five or six, and one of those was spoiled. Collins recalled that on January 9, 200 men from Mahone's division rushed some commissary wagons. The following day, Collins wrote they only got "one tea-cup full of unsifted corn meal."[43]

In early February, the 18th, 28th, and 37th Regiments all pledged to serve for the duration of the war, rejected the "absurd proclamations of Abraham Lincoln," and promised to devote "our property, our lives, and our honor and our all, never to submit to the Abolition tyranny nor Yankee rule." Despite their

41 Inspection reports, Records of the Adjutant and Inspector General's Department, M935, NA.

42 *Fayetteville Semi-Weekly Observer*, January 9, 1865; Lane, "Glimpses of Army Life in 1864," *SHSP*, 18:418-19; Harris, *Historical Sketches*, 59.

43 Collins, "Reminisces," 68, 69; Hancock, *Four Brothers in Gray*, 286.

sturdy reenlistment resolutions though, desertion intensified as conditions deteriorated.[44]

A steady stream went back to North Carolina or into Federal lines. Ten members of Company F, 33rd NC, slipped away on December 9, while the brigade was on the march. Men who had witnessed almost four years of toil and bloodshed were losing heart. "The soldiers are going home and to the yankees stedy," Proffitt wrote on February 15. "At last . . . [we] got so hungry that the site of a well fed yankee troop was too much," John Adams (37th NC) recalled. "Taking a flag of truce, [I] crossed to the other sid." At least seven desertions occurred in January, 122 in February, and 51 in March. Some of these men left by themselves, like John Warner (28th NC), who slipped off on February 1. Others left in large groups. Twenty members of Company I, 33rd Regiment, deserted on February 19. They gathered a large number of blankets and presented a comfortable bed to the officer who commanded. As he slept, they slipped across the lines, "bringing arms and equipments—everything they had but those lucky blankets." The number of deserters astounded Alfred Proffitt. "I don't know which takes the day, the yankees or the woods." Of course, Federal authorities did everything they could to encourage Confederate desertions. In January, Grant had promised them food and free transportation, if their homes were within the lines. Or, if a deserter took the Oath of Allegiance, he might be able to obtain a job in one of the various army departments as a laborer. If deserters brought their rifles with them, they were paid for those as well. Between January 10—March 28, Lee's army lost at least 5,928 deserters.[45]

Collins of the 37th had been unhappy with army life for at least two years. He despised his officers and believed the cause hopeless. "I went on picket duty again," he wrote in his diary after the war, "in quite a pensive, or thoughtful, and sad, or sorrowful mood . . . being sorely pressed down in mind." Not only did his "savage treatment" by his officers weigh heavily upon him, but also the failure of government officials to make peace with the North. Nearly "every person possessed of sound reason, both North and South well knew that this

---

44 *Fayetteville Observer*, February 25, 1864.

45 Lane, "History of Lane's North Carolina Brigade," *SHSP*, 9:357-61. Dayton E. Flint to "Dear Sister," February 21, 1865, reprinted in the *Washington Star*, April 20, 1911; Hancock, *Four Brothers in Gray*, 287, 288; Pen Pittard, *Alexander County's Confederates* (n.p., 1960), 65; Jordan, *NC Regiments*, 8:219, 9:222-32; OR 42/2:828-29; John Horn, *The Petersburg Campaign: June 1864 - April 1865* (Conshohocken, PA, 1993), 217.

great Southern Rebellion was virtually crushed at that time." Continuing the fight was simply "willful murder . . . . I consequently resolved to hazzard my life and health no longer for the support of a completely fallen cause." Many Confederate soldiers undoubtedly repeated Collins's next moves during that last frigid winter:

> I voluntarily went out on vidette on the [10] o'clock relief that night, about thirty-yards in front of our skirmish line and taking a post near a large persimmon tree, sat down on the south . . . side . . . and . . . await [ed] the going down of the moon . . . [this] was one of the most pensive, or sad and thoughtful hours I ever experienced . . . I was extremely anxious and impatient for the moon to go down . . . I commenced hurry the moon in such ejaculatory phrases as "Hurry Moon Hurry, Oh Moon hurry, may the Lord hurry the moon down" . . . I heard the 10 o'clock relief alarm start down the line from the right, "Ten O'Clock, Ten O'Clock, Ten O'Clock," and knowing the relief would be there in a very few minutes, as it had but about thirty yards to come, and thinking that might be the last chance that might ever present itself to me, I got down on my hands and knees, thinking I might crawl off, as about half the moon was yet visable over the top of the hill . . . proving to be very slow, I arose to my feet for the purpose of forever abandoning . . . the fallen rebel cause, walked hurriedly and very cautiously over into the Union . . . crossing a ravine . . . and from thence an old road through an open field to a piece of woods . . . thence through the wood, carefully examining every large tree that I passed by, for Union videttes; crossing a small creek . . . till I came within about forty yards of the a union vedette post . . . I looked up and seeing five or six dark figures in the distance, hollowed out "Don't shoot, I am coming over." "Are you?" said they, "Well come on; Come this way. Come this way," Exclaimed about a half a dozen voices.[46]

The desertion problem was so appalling that the 7th NC, under command of Maj. James Harris, was detached from the brigade on February 26, and sent home to Moore, Randolph, and Chatham counties. The regiment, along with the 46th NC Troops, arrived in Greensboro on March 1. The 7th conveyed prisoners, executed a Federal soldier who pled guilty to killing at least two men after he escaped from prison, and then rallied in Salisbury when word arrived of a Union cavalry force under Maj. Gen. George Stoneman moving through the state. When Stoneman's raiders did reach Salisbury, the 7th, back in

46 Collins, "Reminisces," 75-76.

Greensboro, missed the ensuing battle. In Greensboro, the 7th was assigned to guard government stores and even had the opportunity to serenade Governor Vance.[47]

Ebbing out across the no-man's land between the armies was the lifeblood of the Confederacy—tired of the war, of hunger, of disease. "The weather was exceedingly cold, and the suffering of the men were intense," that winter, wrote a member of the 33rd. Still, no doubt many were surprised by how rapidly the end came.[48]

---

47 Harris, *Historical Sketches*, 60-62. Two brigade staff officers probably accompanied the brigade: Ordnance Officer James Bryan and Assistant Quartermaster John Sudderth. Krick, *Staff Officers in Gray*, 86, 278.

48 Clark, *Histories*, 2:576.

Chapter 17

"[Lane's Carolinians] stacked their arms, took off their accouterments, and furled their bullet ridden battle flags, which bore on them the names of all the great battles fought by the Army of Northern Virginia."

To Appomattox

Robert E. Lee was running out of time. His army was spread dangerously thin, and the recent losses in the Shenandoah Valley left food supplies short, not only for his troops, but for the tens of thousands in Richmond as well. In mid-March, the Army of Tennessee attempted to strike a portion of the Federal force advancing from South Carolina into the Tar Heel state. While Confederate forces met with some early success, Federal reinforcements prevailed, and the Army of Tennessee retreated toward Raleigh and Greensboro. Lee believed if he could abandon Petersburg and move west, he might be able to rendezvous with the western army. The combined armies could then trounce the Federals in North Carolina, before Grant could arrive.

Lee assembled nearly half his army near the Appomattox River, choosing Fort Stedman, a Union fortification, for the site of attack. A victory here might force Grant to contract his lines. Two brigades from the Light Division were chosen to participate in the attack. With Wilcox absent sick, Lane sent

Thomas's brigade and his own toward the Confederate left on the evening of March 24. Going into a reserve position on Lieutenant Run, they "lay all night in the streets of Petersburg," Lane wrote. At 4:00 a.m. on the 25th, the Confederates launched their attack, quickly capturing Fort Stedman. Yet a devastating crossfire, coupled with Federal counter-attacks, drove them back, with a loss of more than 1,900 alone captured. Lane's brigade remained in reserve and never joined the action, although one brigade member recalled being intensely shelled by artillery.[1]

Lane was ordered to take the brigades back toward Jones Farm, seven miles away. As the Tar Heels returned to camp, Federal forces assailed the Confederate picket lines. Union officers correctly guessed the Confederates had to be weak somewhere, and a second attack captured the lines along the Light Division's front. Lane's brigade quickly fell in. Its skirmishers managed to hold off a portion of the attackers, while Confederate artillery opened fire. "Our batteries . . . fired right over the heads of our company," a member of the 37th recalled, "opening gap after gap through their ranks." The Federals fell back, reformed, and charged the picket line once more, this time capturing it. At least a half-dozen brigade members were captured at the battle of Jones's Farm. The Union soldiers now occupying the Confederate picket posts were within a half mile of their main line. Lane's men hastily dug new picket posts that evening.[2]

"This is the Sabbath all quiet," John Alexander (37th NC) scribbled in his diary on March 26. That night, Lee instructed Lane to capture McIlwaine's Hill. Lost the previous day, the knoll provided enemy guns a good position from which to dominate much of the Confederate entrenchments. The Light Division's sharpshooter battalions were tasked with the operation. As Lane and Wooten inspected the lines, one Tar Heel remarked: "Look yonder, fellows, at the general and the major. That means something. It looks like somebody will be getting hurt soon." In the pre-dawn darkness, Wooten led his sharpshooters out of camp. In the staging area Lane's sharpshooters were on the right, with McGowan's to his left. Scales's and Thomas's sharpshooters were posted in support. Masked by the darkness and fog, the sharpshooter battalions stepped off about 5:00 a.m. toward the hill. Reforming after passing through Rohoic Creek, they pressed ahead, until forty-yards from McIlwaine's Hill, an enemy

---

1 Lane, "History of Lane's North Carolina Brigade," *SHSP*, 9:494; Clark, *Histories*, 2:481, 670.

2 Collins, *Reminisces*, 71-72; Lane, "History of Lane's North Carolina Brigade," *SHSP*, 9:494-95.

picket issued a challenge, answered by a Rebel Yell. A smattering of rifle fire greeted the rushing sharpshooters. Near the crest of the hill, Wooten's battalion wheeled to the right, McGowan's to the left. Without a loss, they swept the hill of Federals in a matter of moments Lane led his brigade forward in support as soon the yell pierced the darkness. For the rest of the day, sniping shots by both sides produced a few casualties. An 11:30 a.m. truce allowed the sides to retrieve some of the dead and wounded from the field. It lasted until 1:00 p.m. After the war, Lane recalled seeing Federal soldiers dragging a cannon through the woods and placing it in a ravine. "Your Major Hooten [sic] is so fond of running up these hollows," a Federal explained, "and breaking our lines we are putting a gun here to give him a warmer welcome the next time he comes."[3]

March 28 was quiet, John Alexander recorded, but the following day, he could hear fighting off toward the right. Lee's headquarters had learned Federals were headed west toward Dinwiddie Court House. Lee began pulling troops out of the lines to build a force to strike back. He sent McGowan's brigade, to Lane's right, to reinforce Confederate soldiers at Burgess Mill. Lane's four regiments extended their lines to the right: his left anchored by the 33rd, followed by the 18th, 37th, and 28th Regiments. A tributary of Arthur's Swamp flowed through the works between the 37th and the 28th, through a depression of 50-60 feet that flattened into a marsh close to the Federal picket line. Trees previously covered the ravine, but over the winter, Confederates cut the timber for heat, cooking, and huts, leaving only stumps. Confederate artillery covered both sides of the ravine. Wiggins recalled he and his comrades in the 37th Regiment were spread 10 paces apart behind the works, no more than a skirmish line. In the 18th NC, they were 20 feet apart.[4]

Rain began falling the evening of March 29, drenching the soldiers in the trenches; it continued through March 31. On April 1, an ailing A. P. Hill toured Confederate lines, twice. Late that afternoon word arrived of the Confederate

3 Alexander, Diary, March 26, 1865; Lane, "History of Lane's North Carolina Brigade," *SHSP*, 9:495; *The Charlotte Observer*, August 20, 1893; Dunlap, *Lee's Sharpshooters*, 251-54. There is some confusion regarding command of the division. Lane wrote after the war that Cadmus Wilcox was sick, and he himself was in command; see *Charlotte Observer*, August 20, 1893. A recent account has Wilcox exercising command during the attack; see A. Wilson Greene, *Breaking the Backbone of the Rebellion: The Final Battles of the Petersburg Campaign* (Knoxville, TN, 2008), 144-47.

4 Alexander, Diary, April 1, 1865; Greene, *Breaking the Backbone*, 192; Clark, *Histories*, 2:61, 670.

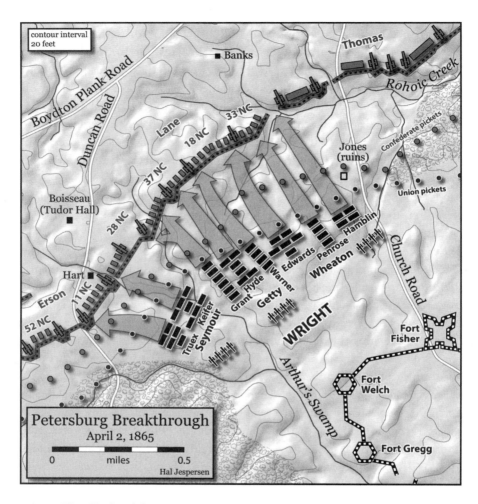

Petersburg Breakthrough
April 2, 1865

rout at Five Forks. After 10 months, Grant finally turned Lee's right flank. Lee could either evacuate his army or risk its capture. He therefore prepared to withdraw and called Longstreet's corps to the Petersburg front to bolster his lines.

About 10:00 p.m., some 150 cannons opened on the Confederate lines. Wilcox described the bombardment as "an almost incessant cannonade, solid shot and shell whizzing through the air and bursting in every direction, at times equal in brilliancy to a vivid meteoric display." The barrage slackened about 1:00 a.m., although it resumed periodically throughout the night. Not long after the bombardment ceased, at least 14,000 enemy infantry moved into the open ground between the lines in front of Lane's position. At least once, Confederate

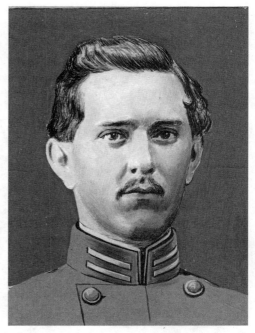

Lieutenant Octavius Wiggins, 37th North Carolina, survived a blast to the head and capture during the final assault at Petersburg.

Histories of the Several Regiments and Battalions from North Carolina

pickets to open fire at a noise, but Federal infantry were not allowed to squeeze their triggers and reveal their position by returning it.[5]

A single cannon shot reverberated through the morning darkness on Sunday, April 2, and Federal soldiers were up and moving toward the Confederate lines. Pickets fired a few rounds to alert those in the main works and scampered back. Federal pioneers hacked at the abatis as Confederate artillery belched into the darkness. One of the first Federals to surmount the works was a Vermont officer, who was bayoneted twice and slashed in the head by a sword before being dragged back over the wall. Too few defenders manned the entrenchments, however, and other Federals swarmed across the works. Several met the 37th's color bearer, a nameless Tar Heel who was knocked down and lost his banner, but not before he killed two men and wounded a third. As the Federals overran the works, one pointed his rifle at the head of Lt. Wiggins (37th NC) and pulled the trigger. The round grazed and blinded him, knocking "him senseless upon the ground." Wiggins was one of 168 members of the 37th captured that day, and hurried to the rear.[6]

5   Cadmus M. Wilcox, "Defence of Batteries Gregg and Whitworth, and the Evacuation of Petersburg," *SHSP*, 4:25.

6   Cpl. Richard Welsh, 37th Massachusetts Infantry, was awarded the Medal of Honor for capturing the flag of the 37th North Carolina. The flag was sent to the War Department and the number 384 was stenciled on it. For years, the flag hung in Lee Chapel at Washington and Lee University. It is in possession of the Museum of the Confederacy, at times on display at its

The flag of the 37th North Carolina, issued in December 1862, was captured on the morning of April 2, 1865. *Museum of the Confederacy*

Elsewhere along Lane's line, Federals stormed over the entrenchments. "We fought desperately," James Weston (33rd NC) wrote. Three of Lane's regiments, continuing to fight, "each man for himself," retreated through their winter quarters. "I was driven from the works, the line on the right and left of me in the regt. was broken and the enemy were filing down in the rear of our works towards Petersburg," remembered Jackson Bost, the 37th NC's commander. "I had to fall back directly to the rear and formed a skirmish line as

Appomattox Museum. Dedmondt, *The Flags of Civil War North Carolina*, 143; Clark, *Histories*, 2:670-71.

This Fourth Bunting battle flag replaced the flag lost by the 18th North Carolina at the first battle of Deep Bottom. It was captured on April 2, 1865, below Petersburg. *North Carolina Museum of History*

best I could to keep the enemy from advancing too fast in our rear, in order to give our wagons time to get out." In the melee, the 18th Regiment's color bearer was knocked down and his flag too was captured. Lane sent Hale hurrying toward Wilcox's headquarters with news of the breakthrough.[7]

7   Ibid., 576; Jackson Bost to "Dear General," July 31, 1867, Lane Papers, AU; Lane, "The Defence of Battery Gregg-General Lane's Reply to General Harris." *SHSP*, 9:105. Frank Fesq was credited with the capture of the flag of the 18th Regiment. He was awarded a Medal of Honor on May 10, 1865. The flag was forwarded to the War Department with number 385 stenciled on it. It was sent to the Hall of History in Raleigh in 1905, stolen from the museum, possibly in the 1960s, and recovered in 2005. The flag is now preserved at the North Carolina Museum of History (NCMH) in Raleigh.

On Lane's left, the 28th regiment was cut off from the rest of the brigade. Hale recalled seeing unknown men in the area:

> I remarked to some one "why there are the skirmishers, driven in,"& called out to know how near behind the enemy were. Just at that moment I observed a stand of colors in the work[s] & the person in command ordered his followers to fire. This was just before, or just at, dawn, and it was impossible to distinguish anything more than the color aforesaid (though not the color of the colors) & outlines of men against the sky.

According to Hale, the confused Tar Heels "fought these people & all the hordes that passed over, step by step." Despite a brave stand, the 37th was pushed back toward the Boydton Plank Road, attempted to reform, but was pushed back again toward the Cox Road. The 28th NC's Hugh Torrence was shot in the face, the ball striking him in the right eye and exiting through the left eye socket. "I was officially reported killed," Torrence recalled many years after the war.[8]

Unable to sleep, A. P. Hill rode to Lee's headquarters in Petersburg. At the word of the Federal breakthrough, he rode off toward Heth's headquarters, trying to assess the damage and help rally the men. Near the rear of Lane's position, Hill and a staff member encountered the enemy. Two Federal soldiers fired on Hill and killed him instantly, while the courier escaped. The 5th Alabama Battalion received credit for recovering Hill's body. [9]

Lane worked his way to the rear, encountered Wilcox, and the two managed to rally about 600 members of Lane's and Thomas's brigades near Battery Gregg. Wilcox placed Thomas on the right and Lane on the left and ordered them forward. He hoped the counter-attack would buy enough time for reinforcements to arrive from north of the Appomattox River, and possibly restore the broken lines. Lane placed Maj. Wooten in charge of the unknown number of men from his command. Wilcox testified to the promptness and spirit of the men when ordered to advance. They pushed forward, driving the

---

8   Edward Hale to JL, June 13, 1884, Lane Papers, AU; Clark, *Histories*, 2:482; Hugh Torrence, Memoir, Military Collection, Box 72, Folder 19, NCDAH.

9   Robertson, *Hill*, 319. Note, however, an article in *The Southern Home*, May 5, 1870, that maintains Hill's body was found by several North Carolinians, including James Cody, Eric Erson, J. M. Young, Daniel Hanes, "and a Sergeant of Lane's Brigade."

Federals "beyond the branch, near the house occupied by Mrs. Banks," according to Lane. For 15 minutes, the Confederates held some of their previous works, along with a new line perpendicular to those works. Dallas Rigler (37th NC) recalled, "when we reached the [Church] road they was not more than 30 men and five officers namley Lieuts Snow, Craige & Howard of the 33rd Regt and myself and Lieut Orman of the 37th." Harris's brigade from Mahone's division arrived and moved toward Lane's right. Yet enemy numbers were overwhelming. Lane sent Hale to Wooten, ordering him to withdraw the troops back to Battery Gregg. It was probably close to 9:00 a.m. when "positive orders" to retire were given. During this attack, Hale returned to their former camp to retrieve some hams while William McLaurin rescued the records of the 18th Regiment.[10]

Some of Lane's men filed into Battery Gregg while the majority were sent to a position near Battery 45, called the "Dam." Just to the north, Batteries Gregg and Whitworth had been built as an inner line of fortifications stretching from Battery 45 to the Appomattox River to protect Lee's line of retreat. However, the trench line connecting these positions had not been finished. Adjutant Hale considered the forts "monstrosities of engineering in modern warfare" and "nothing but man traps." Lane, too, had already told Wilcox his misgivings about holding the works; pulling all the Confederate forces back was the wiser choice, he thought. Yet Wilcox needed to slow the victorious Federals, allowing time for reinforcements to arrive. Lane dispatched an officer to Fort Gregg, ordering a "sufficient number of my men" to enter the fort, and the others to the "Dam" area. Lane himself soon arrived and took command. He ordered extra ammunition brought up. Yet he did not wish to remain. Most of his brigade was positioned at the "Dam." Wilcox had ordered Lane to Battery Gregg, an assignment "against my wishes and judgment," Lane wrote later. Wilcox soon departed, and Lane met with two of his staff officers together outside the fort. "[W]e were unanimous in not wishing to remain in the fort [and] I [was] determined to ask permission to leave." Wilcox soon returned, mounted his horse, and addressed the soldiers— a combination of men from the brigades of Lane, Harris, and Thomas, along with members of the Washington Artillery and Chew's Artillery. "Men," he yelled above the din, "the salvation of Lee's army is in your keeping." If they could hold for just two

---

10 OR, 46/1:1285; C. M. Wilcox, "Battery Gregg-Reply to General N. H. Harris." SHSP, 4:170; Dallas Rigler to JL, June 17, 1867, Lane Papers, AU; Clark, Histories, 2:62.

hours, Longstreet would be up. Lane gained permission to leave the fort. But before doing so, he ordered Hale to count the men he had in Battery Gregg.[11]

Artillery rounds from Federal guns began slamming into the fort. Wilcox rode away amidst the showering of shrapnel while Hale tried to count the number of Tar Heels within. He couldn't be heard above the roar of the artillery. Quickly working his way around the small enclosure, Hale found "some lying fast asleep from exhaustion, some in that listless stupor produced by over-heat, over-work, and the deafening noise of battle; others too busy loading & firing to heed anything, or jostling each other for eligible situations for sharp-shooting." He estimated the number of brigade members in the fort at 32, not counting Lane and a couple of staff officers, but he believed the number was probably double. As Lane left, he placed Lt. George Snow (33rd NC) in charge of his men in Battery Gregg. Lane, Hale, Lt. Meade, and Lt. Thomas Wiggins (37th NC) headed toward the "Dam." At first they moved at a "dignified quick-step," but as enemy fire in their direction intensified, their quick-step became a double-step, and finally, a run. They reached the "Dam" safely.[12]

Dallas Rigler, a lieutenant in the 37th Regiment in the battery, survived the oncoming onslaught. He believed a total of 75 members of Lane's brigade fought alongside him. Sometime around 11:00 a.m., the Federals commenced their attack. Rigler explained that the Confederates held their fire until the Federals were within

> forty yards and then we gave them one deadly volley, they then wavered and the first line gave way, the second came forward and came in thirty yards of the fort. We yelled and fired they stood a few seconds and then broke the 3rd [retreated] also But the forth and fifth came to the ditch around the Fort. While this fighting was in the front one line came in the rear and almost got inside the fort through the door[.] about twenty men charge them and drove them back[.] about Eleven o'clock they scaled the walls of the fort and for several minutes we had a hand to hand fight[.] we used the bayonet and killed almost all of them that came over the top - About half past Eleven they attempted to scale the walls again[.] we met them with the bayonet and for several

11 Edward Hale to JL, June 13, 1884, Lane Papers, AU; James Lane, "The Defence of Battery Gregg," 106; Archibald Jones, "The Battle of Fort Gregg." *SHSP*, 31:56-58.

12 Edward Hale to JL, May 20, 1867, AU; Lane, "The Defence of Battery Gregg," *SHSP*, 9:106.

minutes it was of the most desperate struggle I ever witnessed but it did not last long[.] soon they was all killed or knocked back and then a deafing shout arose from our boys[.] near twelve they tried to force their way through the door in rear of the fort and succeeded in getting almost in but we met them with the bayonet and drove them back[.] this time the amunition was almost out and our men threw bats and rock at them in the ditch. no amunition could we get and about twelve they scaled the walls and after a short struggle they took the fort and some few did fire on after they got posession but their officers tried to stop them.[13]

Rigler recorded five charges, though there were probably only three. He was simply witnessing different groups of advancing Union soldiers. By 3:00 p.m., the fort had fallen. George Benson (33rd NC) recalled firing his last shot, throwing away his rifle, and surrendering. As he was marched from the fort, he could see "some of my Brother Soldiers lying there to rise no more while others were there crying for help and no one to assist them." He regretted this had all occurred on a Sunday. The savage fighting to take Battery Gregg, many agreed, exceeded that at places like the Sunken Road at Antietam and around the Bloody Angle at Spotsylvania Court House. Yet the gallant stand, by a handful of Confederate soldiers within Batteries Gregg and Whitworth, bought the time needed to shore up the inner Confederate works. Total Confederate losses were placed at 333: 57 killed, 243 wounded and captured, and an additional 33 captured. Federal losses were placed at 714 killed and wounded.[14]

At least one soldier escaped: Cpl. James Atkinson, who apparently served as color-bearer of the 33rd Regiment for the last year of the war. He had his regiment's banner with him in Battery Gregg. During the struggle, he made his escape. At some point between the Battery and the inner Confederate lines, Atkinson "unfurled the flag which he bore, and, taking a position not a great way off, he waved the tattered colors in their very teeth." Federal soldiers fired several "volleys" at Atkinson, but he was never hit. A moment later, he stuck the "flag staff in his belt" and "coolly marched away, the volleys still

13 Dallas Rigler to JL, June 17, 1867.AU.

14 George Benson, "My Last Fighting and Prison Life," Robert Cutler Collection. Copy in author's possession; John Fox, III, *The Confederate Alamo: Bloodbath at Petersburg's Fort Gregg on April 2, 1865*, (Winchester, VA, 2010), 229. Fox provides a list of soldiers assumed to be in Battery Gregg from the various regiments. They seem to be almost entirely from the 33rd and 37th NC. The *Durham Globe* reported on August 29, 1891, that Lane ordered these two regiments into Battery Gregg.

Captain John Fain, 33rd North Carolina, was reported killed on April 2, 1865.

Histories of the Several Regiments and Battalions from North Carolina

continuing—he with head aloft and colors flying, down the ravine, up upon the dam connecting the two forts, and finally safely" into the Confederate lines. Many years later, Hale wrote at some point he heard the Federals yell, "Do not shoot any more: he is too brave a man to kill!"[15]

Confederate soldiers all along the line witnessed the bitter and bloody struggle for Batteries Gregg and Whitworth. "I was glad to be on the outside," admitted William McLaurin (18th NC). James Weston (33rd NC) remembered seeing Atkinson with his flag, and that the men "cheered him long and loud, even after he had reached the Confederate works." Though not exposed to the mayhem in the redoubts, the remnants of the brigade were also under fire. Weston watched the attack with other officers, including Capt. John Fain. "Presently we heard that unmistakable thud, and Captain Fain fell heavily forward, mortally wounded. He begged us to take him off the field, but it was impossible. . . . In five minutes he was dead." Lane officially reported that after the fight for Battery Gregg, his line was attacked and driven back to the former works near Battery 45. At one point during the fighting, Capt. Hale was spotted on one of the traverses cheering the men as they redeployed. Lane ordered him to come down, but the

---

15 *The Charlotte Democrat,* July 6, 1883; *Fayetteville Observer,* September 30, 1909; *The Observer,* May 15, 1878. An article in the *Fayetteville Observer,* August 23, 1899, stated Atkinson stopped, perhaps twice, to "wave defiantly at the enemy." See also *The Charlotte Observer,* January 14, 1900. William McLauren added Atkinson was accompanied by Lt. William Robinson, 18th NC. Clark, *Histories,* 2:62.

brave captain refused and maintained his exposed post amid a shower of shot and shell until the last of the brigade had passed.[16]

The flight from Petersburg and Richmond began in earnest that evening. Government stores that could not be transported out of town were put to the torch. At 11:00 p.m., Jefferson Davis and most of his cabinet boarded the last train out of Richmond, bound for Danville. Near the same hour, Lane's brigade left the trenches. When Federal soldiers marched into the two cities later that day, they found thousands of sick and wounded Confederate soldiers in area hospitals. At least 78 incapacitated members of Lane's brigade were captured on April 3. Wilcox recorded the remnants of the Light Division made their way toward Goode's Bridge, which they crossed near dark on April 3.[17]

Lee planned to concentrate his forces at Amelia Court House, 36 miles west of Petersburg. Tired and hungry, the brigade bivouacked near there on the night of April 4. The 350,000 rations Lee ordered to Amelia were not there. Wagons were sent out to scour the countryside for provisions but came back nearly empty. After paring down the army's transportation and artillery, the soldiers resumed the march toward Jetersville on April 5. Sometime during the day, Lane's brigade formed a line of battle. Wooten led out the brigade's sharpshooters and engaged the Federals. The march resumed that night.[18]

Soldiers trudged through the Virginia springtime countryside on April 6, passing through Rice's Station. About 10:00 a.m., supply trains reached the brigade, and the men were issued rations, medical items, and ordnance stores. Hill's old corps was now under the command of Longstreet, who at one point ordered his divisions off the road and into position in anticipation of a possible attack. Field's and Wilcox's divisions manned the front, with Mahone's and Heth's men in reserve. Save possibly for the sharpshooters, Lane's brigade was not involved in any serious fighting. Just after dark, the trains started to Farmville, with the soldiers following soon thereafter.[19]

16 Clark, *Histories*, 2:62, 576-77; Lane, "History of Lane's North Carolina Brigade," *SHSP*, 10:58; *Fayetteville Observer*, November 9, 1893.

17 The number of soldiers captured comes from a survey of Jordan, *NC Troops*, volumes 4, 6, 8, & 9; Wilcox, Official Report, VHS.

18 Wilcox, Official Report, VHS.; Lane, "History of Lane's North Carolina Brigade," *SHSP*, 10:58.

19 Alexander, Diary, April 6, 1865, SHC/UNC; William Marvel, *Lee's Last Retreat: The Flight to Appomattox* (Chapel Hill, NC, 2002), 75-94.

April 7 found Wilcox's division bringing up the rear of Longstreet's column. Shortly after sunrise, the column moved through Farmville, collecting rations and crossing the Appomattox River before halting. Scales's brigade remained at Briery Creek, with cavalry, to protect the rear of the column. When the enemy began encroaching on the rear guard, Wilcox hurried the rest of his division back through Farmville and up the heights. How much of Wilcox's command got into position before Federal infantry and cavalry began to close in is not clear. He managed to get the majority back through Farmville before the bridge across the Appomattox was burned. The weary Carolinians then had a short period of rest, before news arrived that Mahone's division, to their north, was under attack. Longstreet rushed two divisions to Mahone's support. Mahone was on the left, then Field's division, then Wilcox's. The heaviest of the attacks fell on Mahone's front, but Wilcox later wrote his division's lines were charged at some point. His weary soldiers held. Lane's official report was silent on his brigade's role in the afternoon fight.[20]

Hospital Steward William Alexander (37th NC) noticed passing burning wagons during the march. The army moved faster without the encumbrance of a large number of wagons. About midnight, Longstreet began withdrawing his troops. "[W]e traveled all night," Alexander complained, only stopping once for two hours. "[T]his is the second night that we did not halt or camp." Lane's brigade moved down the Buckingham Plank Road, learning of an order from Longstreet discouraging straggling. It further stipulated every division must mass on the one in front when it came time to stop. By mid-afternoon, Longstreet's column was approaching New Store. They eventually encamped not far from New Hope Church, about six miles from Appomattox Court House. That evening, Alexander pulled his medical wagon into a field. He unhitched his team and set the wagon on fire.[21]

Before daylight on April 9, Lane's brigade was up and moving with the rest of the former Light Division toward Appomattox Court House. They were following Stonewall Jackson's original command, now led by Maj. Gen. John B. Gordon. Gordon had orders to punch through the Federal cavalry, allowing the army to continue south in hopes of linking up with other Confederates in North Carolina. Not far from town, the Light Division's advance bogged down amidst

---

20 Wilcox, Official Report; Lane, "History of Lane's North Carolina brigade," *SHSP*, 10:58; Marvel, *Lee's Last Retreat*, 122-35.

21 Alexander, Diary, April 6- April 8, 1865; Marvel, *Lee's Last Retreat*, 137-53.

the wagons, artillery, and stragglers. Wilcox rode ahead to assess the problem, and soon heard musketry and artillery fire. He then received orders to support Gordon's attack.

As the Light Division moved toward Appomattox Court House, Wilcox could see Federals on his right, and he sent two brigades off, deploying skirmishers as they went. The other two brigades, including Lane's, continued toward the sound of the fighting. With orders to form to the right of Col. Thomas Talcott's Engineer Regiment, Lane rode ahead to a stream. When the "tattered and starving remnant of my glorious brigade approached," Lane recalled, "I called out to the men to take to the water, without using the narrow crossing." With a cheer, Lane's brigade crossed the stream and moved forward up a hill. As Wilcox neared Gordon, they spotted a man "waving a white handkerchief." A cavalryman asked Lane what he thought of Lee's surrender. "What?" the general replied. Not long after, he spotted a Union and Confederate officer riding together behind the lines. Major Joseph Englehard, who had transferred from brigade staff to division staff a couple of years earlier, rode up to Lane and confirmed the news, ordering him to move his brigade into some woods nearby. "Only think what you and I and these brave fellows have endured and all for nothing," Hale reportedly told Lane.[22]

The troops stacked arms, and Lane called his regimental commanders together. All he knew at the time was Lee had surrendered. Rumors spread quickly through the ranks. James Weston (33rd NC) recalled seeing a Federal officer ride down the brigade's line. "He smiled as he rode quickly on, but it was the wickedest smile I ever saw on any man's countenance." Lee soon met with Grant at the home of Wilmer McLean. They agreed to terms by which the Army of Northern Virginia would stack arms and be issued paroles, the men free to return to their homes. When Lane confirmed the news, many found it hard to accept. "Major, let's not surrender," a lieutenant muttered to Weston. "Let's cut our way through." Weston stayed, but confessed as they spread their blankets that night to sleep, they "shed bitter tears, feeling that we had no home and no country."[23]

April 10 dawned as gloomy as the Tar Heels' spirits. It rained most of the day. Early on, Longstreet ordered his men into the adjoining fields to stack their

---

22 Wilcox, Official Report, VHS; Clark, *Histories*, 2:577; Lane, "A History of Lane's North Carolina Brigade," *SHSP*, 10:58; *Fayetteville Observer*, June 8, 1897.

23 *Fayetteville Observer*, June 8, 1897; Clark, *Histories*, 2:577, 578.

rifles. He wanted to prevent any ongoing hostilities between the two sides, while six generals, three from each side, resolved the details of the surrender at the McLean House. They agreed upon a place to stack arms and surrender flags. The cavalry would be paroled first, due to the lack of forage nearby and the need to move the animals. By mid-morning, rations were starting to filter into the Confederate camps, many from Confederate stores captured earlier, but some from the Federal supply trains. Earlier, Weston had asked a Federal commissary officer for some food. He had none to give, he said, but told the major to "walk about the tent carelessly and fill your haversack with crackers and loaf sugar, and your canteen with whiskey, and I won't see you."[24]

That same day, Lane's Tar Heels heard Lee's farewell address. In a mere six sentences, Lee told his men they had been forced to surrender due to overwhelming numbers. "You will take with you the satisfaction that proceeds from the consciousness of duty faithfully performed," Lee wrote. Lane took time to write his last official report, covering the period April 1-9. Non-arms bearing men, those who had been driving wagons or been posted elsewhere, made their way into the brigade's camp. Lane opposed these men surrendering with the brigade. He believed they should be surrendered as a part of the headquarters staff. "I did not wish to surrender any but those brave fellows who had followed us under arms."[25]

Although against orders, many Federals stole across the lines to visit with their former enemies. One New York soldier met a lieutenant from the 28th Regiment, who invited the New Yorker to the Tar Heel camp. On their way, they passed the apple tree where Lee had rested while awaiting a reply from Grant. Other soldiers were in the process of felling the tree when they arrived, and the Federal soldier filled his pockets with chips. After spending the day within Confederate lines, their "guest" returned to his regiment, passing some of the chips to others in his company.[26]

It was still dank and rainy the next day. Orders for the march circulated among the infantry. Lane issued his own orders regarding the surrender, and Col. Cowan and Maj. Weston were sitting under a tree when those orders arrived. After reading the orders, Cowan "jumped up, his eyes flashing fire . . . I

---

24 Clark, *Histories*, 2:580

25 Dowdey and Manarin, *The Wartime Papers of R. E. Lee*, 934-35; Lane, "History of Lane's North Carolina Brigade," *SHSP*, 10:57-58; *Fayetteville Observer*, June 8, 1897.

26 *The National Tribune*, April 5, 1894.

Lieutenant Evander Robinson, 18th North Carolina, was one of just a handful to serve from April 1861 until the surrender at Appomattox on April 9 1865.

Histories of the Several Regiments and Battalions from North Carolina

won't surrender. . . . Major Weston, take charge of the regiment." Cowan mounted his horse and rode away. Soon thereafter, brigade after brigade began the trek across the river to Appomattox Court House, where Federal soldiers were drawn up, waiting. John B. Gordon's men came first, followed by Charles Field's division, George Pickett's handful of survivors, Henry Heth's division, and the former Light Division. William Mahone's soldiers brought up the rear. Lane recalled four lines of Federal soldiers, two on each side. His Carolinians "stacked their arms, took off their accouterments, and furled their bullet ridden battle flags, which bore on them the names of all the great battles fought by the Army of Northern Virginia. True to my promise, our beautiful Head Quarters flag was the last one to be furled and laid on the stacks." Rufus Carson (28th NC) recalled stacking arms in front of the 155th Pennsylvania Infantry. How many flags Lane's brigade surrendered at Appomattox is not known. Only the flag of the 28th Regiment appears to survive.[27]

Slowly the remnants of Lane's brigade made their way back to camp. "Then came the tender hearted partings of brave men, who had marched through all kinds of weather, starved, fought and bled together," Lane recalled. Someone

27 Clark, *Histories*, 2:578; *Fayetteville Observer*, June 8, 1897. It is believed a 4th bunting issue flag sent to the 28th in the summer of 1864 was surrendered at Appomattox. It was forwarded to the War Department and #364 stenciled on it. The flag was returned to North Carolina in 1905 and is held at the NCMH in Raleigh. Dedmondt, *The Flags of Civil War North Carolina*, 125, and R. W. Carson, "Reminiscences of Civil War." Civil War Collection, Box 70, Folder 30, NCDAH.

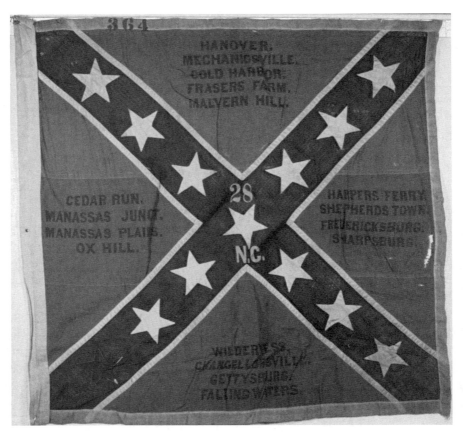

On April 9, 1865, the 28th North Carolina surrendered its flag at Appomattox Court House. *North Carolina Museum of History*

---

called for "Three cheers and a tiger for our Little General," a compliment Lane considered the greatest ever paid to him. Once the paroles were issued to the men, they were free to make their journeys homeward.[28]

Commissary Sergeant William Mauney (28th NC) wasn't with the brigade. After the breakthrough on April 2, he had wandered the countryside, evidently with others from the 28th. On April 8, he was at Roanoke Station. A train took him to Danville and then on into North Carolina. Mauney reported being at the 7th NC's camp on April 10, in Greensboro two days later, and finally in Charlotte on April 23. For a few days, he worked in the office of post

28 *Fayetteville Observer*, June 8, 1897.

commander Col. William Hoke before being paroled in Charlotte on May 3. He finally arrived home in Gaston County on May 9.[29]

Quite a few members of Lane's brigade were already back in North Carolina. The 7th Regiment had been on duty there since late February 1865, charged with rounding up deserters in the Piedmont area. Part of the regiment was ordered back to Danville on April 5, but returned to Greensboro on April 11. Some of the regiment was in Greensboro guarding commissary stores, while another detachment was sent out on April 19 to rebuild a bridge near Jamestown destroyed by Federal cavalry.[30]

While Lee's Army of Northern Virginia was fighting Grant in the Overland and Petersburg campaigns, its counterpart, the Army of Tennessee, fought Maj. Gen. William T. Sherman's army in north Georgia, around Atlanta, through south Georgia and into South Carolina. In mid-March 1865, combined forces from the Army of Tennessee and coastal garrisons attempted to stop the Federals. After losing at the battle of Bentonville, NC, Confederate forces retreated through Raleigh and toward Greensboro. At the end of April, the army's commander, Gen. Joseph E. Johnston, began meeting with Sherman at the Bennett farm near Durham. On April 26, Johnston surrendered not only the Army of Tennessee, but all Confederate soldiers under his command.

This included the 7th Regiment. James Harris recorded that official orders regarding the surrender arrived while the 7th Regiment was posted in Lexington on April 27. On April 29, the regiment stacked all but one-fifth of their arms, and, as with Lee's army, the officers were allowed to keep their side arms. Unlike the 28th Regiment, the 7th did not surrender its flag. Instead, the few remaining soldiers of the regiment ripped it into fragments, many of them taking pieces of their beloved and battle-stained banner as mementoes, safe from enemy hands.[31]

The 7th Regiment surrendered 13 commissioned officers and 139 enlisted men, Harris wrote. Added to this number were two staff officers. At Appomattox, Lane's brigade surrendered 579 men, plus the general and four other staff officers. Lane's brigade totaled 738 members under arms when they were paroled at Appomattox or in Lexington. With parole papers in hand, the

29 Mauney, diary, April 3-May 9, 1865.

30 Harris, *Historical Sketches*, 61-62.

31 Ibid., 62. A piece of the Seventh's battle flag was given to the Hall of History in October 1892 by John Morning. While fraught with errors, see *The Dispatch*, October 6, 1892.

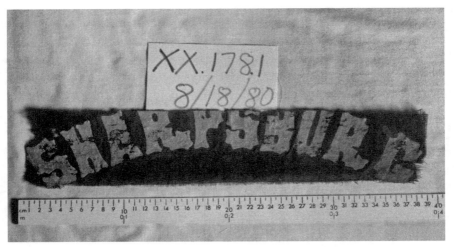

Instead of surrendering their flag, surviving members of the 7th North Carolina ripped up the banner. This fragment is the only one known piece that has survived. *North Carolina Museum of History*

men set out for their homes across the Old North State. They were now "war worn veterans," wrote James Harris many years later, and set off "towards their several homes to engage in the battle of life."[32]

32 Harris, *Historical Sketches*, 62; William Nine and Ronald Wilson, *The Appomattox Paroles, April 9-15, 1865* (Lynchburg, 1989), 113, 121, 142, 158, 159, 253-54.

"There are other instances in which he did my command injustice."

Remembering the Branch-Lane Brigade

They came by the thousands to Raleigh on a spring morning in May 1895. There were young men in smart military uniforms, families from both near and far, politicians, and veterans who had worn the gray. Among the dignitaries on the platform was Nancy Branch, dressed in the shades of mourning she had worn ever since the death of the general in September 1862. She sat beside Nancy Morrison Jackson, the widow of Stonewall. Soon, Jackson's granddaughter pulled the rope, unveiling the Confederate monument on the grounds of the state capital.

Only a year had passed since the end of the war when Nancy Branch helped organize the Ladies Memorial Association of Wake County. She was the group's first president. Their goal was to protect the graves of Confederate dead in the area. After acquiring a piece of property, the ladies, with the help of male members of their group, began moving the remains of hundreds from the Rock Quarry Cemetery, as well as from other cemeteries, to a new plot of land, later named Oakwood Cemetery. In May 1867, they held their first decoration day, cleaning and decorating the graves with flowers not only at Oakwood, but also in the old City Cemetery, where General Branch was buried. A few years later,

Thousands of men, women, and children gathered in May 1895 to participate in the dedication of the Confederate Monument on the grounds of the statehouse in Raleigh.
North Carolina Department of Archives and History

the Ladies Memorial Association of Wake County took charge of the re-internment of identifiable North Carolinians from the Gettysburg dead, and then from Arlington, all buried at Oakwood. Nancy Branch was considered "one of the best informed students of war history in the South." For the remainder of her life, she was involved in the affairs of local Confederate veterans, participating in reunions and visiting the Confederate Veterans' home in Raleigh. Nancy Branch died in 1903 and is buried beside the general in the City Cemetery in Raleigh.[1]

As it did for many other Confederates, the end of the war caught Branch's successor with no home, no employment, and no direction to pursue. "I am without property and without money," James H. Lane wrote on July 10, 1865. After receiving his parole, Lane started to his parents' home in Matthews Court House, Virginia. Lane considered that ride "the saddest part of all. No longer

---

1   Margaret Collier, *Representative Women of the South,* 6 vols. (College Park, GA, 1920-1938), vol. 5, 175-178; *The Morning Post,* November 10, 1903.

Lawrence Branch lies beside his wife Nancy in the Old City Cemetery in Raleigh, North Carolina. *Michael C. Hardy*

was there the thrill of fighting and the companionship in danger. Nothing remained but utter desolation." At home, Lane found plundered houses and ruined farms. His parents were crushed by the war. Not only were their livelihoods gone, but two sons, both serving on the General's staff, did not return.[2]

For the time being, Lane worked his father's garden and cornfields. On July 11, he appeared before the local provost marshal and took the Oath of Allegiance. As prescribed by the president of the United States, Lane wrote requesting a pardon for his role in the late rebellion. Lane was brief: he had entered Confederate service from North Carolina, serving until the surrender of the Army of Northern Virginia. Lane was most likely granted his pardon on July 4, 1868.[3]

Though Lane farmed throughout the summer, his war wounds excluded him from long-term agriculture. He looked for teaching positions in Wilmington and at VMI. A later sketch of Lane reveals he borrowed $150 from a friend and set out to find employment. He opened schools in Concord, NC, in February 1866 and then in Richmond in 1868.[4]

In September 1869, Lane married Charlotte Meade. The couple lived in Richmond until 1872, when Lane accepted the position of instructor of natural philosophy, chemistry, and military tactics at the Virginia Agricultural and Mechanical College in Blacksburg, a position he enjoyed until 1878, when a disagreement with fellow faculty, students, and townspeople led to a fistfight between Lane and school president Charles Minor. Both were hauled into court and cited for disturbing the peace. Lane, and many of the townspeople, wanted the college to be organized as a military school, with strict discipline. Minor and several other professors disagreed. Matters cooled until November 1878, when the board of visitors adopted Lane's plan. The school president and several faculty members were replaced. Eventually, a committee appointed by the Virginia General Assembly recommended both the board and all faculty be

2   James H. Lane to Andrew Johnson, July 10, 1865; Case files of Applications from Former Confederates for Presidential pardons, 1865-67, M1004, RG 94, NA; Petrie, *General Lane*, 6.

3   *Charlotte Observer*, March 22, 1894; The *Daily Illinois State Journal*, reported on July 19, 1865, the "Pardon bureau is still overrun with applications, among them are those of . . . James H. Lane, Brigadier General of the rebel army." There was a mass pardon of former Confederate officers on July 4, 1868, so it is likely Lane's pardon was included.

4   JL to F. H. Smith, September 15, 1865, James H. Lane Papers, Virginia Tech; Edward Hale to JL, July 31, 1865, James H. Lane Papers, AU; *Fayetteville Observer*, March 22, 1894.

fired. So, although the school was organized according to Lane's plan, he was dismissed in June 1880. He next taught in Wilmington, and, in 1881, began teaching mathematics at the Missouri School of Mines. Charlotte's poor health forced their return to Richmond before the term ended.[5]

Lane applied for the positions of commandant and professor of engineering at Alabama Agricultural and Mechanical College in Auburn in June 1882. With his letter, he enclosed a pamphlet containing commendatory letters from 37 well-known men of the South, including Robert E. Lee. With such glowing recommendations, Lane was hired, becoming the chair of the Civil Engineering and Mining Engineering department, where he taught for the next 25 years. When he retired in the spring of 1907, the school bestowed upon Lane the honor of "Emeritus Professor of Civil Engineering," the first such distinction for what is now Auburn University. In late 1891, the US Department of Agriculture appointed Lane as the state statistical agent of Alabama, a position he held until his death. He also won awards for some of his civil engineering drawings.[6]

During the course of his postwar life, Lane was also building a reputation as the staunch defender of the role of North Carolina during the war. The "battle of the books," which lasted for decades, often found Lane at the forefront, defending the exploits of his former soldiers during the war. Some of his most virulent confrontations revolved around the defenders of William Mahone's command. Three times during the war, at Spotsylvania Court House, Reams Station, and Battery Gregg, these two commands had clashed with each other as well as with the enemy. They continued sparring through various newspapers and periodicals through the post-war years. Just two years after Appomattox, the editors of the *Petersburg Index* lambasted the performance of Wilcox's division in a review of Edward Pollard's *Lee and his Lieutenants* at several engagements. For example, the newspaper asserted: at the Wilderness, "Wilcox was not engaged, except slightly, on the first evening"; at Spotsylvania, "Wilcox's troops did not hold their own on the 12th of May"; at Jericho Ford, the brigades of Lane and McGowan "behaved most disgracefully, and were replaced"; and at Battery Gregg, the "infantry garrison . . . was composed entirely of members of the Mississippi brigade of Harris." Lane refuted each

5   Lane is mentioned as being courted as principal of the rebuilt Hillsboro Military Academy in 1873. *The Wilmington Morning Star*, January 24, 1873.

6   Philips, "James Henry Lane," 230-32.

and every one of these derogatory assertions, at times quoting from official battle reports, and, in the case of Spotsylvania, with a copy of a letter from Gen. Robert E. Lee to Cadmus Wilcox concerning captured battle flags William Mahone claimed.[7]

Lane wrote more on the battle of Chancellorsville than on any other engagement. In 1873, he addressed an article to the *Richmond Dispatch* in which he once again defended his brigade. Making the rounds at the time was a story about how no night attack was contemplated on May 2. Lane provided more details on the terrain, the position of his brigade, and his encounter with Jackson while seeking out A. P. Hill for further orders. When a former soldier claimed Jackson's wounding took place before dark, Lane referred everyone to his 1863 report and 1873 letter, and provided a few more details of his conversation with Jackson in the darkness along the Orange Plank Road. A year later, Lane wrote to Henry B. McClellan, a former staff officer for J. E. B. Stuart and Wade Hampton, who was writing a biography of the famed cavalry commander. In December 1888, Lane penned his own account of Jackson's wounding, but it never appeared in print.

In 1892, Lane began corresponding with Augustus C. Hamlin, a former Union soldier researching a history of O. O. Howard's XI Corps at the Battle of Chancellorsville. Lane repeated much of what he had written in the first two accounts, but he added a few additional, if minor, details. Though they were never published, these accounts influenced Hamlin's book. Hamlin eventually persuaded the former Confederate general to visit the battlefield with him. The subsequent September 1894 visit to Virginia is the only known time that Lane is is known to have walked one of his former battlefields. Of all the places Lane fought, his postwar writings clearly demonstrated that no other place haunted him as much as Chancellorsville.[8]

---

7 The full title of Pollard's work is *Lee and His Lieutenants: Comprising the Early Life, Public Services, and Campaigns of General Robert E. Lee and his Companions in Arms, With a Record of Their Campaigns and Heroic Deeds* (New York: E. B. Treat & Co., 1867). For more on the battle of the books, see Craig Symonds, *Joseph E. Johnston: A Civil War Biography* (New York, NY, 1992), 358; *The Raleigh Sentinel*, September 23, 1867.

8 *Wilmington Morning Star*, July 4, 1873; JL to Henry McClellan, May 14, 1885, *The Life and Campaigns of Major General J. E. B. Stuart* (Boston, MA, 1885), 241-42; JL to Augustus Hamlin, 1892, James H. Lane Papers, AU; JL, "Reminiscences of Jackson." Lane informed his readers that the 1873 letter was written while he was visiting Richmond, at the request of Moses Hardy. Lane, "History of Lane's North Carolina Brigade," *SHSP*, 8:489-96.

James Lane would have viewed this monument to Stonewall Jackson when he visited the Chancellorsville battlefield after the war. *Library of Congress*

It appears Lane wrote only once about Gettysburg, and it was in reply to Walter Taylor. In 1877, Lee's former staff officer published his memoir entitled *Four Years with General Lee.* In it, Taylor claimed that, on July 3, the "assaulting column really consisted of Pickett's division," and Pickett's men were "the only organized body that entered the works of the enemy." Furthermore, claimed Taylor, the open terrain and entrenched Federal positions of infantry and artillery demoralized Pettigrew's and Trimble's commands, causing "them to falter, and finally retire."[9]

The staff members of the *Raleigh Observer* stepped up to the challenge and sent a list of questions to every Tar Heel officer they could find. Much of the October 30, 1877, edition of the newspaper addressed the issue. A dozen different brigade officers took the time and trouble to respond. Lane's letter, dated September 7, 1877, was the longest and most detailed of them all. In it, Lane quoted Taylor, his own official report, and a letter from General Isaac Trimble before closing with his own observations. Although his was not a blistering rebuttal, Lane's words offered an honest and sincere account. "I know too well what it is to be a soldier to wish to rob any command of any of its laurels, and as a Virginian, I by no means wish to cast any reflections whatever upon the gallant troops from my native State," explained the former general. "What I have written is solely in defence of a most heroic body of North Carolinians, of whom Gen. Lee told me, in person, that North [Carolina] had just cause to be proud."[10]

Lane's thoughts on the war also appeared in other publications. In 1874, he wrote a couple of articles on the battle of the Wilderness, and another on the 28th Regiment, for the relatively new *Our Living and Our Dead*, a literary-historical periodical published out of New Bern. Quite possibly his biggest contribution began in October 1879, when Lane started publishing the reports from his brigade in the *Southern Historical Society Papers*. He concluded the series in 1882. Later, the general added excerpts from his own letters in an 1890 article and sketches of the history of the 28th Regiment in 1896 and his sharpshooter battalion in 1900. Lane revisited the Mahone controversies three different times in the pages of the *Southern Historical Society Papers*: 1877, 1881, and 1890. In "The Truth of History," published in 1890, Lane concluded that the "false claim set up for Harris's brigade" had been instigated by Mahone himself. "There are other instances in which he did my command injustice." However, as a gentleman of his era, after sending portions of various reports and letters of eye witnesses, Lane claimed simply wanting to call "attention to historical facts,

9   Walter Taylor, Jr. *Four Years with General Lee* (New York, NY, 1877), 105-107.

10 *Raleigh Observer*, November 30, 1877.

James Lane in a postwar photo at Auburn University.

North Carolina Department of Archives and History

without any coloring at all, and, as far as possible, let others speak in behalf of my gallant brigade of North Carolinians."[11]

It was not entirely beyond Lane to take a swipe at Mahone. Aging Confederates had been evincing some hostility toward Mahone ever since 1870, when a biography of the Virginian appeared in a New York newspaper and then in the *New York Historical Magazine*. The biographer recognized only Mahone's brilliance toward the end of the war, placing him on par with George Washington, Napoleon, and Stonewall Jackson, while portraying Robert E. Lee as incompetent. Mahone spent his postwar years in politics, serving a term in

11 Lane, "The Truth of History," *SHSP*, 18/71-80.

the United States Senate. However, he sided with the hated Republicans. As he stumped for James B. Weaver, the Populist presidential nominee in 1892, Lane quipped that their platform was "enough to make an old rebel use a few 'cuss words.' I cannot help thinking that his Santanic [sic] Majesty has some very warm 'reserved seats' in hell for all such creatures."[12]

In 1894, the North Carolina Confederate Veterans Association decided a member of each Tar Heel regiment should write a history to be published by the state. James Harris had already written a history of the 7th Regiment and simply scaled back his previous work. William McLaurin and Thomas Sutton each wrote sketches of the 18th Regiment. James Weston chronicled the history of the 33rd, while Octavius Wiggins wrote on the 37th Regiment. Twice before Lane had written short pieces on the 28th Regiment, and he provided project editor Walter Clark with the requested information, including some wartime images of officers and men from the various regiments. Lane corresponded with numerous old soldiers to obtain photographs to be included with the text. The headshots were then placed on pre-painted or engraved bodies. Clark's histories were published in 1901.[13]

Four daughters were born to James and Charlotte Lane. Charlotte died in 1888 and was buried in Auburn, where Lane continued to teach. As the twentieth century dawned, Lane's health declined. He confessed in a letter to his brother Thomas in 1904 that he was suffering from the "grippe." Four years later, Lane told his sister he had partial paralysis in his right arm and leg, possibly indicating he had experienced a stroke. His health prevented the old general from attending a reunion in Gaston County that year. Though he had regained the use of his arm, his right leg still bothered him. "I write with difficulty now and very slowly," he confessed. "My walking is slow and uncertain though I use a cane."[14]

James Henry Lane, dubbed "the Little General" by his men, died at his home in Auburn on Saturday night, September 21, 1907. "He was a man of singularly pure and simple character," a professor from the University of

---

12 Noe, "The Lane-Mahone Controversy," 1103. The letter, written from Auburn, AL, on October 19, 1892, was signed "Old Rebel." The editor of the *Wilmington Messenger* attributed it to Lane on November 2, 1892.

13 C. L. Patton to JL, August 13, 1901, James H. Lane Papers, AU.

14 JL to "My Dear Brother," April 16, 1900, Lane Family Papers, College of William and Mary; JL to "Dear Sister," April 22, 1907, James H. Lane Papers, AU; *The Gaston Gazette*, July 19, 1907.

James H. Lane died in 1907 and is buried with his wife Charlotte in the Pine Hill Cemetery in Auburn, Alabama. *Author*

Virginia eulogized six weeks later, "absolutely straightforward and sincere, without fear, a soldier every inch of him, whose scorn no student dared to provoke, and a stanch [sic] friend whose loyalty none ever doubted." Lane was laid to rest beside his beloved Charlotte at Pine Hill Cemetery in Auburn.[15]

15 *Confederate Veteran* (September 1908), 17/9:469.

"[O]ne of the finest fighting records."

The Branch-Lane Brigade's Place in History

In March 2016, a monument was dedicated to the Branch-Lane brigade at Pamplin Historical Park in Petersburg, Virginia, commemorating the brigade at the spot where the breakthrough took place on April 2, 1865. Efforts were also underway to raise funds for the conservation of Branch's headquarters flags. After 150 years, the Branch-Lane brigade finally seemed to be getting the recognition Riddick Gatling, Jr., sought in 1888 when he lamented the lack of a history for his comrades.

The Branch-Lane brigade was renowned during the war, with as illustrious a reputation as the Stonewall Brigade or the Iron Brigade. In September 1862, Raleigh's *Semi-Weekly State Journal* said that the brigade "had gained a dangerous notoriety, for, whenever Jackson or A. P. Hill has a desperate undertaking Branch's men are ordered in." After documenting the various engagements the brigade had fought in just six months, the writer concluded, "We trust enough of these glorious fellows may yet be spared to enjoy the well-earned reputation of their brigade." Unfortunately, a vast segment of this extraordinary group did not live to see the end of the war, and many who did survive could not merely enjoy the brigade's impressive reputation. Rather, they often had to struggle for

On March 19, 2016, a monument was dedicated to Lane's brigade at Pamplin Historical Park near Petersburg, Virginia. *Brian Duckworth*

the recognition they justly deserved, both during and after the war, despite being frequently praised.[1]

Even after the war, friend and foe alike continued singing the brigade's praises. Former Federal officer Augustus C. Hamlin, in his book on the battle of Chancellorsville, wrote: "The history of this command [Branch-Lane brigade], under its dauntless leader, throughout the war, and ending at Appomattox, will always be admired and respected by those who believe in American manhood. And the student who seeks to discover a higher degree of courage and hardihood among the military organizations of either army will look over the true records of the war for a long time, if not in vain."[2]

That acclaim continues into the twenty-first century. Historian Alfred Young III, to cite just one, examining the numbers of men in Lee's army during the Overland Campaign, believed Lane's brigade had "one of the finest fighting records in the Army of Northern Virginia."[3]

There were of, course, detractors, former soldiers like Walter Taylor, and at times, historians like Douglas Southall Freeman. The latter contended Lane should have notified Longstreet on July 3 that his line did not extend to cover the entire distance behind Pettigrew's division. In *Lee's Lieutenants*, his three-volume history of the leadership of the Army of Northern Virginia, Freeman fails to mention any contribution of Lane's brigade at Spotsylvania Court House on May 12, assigning the salvation of Lee's army to John B. Gordon's brigade; Freeman also neglects to cover the brigade's role at Battery Gregg on April 2, 1865. He writes much more sympathetically of General Branch. Hanover Court House was "in no sense discreditable to Branch, and Branch's failure to support Longstreet at Frayser's Farm was due to the fact Branch had his hands full on his own front."[4]

In the end, the Branch-Lane brigade played an enormous role in the ordeals of the Army of Northern Virginia. Battles such as Cedar Mountain, Second Manassas, Spotsylvania Court House, and Reams Station might have ended differently had it not been for these Tar Heels. With victories, however, came battlefield defeats, like Hanover Court House, and the breakthrough below

---

1   *Semi-Weekly State Journal*, September 17, 1862.

2   Hamlin, *Chancellorsville*, 114.

3   Young, *Lee's Army*, 139.

4   Freeman, *Lee's Lieutenants*, 1:220, 651; 3:184, 388-410.

Petersburg on April 2. And the death of the beloved Jackson at the hands of the brigade cast a pall over its otherwise stellar history. Perhaps it also explains why, despite its many accomplishments, the Branch-Lane Brigade has not always enjoyed the attention its reputation deserves.

"Bravest of the brave" and a brigade with "a dangerous reputation" were terms frequently used to describe the Branch-Lane brigade. Of the 8,975 men who served those four years in the brigade, at least 3,151 died while in service—1,197 on the battlefield. The others died of disease, in prison, or of unknown causes. In the end, the Tar Heels in the Branch-Lane brigade were not necessarily braver than the men of the Stonewall brigade or of Kershaw's brigade, but these Tar Heels most certainly did earn their dangerous reputation.

Bibliography

Primary Sources

Auburn University, Auburn, AL
    James H. Lane Papers

Duke University, Durham, NC
    Leonard Alman Papers
    Jackson L. Bost Letters
    Confederate States of America Collection, 37th North Carolina Troops
    John H. Kinyoun Papers
    Alexander M. McPheeters Papers
    C. F. Mills Papers
    Munford-Ellis Family Papers
    Thomas Nixon Papers
    Thorton Sexton Letters
    A. L. Sterns Letters

Gaston County, North Carolina, Museum, Dallas, NC
    M. L. Holland Letters

Emory University, Atlanta, GA
    Bell Wiley Papers

Kings Mountain Historical Museum, Kings Mountain, NC
    William A. Mauney Diary

Library of Congress, Washington, D.C.
    Cadmus Wilcox Papers

National Archives, Washington, D.C.
    Ezra Carman Papers

North Carolina Division of Archives and History, Raleigh, NC
    R. W. Carson Reminiscences
    Henry T. Clark Letterbooks
    Noah Clark Papers
    Noah Collins Papers, 1861-1865
    John Thomas Conrad Papers
    William B. Howard diary
    George B. Johnston Papers
    Mrs. Ben Lacy Papers
    Isaac Spencer London Collection
    Military Collection
    J. H. Johnston Diary
    Hugh Torrence Memoir
    O. J. Lehman Reminiscences
    John B. Neathery Papers
    Lawrence O'Bryan Branch Letterbook
    Mrs. Lawrence O'Bryan Branch Papers
    John F. Shaffner Papers and Diary
    Mary Lee Tickin Papers
    Williams-Womble Papers
    John Wright's Papers

Private Collections
    Boger Letter
    Bennett Smith Papers
    Robert Francis Letters
    George W. Benson "My Last Fighting and Prison Life"

Richmond National Battlefield Park, Richmond, VA
    Richard Martin Van Buren Reeves Letters

Southern Historical Collection, University of North Carolina, Chapel Hill, NC
   William D. Alexander Diary
   Battle Family Papers
   W. J. H. Bellamy Diary
   Fries-Shaffner Papers
   Heartt-Wilson Papers
   Joyner Family Papers
   Francis M. Kennedy Dairy
   Lenoir Family Papers
   William G. Morris Letters
   Proffitt Family Papers
   Royster Family Papers
   Joseph H. Saunders Letters
   Ann Linebarger Snuggs Papers
   George S. Thompson Quartermaster Papers

United States Army Military History Institute, Carlisle Barracks, PA
   "Sketch of the Life of Lt. Robert McAulay"

University of North Carolina-Charlotte, NC
   John B. Alexander Letters
   Nicholas Riddle Gibbon Papers

University of Virginia, Charlottesville, VA
   Branch Papers

Virginia Historical Society, Richmond, VA
   Lee Headquarters Papers

Virginia Tech, Blacksburg, VA
   Lane Papers

Government Publications

Journals of Congress of the Confederate States of America. 7 volumes. Washington: Government Printing Office, 1904-1905.

The War of the Rebellion: A Compilation of the Official Records of the Union and Confederate Armies, 128 vols. Washington, D.C., 1880-1901.

Periodicals

Atchison Daily Globe
Biblical Recorder
The Bladen Journal
Charlotte Democrat
Charlotte News
Charlotte Observer
Confederate Veteran
The Daily Confederate (Raleigh)
Daily Illinois State Journal
The Daily Journal (Wilmington)
Daily Progress (NC)
Detroit Free Press (MI)
The Dispatch (VA)
Durham Globe
Fayetteville Observer
Gastonia Gazette
Hillsborough Recorder
Lenoir Topic (NC)
Monroe Journal (NC)
The Morganton Herald (NC)
The Morning Post
Mooresville Tribune (NC)
The National Tribune
News and Observer (NC)
News Herald (NC)
North Carolina Standard (NC)
North Carolina Whig
Oneida Weekly Herald (NY)
Our Living and Our Dead
Philadelphia Times (PA)
The Raleigh Sentinel
Register (NC)
Richmond Enquirer (VA)
Richmond Times (VA)
Rochester Democrat and American (NY)
San Angelo Daily (TX)
Semi-Weekly State Journal (NC)
Semi-Weekly Standard (NC)
Southern Historical Society Papers
The Southern Home

Spirit of the Age (NC)
Statesville Landmark (NC)
The Tarborough Southerner (NC)
The Union Republican (NC)
Washington Star (NC)
Watauga Democrat
Western Democrat (NC)
Wilmington Journal Weekly
Wilmington Messenger
The Wilmington Morning Star

Published Sources

Primary Sources

Alexander, John B. *Reminiscences of the Past Sixty Years.* Charlotte, NC: privately printed, 1908.

Caldwell, J. F. J. *History of a Brigade of South Carolinians.* Philadelphia, PA: King and Baird, 1866.

Chamberlain, William W. *Memoirs of the Civil War.* Washington, D.C., Press of Bryon S. Adams, 1912.

Chisolm, J. Julian. *A Manual of Military Surgery for the Use of Surgeons in the Confederate Army.* Richmond: West & Johnston, 1861.

Cochran, George W. *A Brief Sketch of the Cochran Family.* n.p., n.d.

Davis, Jefferson. *The Papers of Jefferson Davis: 1862.* Baton Rouge: Louisiana State University Press, 1995.

Denny, Joseph W. *Wearing the Blue in the Twenty-fifth Mass. Volunteer Infantry.* Worcester: Putnam and Davis Publishers, 1879.

The Diary of Elizabeth Ellis Robeson, Bladen County, North Carolina, 1847-1866. n.p., n.d.

Douglas, Henry Kyd. *I Rode With Stonewall.* Chapel Hill: University of North Carolina Press, 1940.

Dowdy, Clifford, and Louis Manarin, eds. *The Wartime Papers of R. E. Lee.* New York: Bramhall House, 1961.

Early, Jubal A. *Autobiographical Sketch and Narrative of the War Between the States.* Philadelphia, PA: J. B. Lippincott Co., 1912.

Freeman, Douglas Southall. *Lee's Dispatches.* New York: G. P. Putnam's Sons, 1915.

Fremantle, Arthur J. L. *Three Months in the Southern States.* London, 1863.

Hancock, M. A., ed. *Four Brothers in Gray.* Sparta, NC: Star Route Books, 2013.

Harris, J. S. *Historical Sketches, Seventh Regiment North Carolina Troops.* Mooresville, NC: Mooresville Printing Co., 1893.

Hassler, William, ed. *One of Lee's Best Men: The Civil War Letters of General William Dorsey Pender.* Chapel Hill: The University of North Carolina Press, 1965, 1999.

Hatley, John, and Linda Huffman, eds. *Letters of William Wagner, Confederate Soldier.* Weldon, NC: Broadfoot, 1983.

Hewett, Janet Hewett, et. al., *Supplement to the Army Official Records,* 100 vols. Wilmington, NC, Broadfoot, 1994-2001.

Jones, J. William, ed. *Personal Reminiscences, Anecdotes, and Letters of Gen. Robert E. Lee.* New York: D. Appleton and Company, 1875.

Kautz, August V. *Customs of Service for Non-Commissioned Officers.* Philadelphia, PA: J. B. Lippincott & Co., 1864.

———. *The Company Clerk.* Philadelphia: J. B. Lippincott & Co., 1865.

Koonce, Donald, ed. *Doctor to the Front: The Recollections of Confederate Surgeon Thomas Fanning Wood, 1861-1865.* Knoxville: The University of Tennessee Press, 2000.

Lane, James H. "History of Lane's North Carolina Brigade." *Southern Historical Society Papers,* vol. 7 (1879), 513-522.

———. "History of Lane's North Carolina Brigade." *Southern Historical Society Papers* vol. 8, no. 1 (January1880), 1-8.

———. "History of Lane's North Carolina Brigade." *Southern Historical Society Papers* vol. 8, no. 2 (February 1880), 67-76.

———. "History of Lane's North Carolina Brigade." *Southern Historical Society Papers* vol. 8, no. 3 (March 1880), 97-104.

———. "History of Lane's North Carolina Brigade." *Southern Historical Society Papers* vol. 8, no. 4 (April 1880), 145-154.

———. "History of Lane's North Carolina Brigade." *Southern Historical Society Papers* vol. 8, no. 5 (May 1880), 193-202.

———. "History of Lane's North Carolina Brigade." *Southern Historical Society Papers* vol. 8, nos. 6, 7 (June, July 1880), 241-248.

———. "History of Lane's North Carolina Brigade." *Southern Historical Society Papers.* 8, nos. 8, 9 (August, September 1880), 396-404.

———. "History of Lane's North Carolina Brigade." *Southern Historical Society Papers.* vol. 8, nos.10, 11, 12 (October, November, December 1880), 489-496.

———. "History of Lane's North Carolina Brigade." *Southern Historical Society Papers.* vol. 9 no. 1 (January 1881), 29-35.

———. "History of Lane's North Carolina Brigade." *Southern Historical Society Papers* vol. 9, no. 2 (February 1881), 67-76.

———. "The Defence of Battery Gregg – General Lane's Reply to General Harris." *Southern Historical Society Papers* vol. 9, no. 3 (March 1881), 102-107.

———. "History of Lane's North Carolina Brigade." *Southern Historical Society Papers* vol. 9, no. 3 (March 1881), 124-129.

———. "History of Lane's North Carolina Brigade." *Southern Historical Society Papers* vol. 9, no. 4 (April 1881), 145-154.

———. "History of Lane's North Carolina Brigade." *Southern Historical Society Papers* vol. 9, no. 5 (May 1881), 193-202.

———. "History of Lane's North Carolina Brigade." *Southern Historical Society Papers* vol. 9, no. 6 (June 1881), 241-248.

———. "History of Lane's North Carolina Brigade." *Southern Historical Society Papers* vol. 9, no. 7,vol. 8 (July, August 1881), 353-360.

———. "History of Lane's North Carolina Brigade." *Southern Historical Society Papers* vol. 9, no. 10, 11, 12 (October, November, December 1881), 489-496.

———. "History of Lane's North Carolina Brigade." *Southern Historical Society Papers* vol. 10, no.1, (January, February 1882), 57-59.

———. "History of Lane's North Carolina Brigade." *Southern Historical Society Papers* vol. 10, no. 5 (May 882), 206-213.

———. "History of Lane's North Carolina Brigade." *Southern Historical Society Papers* vol. 10, no. 6 (June 1882), 241-243.

———. "Lane's Corps of Sharpshooters." *Southern Historical Society Papers* vol. 28 (1900),1-8.

———. "Personal Reminiscences of General Lee." *The Wake Forest Student*, vol. 26, no. 5 (January 1907), 310-11.

———. "The Truth of History." *Southern Historical Society Papers*, vol.18 (1890), 71-80.

Lehman, O. J. "Reminiscences of the War Between the States. 1862 to 1865." *The Union Republican*, October 19, 1922.

Matthews, James M. ed., *The Statutes at Large of the Provisional Government of the Confederate States of America*. Richmond, VA: R. M. Smith, 1864.

Mills, George H. *History of the 16th North Carolina Regiment (Originally 6th North Carolina Regiment)* Rutherfordton, NC, 1901.

Mobley, Joe A., ed. *The Papers of Zebulon Baird Vance*. Vol. 2. Raleigh: Division of Archives and History, 1995.

Moorman, Marcellus. "Narrative of Events and Observations connected with the wounding of General T. J. (Stonewall) Jackson." *Southern Historical Society Papers* 30 (1902), 110-117.

Norton, Oliver. *Army Letters, 1861-1865,* Dayton, OH: Morningside, 1903, 1990.

Porter, Horace. *Campaigning with Grant.* New York: Century Company, 1906.

Sears, Stephen, ed. *The Civil War Papers of George B. McClellan: Selected Correspondence, 1860-1865*. New York: DaCapo Press, 1992.

Shaffner, Louis. "A Civil War Surgeon's Diary." *North Carolina Medical Journal* 23 (September 1966), 409-416.

Simpson, Kenrick N., ed. *Worthy of Record: The Civil War and Reconstruction Diaries of Columbus Lafayette Turner.* Raleigh: North Carolina Department of Cultural Resources, 2008.

Smith, Locke W., Jr., ed. "'God Save Us All In Heaven.'" The William Rufus Barlow Letter Collection." *Company Front.* 27, No. 2, (2013), 5-60.

Sorrel, G. Moxley. *Recollections of a Confederate Staff Officer.* Jackson, TN: McCowat-Mercer Press, 1958.

Speer, Allen P., ed. *Voices from Cemetery Hill: The Civil War Diary, Reports, and Letters of Colonel William Henry Asbury Speer (1861-1864).* Johnston City, TN: The Overmountain Press, 1997.

Taylor, Robert, Jr. *Four Years with General Lee.* New York: Appleton, 1877.

Tolbert, Noble. J., ed. *The Papers of John Willis Ellis.* 2 vols. Raleigh: North Carolina Department of Archives and History, 1964.

von Borke, Heros. *Memoirs of the Confederate War of Independence.* 2 volumes. New York: Peter Smith, 1938.

Wilcox, Cadmus. "Defence of Batteries Gregg and Whitworth, and the Evacuation of Petersburg." *Southern Historical Society Papers* 4 (1877), 18-33.

———. "Lee and Grant in the Wilderness." *The Annals of the War Written by Leading Participants North and South.* Philadelphia, PA: The Times Publishing Company, 1879.

Williams, Max, ed., *The Papers of William Alexander Graham.* 8 vols. Raleigh, NC, 1984.

Wittenburg, Eric. *"We Have it Damn Hard Out Here:" The Civil War Letters of Sergeant Thomas W. Smith, 6th Pennsylvania Cavalry.* Kent, OH: Kent State University Press, 1999.

Secondary Sources

Allardice, Bruce. *Confederate Colonels: A Biographical Register.* Columbia, MO: University of Missouri Press, 2008.

Arthur, John P. *Western North Carolina: A History from 1730 to 1913.* Johnson City, TN: The Overmountain Press, 1914, 1996.

Ballard, Sandra L., and Leila E. Weinstein, eds., *Neighbor to Neighbor: A Memoir of Family, Community, and Civil War in Appalachian North Carolina.* Boone, NC: Center for Appalachian Studies, 2007.

Barrett, John G. *The Civil War in North Carolina.* Chapel Hill, NC: University of North Carolina Press, 1963.

Bicentennial of Bethania Moravian Church, 1759 - 1959. Winston-Salem: Bradford Printing Service, 1959.

Blight, David W. *Race and Reunion: The Civil War in American Memory.* Cambridge: Belknap Press of Harvard University Press, 2011.

Bradley, Paul. "Was General Lane a Scapegoat?" *America's Civil War.* Vol. 26, (May 2013), 51.

Brown, Kent Masterson. *Retreat from Gettysburg: Lee, Logistics, and the Pennsylvania Campaign.* Chapel Hill: University of North Carolina Press, 2005.

Bunch, Jack A. *Roster of Courts-Martial in the Confederate States Armies.* Shippensburg, PA: White Mane, 2001.

———. *Military Justice in the Confederate States.* Shippensburg, PA: White Mane, 2000.

Calcutt, Rebecca. *Richmond's Wartime Hospitals.* Gretna, LA: Pelican, 2005.

Carman, Ezra. *The Maryland Campaign of September 1862.* Volume 2. Ed. by Thomas Clemens. El Dorado Hills, CA: Savas Beatie, 2012.

Carmichael, Peter S. "Letters Home: Correspondence from Men at War." *The Civil War Monitor.* (Summer 2014), 67-71.

Casstevens, Frances. *The Civil War in Yadkin County, North Carolina.* Jefferson, NC: McFarland and Company, 1997.

———. *The 28th North Carolina Troops Infantry.* Jefferson, NC: McFarland, and Co., 2008.

Cheney, Newel. *History of the Ninth Regiment, New York Volunteer Cavalry.* Jamestown; Martin Merz and Son, 1901.

Clark, Walter. *Histories of the Several Regiments and Battalions from North Carolina in the Great War 1861-'65.* 5 volumes. Raleigh: E. M. Uzzell, Printer and Binder, 1901.

Coco, Gregory A. *A Vast Sea of Misery: A History and Guide to the Union and Confederate Field Hospitals at Gettysburg, July 1-November 20, 1863.* Gettysburg, PA: Thomas Publications, 1988.

Collier, Margaret, *Representative Women of the South,* 6 vols. College Park, GA, [By the author], 1920-1938.

Cunningham, H. H. *Doctors in Gray: The Confederate Medical Service.* Baton Rouge: Louisiana State University Press, 1958.

Dedmondt, Glenn. *The Flags of Civil War North Carolina.* Gretna, LA: Pelican Publishing Company, 2003.

Dowdy, Clifford. *Experiment in Rebellion.* Garden City, NY: Doubleday, 1946.

Dunlap, W. S. *Lee's Sharpshooters.* Dayton: Morningside, 1899, 2000.

Edwards, Shayle. *The Lanier Brothers: "Apples and Green Corn."* [n.p.] 2000.

Evans, Clement A. *Confederate Military History.* 12 vols. Atlanta: Confederate Publishing Co., 1899.

Faust, Drew Gilpin. *This Republic of Suffering: Death and the American Civil War.* New York: Alfred A. Knopf, 2008.

Fox, John J. *The Confederate Alamo: Bloodbath at Petersburg's Fort Gregg on April 2, 1865.* Winchester, Virginia: Angle Valley Press, 2010.

Freeman, Douglas Southall. *R. E. Lee: A Biography.* 4 volumes. New York: Charles Scribner's Sons, 1934-1935.

———. *Lee's Lieutenants.* 3 volumes. New York. Charles Scribner's Sons, 1942.

Furguson, Chris. *Southerners at Rest: Confederate Dead at Hollywood Cemetery.* Winchester, VA: Angle Valley Press, 2008.

Furgurson, Ernest B. *Chancellorsville 1863: The Souls of the Brave.* New York: Alfred A. Knopf, 1992.

Gillispie, James. *Cape Fear Confederates: The 18th North Carolina Regiment in the Civil War*. Jefferson, NC: McFarland and Company, 2012.

Gottfried, Bradley M. *Brigades of Gettysburg: The Union and Confederate Brigades at the Battle of Gettysburg*. New York: Skyhorse Publishing, 2012.

Green, A. Wilson. *Breaking the Backbone of the Rebellion: The Final Battles of the Petersburg Campaign*. Knoxville: The University of Tennessee Press, 2008.

Guelzo, Allen C. *Gettysburg: The Last Invasion*. New York: Alfred A. Knopf, 2013.

Hahn, George. *The Catawba Soldiers of the Civil War*. Hickory, NC: Clay Print Co., 1911.

Hamlin, Augustus C. *The Battle of Chancellorsville*. Bangor, ME: [By the author], 1896.

Hardy, Michael C. "The 37th North Carolina Troops." *America's Civil War* (May 2003), vol. 16, 2, 115-117.

——. *The Thirty-seventh North Carolina Troops: Tar Heels in the Army of Northern Virginia*. Jefferson: McFarland and Company, 2003.

——."The Gettysburg Experiences of Lt. Iowa Michigan Royster." *Gettysburg Magazine* (July 2003), vol. 29, 121-124.

——."A Day of Carnage & Blood." *America's Civil War* (March 2005), vol. 18, 1, 98-104.

——. *The Battle of Hanover Court House*. Jefferson, NC: McFarland and Company, 2006.

——. "McClellan's Missed Opportunity." *America's Civil War* (March 2007), vol. 20, 1, 154-160.

——. *Watauga County, North Carolina, in the Civil War*. Charleston, SC: The History Press, 2013.

Harsh, Joseph L. *Confederate Tide Rising. Robert E. Lee and the Making of Southern Strategy, 1981-1862*. Kent, OH: The Kent State University Press, 1998.

Hartwig, D. Scott. *To Antietam Creek: The Maryland Campaign of September 1862*. Baltimore: The John Hopkins University Press, 2012.

Henderson, William D. *The Road to Bristoe Station: Campaigning with Lee and Meade, August 1 - October 20, 1863*. Lynchburg, VA: H. E. Howard. 1987.

Hennessy, John J. *Return to Bull Run: The Campaign and Battle of Second Manassas*. New York: Simon and Schuster, 1993.

Heritage of Ashe County, North Carolina. 2 vols. Winston-Salem, NC: Hunter Publishing Co., 1984.

Hess, Earl. *Lee's Tar Heels: The Pettigrew-Kirkland-MacRae Brigade*. Chapel Hill: University of North Carolina Press, 2002.

Hickerson, Thomas F. *Echoes of Happy Valley*. Chapel Hill, NC: privately printed, 1962.

Horn, John. *The Destruction of the Weldon Railroad*. Lynchburg VA: H. E. Howard, 1991.

————.*The Petersburg Campaign: June 1864 - April 1865.* Conshohocken, PA: Combined Books, 1993.

Humphreys, Margaret. *Marrow of Tragedy: The Health Crisis of the American Civil War.* Baltimore, MD: The John Hopkins University Press, 2013.

Husk, Martin. *The 111th New York Infantry.* Jefferson, NC: McFarland and Company, 2009.

Jones, Archibald. "The Battle of Fort Gregg." *Southern Historical Society Papers* (1903), Volume 31, 56-58.

Jones, Austin A. *The Capture of Harper's Ferry.* n.p., 1922.

Jones, J. William. *Christ in the Camp, or Religion in the Confederate Army.* Atlanta, GA: Martin and Hoyt, 1904.

Jordan, Weymouth, Louis Manarin, et. al. *North Carolina Troops, 1861-1865: A Roster.* 19 volumes. Raleigh: North Carolina Division of Archives and History, 1961-present.

Joslyn, Mauriel Phillips. *Captives Immortal: The Story of the Six Hundred Confederate Officers and the United States Prisoner of War Policy.* Shippensburg, PA: White Mane Publishing, 1996.

————. *The Biographical Roster of the Immortal 600.* Shippensburg, PA: White Mane Publishing, 1992.

Kelly, C. Brian. *Best Little Stories: Voices of the Civil War.* Naperville, IL: Cumberland House, 2006.

Krick, Robert E. L. *Staff Officers in Gray.* Chapel Hill: The University of North Carolina Press, 2003.

Krick, Robert K. *Civil War Weather in Virginia.* Tuscaloosa: The University of Alabama Press, 2007.

————. *Stonewall Jackson at Cedar Mountain.* Chapel Hill: University of Chapel Hill Press, 1990.

————. *The Smoothbore Valley that Doomed the Confederacy.* Baton Rouge: Louisiana State University Press, 2002.

Marvel, William. *Lee's Last Retreat: The Flight to Appomattox.* Chapel Hill: University of North Carolina Press, 2002.

Mast, Greg. *State Troops and Volunteers.* Raleigh: North Carolina Department of Archives and History, 1995.

McClellan, Henry. *The Life and Campaigns of Major General J.E.B. Stuart.* Boston: Houghton, Mifflin and Company, 1885.

McGrath, Thomas. *Shepherdstown: Last Clash of the Antietam Campaign, September 19-20, 1862.* Lynchburg, VA: Schroeder Publications, 2007.

Miller, J. Michael, "Perrin's Brigade on July 1, 1863." *Gettysburg Magazine*, vol.13 (July 1995), 22-32.

Newton, Steven H. *The Battle of Seven Pines.* Lynchburg, VA: H. E. Howard, 1993.

Nine, William G., and Ronald G. Wilson. *The Appomattox Paroles, April 9-15, 1865.* Lynchburg, VA: H. E. Howard, 1989.

Noe, Kenneth W. *Reluctant Rebels: The Confederates Who Joined the Army after 1861.* Chapel Hill: The University of North Carolina Press, 2010.

O'Daniel, Julia. *Kinfolk of Jacob Conrad.* n.p., 1970.

O'Reilly, Francis. "Busted Up and Gone To Hell: The Assault of the Pennsylvania Reserves at Fredericksburg." *Civil War Regiments: A Journal of the American Civil War.* 4, no. 4 (1995), 1-27.

———. *The Fredericksburg Campaign.* Baton Rouge: Louisiana State University Press, 2003.

Patterson, Gerard A. *From Blue to Gray: The Life of Confederate General Cadmus Wilcox* Mechanicsburg, PA: Stackpole Books, 2001.

Perry, Aldo S. *Civil War Courts-Martial of North Carolina Troops.* Jefferson, NC: McFarland and Company, 2012.

Pfanz, Harry W. *Gettysburg: Culp's Hill and Cemetery Hill.* Chapel Hill: University of North Carolina Press, 1993.

———. *Gettysburg: The First Day.* Chapel Hill: University of North Carolina Press, 2001.

Pickenpaugh, Roger. *Captives in Gray: The Civil War Prisons of the Union.* Tuscaloosa: University of Alabama Press, 2009.

Pittard, Pen. *Alexander County's Confederates.* n.p., 1960.

Pohanka, Brian C. *Vortex of Hell: History of the 5th New York Volunteer Infantry.* Lynchburg, VA: Schroeder Publications, 2012.

Powell, William, ed., *Dictionary of North Carolina Biography.* 6 volumes. Chapel Hill: University of North Carolina Press, 1979.

Puett, Minnie S. *History of Gaston County.* Charlotte: Laney-Smith, 1939.

Purser, Charles, and Frank Powell, III. *A Story Behind Every Stone: The Confederate Section of Oakwood Cemetery, Raleigh, North Carolina.* Wake Forest, NC: Scuppernong Press, 2005.

Remini, Robert V. *The House: The History of the House of Representatives.* New York: Smithsonian Books, 2006.

Rable, George C. *God's Almost Chosen Peoples: A Religious History of the American Civil War.* Chapel Hill: The University of North Carolina Press, 2010.

Ray, Fred L. *Shock Troops of the Confederacy: The Sharpshooter Battalions of the Army of Northern Virginia.* Asheville, NC: CFS Press, 2006.

Rhea, Gordon C. *The Battle of the Wilderness, May 5-6, 1864.* Baton Rouge: Louisiana State University Press, 1994.

———. *The Battles for Spotsylvania Court House and the Road to Yellow Tavern, May 7-12, 1864.* Baton Rouge: Louisiana State University Press, 1997.

Robertson, James I. *General A. P. Hill: The Story of a Confederate Warrior.* New York: Vintage Books, 1987.

———. *Stonewall Jackson: The Man, the Soldier, the Legend.* New York: Macmillan Publishing, 1997.

Rodriguez, Richard J. *Black Confederates in the U.S. Civil War: A Compiled List of Africans who Served the Confederacy.* Charleston, SC: Create Space, 2010.

Rollins, Richard. *"The Damned Red Flags of the Rebellion": The Confederate Battle Flag at Gettysburg.* Redondo Beach, CA: Rank and File Publications, 1997.

Schantz, Mark S. *Awaiting the Heavenly Country: The Civil War and America's Culture of Death.* Ithaca, New York: Cornell University, 2008.

Schenck, Martin. *Up Came Hill: The Story of the Light Division and its Leaders.* Harrisburg, PA: The Stackpole Company, 1958.

Schroeder-Lein, Glenna R. *The Encyclopedia of Civil War Medicine.* Armock, NY: M. E. Sharpe, 2008.

Sears, Stephen. *Chancellorsville.* New York: Houghton Mifflin Company, 1996.

———. *Landscape Turned Red: The Battle of Antietam.* New York: Ticknor and Fields, 1983.

———. *To the Gates of Richmond: The Peninsula Campaign.* New York: Ticknor & Fields, 1992.

Shattuck, Gardiner H., Jr. *A Shield and Hiding Place: The Religious Life of Civil War Armies* Macon: Mercer University Press, 1987.

Silkenat, David. *Moments of Despair: Suicide, Divorce, and Debt in Civil War Era North Carolina.* Chapel Hill, the University of North Carolina Press, 2011.

Sitterson, Joseph. *The Secession Movement in North Carolina.* Chapel Hill: The University of North Carolina Press, 1939.

Smith, John L. *History of the 118th Pennsylvania Volunteers.* Philadelphia: J. L. Smith, 1905.

Sommer, Richard J., *Richmond Redeemed: The Siege at Petersburg.* Garden City, NJ: Doubleday, 1981, 2014.

Speer, Lonnie R. *Portals to Hell: Military Prisons of the Civil War.* Mechanicsburg, VA: Stackpole Books, 1997.

Sprunt, James. *Chronicles of the Cape Fear River, 1660-1916.* Raleigh: Edwards and Broughton Printing Co., 1916.

Stanly County Heritage, Vol. 1. Waynesville, NC: Walsworth Publishing Co., 2001.

Symonds, Craig. *Joseph E. Johnston: A Civil War Biography.* New York: W. W. Norton, 1992.

Tucker, Leslie R. *Major General Isaac Ridgeway Trimble: Biography of a Baltimore Confederate.* Jefferson, NC: McFarland and Company, 2005.

Tyler, Lyon, ed. *Encyclopedia of Virginia Biography.* 3 volumes. New York: Lewis Historical Publishing Company, 1915.

Warner, Ezra. *Generals in Gray.* Baton Rouge: Louisiana State University Press, 1959.

———, and W. Buck Yearns. *Biographical Register of the Confederate Congress.* Baton Rouge: Louisiana State University Press, 1975.

Wegner, Ansley. *Phantom Pain: North Carolina's Artificial-Limbs Program for Confederate Veterans.* Raleigh: North Carolina Department of Cultural Resources, 2004.

Weitz, Mark. *More Damning than Slaughter: Desertion in the Confederate Army*. Lincoln: University of Nebraska Press, 2005.

Wiley, Bell. *The Life of Johnny Reb: The Common Soldier of the Confederacy*. Baton Rouge: Louisiana State University Press, 1943, 1978.

Wills, Brian S. *Confederate General William Dorsey Pender: The Hope of Glory*. Baton Rouge: *Louisiana State University,* 2013.

Wood, Thomas. "James Fergus McRee, M.D." *North Carolina Medical Journal*. vol. 29, no. 1 (January 1892), 10-20.

Yates, Robert. "Governor Vance and the Peace Movement." *North Carolina Historical Review*. vol. 27, no. 1, 1-26, 89-113.

Yeary, Mamie. *Reminiscences of the Boys in Gray, 1861-1865*. Dallas, TX: Smith and Lamar, 1912.

Young, Alfred C., III, *Lee's Army During the Overland Campaign: A Numerical Study*. Baton Rouge: Louisiana State University Press, 2013.

Theses and Dissertations

Alexander, William K. "Fought them like Tigers: The Life and Times of the Thirty-third North Carolina Infantry Regiment." Master's Thesis. Western Carolina University, 2003.

Brawley, James S. "The Public and Military Career of Lawrence O'Bryan Branch." Master's Thesis. University of North Carolina, Chapel Hill, 1951.

Dozier, Graham. "The Eighteenth North Carolina Infantry Regiment, C. S. A." Master's Thesis. Virginia Polytechnic Institute and State University, 1992.

Gianneschi, Matthew Everett. "A Man from Mecklenburg: 1st Sergeant John Tally and the 'Hornet's Nest Riflemen,' North Carolina 37th Regiment, Company I." Master's Thesis. University of Denver, 1998.

McDaid, William. "Four Years of Arduous Service: The History of the Branch-Lane Brigade in the Civil War." Ph. D dissertation. Michigan State University, 1987.

Phillips, Kenneth E. "James Henry Lane and the War for Southern Independence." Master's Thesis. Auburn University, 1982.

Websites

"Among Most Widely Used Confederate Infantry Manuals." *Raynor's Historical Collectible Auctions*. August 3, 2004. Last accessed on August 4, 2015. http://www.Hcaauctions.com/lot-3463.aspx.

Index

reviews brigade, 254; comments on the breakup of brigade, 257; comments on the reenlistment of regiments in brigade, 261n; meets with Lane at Spotsylvania, 281; attempts to lead brigade attack, 282n; advocates charges against Col. Haywood be dropped, 302; refuses to allow Lane to return to brigade command, 318; directing troop movements at Deep Bottom; congratulates role of brigade at Reams Station, 327; gives Lane peaches, 328; 37th Regiment flag at Lee Chapel, 344

Lincoln, Abraham, 3, 4, 5, 21, 31, 32, 37, 71, 73, 145, 218, 248, 335

Longstreet, Lt. Gen. James, division/corps of, 65, 66, 72, 81, 82, 85, 88, 89, 90, 93, 98, 107, 145, 146, 147, 155, 190, 192, 216, 217, 218, 222, 223, 225, 226, 227, 233, 234, 235, 254, 269, 272, 342, 348, 351, 352, 353

Lovell, Capt. Edward, 152, 270, 292; photo, 153

Lowe, Sgt. Maj. Milton, 65,

Lowe, Col. Samuel D., 28, 187, 190, 226; photo, 210

Lowe, Lt. Col. Thomas, 23; photo, 124

Mahone, Maj. Gen. William, 282, 286, 287, 315, 316, 322, 324, 335, 347, 351, 352, 355

Maine Military Units
  2nd Infantry, 42, 44, 45
  16th Infantry, 154

Malvern Hill, battle of, 67-68

Manassas, second battle of, 85-89

Manassas Junction, battle of, 83-84

Martinsburg, Virginia, 98, 99, 109, 236

Mauney, Sgt. William, 154, 220, 322, 356

McClellan, Maj. Gen. George B., 31, 32, 33, 34, 37, 38, 39, 50, 53, 56, 57, 58, 65, 67, 70, 71, 81, 82, 98, 101, 109, 112, 145, 288, 295

McDowell, Maj. Gen. Irvin, 37, 38, 39, 50, 53, 112

McGowan, Brig. Gen. Samuel, and brigade of, 193, 205, 206, 208, 210, 221, 222, 262, 267, 268, 291, 293, 295, 315, 319, 324, 325, 329, 330, 331, 332, 335, 341

McLaws, Maj. Gen. Lafayette, and division of, 52, 98, 101, 192

McLaurin, Lt. William, 33, 130, 145, 166, 171, 181, 187, 193, 199, 203, 204, 268-269, 272, 280, 286, 290, 292, 333, 347, 350; photo of, 167

MacRae, Brig. Gen. William, brigade of, 325, 326, 329, 332

Meade, Maj. Gen. George, 254, 264, 288, 328

Michigan Military Units
  5th Infantry, 272
  17th Infantry, 284, 285, 287

Mine Run, battle of, 257-259

Morris, Lt. Col. William, 25, 27, 30, 51, 53, 69, 70, 92, 94, 97, 100, 103, 104, 118, 122, 125, 135, 143, 144, 153, 164, 167, 170, 171, 172, 175, 183, 184, 185, 186, 196, 203, 211, 230, 238, 245, 247, 248, 308, 309

Morris Island, South Carolina, 245, 246

New Bern, battle of, 1, 7-10, 15, 17, 18, 29, 30, 69, 72, 101, 112, 138, 185, 238, 242

New York Military Units
  5th Infantry, 47
  9th Cavalry, 320, 321
  14th Infantry, 48
  17th Infantry, 47
  19th Light Artillery, 283, 287
  25th Infantry, 40, 42, 45
  44th Infantry, 42, 44, 45
  126th Infantry, 228, 231

Nicholson, Capt. William, 45, 50, 51, 67, 205, 259, 261, 282, 287; photo of, 281

Norwood, Lt. Thomas L., 183, 217, 230, 234, 235, 242, 308

North Anna River, Virginia, 145, battle of, 289-292

North Carolina Military Units
  1st Infantry, 257
  1st Volunteers, 16, 17, 20, 88
  2nd Cavalry, 7, 8
  3rd Infantry, 257
  4th Cavalry, 135
  4th Infantry, 116
  7th Infantry, organization of, 11-13, 22; desertion, 304-312; Hanover Court House, 45-46; Beaver Dam Creek, 58; Gaines Mill, 58-64; Frayser's Farm, 66-67; Malvern Hill, 67-68; Cedar Run 75-80; Manassas Junction, 83-84; Second Manassas, 86, 88; Chantilly, 91-92; Harper's Ferry, 98-100; Antietam, 102-104; Shepherdstown, 108-109; Fredericksburg, 147-154; Chancellorsville, 193-213; Gettysburg, 221-232; Falling Waters, 235-236; Bristoe Campaign, 255-256; Mine Run, 256; Wilderness, 265-272; Spotsylvania Court House,

Acknowledgments

A project like this, which took me over twenty years to research, would be impossible to complete without the help of many others. It is often difficult to know where to start and stop when it comes time to thank people, but I am extremely grateful for all the assistance that I received along the way.

I am deeply thankful for my publisher Savas Beatie, Managing Director Theodore P. Savas, and for the many wonderful folks on the Savas Beatie team for their efforts in seeing this book through to completion, including editor Thomas Schott, whose pen helped make this manuscript stronger, and Marketing Dirctor Sarah Keeney, Media Specialist Sarah Closson, Account Manager Donna Endacott, and others on the marketing team who are wortking hard to position my book for success.

Special thanks go to the many people who volunteered their time and knowledge over the years: Julie Henry, librarian, University of North Carolina—Charlotte, for information on John B. Alexander and Col. Charles C. Lee; T. H. Robbins, of Elm City, North Carolina, for information on the 33rd North Carolina Troops; Tom Clemens of Maryland, for copies of the Carman Papers relating to Branch's brigade at Antietam; Eric Mink for allowing me access to the files at the Fredericksburg-Spotsylvania

National Military Park, and to Robert E. L. Krick, historian at the Richmond National Battlefield Park, for not only allowing me access to the park's files, but also for answering questions from time to time. Many thanks to my readers Gregg Cheek, Stephen Harris, Joe Owens, Eric J. Wittenberg, and Tom Clemens. This book would not have been possible without the love of my life, Elizabeth Baird Hardy; she has spent countless hours searching in archives, tramping through battlefields, listening to my ideas, helping me solve mysteries, reading, and re-reading. I think she loves these men almost as much as I do.

Profound thanks are also due to the men of the Branch-Lane brigade, many of whom left us their words and thoughts about their experiences, from the mundane and humorous to the tragic and transformative. This story would not be possible if they had not started telling it first, as they lived it, as they earned their dangerous reputation and became immortal.

About the Author

Michael C. Hardy is a widely recognized expert and author on the Civil War. He is a graduate of the University of Alabama and was named North Carolina Historian of the Year in 2010. His work has appeared in national magazines, and he blogs regularly at *Looking for North Carolina's Civil War*. When he is not researching and writing, Michael and his family volunteer as interpreters at several historic sites in western North Carolina and East Tennessee.